Becoming
a Therapist

Becoming
a Therapist

On the Path to Mastery

Thomas M. Skovholt

JOHN WILEY & SONS, INC.

Published by John Wiley & Sons, Inc., Hoboken, New Jersey.
Published simultaneously in Canada.

Library of Congress Cataloging-in-Publication Data:

Skovholt, Thomas M.
    Becoming a therapist : on the path to mastery/Thomas M. Skovholt.
        p. ; cm.
    Includes bibliographical references and index.
    ISBN 978-0-470-40374-7 (pbk. : alk. paper); ISBN 978-1-118-17818-8 (ebk);
    ISBN 978-1-118-17819-5 (ebk); ISBN 978-1-118-17817-1 (ebk)
    I. Title. [DNLM: 1. Psychotherapy. 2. Counseling. 3. Mental Disorders—therapy.
4. Professional Role. 5. Vocational Guidance. WM 420]

616.89'14—dc23

2011029296

Printed in the United States of America.

10 9 8 7 6 5 4 3 2 1

For Lisa

Contents

Preface

The therapy and counseling professions offer hope and promise for those who enter through their educational gates toward professional development. To learn a lot and then use that knowledge to help people translates into rewarding and meaningful work. Welcome to this world!

This book describes the world of the therapy and counseling professions and specifically the landscape of the novice journey. I aim to paint a portrait of key features of the world of the beginner and what is called the universality of experience effect. More specifically, my intention is to provide a positive trinity of validity, clarity, and hope for novices, their teachers, and their supervisors.

I aim to create a map of sorts—one that highlights the peaks as well as the valleys, one that outlines the routes that lead to higher ground. I am hopeful that some readers will have a recognition reflex to terrain descriptions, such as the valleys and hills, the rocks and soil, and the watering holes. I hope that the map of terrain descriptors will help in navigating the journey all of us, as novices, must take. The goal is to lay out the future regarding the work life of therapists and counselors. It is a here-is-what-to-expect approach, especially regarding the inner landscape of the world of the therapist and counselor.

The different therapy and counseling professions are a loose grouping of career fields that are both distinct and similar. These distinct fields include counseling and clinical psychology, social work, school counseling, addictions counseling, marriage and family therapy, medicine, community counseling, pastoral counseling, nursing, academic advising, health and life coaching, family law, and other related fields where the professional helping relationship—the working alliance—is a central curative factor. The helping relationship is central to teaching, too. Many books focus on the unique features of each of these fields and how they deserve a place in the occupational sunshine of the helping professions.

This book is different and focuses much more on the similar aspects of the various fields. Decades ago, Henry, Sims, and Spray (1971) examined four of these fields and concluded that they were so alike they should merge and become the fifth profession of psychotherapist. Although that never happened, the Henry book made a big impression on me. In this book, I bridge the microdifferences between specific therapy and counseling career fields as part of a bigger view. The key similarity is that all of these fields focus on using the helping relationship to improve the life of the other. We are fellow travelers with those who are in the client-patient-student role as we seek and explore and try out solutions to enrich human life, often one life at a time.

Ethics are the bedrock of the work. The other's well-being is illuminated and at center stage. Novices are often frightened by ethics because they worry that they will easily make a major ethical blunder. I think it is better not to be so anxious about making mistakes but rather to take a positive view and dedicate oneself to being highly ethical in one's work life as a therapist or counselor. Knapp and VanderCreek (2012) have contributed a wonderful book on positive ethics.

Another point relates to the importance of questions versus answers. When each of us enters a career field, we naturally search for answers. If we know the answers, then we do not feel so lost, so stupid, so incompetent. That makes sense. But I have come to the conclusion that good questions are just as important as answers. Why is that? you may ask. The reason is because the answers change as the field evolves. So much in this field—in terms of specific answers—has changed over the last decades. Humans are so complex that answers, while attempting to reduce the complexity, often end up becoming disappointments. Clear, concise ways of seeing and doing things (e.g., three steps to this, a quick method for that, one theoretical approach as best for everything) get replaced. Over the past decades, this has happened over and over again in the therapy and counseling fields. So, when the person no longer can trust the former clear answers, it is so valuable to have good, solid questions to rely on. Really good questions keep us in the search—the exciting career long search—for ways to understand people and help them live positive and meaningful lives.

With a balance between answers and questions and a focus on the inner world of the therapist and counselor, we go forward with this book. Now, on to Chapter 1 and our exploration of this career area of therapy and counseling.

REFERENCES

Henry, W. E., Sims, J. H., & Spray, S. L. (1971). *The fifth profession.* San Francisco, CA: Jossey-Bass.

Knapp, S. J., & VanderCreek, L. (2012). *Practical ethics for psychologists: A positive view,* 2nd edition. Washington, DC: American Psychological Association.

Acknowledgments

I would first like to acknowledge my editor at John Wiley & Sons, Inc., Marquita Flemming. Job of the Old Testament is famous, very famous for his patience. Marquita has shown Job-like patience with me and the writing of this book. It has taken a long time to try to say what I think is important for novice therapists and counselors. Marquita has been wonderful with her vision, leadership, and support of my efforts over a number of years with this book. Thanks to her.

My thanks also to editor Lisa Gebo. Like many other authors in the human services, I benefited from her editorial generosity and her passion for the work in this field and its potential to reduce human suffering and increase human happiness.

Sherry Wasserman at John Wiley & Sons gave encouraging direction as I searched through the world of permissions hell. Without her, I would still be there and this book would be like an airplane waiting in line for takeoff.

I was fortunate that professor and counselor educator Sherri Cormier agreed to carefully read the whole manuscript. She provided expertise in counseling and therapy, high-level editing skill, and feedback—that great avenue for improvement. Of course, the roads not taken with his book and its deficiencies are mine alone to claim.

Appreciation to these people for graciously offering their opinions on various parts of these chapters: Yvonne Beech, Carolyn Burke, Sally Hage, Julie Heidemann, Moshe Israelashvili, Lisa Langenhahn, Mary Mullenbach, Rosie O'Brien, L. P. Smith, Alexandra Stillman, and Rhonda Wood.

Sandie Wick, Fran LaFave, Ed Hughes, and John and Marie Braun provided professional environments in Minnesota where I have been able to work as a practitioner. It has made all the difference.

The many, many counseling and therapy students at the University of Florida, the University of Minnesota, and Hacetteppe University in Turkey who have taught me so much about our field—thanks to you. A special note of appreciation to my doctoral advisees—such treasured working relationships for me and so much pleasure too as I watched them enter the professional world. The University of Minnesota has been a wonderful academic home for over 30 years. I have been lucky to have a position there—and in my home state too!

There were the fortunate years of graduate study at the University of Missouri and the formative years of working at the University of Chicago Hospital and studying in Chicago too.

I have been a fellow traveler with many, many clients in therapy and counseling. They have taught me so much during those courageous times when they have sought to find a way to feel less distress and be more joyful, often when no solution seemed apparent. How could I know about the complex ambiguity of counseling without all the clinical hours? Clients have taught me about the great hope and promise of therapy and counseling. It is gratifying to be the practitioner when the client finds a way to an emotionally richer, happier, more meaningful life; to a life of contribution and positive attachments. During those times I feel fortunate to be in this field.

Appreciation is also expressed to my advisor at Missouri, Joe Johnston, and mentors Phyllis Epley, George Meyer, Norman Moen, Helen Roehlke, Paul King, Harry Grater, and Sam Scher.

Gratitude for my parents, Joe and Elvera, and my family of Glen, Anna, Jane, Annie, Rachel, David, Iztchel, Lisa, and Rachel. And Danny, Hanna, Julius, and Abby. And a special note of welcome to niece Karla who has joined the counseling field.

A special thanks to five friends who have given the gift of friendship over many years: Dan Detzner, Mike Pearson, John Romano, Helge Rønnestad, and John Sullivan.

In 1990, I heard Rollo May speak at a conference. Later I asked him to autograph his book, *The Courage to Create.* Ever since, I have had that book where I write, hoping for inspiration and direction. Looking at the book title has given me encouragement—the oxygen that keeps us humans hopeful as we keep trying to express our ideas and make a contribution.

1

Opening Up Your Life to the Excitement of the Therapy and Counseling Professions

15 QUALITIES FOR THE THERAPIST/COUNSELOR

All career fields have key qualities, attitudes, and skills that are needed for success. For the architect, it includes proper spatial calculations; for the tree trimmer, obsession with safety is valuable; the psychometric psychologist hates measurement error; the chef seeks a well-timed mix of ingredients; for the baseball player, it is seeing the ball and its secrets when coming out of the pitcher's hand. In order to excel at the work, each of these occupations calls for the mastery of specific attitudes and skills. What are therapists' difficult-to-master attitudes and skills? What key qualities do we need? These are important questions for emerging practitioners.

Key Quality 1: Enthusiasm Within Insecurity

Helge Rønnestad and I wrote years ago about the emotional reactions of the beginner in our field. These emotions seem to be timeless and are part of the rite of passage into the work whether one begins in the early decades of the 21st century or decades earlier.

> Enthusiasm and insecurity are predominant affective expressions. The beginning graduate student feels very excited about learning how to help others yet very insecure about her/his knowledge of therapy/counseling procedures and one's own ability to succeed.
>
> —*Skovholt & Rønnestad, 1995, p. 24*

Some of the material in this book appeared earlier in: Skovholt, T. M. (2001). Elevated Stressors of the Novice Practitioner. *The Resilient Practitioner* (pp. 55–75). Boston, MA: Allyn & Bacon; Skovholt, T. M. & Trotter-Mathison, M. (2010). Elevated Stressors of the Novice Practitioner. *The Resilient Practitioner* (2nd ed., pp. 79–104). New York, NY: Routledge; and Skovholt, T. M., & Rønnestad, M. H. (2003), "Struggles of the Novice Practitioner," *Journal of Career Development, 30,* 45–58.

The excitement and the fear, the known and the unknown, the certain and the uncertain. These are the conditions for novices entering the therapy and counseling professions. Like other explorers, such as Lewis and Clark in North America and Jane Goodall in Africa, novices enter a personally unexplored wilderness.

A bounty of unknown sensations, stretching experiences, new perspectives, and skills await them. Our profession, wherein we commit ourselves to being helpful to others, is at the center of this world. There is a thrill about the novice practitioner voyage into this world, about the steps taken to be a practitioner of helping and human development. To get there, novices must enter the vast unknown. Explorers are to be applauded for their risk taking. The joy when entering the helping professions is the anticipation of an effective professional career of service to others. Professional development is about cultivating a style and skill level that optimizes the human development of those clients who invite us into their lives. If done right—with respect, caution, and skill—the counseling process can be of benefit to others.

Key Quality 2: Courage

> If you pay attention to the world you see a lot of pain. . . . Francesca was in therapy after a brutal date rape. Sue Anne came because her husband had just killed himself.
>
> —*Pipher, 2003, p. 53*

Therapists/counselors must possess immense courage. Our enemies are the distress trilogy of anger, anxiety, and depression that invade the lives of our clients. We must stand up to these crippling emotions and not be afraid. How can we help our clients if we are afraid of their distress?

We must wade into the anxiety and fear, despair and hopelessness, anger and rage, and stand in the pool of the client's distress with fortitude, patience, and serenity. We must show the client that we are not afraid; if they see that we are not afraid, they need not be afraid. We stand up to fear, we do not give in to despair, and we are relentless in understanding the sources of rage while helping the other to heal. Courage must envelop us as we attack the limits that these emotions put on our clients as they try to live, grow, and extend themselves into full lives. It is easy to back down from life, from the existential realities that are in front of us as human beings, to shrivel into the routines that give us comfort and security. Just as muscles become less flexible when not stretched, the human will is more susceptible to ongoing emotional distress when it is not engaged.

Courage also involves not being intimidated by our clients. One of the reasons to get more education and have more degrees is to be immunized from being afraid of accomplished people who come to us as clients. Our clients do not need us to be intimidated by them or be jealous of them. These things get in the way of what they need—our intense focus on helping them. So, if your client is a lawyer, a doctor, a chief executive, a professor, a wealthy person, a beautiful person, a wonderful artist, or has one or another admired trait, it does not matter. Or if your client seems so different from you, lives differently from you, has made choices different from yours, it is the same. All our clients need the same thing, no more or less: our best efforts at being a helpful practitioner in their lives.

Having courage when working as therapists and counselors, as guests in the lives of our clients, can be difficult. Meeting this challenge is helping to head off the client's ontological anxiety, a term used by theologian Paul Tillich (1952) to describe that life is not on track. This courage of practitioners, a more subtle kind than that of the boxer and firefighter, is still courage. It is an occupational essential for effective counselors and therapists. During education and training, emerging practitioners learn how to have and show this courage.

There is also the courage of novices when entering practice as students in training. Novices enter practice as a new canoeist enters white water—with anxiety, some instruction, a crude map, and some previous life experience. However, all of a sudden, the client is in front of student practitioners, telling a very personal, real story. The story often comes in a form and structure that is unique. The student experience is like the sudden rush of water, rocks, and rapids demanding instant understanding and reaction. Novices often have the urge to both call the emergency phone number 911 and appear calm, collected, and professional—whatever that is. In a study of novices in the related field of medicine, the most stressful situation was the white-water experience—having to make clinical decisions while very confused (Zeigler, Kanas, Strull, & Bennet, 1984).

Key Quality 3: Profound Empathy and Cultural Competence

We tend to forget the complexity of the process [of being empathetic]. It is extraordinarily difficult to know really what the other feels; far too often we project our own feelings onto the other.

—Yalom, 2002, p. 21

The work of therapists/counselors is also difficult because it demands that we gather information and understand the other in a way that goes against our basic nature. The human senses of touch, sight, hearing, smell, and feel are all designed to give each of us information to be safe as an individual. The information is to help each of us in our own personal survival and well-being.

We process data in our brains to understand the situation we are in and to make judgments. We do this to increase our own safety in many areas, such as physical, emotional, spiritual, financial, interpersonal, and intellectual. This constant sensory perception and processing is an amazing way that we, as a species, have developed to live and thrive. It has given us the capacity to grow, multiply, and dominate all living things.

Opposed to this ingrained natural response, therapists/counselors are required to use their hearing, smelling, feeling, seeing, and touching to sense the world and life of the other, to experience the movie of the other's life. It is *not* natural. It a difficult and potentially exhausting request. And it is an enormous gift to the other. This gift propels much of the positive power of our work.

In my classes, I often ask students to describe their reactions to a common experience, such as the view outside the classroom window. During this exercise, all students look at the same view yet their descriptions differ dramatically: One student says she sees the far, large white building; another, the close oak trees; a third, the people on the sidewalk, a fourth brings up the pale blue sky as that which got his attention. Most often we dismiss such differences as cute, interesting, and funny and then move on. Yet thinking deeply about these instant perceptual differences can shake us as we realize that we actually live in a world that appears the same but can be experienced very differently.

Years ago, in an interviewing class, I asked a Jewish Israeli woman and Palestine Muslim man to talk about their common world. They could not do it. Although they were both English speakers, they had no shared language. Neither had the ability to see and feel the other's perspective. Each had a worldview that was too ingrained. I remember a similar experience in the prime days of the nuclear showdown of the Cold War. On a television show, Soviet and American citizens were asked to have a dialog. I recall feeling frightened when they could not do it. They had so little understanding of each other. I thought, at a time when each has scores of missles directed at the people of the other country, how could USA-USSR differences ever be bridged?

Cultural competence is a central skill here. It consists of having awareness, knowledge, and skills that can connect the practitioner to the client regardless of diversity differences such as ethnicity and social class (Goh, 2005; Sue, Arredondo, & McDavis, 1992; Vasquez & Vasquez, 2003; also see Chapter 5 in this book).

The job of therapists/counselors is to excel at seeing and feeling the world of the other. It is hard work. It is not natural; it is like swimming not with the current but instead voluntarily going upstream *against* the current. It is an occupation that stretches the natural self like yoga or as the physical therapist stretches us. We must understand the world through the eyes of the other in order to be highly effective in helping. It is not natural to swim upstream, to put ourselves in such a challenging empathy situation, but it is an occupational essential.

Practitioners must also maintain the self while perceiving the world through the eyes and ears of the other. The task of counselors/therapists is to maintain their human perceptual system while taking on the client's at the same time.

This is a way that counseling and therapy work is different from the interpersonal help offered by family and friends. Practitioners must maintain a dual reality: a strong sense of one's self while at the same time accurately perceiving the world through the senses of the other. Some naturally skilled helpers, early on in life, develop the capacity to easily and accurately feel another's distress; they have the perceptual maturity and empathy to hold onto multiple perspectives and gather data through multiple channels at the same time.

Key Quality 4: One-Way Helping Relationship Embedded in the Cycle of Caring

Therapists must be experts in fostering relationships with individuals who have difficulty doing so.

—Clarkin & Levy, 2004, p. 211

The one-way helping relationship gives the work its power. Clients' lives, and all their nuances, command center stage. Their hopes, their joys, their fears, their needs draw therapist energy and focus. It is like the parent's focus on the young child—the focus is on the needs of the child. So too, the teacher, the nurse, the family law attorney, the physical therapist, and many other helping fields focus on the needs of the other as part of the power of the occupation. My life might be about me, but the work is about the client.

This focus on the other is not easy. One study of physician–patient relationships, for example, found that physicians focused on themselves to a surprising amount; physician self-disclosure occurred in 34% of first-patient visits. The article title shows the problem: "Physician Self-Disclosure in Primary Care Visits: Enough about You, What about Me?" (McDaniel et al., 2007).

It can be especially hard to focus on the client when the client is not able to be positive and engaging. For example, Strupp and Hadley (1977) found an appallingly poor pattern of reaction by trained therapists to challenging client behavior. When clients expressed negativity, the therapists responded with negativity, often in a subtle way unrecognized by the therapists themselves. And these were trained therapists. It is important to be able to respond to client negativity in more therapeutic ways than just with more negativity. Anybody can respond negatively to negativity. Doing so is just basic human 101.

Those in the helping professions offer a one-way caring relationship—that is the meaning of the helping professions, the caring professions, the helping/healing/teaching professions, whatever term we use. But it is difficult because we too are human. We too have needs. We too want to be heard. We too want to explain our position. We too want to defend ourselves.

Therapy is a one-way caring relationship; it is not two-way. When the one-way becomes the two-way, the ethical becomes the unethical, the effective becomes the ineffective, the great gift becomes of little value. What is the work like in the ideal therapeutic relationship? It is a one-way caring relationship.

The Cycle of Caring, described in more detail in Chapter 8, is a blueprint of the work of helpers. Practitioners have to develop competence in all four seasons of the four-season cycle. When we begin with a new person, it is like the spring of new beginnings. Here, hope and an empathetic connection with the other (client, student, patient, advisee, supervisee, mentee) take hold. Then there is the summer of engagement, when hard work and sweat take over. Finally, it is time for autumn, when it is time to part.

The engagement between practitioner and client may be brief, and autumn may arrive quickly, as with a one-session meeting. But autumn always comes, just as all relationships have both beginnings and endings. And autumn is the time for noticing the changes and getting ready to disengage. Winter is a time for self-care, a time of solitude, retreat, reflection, and re-creation. Winter is necessary for spring to occur. And spring comes again in the Cycle of Caring, and the practitioner engages again with another person. The one-way helping relationship within this four-season cycle is the essence of the work. Practitioners repeat it thousands of times during a 30- to 40-year career.

Key Quality 5: Intensive Listening

A basic pact about communication is the ever present reality of miscommunication. When others talk at us, we often hear most of all the echoes of our own thoughts and feelings.

The ability to listen intensively is fundamental to the work. Listening appears easy; in fact, however, the intensive listening of therapy and counseling is very difficult. Why is it so difficult to do a behavior that is so simple that everybody does it? It does not make sense. Something so common cannot be so difficult.

Evolutionary psychologist Geoffrey Miller (2000) argues that the evolved human is set up for the advantages that talking gives: "Scientists compete for the chance to give talks at conferences, not the chance to listen" (p. 350). Given that the evolutionary advantage is with talking, Miller says that the kind of intensive listening done by therapists and counselors "requires an almost superhuman inhibition of our will to talk."

Listening and not talking, Miller says, is unnatural. We have evolved to talk more than listen. "Our hearing apparatus remains evolutionarily conservative, very similar to that of other apes, while our speaking apparatus has been dramatically re-engineered . . . this anatomical evidence suggests that speaking somehow brought greater hidden evolutionary benefits than listening" (Miller, 2000, p. 351).

The act of intensive listening takes enormous energy both because it is hard work to focus so much and because it is unnatural, given our evolved natural talking self. In addition, the listening has to be at a deeper level than just cataloging content. Affective sensitivity is crucial. As we listen, we have to be tentative about our understanding of what we hear and try very hard to understand the complexity of another person. Those we listen to try to explain their 3-dimensional reality within the limitations of language. Language is such a limitation because it is such an abstraction of symbols used to describe something much bigger and more complex.

Key Quality 6: Embracing the Unknown, the Murky, and the Paradoxical as the Concrete

Another difficulty is the nature of the work and how it is so hard to quantify. As a society, we value work that we can touch, see, and know using traditional ways of knowing:

logical, linear, sequential thinking and content areas like math, science, and engineering. We all know what this kind of thinking is and can do it, or not do it, to some degree. This is a known world. The therapy and counseling field is different, and the difference makes it hard for others to understand and value it. In our professional lives, we are privy to a flow of emotions and patterns that is similar to abstract art. Competence in navigating this world is very different from competence in navigating the logical, linear world.

In addition, in therapy and counseling, we enter the personal lives of the people we serve; we are guests in their lives. And our conversations with them are private. So, comfort with the unknown, the private, the unexplainable, the ambiguous is another key quality in therapy and counseling work. There is less concrete data of success than we would like, especially in a world that likes to measure and quantify. We work in the abstract art of emotions rather than linear patterns, and we do it within a confidential world that cannot be shared with others.

Sometimes our deeper realities are paradoxical, like the word "bittersweet," which is a rich word because it contains a more complex reality: bitter *and* sweet. The realities of counseling are often like this, and people are often drawn to the field because of these more nuanced ways of understanding. Table 1.1 is a chart using paradoxical language to understand master therapists from our research projects.

Table 1.1   Paradoxical Characteristics of the Master Therapist

Drive to mastery	AND	Never a sense of having fully arrived
Able to deeply enter another's world	AND	Often prefers solitude
Can create a very safe client environment	AND	Can create a very challenging client environment
Highly skilled at harnessing the power of therapy	AND	Quite humble about self
Integration of the professional/ personal self	AND	Clear boundaries between the professional/ personal self
Voracious broad learner	AND	Focused, narrow student
Excellent at giving of self	AND	Great at nurturing self
Very open to feedback about self	AND	Not destabilized by feedback about self

Source: Skovholt, Jennings, & Mullenbach, 2004, p. 132.

Key Quality 7: Accepting and Managing the Public's Uncertainty about Us

Managing the public's uncertainty about us as therapists is one of the most difficult parts of the work. If someone at a party or public gathering asks our occupation and hears "psychologist," a variety of different reactions are common. Some respond with admiration and respect and are drawn to the word "psychologist" because they know that practitioners in this field are good people who are trying to help others. Others are drawn to it because the academic field is the science of human behavior, and that seems fascinating. But another reaction can be, in the long run, very stressful for mental health practitioners. It is the reaction of caution, of fear, of discomfort, of dislike.

Some people's discomfort is based, in part, on the assumption that we can perhaps almost read minds. This reaction seems to come out of the psychoanalytic tradition and the impact of Freud that has entered the cultural fabric at an unarticulated level. Freud spent a lot of time describing his theory of humans as being governed by unacceptable impulses that are mostly unconscious. According to this theory, they can be dug up and accurately interpreted by the practitioner. (Note: This is not a current view of most practitioners.) The Freudian and psychoanalytic way of thinking about human life, at least the public view of it, has deeply affected how the public thinks about psychological practitioners. The term "shrink" is not a term of endearment. If positive psychology or cognitive-behavioral methods had been developed first, before psychoanalysis, the fear factor would not be so strong.

I remember the time a female client, at a first appointment, said, "I don't know what is worse: going to the dentist, the gynecologist, or you, the psychologist." I said to her, "So, that is the list I am on. I hope I am not in first place." She just smiled. Then I turned to her husband and said, "I suppose for you, it would be the dentist, the urologist, and me." I had hoped he would vigorously object, but he nodded in agreement. Oh my, I thought—to be feared by people one is trying to help. That is unfortunate. The couple's indicators of discomfort did lead us to discuss how difficult it can be to ask for help with very personal concerns. So, that was a positive part. But this example shows the ambivalence others have about practitioners in the helping professions.

Coming to a helping practitioner often means facing and discussing painful realities of the past and the present and having to face decisions that can be terrifying. The soft lights, pastel colors, comfortable chairs, and available tissues of the counseling room are intended to help soak up the pain and reduce the anxiety. It may help a little—although male clients usually are not comforted by such settings. No matter the setting, counseling work for the client is often very difficult.

It is an occupational stressor to be a kind, nice person who wants to help others and to be greeted by discomfort and suspicion. Learning how to manage this reality is important for practitioners. It starts in the novice years, when others start reacting to us differently because we are training to be a counselor or therapist.

Key Quality 8: Energized by Asking Questions and Searching for the Truth

Most of the craziness in the world—violence, addictions, and frenetic activity—comes from running from pain.

—Pipher, 2003, p. 54

When starting a therapy relationship, I tell the other person that one of the first goals is to fill out a blank canvas. When it is filled out, the client can say "Yes, that is my life." It is so empowering to be accurate about one's life. That way, a person can know what is right and what is wrong, what needs to be fixed, what can be left alone, and what is shining bright right now. It is like having a home inspection before purchasing, but in a more personal way. Clarity about our own good news and not-so-good news helps us move forward in an accurate way.

Yes, the truth can be empowering, but we have a strong system of defenses to keep the pains of the truth at bay. Yoga stretches the body, but sometimes the body, especially when it is tight and inflexible, does not want the pain of being stretched no matter how it might—eventually—help. Think of these words: "The only thing worse than feeling pain is not feeling pain" (Pipher, 2003, p. 54). We often actively keep away from truths that ultimately can set us free. Going fast down the wrong road ultimately does not work very well, but stopping, turning around, and then going down the right road is difficult. Having a trained therapist help us find our right road can be very helpful.

To help others go after their human truth, we must do that ourselves. Therapist Pipher (2003) writes: "I am blind in one eye, moody, unfashionable, directionally impaired, claustrophobic, and easily tuckered out. And those flaws are just the ones I'll confess to" (p. xviii). We must, like Pipher, learn to be accepting and comfortable with our own flawed humanness. Then we can help our clients fill out the blank canvas. And they can then go on illuminated by their truth.

To help clients—and ourselves too—find the truth, we need to love questions. Here, Alice Walker tells us about loving questions:

> I must love the questions
> themselves
> As Rilke said
> like locked rooms
> full of treasure
> to which my blind
> and groping key
> does not yet fit.
>
> and await answers
> as unsealed letters
> mailed with dubious
> intent
> and written in a very foreign
> tongue.
>
> and in the hourly making
> of myself

> no thought of Time
> to force, to squeeze
> the space
> I grow into.
> *—Alice Walker, in White, 2004, pp. 227–228*

Key Quality 9: Knowing Suffering and Going Beyond It

She had a deformity of the upper back/spine. And that is probably what saved her.
—Alice Walker, in White, 2004, p. 221

Here Alice Walker is discussing the sensitivity and intensity of the work of Eudora Welty, a white Southern woman writer of privilege, whose own suffering helped her see and feel beyond her privilege and write powerful prose about race and segregation.

We do not work in joy clinics, where people rush in because they are bursting with good news and are about to explode with the thrill of it all. No, we specialize in despair, betrayal, fear, hopelessness, ignorance, and the lack of the privileges bestowed on some by class, race, gender, trauma, immigration, lack of education, disability, and other unfortunate realities.

We must know suffering personally and not shut it off. In our study of master therapists (Skovholt et al., 2004), we found that they did just that: They had personal histories of suffering. But the suffering of the master therapists was not so intense, with scarring so deep, that they were unable to reach out to others. Nor did they have to manage scarring pain by shutting it off at a deep level. Shutting it off at a deep level means the individual has no access to profound emotion and runs from an internal, or external, confrontation with strong emotions. This shutting off at a deep level means the person cannot succeed as a therapy and counselor practitioner.

For many therapists, their own intense losses; their own confusion and self-distress; their own anger, anxiety, depression is the fuel for the suffering. There are also plenty of other sources of suffering: the cultural alienation that happens with the global movement of so many refugees and immigrants, the rejection within peer hierarchies, the ever-present culture of competition with its winners and losers, among others. All of these can serve as suffering factories.

One kind of suffering is that described by the existential writers like Rollo May (1983). These writers tell us about the fallout that awareness of mortality brings: being forgotten, being insignificant, only passing through, being pushed off the planet by the next generation. For example, about being forgotten: How often do you think about your great-grandparents or visit their graves?

The existential realities should be enough to generate a factory's worth of painful feelings. Usually other painful realities propel us to this work. Knowing suffering from the inside is invaluable for practitioners. The internal experience of suffering helps as practitioners enter the cave of pain and hurt that fills the client's world. You cannot just read about suffering; to be really known, it has to be felt. Even this necessity is not sufficient. Although we need to know what suffering feels like, we cannot assume that our experience of suffering is similar to that of our clients or that our remedies will work for everyone.

One of the great ironies of the helping professions and especially the helping fields like counseling and therapy is that often it is healing our own distress that propels some of our interest in the work. Here is the irony: We enter very altruistic work out of self-needs, yet eventually we must be transformed. We must go from cocoon to butterfly and become altruistic caregivers of others in order to be skilled helpers. I say more about this under key quality 11.

Those entering the field are most effective if they can access their own personal suffering to use as an internal mental schema for the enormous energy of connecting with and caring about their clients. It is best if practitioners are happy and joyful in their lives and also can access suffering. Understanding the world of distress and using it to make a profound impact in the lives of others—that is the idea for practitioners.

Key Quality 10: Exciting to Be *in* the Novel Rather than Read It

Generally people read novels and watch movies to experience a broader intensity about human life. Therapists and counselors do that too. But we also have a more profound version of human reality, which we experience when meeting with our clients. Right in front, yes, right in front of us, is the intensity of human life.

The novel is the life of the client. Novices can no longer sit back, watch, and have the privilege of passivity, free to critique other players on the stage or to daydream about other realities. Now it is riveting and real. Novices are in the counseling session as the helper. And as real as anything is the need to do more than feel or to think. Now novices must act. But, how to act and in what measured ways about what dimensions? It is like watching a movie going at double speed and being asked to react to what is most important. It is all coming fast, and everything seems important. With the first client meetings, the novice experience of being overwhelmed and unsure can emerge and be expressed in one or more forms of anxiety. Much of the doing something is staying the course of intense dedication to the client and his or her welfare. Trusting the process, an elusive idea, is central to the acting and doing of the work.

In the counseling interaction, we are in a vivid human drama, a human drama that is much more engrossing than the average novel.

Key Quality 11: Signing Up for the Intense Will to Grow

For most people, commencement is an end. It happens at graduation when school is finished. It signals being done. However, this is not an accurate definition of the word. The dictionary defines "commencement" as the beginning. And that is a good way of thinking of professional development in the counseling and therapy professions. We become our own internal teachers when school is over and others no longer tell us what to learn and when to learn it. Beginning the novice voyage means signing up for education, learning, development—forever. The master therapists in our sample (Skovholt et al., 2004; Chapter 11 of this book) were committed to their own development; we labeled this attribute the "intense will to grow." It was essential to the emergence of their expertise.

There are many things to learn and ways to learn. One kind is the learning that is part of the intensive academic classes of graduate school. Parallel to this is the learning in practicum, which is just as intense but often very different. And then there is the intensive learning about oneself—the introspection, the psychologizing about oneself that occurs especially early in one's career. Put these three kinds of learning together, and beginners often feel that their education is intense. And it is!

Counseling is about human behavior and how to modify it in a way that brings positive results. Understanding the complexity of the profession is hard, more than anything, because *Homo sapiens* are the most complex of all species. Ants are complicated enough, but people! And that complexity means continual learning as you go, a constant adding and revising. Signing up for this work is signing up to be a student of human behavior in the classroom of life that never has a bell ending the class. It is exhilarating to live this life, but do not sign up for it if you already have the answers or want shortcuts. An important point in therapist and counselor development is when students begin to realize that entering into this knowledge world leads to questions as much as answers and that uncertainty keeps pace with certainty. Some want to get a few answers and apply them and feel competent with one theory or one treatment plan. These are useful short-term solutions. Students also need to keep open and keep learning and let human behavior be as complicated as it is. The intense will to grow is a necessity for this process.

The key for beginners is to realize that learning about human complexity does not stop after school is over. The pace and intensity may be different and the sources of knowledge do not tilt toward classes in the same way. But keeping at it and continuing to understand people at a deeper level is part of walking on the practitioner path for the decades that one is in the field. It is a pleasure most of the time, to keep learning and growing.

Key Quality 12: Addressing Personal Motives for the Work

Often people enter the helping and related career areas because of deeply felt experiences in their personal lives. Physicians sometimes choose their work because of a tragic loss to illness of someone close to them. Teachers may become very invested in teaching others how to learn because of their own frustrations in school. This was true of counselor educator Gerald Corey (2005), who ended up writing very readable books because of his own frustration with the education he received and the horrible feelings he endured concerning his own school failure. Another example is addiction work, which often attracts those who have been caught by chemical abuse.

Derald Wing Sue (2005), a prominent leader in multicultural counseling, describes such a personal motive base for his work. He wrote: "I will never forget that incident [of racial harassment as a child]. It taught me several important lessons in life that have remained with me to this day and form the basis of my professional work" (p. 75).

In the highly altruistic helping fields, the original motivation for the work is often deeply self-focused. The paradox is that the focus must change eventually from deeply self-oriented to deeply other-oriented. There is a big shift necessary in this work. Do novice practitioners, entering this work with strong self-needs, know they are entering work that depends ethically, and for its power and value, on an intense focus on the other rather than the self? This is a great paradox of the work: entering the career for self-needs only to learn in time how the work must be about the other's needs. And in addressing the needs of the other, we can grow ourselves. Addressing this topic of self-needs and the needs of the other is one of the growth areas for the early practitioner.

Key Quality 13: Wanting Meaning More than Money

Therapy-type work usually does not produce a large income. Lower income is generally associated with fields that involve a focus on intense human needs, such as counseling, teaching, social work, and religious careers.

Big money is possible, but it usually comes from owning a large counseling clinic, authoring a very popular inventory or self-help book, or working in a business setting with executives where the fees are much higher. Most practitioners work where there is more need but less money.

Finding meaning and purpose from the work is the bigger currency, as explained in the next quotations.

> I rarely hear my therapist colleagues complain that their lives lack meaning. Life as a therapist is a life of service in which we daily transcend our personal wishes and turn our gaze towards the needs and growth of the other. . . . There is extraordinary privilege here. And extraordinary satisfaction, too.
>
> —*Yalom, 2002, p. 256*

> Our goals of understanding others' points of views, alleviating human suffering, and enhancing relationships are noble goals.
>
> —*Pipher, 2003, p. 179*

Although not a therapist, Ann Dunham, President Obama's mother, worked with poor people in a helping role. The values in this kind of work are similar to the values of therapists and counselors. Her daughter Maya (President Obama's half sister) said about their mother:

She gave us a very broad understanding of the world. . . . She hated bigotry. She was very determined to be remembered for a life of service and thought that service was really the true measure of a life.

—*Scott, 2008, p. 17*

Transcending the self is a key ingredient to higher-level human functioning as outlined by many major religions and by psychological concepts of the happy life. Seligman, Martin, Rashid, and Parks (2006), leaders in Positive Psychology, contend that happiness consists of three parts: the Pleasant Life, where Positive emotions are abundant in the person's life; the Engaged Life, where the person is involved and absorbed with projects and people; and the Meaningful Life, where a strong sense of meaning is present in the person's life. They found that higher life satisfaction was robustly correlated with Engagement and Meaning. In the helping professions we have the possibility of all three pathways to a rich life and happiness.

I came upon a similar idea when I was a graduate student reading Frank Riesman's description of the helper therapy principle, the idea that the helper benefits as much as the client by the interaction. Years ago, I explored this idea in an article (Skovholt, 1974) that discussed how the helper benefits through principles of social exchange theory and direct reinforcement.

Key Quality 14: Energized by Integrity

Integrity as a key quality expresses itself in two ways.

1. There is integrity when the intervention, offered to people in need, has validity.
2. There is integrity when practitioners work within an active ethical stance.

A statement about the first kind of validity comes from an esteemed psychotherapy research book. This volume, consisting of 854 pages and 18 chapters (Lambert, 2004), offers dizzying detail. Lambert and Ogles summarize what psychotherapy does in this way:

Psychotherapy facilitates the remission of symptoms and improves functioning. It not only speeds up the natural healing process but also provides additional coping strategies and methods for dealing with future problems. Providers as well as patients can be assured that a broad range of therapies, when offered by skilled, wise, and stable therapists, are likely to result in appreciable gains for the client.

—*Lambert & Ogles, 2004, p. 180*

A great profession, devoted to public welfare, stands on the rock-strong foundation of validity of its methods. Without validity, a profession devoted to human welfare ultimately offers only the poisonous effects of fraud. When emotionally vulnerable people are manipulated and used, then we have fraud. A helping profession standing on sand, with no validity, ultimately gets washed away. It may take time, but eventually it happens. And for good reason. Most of the invalid methods in the helping professions offer clients methods that involve little practitioner training, are constructed to benefit the practitioner more than the client, and overreach by promising everything to everybody with one strategy.

Part of the validity rock-strong foundation of counseling and therapy is not promising too much. "Change that looks too good to be true most generally is" (Pipher, 2003, p. 43). Lawyers can help us when we have legal difficulties, but they cannot make us free of legal worries; physicians can help us ward off disease but cannot make us bacteria free for life; so too with therapists and counselors. When we are highly trained and dedicated to the highest skill and ethics of practice, we can offer help but not a problem-free life.

Our profession of therapy and counseling, devoted to reducing human suffering and increasing human competence, does not overpromise. As described by Lambert and Ogles (2004), the research suggests that overall we can, with the right conditions, offer positive change for our clients; some really benefit, some do not benefit at all, and many fit in between. There is overall validity to the work but few quick miracles.

The second kind of integrity concerns client welfare. Clients can easily feel vulnerable in therapy and counseling. It is very important for practitioners not to misuse this vulnerability. This is the core of ethics and integrity in the work. The welfare of the client is the number-one concern; all other issues are secondary.

Signing up to act with integrity and be energized by it is a key when entering this field.

Key Quality 15: Learning to Be Very Patient

Why can't we offer what some self-help and pop psychology books offer: a simple, easy-to-learn formula explaining human behavior terms with a few, easy-to-learn remedies for quickly solving problems? Doing so is a powerful seduction because terrified and suffering people are not comforted by hearing that human life is complex and that change takes time.

In the United States, we aspire to be a country of equal opportunity and equal achievement. Yet there remains a great canyon between the ideal and reality. Why? Why can't we fix this gap? University of Kansas researchers have found that by age 3, children of professional parents knew 1,100 words and children of parents on welfare knew 525 words (Tough, 2006). Paul Tough goes on to say:

> By age 3, the average child of a professional heard about 500,000 encouragements and 80,000 discouragements. For the welfare children, the situation was reversed: they heard, on average, about 75,000 encouragements and 200,000 discouragements. (p. 48)

By age 3, such gaps! The gap between deficit and growth in human development can be closed, but doing so is not quick, fast, or easy. We can do profoundly good work, but we should not overpromise.

Intensive training in the behavioral sciences informs practitioners that human life is complicated. Improving it takes time. This is the way it is. We cannot offer a shortcut around suffering, loneliness, and despair. Reflecting on the time issue, Pipher (2003) says:

> Last night I read a case history about deep brief therapy, an approach that lasts a few sessions but profoundly changes the clients involved. It struck me as a bonus concept. Relationships take time. When we suggest that high-quality advice can be given under rushed conditions, we undercut what we can offer people—a calm place to carefully explore their situations. Furthermore, we are likely to harm people if, while we are ignorant about many aspects of their lives, we jump in with radical advice and grandiose plans to transform them. (p. 26)

We do offer an incubator of human growth and development that can, over time, gradually transform lives. The hope that change is possible sustains all of us, including seasoned practitioners.

These are 15 key qualities for the work. Now on to a few more topics in this chapter.

CENTRAL EXCITEMENT OF THE WORK

What was once accepted as human fate can now be changed. We now have words for conditions that can be defined and changed, such as chemical dependency, test anxiety, depression, domestic abuse, learning disabilities, psychological trauma, attachment disorder, and body image. In the past, we were born into a genetic vulnerability and, perhaps later, developed a condition (e.g., alcoholism), and that was our lot. Now therapy and counseling, and many other methods too, can improve our lives.

People often come for help because they have an unsolvable problem that needs to be solved. People are usually very active and skilled problem solvers. They find ways to solve problems every day. Even daydreaming can be a useful way to solve problems.

Sometimes, as people, we encounter problems that do not need to be solved. We shelve them, forget about them, and find other ways to do things. The crisis floats away. At other times, our problem-solving methods are not creative enough and even avoidance does not work. Then we have the unsolvable problem that has to be solved. In the body, this situation is often expressed in the form of one or more parts of the distress trilogy of anger, anxiety, and depression, similar to the engine light coming on in the car to signal a problem. And there also arises the demoralization that Frank and Frank (1991) have so eloquently described as central to clients when they come to us. This situation of being stuck (cannot live with him, cannot live without him) with a profound loss attached to all options means that therapy and counseling can be an effective—but slow—method of helping people. There are few quick cures. The slowness can be hard for novice practitioners, who may need the quick validation of their own work to avoid falling into the hole of the heroic helper who pushes for quick and powerful change. Veteran practitioners, who have accepted the slow pace, can know the excitement of gradually helping clients find a way out of the haze into a better, deeper, richer life.

TO THE NOVICE PRACTITIONER—WELCOME!

But who would be Nietzsche's therapist? After much historical research, it was apparent that there was no such creature in 1882—only 120 years ago.

—Yalom, 2002, p. 218

Therapy and counseling is one of the great inventions of the last half of the 20th century. Unlike medicine and ministry, which have long healing histories, in the past therapy and counseling did not exist as a formal professional field. Now it transforms lives. When embarking on the novice practitioner voyage, beginners ask questions such as "What am I getting into?" "Will I be any good at it?" "How hard is it?" Let us start with the last question: how hard is it? I do not want to scare away readers, but I will start with a quote that indicates that the work—in its own way—is hard.

Being a psychotherapist is no Caribbean cruise with bonbons and bourbon.

—Pipher, 2003, p. 75

The work is difficult. Yes, it is. Fortunately, succeeding at a difficult task is one source of work satisfaction. It is ironic that the work of the therapist and counselor can be hard. How can it be hard to talk and listen with another when it is done routinely every hour, around the clock, by millions of people in our global community. In Shanghai, sisters are sharing their dilemmas about boys; in Oslo, fathers are consoling their daughters; in rural eastern Turkey, men are sharing their fears about how they are going to leave their village for the prospects of Istanbul. A teacher in Nairobi is telling a disobedient boy to pay attention to the lesson because he will need it later; in Paris, an older couple tells one another that their love is frayed; in Lima, a boy is listening to his friend cry while a mother is dying.

There are counselors and therapists everywhere; they are called mothers, sisters, fathers, friends, grandmothers, brothers, elders, wise persons, and many other names. They give enormous emotional love to others. This outpouring of human love is one of the essential ingredients for physical health and a happy life. A long period of social isolation can be so difficult to endure.

What makes being a helping professional so different from providing emotional support as a family member and friend? Why does the job of being a helping professional become so difficult? For one thing, it is hard to sit with suffering, to see a shattered life be described in vivid detail. None of us wants to feel so helpless, so powerless, so close to hell. Even if it is not our life, we want to scream, run, fight it. When a client talks about wanting life to end, as people we want to say "Buck up. Don't say or feel that." To sit with suffering is so hard . . . and that is why doing so is such a gift to the other.

Counseling and therapy is easy when it consists merely of telling the other person how and what to do, using a script of the right answers. In these situations, the content of the script comes in a pure form from personal experience or a memorized ideology/theory. Quick problem solving and fast improvement is the goal. Sometimes this caring for the other, such as sister to sister, is a balm; sometimes it is a useful solution; sometimes it does not help; and sometimes it is harmful.

Professional therapy and counseling is more complicated, like the difference between tossing one ball and juggling three balls. And the difficulty of the work gives some of the work its joy.

SUMMARY

The great majority of therapists [M=11 years of experience] reported recently having high levels of *Flow* feelings: stimulated (80%), engrossed (80%), inspired (79%), and challenged (70%).

—*Orlinsky & Rønnestad, 2005, p. 57*

Have patience with everything unresolved and try to love the questions themselves.

—*Rainier Marie Rilke, cited by Yalom, 2002, p. 10*

There are 7 billion human beings now, in all corners and places on our earth. We are more united than ever, thanks to technology, and, paradoxically, we more clearly see the differences. Differences by nationality, by age, by gender, by income level, by religion, by geographic position in the world, and by so many other wedges. Yet the common DNA, the common human joys and celebrations, the common dilemmas and diseases are there too. As counselors and therapists, this is our work world: the world of people and being helpful in it.

Counseling and therapy work is full of joy and excitement: the joy of helping others and the excitement of having a valid and valuable method to use. As we embark on the novice voyage—and we all do it—it is best, but often so difficult, to try to enjoy the process, to be open to the experiences as we go along. And remember, many mentors and teachers are available as guides.

In *Letters to a Young Therapist*, Mary Pipher (2003) writes to a new practitioner, Laura, whom she is supervising: "Laura, there is no better work than the work we do.

It has been a pleasure to watch you flower and bloom over the year. You will be an excellent therapist. Welcome to our field". (p. 180)

I add my own welcome to you the reader, the new practitioner. Now, on to the good news of Chapter 2.

REFERENCES

Clarkin, J. F., & Levy, K. N. (2004). The influence of client variables on psychotherapy. In M. Lambert (Ed.), *Bergin and Garfield's handbook of psychotherapy and behavior change* (pp. 194–226). Hoboken, NJ: Wiley.

Corey, G. (2005). A meaningful life—personal and professional—has many twists and turns. In R. K. Conyne & F. Bemak (Eds.), *Journeys to professional excellence: Lessons from leading counselor educators and practitioners* (pp. 57–72). Alexandria, VA: American Counseling Association.

Frank, J. D., & Frank, J. B. (1991). *Persuasion and healing*. 3rd ed. Baltimore, MD: Johns Hopkins University Press.

Goh, M. (2005). Cultural competence and master therapists: An inextricable relationship. *Journal of Mental Health Counseling, 27*, 71–81.

Lambert, M. (2004). (Ed.) *Bergin and Garfield's handbook of psychotherapy and behavior change*. Hoboken, NJ: Wiley.

Lambert, M., & Ogles (2004). The efficacy and effectiveness of psychotherapy. In M. Lambert (Ed.), *Bergin and Garfield's handbook of psychotherapy and behavior change* (pp. 139–193). Hoboken, NJ: Wiley.

McDaniel, S. H., Beckman, H. B., Morse, D. S., Silberman, J., Seaburn, D. B., & Epstein, R. M. (2007). Physician self-disclosure in primary care visits: Enough about you, what about me? *Archives of Internal Medicine, 167*, 1321–1326.

May, R. (1983). *The discovery of being: Writings in existential psychology*. New York, NY: Norton.

Miller, G. (2000). *The mating mind*. New York, NY: Anchor Books.

Orlinsky, D. E., & Rønnestad, M. H. (2005). *How psychotherapists develop: A study of therapeutic work and professional growth*. Washington, DC: American Psychological Association.

Pipher, M. (2003). *Letters to a young therapist*. New York, NY: Basic Books.

Scott, J. (2008, Mar. 13). A mother's unconventional life is reflected within Obama: Barack Obama's mother had a varied international career, *International Herald Tribune*.

Seligman, M. E. P., Rashid, T., & Parks, A. C. (2006). Positive psychology. *American Psychologist, 61*, 774–788.

Skovholt, T. M. (1974). The client as helper: A means to promote psychological growth. *Counseling Psychologist, 4*(3), 58–64.

Skovholt, T. M., Jennings, L., & Mullenbach, M. (2004). Portrait of the master therapist: The highly-functioning self. In T. M. Skovholt & L. Jennings (Eds.), *Master therapists: Exploring expertise in therapy and counseling* (pp. 125–146). Boston, MA: Allyn & Bacon.

Skovholt, T. M., & Rønnestad, M. H. (1995). *The evolving professional self: Stages and themes in therapist and counselor development*. New York, NY: Wiley.

Strupp, H. H., & Hadley, S. W. (1977). A tripartite model of mental health and therapeutic outcomes: With special reference to negative effects in psychotherapy. *American Psychologist, 32*, 187–196.

Sue, D. W. (2005). The continuing journey to multicultural competence. In R. K. Coyle & F. Bemak (Eds.), *Journeys to professional excellence: Lessons from leading counselor educators and practitioners* (pp. 73–84). Alexandria, VA: American Counseling Association.

Sue, D. W., Arredondo, P., & McDavis, R. J. (1992). Multicultural competencies and standards: A call to the profession. *Journal of Multicultural Counseling and Development, 20*, 64–88.

Tillich, P. (1952). *The courage to be*. New Haven, CT: Yale University Press.

Tough, P. (2006, Nov. 26). Can teaching poor children to act more like middle-class children help close the education gap? What it takes to make a student. *New York Times Magazine*.

Vasquez, L. A., & Vasquez, E. G. (2003). Teaching multicultural competence in counseling curriculum. In D. B. Pope-Davis, H. L. K. Coleman, W. M. Liu, & R. Toporek (Eds.), *Handbook of multicultural competency in counseling and psychology* (pp. 546–561). Thousand Oaks: Sage.

White, E. C. (2004). *Alice Walker: A life*. New York, NY: Norton.

Yalom, I. D. (2002). *The gift of therapy: An open letter to a new generation of therapists and their patients*. New York, NY: Harper Perennial.

Zeigler, J. N., Kanas, N., Strull, W. M., & Bennet, N. E. (1984). A stress discussion group for medical interns. *Journal of Medical Education, 59*, 205–207.

2

Novice Advantages

W hat are the novice advantages? This chapter presents four. Perhaps this discussion will be welcome for beginners who may feel like poker players with the worst hands. In fact, there may be a few aces in the cards that novice therapists or counselors have been dealt.

NOVICE ADVANTAGE 1: INTENSITY AND ENTHUSIASM

One novice advantage is the intensity of youth entering the new world. Even older novice students can have this kind of enthusiasm. You can feel the intensity if you put yourself in the following situations. These are life examples where people often feel the intensity of engagement. For example:

It is a major gymnastics meet and you are competing in multiple events.
It is your wedding dance, and you and your spouse are entering the dance floor.
It is watching your first child being born.
It is waiting in the back hall to begin a solo piano recital—a first big one—in front of a large audience.
It is walking out to do the eulogy for your best friend.
It is being the driver, roaring down the drag strip at 100 miles an hour, in a high-performance car.

This novice advantage is about the emerging practitioner's intensity of presence. The beginning of a great new adventure is full of excitement. There is more excitement if the adventure is a major undertaking; is not fully mapped; will take enormous energy; and if the outcome, although very important, is unknown to the individual. Part of novice practitioner intensity is generated by a fear of the unknown; these practitioners do not yet have an internal professional schema and an external set of skills to handle situations. This intensity describes the early days in the lives of emerging therapists and counselors.

Ann Bancroft, had the great adventure of being the first woman to reach the North Pole on foot and by sled. She was intensely present during those days and nights of the trek across the unknown ice and open water. Polar bears could emerge at any time in the white of the snow and ice. After reaching the North Pole, her group was airlifted out. Sponsored in part by the Science Museum of Minnesota, Ann and the other Arctic explorers came to the Twin Cities, where I live, directly from the Arctic via the Northwest Territories. I took my 13-year-old daughter to see the group. There was Ann, the novice North Pole explorer . . . still in the intensity of the adventure!

So much intensity, so much excitement, so much fear. This is the life of novice counselors and therapists. As I said in Chapter 1, in our counselor and therapist development research, we described the central affect of the beginner as enthusiasm and insecurity (Rønnestad & Skovholt, 2003, 2012; Skovholt & Rønnestad, 1995). Put the two emotions—enthusiasm and insecurity—together, and you have novice intensity. Hours are spent with classmates discussing cases, classes, conflicts, and confusion. The new adventure fills up the life of novice therapists.

The novice advantage can also be understood by examining the lives of veteran practitioners. Veteran practitioners, like mature adults, have somewhat of an attitude of "Been there, done that." Another saying is "Old fish in new wrappers." Instead of launching the boat for the epic trip across unknown seas, a first meeting with a new client feels more like going fishing on a small lake totally known to the fisherman. It is the 20-year-veteran math teacher going in to teach algebra to kids . . . again. It is not the first baby being born but the fifth. It is the 43rd northern winter enjoyed and endured, not a first, second, or tenth.

The affect of veteran practitioners is more measured and restrained, with fewer of the great novice swings between elation and despair. Yes, veterans have many advantages; but they do not include the intensity of novice advantage. Experience in life can alter the reality of the situation, often for the better. I remember as a teenager being worried about ordering at a restaurant. My first attempt at 14 to eat alone did not go so well. I ordered a pheasant sandwich. The waitress replied, "Do you mean the peasant sandwich?" I was busted. My veneer dissolved. We could go to the spot where it occurred and I could recite the sequence. Now I ask: What is there to worry about in a restaurant? Not knowing what to order? Worried about knocking over a glass? Wondering about who will pay and how that will be decided? Unsure what to talk about? I have been through all of this and have come out okay. Only so many things can go wrong when eating out, and when you have encountered most of them, there is less worry. Lost too is the most intense excitement of novelty. I no longer can have the intensity of the first encounter with a peasant sandwich.

Novice practitioners' intensity can make a big difference in outcome. Those who come to counseling often feel discouraged and defeated; a very energized therapist or counselor can invigorate clients, and that can make a big difference.

How Important Is Therapist/Counselor Experience in Delivering Positive Client Outcome?

It is hard to argue against education or experience as important in work performance.

Certainly, as a foundational premise, professional credentialing is built on the assumption that education and experience really matter. Although it is common sense to think that more experience in counseling and therapy will produce superior outcomes, things are not that simple. What does the research say about the success rate for novice therapists versus highly experienced therapists? The data are confusing, as the relationship between experience and outcome is mixed. Lambert and Ogles (2004) found that in earlier studies, "[T]here was no differences between the outcome of patients treated by trained and untrained persons" (p. 170). They then cite a more recent study that found that "[i]n all cases, therapists with more training had better outcomes" (p. 170). Why the mixed results?

I think it works like this. One of my colleagues flies a small plane. He no longer gets excited about routine landings because he has done so many. A new pilot can do just as well with routine landings. However, when things get complicated or unique or difficult, or when things combine in an unusual way, my colleague gets energized and is fully engaged. That is when the veteran pilot does better than the inexperienced novice. It is the result of all the sweat, toil, and tears that is part of becoming experienced. Chapter 11, the practitioner mastery and expertise chapter, explores this dimension in more detail.

I think having a lot of reflective therapy practice experience does matter with complex, multilayered human problems. For one thing, veteran practitioners are more patient with lack of apparent progress; novices, who lack confidence, need the reassurance of client progress and expressed appreciation. For example, client anger expressed toward practitioners is easier for veterans to deal with; it often rattles novices.

Lin (2005), in his dissertation, found no differences between experienced and less experienced counselors in providing e-mail-based counseling. In these cases, the problem presented was fairly simple. Often, but not always, the concerns brought to practicum counseling students are developmental, transitory, and situational. I am not making light of this level of client distress, but it is often more like the flu than like stage 4 cancer or Parkinson's disease. Of course, we know from the tragedies at colleges and universities where students have been killed that college counselors often have very difficult clients to work with. It is important that practicum counseling and therapy students are not assigned these clients.

Another note on experience and outcome. Teaching is a high-relational profession, just like therapy and counseling. Recent research has not found a strong relationship between teaching experience and student performance. In fact, some teachers with less experience produce higher student achievement than more experienced teachers (Harris & Sass, 2009).

Part of the answer to the puzzle regarding therapist experience and client outcome concerns the interpersonal qualities that practitioners bring to the work. In a study by Anderson et al. (1999), cited by Lambert and Ogles (2004), graduate students with high interpersonal skills, regardless of department and major, did better than those with a lower level of interpersonal skills. "This suggests that individual therapist variables, such as interpersonal skills, may be more important than training" (p. 171).

Enthusiasm is a dimension that correlates highly with interpersonal skills. Novices bring to practice the advantage of excitement–animation–exhilaration–positive curiosity. The novelty of the work, with practitioners *excited* to learn more about the lives of others, adds great cognitive stimulation. Conversely, veteran practitioners, working in a limited domain (i.e., only doing chemical dependency assessments, only helping high school students with college planning, only teaching basics of domestic abuse prevention over and over again) are at great risk for boredom. Novices are flooded with novelty; there is no room for boredom here.

As I discussed in Chapter 1, people do not go to practitioners because they have a simple problem. We all confront problems all the time. We solve them, put them away, or forget about them. We go to others for help most often only when we have an unsolvable problem that has to be solved. A problem that has these two dimensions—unsolvable and has to be solved—is often accompanied by a lack of what Bandura (1997) calls self-efficacy, a sense of being able to control, solve, and succeed. Over a period of time, an inability to solve our own problems can easily lead to feeling discouraged. Lack of courage, as in the word "dis-couraged," leads to dis-ease, whereby the person slows or totally stops all active coping. Frank and Frank (1991) coined the term "demoralization" to describe a person's emotional state when asking for help.

In this situation, consider the value of novice helpers with their excitement–animation–exhilaration–positive curiosity. I remember reading a study years ago that found that volunteer students at a state mental hospital had more success than experienced social workers. In the context of this novice advantage of intensity, studies like these make sense.

Related here is the idea that practitioners are a catalyst to release the clients' capacity for self-healing. Bohart (2006) argues strongly for this client-as-healer view as the predominant agent for change, saying that the "client's active self-healing abilities are primary determinants of psychotherapy outcome" (p. 218). If the therapist and client can match readiness for change and have a good working alliance, and if the practitioner conveys interest and excitement about the possibilities for the client's discouraged life, great things can happen. Again, in such situations, novice intensity and excitement can be an active agent in releasing the client's capacity for self-healing.

NOVICE ADVANTAGE 2: DEMOGRAPHIC EDGE

One of our graduate students at the University of Minnesota, Joan, was looking back at her first practicum the year before and lamenting her incompetence. I told her, "You would be more preferred by college students seeking counseling than I would." She said, "No way!" I replied, "Yes, for many of your clients, you would." She did not agree. Now, we always have to factor in student deference to faculty members due to the power imbalance that students perceive. Yet I also know this student as sincere, conscientious, and a talented helper of others.

When we talked, Joan had a total of 150 hours of counseling experience, I had 16,000 hours; she had no professional credentials, I had lots of them. Why was she preferred and often better in counseling situations? Joan was a 29-year-old female; I was a 67-year-old male. Her college student clients were females 18 to 23 years old. People naturally prefer others like themselves, assuming they will understand us better than someone who is "foreign."

The young college women who were counseling clients at the practicum site last year saw Joan the counselor as someone who could understand them and someone who had similar experiences. They had a natural internal schema that 29-year-old Joan would understand them better than someone who appeared very different. These clients often came to the counseling center because of some combination of internal female confusion and relationship distress. For example, they may have gone for therapy because dating was not going well. Perhaps the partner was not available, was disappointing, recently broke up with her, or was too present. For these concerns, it was most natural for these 18- to 23-year-old females to establish a trusting therapeutic relationship with 29-year-old Joan. How could a 67-year-old male possibly understand their current difficulties?

During my training at three different universities, I was a college counseling intern when I was 26, a doctoral psychology intern when I was 28, and a new assistant professor and counselor when I was 29. The clients/students often quickly identified with me. Some of their identifying with me was because of the undergraduate students' search for an identity separate from their parents. I served this function and felt their bonding within the professional relationship with me as therapist or teacher.

Now I am not of college age, although I do have some ideas about being 18 to 23. I was one, I parented two of them, and I did counseling with many of them at the three college counseling centers. Since then, I have similar clients at my practice. I have taught many of them. I have also taught courses on adolescence and college student counseling. The life of a person 18 to 23 years of age has only so many permutations and combinations. Usually the problems include some combination of the age-related themes of autonomy versus dependency, identity development, value clarity, career hopes and confusion, achievement and failure, shame and guilt about behavior excesses, financial stress, and peer relationships of rejection or confusion.

For me, today there is also the advantage of being older with a perspective on the stages and tasks of the young adult years. Looking at 20 when one is in one's 60s gives one patience and a low panic level regarding all the dilemmas and crises of those years. Yet, given the perspective of many decades of living, I also have limitations. I am not age 20. That means that there is a lot that I do not know or understand. We could go through a long list of these issues, including cultural expectations of young people, internal hormone-related realities, being female versus being male, and the multitasking technology world. I went to college when sociology was a popular major and business was not popular; now these two areas have switched places. I would not "get it" on a lot of issues.

There is another reason it seems to me why we prefer a close demographic match when we search for a counselor and why we are ambivalent about someone much older being able to understand us. It is reassuring to think we are unique, special, and unusual.

How painful, at the existential level, to think we are common and marching through the short human life span just like everyone else. Marching through with no uniqueness to be forgotten like those before. An older person can understand us because our story is the same. This awareness can be too much to bear!

There is a long literature regarding the impact of practitioner characteristics on process and outcome. Stanley Strong (1968) had a big impact in the field with the use of social psychology variables in counseling. He and colleagues made a compelling case for the theory that birds of a feather fly together. Specifically, they found that initial client perceptions of similarity, attractiveness, and expertness had a bonding influence on the client's commitment. College students seeking a counselor want to be able to trust her or him. This is especially true when the help seeking occurs under intense stress. Generally, females are socialized into a culture where they share personal feelings with their mother, sisters, female teachers, and female friends. Joan, the 29-year-old therapist, fits this internal schema of whom to trust.

The gender demographic in help seeking has not been explored as much as the ethnic demographic. Many researchers have examined the variable of ethnicity and help seeking. Early researchers here were S. Sue (1988) and Atkinson (1985). Two classic books on this topic are *Counseling the Culturally Different: Theory and Practice,* in its fifth edition, by D. W. Sue and S. Sue (2007), and *Ethnicity and Family Therapy,* in its third edition, by McGoldrick, Giordano, and Garcia-Presto (2005). These and other authors have examined aspects of counselor and client ethnicity match in the practice setting. For example, Rodriguez (1997) illuminates the stretching—and confusing—experience of growing up bilingual. The practitioner with recent experience with this reality can be attuned to a client in this world. We discuss culturally competent practice in more depth in Chapter 5.

Here is an example of the importance of birds of a feather flying together. Great professional-level basketball players seek out John Lucas for help in living successfully in that world. Why? John Lucas is an African American male who played in the National Basketball Association. While competing professionally, he struggled with personal life choices. He has a lot of personal experiences to use in his work with these young men who play professional basketball. Although Lucas is not a licensed mental health practitioner, that does not stop young athletes from calling and visiting him. Demographic and experience matches are important in our work, especially at the initial level of contact and comfort for clients. Again, therapy matches on such variables as age, ethnicity, gender, and common experiences can be valuable.

The demographic advantage is not automatic. One licensed therapist colleague had two clients near her age of 34; one of them, a 36-year-old female, said the therapist was too young to know anything; the other, also a 36-year-old female, thought the therapist would be helpful because she had so much life experience. And just because we are like our clients in age, gender, ethnicity, education level, and so on does not mean that we automatically track their experience, especially at the important emotional level. The risk of projections by practitioners can be higher in these situations.

The demographic advantage is also not automatic because understanding another person is a complex process with many twist and turns. *Memoirs of a Geisha* (Golden, 1997) is, according to reviewers and experts, a very sensitive and accurate account of the geisha culture in Japan. Reading it, I thought that surely the book was written as a memoir by a senior geisha. It was not. It was written by a white man from New York. So, our expectations can get upended. However, as I have said in this chapter, the demographic match on such factors as gender, age, ethnicity, social class, and the practitioner's previous experience with the client's major concerns often provide glue for the initial working alliance.

Most new students in the helping professions, teaching, and many healthcare practitioner fields are female. Most of them are in their 20s and 30s. And most of the student clients going to the over 5,000 colleges and universities for therapy, counseling, and advising in the United States are females in their 20s. Novice practitioners and student clients match on age and gender. In thousands of counselor–client encounters every month, this match produces good outcomes for those seeking help. This idea is supported by one study that found that "graduate students and paraprofessionals were found to be more effective with younger than with older clients" (Lambert & Ogles, 2004, p. 167). This means that every year at many practice sites in agencies, hospitals, clinics, and college centers, female practicum students and interns in their 20s and 30s do good work for female college student clients in their 20s. There are many other examples of positive demographic matches.

Why are the clients mostly female? One idea is that females generally experience more stress than males; another is that males are strongly socialized to show no weakness or vulnerability and, therefore, cannot ask for this kind of help. Historically and cross-culturally, all over the world, young males in their teens and early 20s are sent to combat and war. They are asked to engage in violent and stressful activities without expressing any vulnerable emotions, such as fear, empathy for the enemy, or hopelessness. *War* by Junger (2010) presents a chilling account of the numbing effect of war on men.

Females do not share this burden. Yes, some are in combat, but overall, there are large gender differences in expected behavior. And as one would expect, research has found a consistent gender difference in male and female help seeking, with females having more positive attitudes about expressing a desire to be helped (Walter, Yon, & Skovholt, 2010). Perhaps the gender differences in help seeking come from a combination of stress and openness to seeking help, which produces mostly female clients.

NOVICE ADVANTAGE 3: NEWER KNOWLEDGE

A third advantage is that novices do not have the "hardening of the categories," a term based on the phrase "hardening of the arteries" that Wendell Johnson (1946) used in the book *People in Quandaries*. Can you teach an old dog new tricks? Sometimes. Can you teach a new dog new tricks? Usually you can. Here we have another novice advantage.

As we all know, knowledge develops and turns over at an astonishing rate. New knowledge is being generated at a high rate, and no one can keep up with the research, theory, techniques, and tips in any professional field. A large percentage of all books and articles have been published in the last ten years. Twenty years after graduate school, one well-respected practitioner told me she had replaced about 80% of what she learned in school with new knowledge. However, many veteran practitioners in therapy and counseling are not so intensely focused on continuing to learn and grow and seek out new ideas.

Novices have been in the graduate classroom more recently than veteran practitioners have. Graduate students in counseling and therapy are now being exposed to both new areas and increased concentration in these areas: cultural competence, evidence-based practice, psychopharmacology, the common factors, motivational interviewing, genetic influences, attachment theory, emotionally focused methods, addiction theory, and much, much more.

Some of my friends prefer young physicians because they have just finished medical school and been exposed to the newest research and theory; others prefer seasoned doctors who have a lot of experience. One could argue either way, and for that reason, there is support for the value of novice therapists even when novices feel overwhelmed and unprepared.

Some practitioners work very hard to stay current on academic theory and research. Doing so is difficult. The slope of the curve of getting behind on current academic insights varies between practitioners. Often doctoral students know the most about the entire field when they study for and take the two-day written preliminary exams. Another time is when they take the national exam in psychology. Of course, there is the knowledge base that comes out of practice, which is a rich source for practitioners.

So, the value of newer knowledge versus older knowledge is not a simple issue.

NOVICE ADVANTAGE 4: CLOSENESS TO ONE'S OWN PERSONAL SUFFERING

> My journey into counseling is laden with ironies. Perhaps the most significant is that the focus of my counseling work—helping clients identify and pursue their calling in life—grew out of significant challenges I experienced identifying my own calling.
>
> —*Dik, 2010, p. 34*

Novice therapists often are closer to what we could call the developmental suffering—the struggles of growing up—of many clients. Novices may know, for example, struggles with body image, career confusion, or forming their own sense of self. Older, more experienced practitioners are more expert in flowing through the seasons of life over many, many years and reflecting on the incredible experience of being alive. This should give veterans clear advantages, and, yes, there are many advantages to being older and wiser. However, a research base in teacher education is instructive here. It shows that some people who are very smart in a content area are not very good teachers to beginners.

Nathan and Petrosino (2003) define an "expert blind spot" as a consistent perceptual mistake that can happen with veteran practitioners. Sometimes knowledge is so embedded for highly experienced practitioners that they cannot relate well to a person far from them in life experience. The authors explore this topic when examining the teaching of mathematics. Using a concept from the physiology of the retina, they discuss how experts in mathematics can be so focused on what they know at an advanced level that they are unaware—have a blind spot—that the beginning student is at a very different place. Beginners needs a teacher sensitive to their developmental needs more than a genius who cannot reach down to new students. Nathan and Petrosino mention the "curse of knowledge" that can make for such a divide between the new student and the content expert.

How does knowing so much about a topic relate to novice advantages for therapists and counselors? It may be that older, seasoned practitioners are much wiser in living life but cannot reach down or explain very well the small steps that are part of the suffering process, the maturing process, the growing up process of those newer to certain life concerns. Sometimes highly experienced practitioners cannot access the vivid emotional, cognitive, or behavioral aspects of situations because they occurred so long ago in their own lives. Also, situations that may seem acute for a 19-year-old may seem trite to older practitioners, who believe that "time heals all wounds." One veteran practitioner told me he got tired of offering what he called elementary mental health first aid. Younger, novice therapists probably would not react this way. So here we have data for Novice Advantage 4.

Here are more ideas about this novice advantage. There is often great personal meaning in occupational choice. Many careers are chosen because of a connection to one's personal life. Just today, I read in our local paper about an M.D. who radically changed college majors because of his father's major stroke at that time. Often such choices can bring great meaning, purpose, and satisfaction. Careers in the helping professions often have personal meaning. This felt sense can give novices an advantage because often it provides a well of energy for the work. Sometimes older practitioners have been able to work out the pain, hurt, and emptiness associated with the personal meaning of their career choice and are more at peace. Being more at peace may mean fewer countertransference problems, but it may also mean that seasoned practitioners are more content and less intense.

How does personal life fuel the work? We can think of the practitioner's work as emerging from a three-part learning triangle. Each part provides some of the richness for the work. There is the theory and research part, there is the knowledge from practice part, and there is the personal life part. Together they provide the base for the work. Integrating these three areas of learning is a long-term professional task. We explore this learning triangle more in Chapter 9.

Learning from personal life is based also on our own very personal human psychology. Although it is a scientific field, it is so personal! As therapists and counselors, we are not trying to judge the economic effect of globalization, the reason that bees are not creating hives, the necessary thickness for highway concrete, the composition of carpet for maximum wear, or how to make intravenous drips that drip slowly.

In our work, usually personal concerns provide some of our motivation. And it is good that this is true because personal concerns provide energy, deep meaning, and perhaps some answers as we search with others for the solutions to the concerns. Novices are on the raw edge with the personal concerns that propel them, in part, into the therapy profession.

Practitioners enter our field with one or more of these concerns. In moments of candor we might hear novices say:

"Adoption is important because I was adopted."
"Bullying is important because I was bullied."
"I want to help others who are bi-racial like others helped me."
"Career decision-making skills are important because I wandered around lost for so long."
"Family instability is important to reduce because I had so much of it."
"Molestation has left me unable to trust. It is so destructive and a central issue."
"Depression is so hard to manage; at least, it was for me."

And the topics go on: eating disorders and body image, academic struggles, chronic anxiety, addiction, lying and deceit, cultural and ethnic discrimination and alienation, existential and religious meaning, finding a satisfying partner and intimacy, financial literacy and skill at investing, a hovering despair, managing people in a business and more.

In summary, this fourth novice advantage relates to the motivation and interest of novices in their own personal history and the meaning of their own personal suffering. Curiosity and curative factors about the suffering provide some of the novice intensity, and it is this intensity that provides some of the novice advantage. Of course, novices must learn that the work is about the welfare of the client, the patient, the student, the supervisee. It is not about the self. One of the reasons getting paid for the work is such a good idea is because getting paid is a legitimate and very appropriate practitioner need. Trying to meet personal needs—like friendship—are not.

There are plenty of surprises around the bend of the novice voyage. Many are loss-of-innocence surprises. For example, the power of our work is its deep, selfless nature. This orientation provides so many of the possibilities for healing, education, and development. Yet we have people signing up at the enlistment table who are oriented first and foremost to self-healing. Just as those who enlist in the military or get married are sometimes in for big surprises, so too are many of those entering the helping professions. How the needs of the other and the needs of the self can coexist is a major focus of professional training. It is also a theme in other parts of this book.

The basic point here is that the personal narrative of novice practitioners provides interest and enthusiasm for the work and helps make the bridge to the client. It is a source of energy for the intensity that is a novice advantage.

SUMMARY

The novice advantages are mostly about the advantages of being younger rather than being older: the openness to experience, the excitement of entering the adult world, the innocence when all things are possible. It is the energetic young pup, not the old dog,

greeting the neighbor. It is the excitement of the child jumping up and down, screaming in delight and running, not the measured response of the old chiseled guy. Novice
intensity means that the emerging practitioner can offer a lot when initially getting in
the practitioner saddle.

Novices can do what Yalom says is so important in the next quote.

What do patients recall when they look back, years later, on their experience in
therapy? . . .

More often than not, they remember the positive supportive statements of their
therapist.

. . . Don't be stingy [but] . . . beware of empty compliments. . . . Acceptance and
support from one [the therapist] who knows you so intimately is enormously
affirming.

—*Yalom, 2002, pp. 13–14*

Hold onto these novice advantages because, with Chapter 3, we enter turbulent seas.
There are lots of whitecaps for novices, and we will be entering them in a few pages.

REFERENCES

Atkinson, D. R. (1985). A meta-review of research
on cross-cultural-counseling and development.
*Journal of Multicultural Counseling and Develop-
ment, 13*, 138–153.

Bandura, A. (1997). *Self-efficacy. The exercise of control.* New York, NY: Freeman.

Bohart, A. C. (2006). The active client. In J. C.
Norcross, L. E. Beutler, & R. F. Levant (Eds.),
Evidence-based practices in mental health (pp.
218–226). Washington, DC: American Psychological Association.

Dik, B. J. (2010). On being called to counseling.
In M. Trotter-Mathison, J. Koch, S. Sanger, &
T. Skovholt. *Voices from the field: Defining moments in counselor and therapist development* (pp.
34–37). New York, NY: Routledge.

Frank, J. D., & Frank, J. B. (1991). *Persuasion and
healing.* 3rd ed., Baltimore, MD: Johns Hopkins University Press.

Golden, A. (1997). *Memoirs of a geisha.* New York,
NY: Knopf.

Harris, D. N., & Sass, T. R. (2009). What makes for
a good teacher and who can tell? Working paper
30. Washington, DC: CALDER.

Johnson, W. (1946). *People in quandaries.* New York,
NY: Harper & Row.

Junger, S. (2010). *War.* New York: Twelve.

Lambert, M., & Ogles (2004). The efficacy and
effectiveness of psychotherapy. In M. Lambert
(Ed.), *Bergin and Garfield's handbook of psychotherapy and behavior change* (pp. 139–193).
Hoboken, NJ: Wiley.

Lin, S. (2005). Online versus face-to-face counseling: An examination of session evaluation
and empathy (unpublished dissertation). University of Minnesota.

McGoldrick, M., Giordano, J., & Garcia-Presto, N.
(2005). *Ethnicity and family therapy.* New York,
NY: Guilford Press.

Nathan, M. J., & Petrosino, A. J. (2003). Expert
blind spot among preservice teachers. *American
Educational Research Journal, 40*, 905–928.

Rodriguez, R. (1997) Aria: A memoir of a bilingual childhood. In C. Divakaruni (Ed.), *Multitude: Cross-cultural readings for writers* (pp. 354–370). New York, NY: McGraw-Hill.

Rønnestad, M. H., & Skovholt, T. M. (2003). The journey of the counselor and therapist: Research findings and perspectives on development. *Journal of Career Development, 30*, 1, 5–44.

Rønnestad, M. H., & Skovholt, T. M. (2012). *The developing practitioner: Growth and stagnation of therapists and counselors.* New York: Routledge.

Skovholt, T. M., & Rønnestad, M. H. (1995). *The evolving professional self: Stages and themes in therapist and counselor development.* New York: Wiley.

Strong, S. R. (1968). Counseling: An interpersonal influence process. *Journal of Counseling Psychology, 15*, 215–224.

Sue, D. W., & Sue, S. (2007). *Counseling the culturally diverse: Theory and practice.* Hoboken, NJ: Wiley.

Sue, S. (1988). Psychotherapeutic services for ethnic minorities: Two decades of research findings. *American Psychologist, 43*, 301–308.

Walter, J., Yon, K. J., & Skovholt, T.M. (2010, Aug. 14). College student help seeking. Presented at the APA Convention, San Diego, California.

Yalom, I. D. (2002). *The gift of therapy: An open letter to a new generation of therapists and their patients.* New York, NY: Harper Perennial.

3

The Curse of Ambiguity and Other Ills and What to Do About Them

The requirements for the novice to access, integrate, synthesize and adapt information are exhausting.

—*M. Mullenbach, personal communication, 1999*

Struggling with ambiguity is one of those unspoken aspects of clinical training that students do not comprehend until they begin their graduate programs.

—*Pica, 1998, p. 361*

How should one talk about the powerful breakthroughs experienced in sessions when they are not observable behaviors but more of a felt presence or shift of energy in the room? Some of my most powerful sessions with clients can't really ever be put into words, much less measured.

—*A. Roth, personal communication, 2008*

THE CURSE OF AMBIGUITY

Praemonitus, praemunitas. (forewarned, forearmed)

—*Latin proverb*

We search our whole career for mastery, but we get caught in the mystery of therapy and counseling. Mystery is the curse of ambiguity, the fog we live in, the confusion. And in the mystery we make mistakes. As practitioners, our clients are our greatest teachers, and mistakes can be our friend. It is hard, though, especially for novices, to make such friendships.

Note: A version of this content appeared earlier in Skovholt, T. M. (2001). *The Resilient Practitioner.* Boston, MA: Allyn & Bacon. Copyright Thomas M. Skovholt.

We are all surprised and unprepared while on our own Lewis and Clark exploration through the practitioner's wilderness. New practitioners certainly deserve one chapter in the life journey of surprises. Students are usually accepted into graduate training in the helping professions because they are so good at being students and always trying to do things right while mastering the content of classes. They express it in many ways, such as by getting high grades in classes. Then these individuals decide to be trained in a high-touch human field, in part because people are interesting. If only they knew how interesting the most evolved of all species really is. For each of us, when taking our turn as a novice, practicum in the helping fields is when innocence can hit reality.

Our work in therapy and counseling involves close contact with this highly evolved species. After many centuries of effort, the world's playwrights, head doctors, and spiritual leaders are still trying to figure out people. The kind of problems we attempt to solve in counseling are full of complexity and ambiguity (i.e., what is human competence, and how do we get there? What is effective helping? What is the genesis or cure for depression or anxiety?). To understand this complexity and ambiguity, we often, as practitioners, use thinking patterns that are not logical—linear—sequential because the issues do not lead to engineering-type thinking. Expertise within these webs requires a long time to develop.

ABOUT MYSTERY

Before visiting antidotes to ambiguity, I want to visit mystery and mistakes.

Sometimes when trying to answer the simple question "How can I really help people?" we enter a confusing, distressing, and lonely search through the mystery, through the fog. It is the fog of more questions than answers, of the circle of not knowing expanding as fast as the circle of knowing, of sensing the powerful reality of human variety and depth. This mystery element is about one person being confused while trying to really understand another person at a level of thick description.

Even at conferences where we go to learn more, we can be pulled the other way—to realize how little we know. The mystery dimension means that most of the time as therapists and counselors, we do not know the answers to our important questions:

Did I help?
What mattered?
If I would have done X, would it have helped?
Would method B have been better than method A?
What is success?
Am I any good at counseling?
Do I really help people?
What are the active ingredients?
Will the client and I understand each other?

What specific impact did I have on that client?
These are enduring questions:
In year one of practice,
In year five of practice,
In year ten of practice,
and always in counseling, therapy practice.

It is a mystery. We will never know the answers to most of these questions, and perhaps clients will never know either. The opaque depths where real understanding occurs often do not come lit up with neon signs. For some novices, the ambiguity of therapy and counseling is too stressful. They cannot stand the fog. But if we, as individual practitioners, can accept the mystery and fog, we can be energized by it—energized by the realization that the problem is too complicated to have a clear answer, yet even so, we still can really help another person.

The mystery is produced by human complexity. We are working with people, a complicated species. Why didn't you choose to work with ants—they are plenty complicated? Or leaves? Or to paint houses? Or to give out cash as a cashier? There are plenty of work options with more clarity. Did you realize, when you signed up, that much of our work is never known?

The mystery is made even more difficult because we are led to believe that there can be great clarity and definite answers that can never get challenged. School, we are told, will simplify our quest. Counseling theories are about how to understand. The premise and promise of academic research is that *there are* identifiable answers.

When I was a masters' practicum student decades ago, I developed a six-session career counseling intervention. Each meeting had a specific purpose. I thought the six sessions covered everything and, at the end, the client would be on the right path and there would be success. My supervisor was very positive. I thought that she, as my supervisor, was very positive because I captured the whole deal. Now I think she was just being positive because the six-session package showed I had more ideas of how to proceed than I had at the beginning of practicum (which was zero).

The problem was that I was trying to do something to another, just as how I am now painting a fence in my backyard. The fence is a passive receiver. It is a one-way street with an energetic homeowner painting an inanimate and unmoved fence. But clients are very active in their lives. In fact, a large part of the success of the work in therapy comes from clients. As Bohert and Tallman (2010) say: "[T]he client and factors in the client's life account for more variance in therapeutic outcome than any other factor" (p. 84). So, my six-session package slowly fell apart because clients were not just passive recipients.

Today, after thousands of hours of counseling and therapy work, I realize there is too much mystery to know everything. The other person and I have never met. Neither knows how it will go. Consider yesterday, when I sat with a 42-year-old who was confused, anxious, and depressed. What will happen? How will it go? What might help? In general I knew how to proceed. Yet, each session is like an art form never expressed before. This is what veteran, and expert practitioner, Harry Grater (1988) meant when he wrote an article, "I still don't know how to do therapy."

I know a practitioner who had intensive training in a popular method in the past called trait-factor career counseling. The method is objective, clear cut, and precise. He then used it with all his correctional center clients for years. It was very structured, and there was research support. He knew the theory worked and if the clients did not get it, then they were not ready. He would go on to the next client. He had no struggles.

Then he had a major personal loss: his son died, and he discovered emotions. Really discovered them. And then his counseling had to change because he had discovered emotion from the inside. All of a sudden, things were more complicated. And he had to address the parts he did not know about before. More fog about certainty.

And out of the mystery and the fog come misunderstandings.

Example 1

This example is about a student client who came for career counseling. It was at the time when professional journals had lots of articles about male counselors being sexist in their career counseling with female clients. I thought about that when the student said, "I want to be a nurse!" I said, "How about being a doctor?" We talked some and then she repeated, "I want to be a nurse!" and I came back to medical school as an option. A few minutes later, in order to be heard, she screamed "I WANT TO BE A NURSE!" At that point, I realized that I had forgotten that this was her life and she could choose. I suddenly felt that I was in the hindering professions, not the helping professions.

Example 2

Sometimes the mistakes hurt more. Many years ago, a male client was really depressed. Every week I said, "I think you should go to the hospital." He would say, "I hate the hospital. I don't want to go. I can go on and keep going." And I would think about human freedom and respecting his choice . . . and about how depressed he was . . . and then I would reluctantly say okay. This pattern went on for several weeks.

Then his friend called and said that the client had shot himself. A week later his parents came to see me—they were in such despair over the loss of their son. They had a value system in which suicide is not accepted. It was awful. Their grief filled up the room and tumbled out the door. Days later, I went to his funeral. And I thought often during that time and later about the hospital and how it could have helped him. And about human freedom. And doing a different job. In the first example above, I was too narrow, and in the second, I was too permissive. Are these mistakes, or are they just doing the best one can in a profession filled with uncertainty? As a note, Thomas (2010) has provided a valuable narrative about her experience as a therapist with the stressful reality of a client suicide.

Example 3

There was the time I was teaching community college students. I had a freshman advisee who was low income, a racial minority, a kind of student who is often underrepresented in college. At this college, students had mandatory advising meetings. He came in for advising, and I started into a long career development discussion with him, giving him lots of time, energy, and ideas. I was going to really help him. In a business consulting setting, it would have been worth a lot of money. Finally after 45 minutes, he said impatiently, "Would you sign the slip? I had to come to get the slip signed." Lesson of this example: Getting way ahead of the client does not work.

These three examples are of misunderstandings and mistakes. Yet there are mistakes within the context of the uncertainty of the work and the imprecision of human understanding and communication. Supervisors of student therapists often tell them to learn from their mistakes. These are the kinds of mistakes they mean.

ANTIDOTES FOR THE CURSE OF AMBIGUITY

Have patience with everything unresolved and try to love the questions themselves.
—Rilke cited by Yalom, 2002, p. 10

When I consider what I have learned about myself as a counselor since the beginning of the fall semester, I am most struck by recognizing that I *enjoy* the spontaneity and unpredictability in counseling. Not knowing what my clients will share when they sit down in my office is part of what I find so stimulating about being a therapist. Attending to clients and responding in the moment requires me to think quickly, be creative, and trust my intuition, which is very engaging.

Nicole Park, doctoral counseling student,
personal communication, May 10, 2012

It is hard to accept mistakes, but they are part of the landscape of the practitioner's world. Some accept their own mistakes. Some do not. It is part of the beast that is the practitioner's world. Hitting a baseball at the major league level is considered the hardest thing to do in sports (Mihoces, 2003). I spend time watching players try to succeed at it. Even among major league players, an average of .300 is considered outstanding. That means failure happens 70% of the time. Managing this level of failure and this level of success is a key to a baseball player achieving and staying in the major leagues. Misunderstandings and mistakes are a part of the beast, just as they are with us in the therapy and counseling professions. If you are driven to achieve and do well in school, it is hard to accept the imprecision that goes with the ambiguity of the caring fields. It is just like a college teacher from Tennessee, who looked back at the rookie year of teaching and felt guilt and regret. He wrote:

> I vividly remember thinking of the song title "If it wasn't for my bad luck, I'd have no luck at all," when I was told that I'd be teaching 47 undergraduates. . . . The hundreds of unsuspecting college freshmen who endured my college teaching . . . should receive a coupon redeemable for three hours of instruction.
>
> —*Eison, 1985, p. 3*

We must learn to accept that it is hard to nail Jell-O to the wall! The work is rife, yes, rife, with lack of clarity—uncertainty—confusion—imprecision. Some of us thrive on this; some slowly learn to accept this inevitability; others go into areas in the work that have the most clarity; and others, when they really learn about the Jell-O, the wall, and gravity, ultimately give up and find a career field that has clear answers. Practice work can be very satisfying, and the healing involvement stance of happy practitioners, as described by Orlinsky and Rønnestad (2005), can be a satisfying reality. However, it is essential for novices first to understand, then to accept, and eventually to appreciate the ambiguity of the work. In a paradoxical way, accepting the ambiguity reduces its potential very stressful impact. Forearmed is forewarned.

Perhaps this chapter is difficult novice reading because there is already so much felt uncertainty. I understand that people will read this book in search for clarity and answers. I wish that I could present the foundational information in a way that tells you exactly how to do the work and make the answers easy to understand and follow.

I wish I could do that. It just seems better to confront reality early and head-on. The first answer, as I said, is to realize that vagueness and haziness is part and parcel of this work. After you realize this, you can pursue a realistic search for some tentative answers.

Embrace ambiguity because it promises a work life of intrigue and fascination. We never have to get bored—a fate awaiting hundreds of young workers entering the work world in jobs that have confined and narrow walls of creativity and invention. Helen Roehlke, a 40-year practitioner and supervisor at the University of Missouri, much loved by her students and supervisees, told me she never got bored with her work *during her entire career* because every individual—every client, every supervisee, every student—was unique. This is the payoff when working with ambiguity and human complexity.

Of course, we are stressed by the ambiguity because it makes finding and applying a really good answer to problems much harder. It is hard to overestimate the stress level of exceptional students when they hit the practicum experience. In fact, as I stated earlier, graduate school is set up to be an experience in misery because admissions criteria favor perfectionist students who master the intellectual content material of school and have an A average. Then we put these people in a practicum when in training for the helping professions and tell them to maintain their high standards, but we are not really sure how to help each person because there are so many changing variables . . . and, by the way, we will evaluate (read "criticize" by high-achieving students) you on how you do. This is a pressure cooker for students with high internal standards of success.

One antidote for this slice of ambiguity is for students to realize that the professional gatekeepers—professors and supervisors—know this squeeze and probably felt it themselves at one time. The gatekeepers try to take this dilemma into account and help students through it. Recognizing that the gatekeepers have experienced some of the same feelings can help students in this situation.

EMOTIONAL ROLLER COASTER

Students and interns who experience failure (e.g., clients failing to show up for appointments or dropping out of therapy; clients not improving or deteriorating) may easily experience accelerating doubts about themselves as therapists.

—Orlinsky & Rønnestad, 2005, p. 184

Fear stops all forward movement.

—Axiom

Just as fear and worry are present for the novice, so too are exhilaration and joy when a session has gone well. The novice can be happy about the session, the clients' progress, and the healing power of therapy and counseling. The roller coaster of emotion goes up as well as down.

The first client experiences are seared into the brain. I remember when I began working in an inpatient Chicago hospital unit. My supervisor said, "Go talk to that 15-year-old young woman. She just came last night." So I did. I can now picture it clearly in my mind, although it was decades ago.

I walk, as in slow motion, across the hall toward her. As I get to her, she is slumped over, with her arms curled up around her knees. She is looking down and I cannot see her face. The supervisor said to just talk to her a little but do not expect her to respond. So I try it. It feels strange to talk to someone who is like a mummy. I wondered: How can a person have a conversation without the other person responding? Then, after a few minutes and a few sentences, I say good-bye and leave. And leave with a cascade of questions: Was it the right thing? Did it help her? What is her problem? Do I like this work? Can I be any good at it?

It was my introduction to the one-to-one relationship that is the core of the therapy and counseling fields.

Years later, I had a similar first experience when beginning to teach college students. I remember, as if it were yesterday, entering my first college classroom with University of Florida students. They sat in the seats. Being shy, I wanted to do the same. Instead I went forward, turned around, and saw 46 eyes, in close proximity, staring at me. Thus, with no professional training in teaching, my college teaching career began.

Novices can feel very excited and also feel inadequate when stepping into the professional role, resulting in emotional reactions cascading on them. The moments can be unforgettable. Sometimes anxiety about the unknown and fear about the known combine. Usually the acute anxiety occurs when novices are in a novel situation (i.e., doing a

Figure 3.1   Emotional Roller Coaster

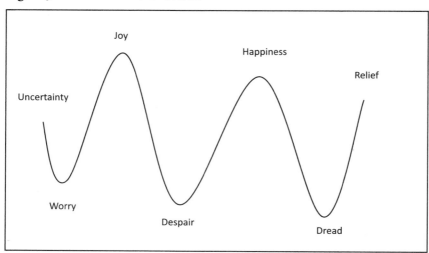

specific professional task for the first time). The situation often becomes arduous because the anxiety of self-consciousness and focusing on oneself makes it more difficult to attend to the complex work tasks. A moderate level of anxiety can improve performance, but high levels of anxiety reduce performance by directing the individual's attention to both reducing the external, visible effects (e.g., trembling and wet hands, unsteady voice) and lowering the internal anxiety level.

Unlike pervasive performance anxiety, hovering like a menacing rain cloud are fears about specific things. The list can be endless, although there are some specific favorites: Being speechless, with no idea what to say to one's client, is a leading candidate for the most popular. Together, anxiety and fear can seriously heighten the stress level for novices.

The emotional roller coaster shown in Figure 3.1 can describe different time periods. I will give examples of the roller coaster over one therapy session and the roller coaster over one month of practicum.

ONE SESSION

Uncertainty is a common novice companion when beginning with a new client. Who knows what will happen when these two people meet? This event of a first meeting between these two people has never happened before. All of their joint humanity will fill the room and spill out into the hallway. *Worry* about specifics can follow. *Will I remember to ask the right questions, give out the right forms, appear professional (whatever that is)?* Then, with things off to a good start—*This is working!*—joy can find room in the novice heart. But, like a roller coaster, the scene can quickly change and suddenly there is *despair. What is this client talking about? What does she want from me? I am so confused.*

The time goes by and there is not much time left. And this brings *happiness. But did we accomplish anything? Dread* arises. *Am I supposed to have a complete diagnosis and be able to explain all of this within a theory? Time to stop. Relief. I guess it wasn't too bad. She said thank you and wants to come back.*

ONE MONTH OF PRACTICUM

Let us say the emerging practitioner is a student in the fourth month of practicum at a community clinic serving adolescent and adult clients. *Uncertainty* can grip. *Am I getting enough hours of experience to fill the requirements? Worry* descends with a sudden feeling: *My personality isn't suited for the work.* A week later, *joy* suddenly arrives when a client is especially thankful for the counseling work. *Telling my supervisor about this feels so good.* But a few days later in case conference *despair* arrives: *I don't want to be responsible for so many people with so many problems.* Yet the week seems to go well with clients and supervision. *My classmates thought my case conference comments were insightful. Happiness* arises, but soon *dread* takes over when a client is in an emergency. *What do I do?* Then *relief. I was able to refer that emergency client. . . . There is light at the end of the tunnel— the semester is almost over.*

ANTIDOTES FOR THE EMOTIONAL ROLLER COASTER

With shifting times and events, intense emotions replace each other. Why such intense emotions? There is no history of many hours of successful work to buffer the confusion. And confusion is a reality in the work. In their large international study, Orlinsky and Rønnestad (2005) reported the number one worry of their practitioner sample, with a mean of 11 years of professional practice, was "unsure how best to deal with a patient"(p. 50). This item was endorsed by 76% of the sample. So, even for those with lots of experience, confusion is the norm. That is an important sentence for the novice. The work of closely interacting with another person and trying to find the right path is like walking through the woods and searching for the path. It is confusing, and that is the norm. Novices do not really know this normative process, so that adds to their worry and frustration. Novices also can easily feel upset about not being taught more, thinking "If they taught me more, the confusion would produce clarity."

The intensity of the early experiences can also be understood by the fact that senior practitioners (when reviewing their long careers) often go back to their early experiences to talk about transforming events with clients. It is as if these early professional client experiences are deeply embedded in their professional schema. So, again I will say that forearmed is forewarned. The emotional roller coaster is part of the novice days, weeks, months, and years. There is aliveness to such affect, so novices should try to accept it and even enjoy it—especially the moments of joy and the times teacher Frank McCourt (2005) describes in *Teacher Man:*

There are some classes you enjoy and look forward to. They know you like them and they like you in return. Sometimes they'll tell you that was a pretty good lesson and you're on top of the world. That somehow gives you energy and makes you want to sing on the way home (p. 77).

TREKKING WITH A DEFECTIVE MAP

Pluralism, along with contextualism, is one of the defining features of the post-modern attitude. . . . [P]luralism considers no single theoretical, epistemological or methodological approach to be superior. . . . Within psychotherapy, theoretical pluralism is reactive to the conventional single-model traditions, each of which holds distinct and often contradictory philosophical and epistemological allegiances.

—Rizq, 2006, p. 614

I didn't teach long enough to know what I was doing.

—Smiley, 1991, p. 384

Ever try to go to a foreign country and use the international language you studied in school? All of a sudden, the book learning hits the practical world; language is used differently from the school room in terms of style and syntax. It is a surprise, and not always a pleasant one. This is the surprise for this section—when lessons from the classroom hit the real world.

Lack of professional experience in counseling and therapy makes everything more difficult. Inexperience creates a host of problems, and the sentence "I didn't know what I was doing" summarizes them. But what does "not knowing" really mean? It means many things. For example, a new therapist sits with a new client who is highly self-critical. The therapist decides that a cognitive therapy approach seems right and tries to apply the theory to the problem. The client does not leap at the ideas suggested by the practitioner. Then the unique elements of the client's presentation puzzle the novice who struggles to find a useful approach. This happens as the session continues with its intensity of ideas, feelings, and exchanges between practitioner and client.

The human solution to confusion and lack of clarity is for someone to write an instruction book and for the rest of us to read it, as with a cell phone manual. This solution works well if the instructions are clearly written—and if we spend the time to read them.

We have followed this path of instruction books often called treatment manuals in counseling and therapy. The confusion problem is followed by instructions. The promise of formal practitioner training is: There will be a useful instruction book. The reality is quite different. Why? I will get to it soon.

EROSION OF THE AUTOPILOT IN COUNSELING AND THERAPY

During World War II, my father worked as an aeronautical engineer designing and testing airplane autopilots. When a plane was crippled by enemy artillery and pilots could not fly it, they would turn on the autopilot and the plane would return to the airbase. After the war, pilots would visit the engineers and thank them for the autopilot.

In the field of counseling and therapy, the reliance on a single method—an autopilot—as the guide has slowly eroded. The "dodo bird verdict" (Lambert, 2004) of all theories producing equal effectiveness has been in the literature for many years. It took a big nudge from the common factors advocates (Hubble et al., 1999) and the stunning research of Wampold (2001) to really slow the train that the theoretical approach really matters in outcome. This is what Rizq (2006) was describing when she said, "Within psychotherapy, theoretical pluralism is reactive to the conventional single-model traditions" (p. 612).

In the past, our autopilot was called a counseling and therapy theory strongly endorsed by a tradition, school, or training institute. Now, with theoretical equivalence in the outcome research, there is no one way to go, there is no one autopilot for us. As Wampold (2010) says, "Despite numerous clinical trials comparing psychotherapies intended to be therapeutic . . . it appears that all the approaches are about equally effective" (p. 110). Throughout the past decades, effectiveness of therapy and counseling rode on the back of method with the practitioner as rider delivering the message. If you had the right horse, then success was just around the corner. And so we had the wars between methods: Jungian psychodynamic versus operant conditioning, directive versus nondirective, cognitive versus interpersonal, and more. Much of this method fighting has ground to a halt with the research that shows almost no success variance attributed to the method the practitioner uses. As Wampold concludes: "There is little evidence that specific ingredients are necessary to produce psychotherapeutic change" (2001, p. 126).

THE NOVICE'S DEFECTIVE MAP WHEN INTERACTING WITH CLIENTS: NO MACRO THEORY GIVES MICRO INSTRUCTIONS

There are a number of reasons why the novice practitioner's map is defective. I have mentioned two of them: lack of practice experience and the lack of a clear winner in the theoretical approach race. Here I go through a number of other factors.

First, remember the ambiguity I described earlier: People are a lot more complicated than cell phones. An example of the complexity of *Homo sapiens* is right there in front of us when we look in the mirror. We try to understand someone else but sometimes cannot even understand ourselves.

Second, the novice practitioner is still working a lot with the internal scheme, the personal epistemology that has developed in his or her own life. Each of us as a lay helper—the first phase in our practitioner development model (Rønnestad & Skovholt, 2003; Chapter 10 in this book)—uses what we know to make sense of the world and offer help to others. Often this way of sensing the interpersonal and intrapersonal world is helpful to others. Unfortunately, our own world does not suffice to help others in part because we are culturally encapsulated by our own small life (Wrenn, 1962). Too often we engage in projections that do not help the other because they are *our* solution to our problems. As Yalom (2002) says: "It is extraordinarily difficult to know really what the other feels; far too often we project our own feelings onto the other" (p. 21). The chemically dependent person in recovery who urges all others to become sober his way is a classic example of this.

Paradoxically, with experience and reflection, seasoned practitioners can use personal experience to help guide professional work. But seasoned practitioners are very careful when doing so. Using personal experience appropriately takes time and lots of reflective practice—ingredients novices do not possess.

So, novice practitioners must try *not* to use personal experience and instead do the work in a professional way while in training. This is what we call an externalization of role while novices are in training (Rønnestad & Skovholt, 2003).

Third, as I have discussed earlier, the current postmodern conceptualizations (Rizq, 2006) and the outcome research (Lambert, 2004; Wampold, 2001, 2010) have combined to knock out the sureness of a single-theory model we can all endorse. And, as documented in the best research handbook (Lambert, 2004), researcher allegiance accounts for much of the difference in outcome research (e.g., cognitive therapy researchers using cognitive measures find cognitive therapy superior). As Rizq (2006) details, this is a distressing reality for the novice in training. Today's emerging counselors and therapists are going through professional training at a time when model equivalence rules the day. Where does that leave students searching for the best map through the thicket?

Even more complicated is the outcome research suggesting that a practitioner's belief in a model is part of positive outcome, although the particular model does not matter (Hubble et al., 1999). This is like asking each of us to sincerely believe in the truth of our religious beliefs while respecting all religions as equally valid ways to profound truth. Asking novices to hold this position concerning theory is taxing for the practitioner.

Fourth, formal theory—narrative, systematic, cognitive, interpersonal, what have you—as a map was developed as a *broad* guide to cover a *variety* of situations, not the particular novel situation the novice has now encountered in this moment with this individual client. Yet novices try to apply the theory broadly, as in this quote from a novice in our research: "At times I was so busy thinking about the instructions given in class and textbooks, I barely heard the client" (Skovholt & Rønnestad, 1995, p. 27).

The micro, specific situation of the novice and client, the dance between them, has never ever occurred before. How can there be a theoretical approach for this micro event? Even after decades of practice, I still am concerned about first client meetings. And why not? We have never met before, and this meeting has never happened before. There is no macro theory to give me micro instructions.

The theory and research map used by inexperienced practitioners comes from others, whether they are writers of theories, supervisors, teachers, or mentors. This is the classic gap between theory and practice that hits all novices in all the helping, teaching, and healthcare fields. The theory-practice gap happens after the practitioner in training has worked hard attending numerous classes, reading countless books and articles, writing many papers, and taking scores of tests. All of a sudden, what one has learned seems irrelevant in practice. One must continually try to access the expert's cognitive map—the theory of another—and use it spontaneously.

Fifth, reflective practice really matters, and our clients are our primary teachers. In a series of critical incidents labeled "clients as teachers," a number of practitioners vividly describe the impact of clients on their growth (Skovholt & McCarthy, 1988). Some of these critical incidents are described in Chapter 5 of this book. In their large international survey, Orlinsky and Rønnestad (2005) found that the number-one source of influence in the life of the practitioner at all career stages (except the novice stage, where it was rated second after supervision) is interacting with clients. And as described by Benner and Wrubel (1982), it is the quality of experience that matters:

> Experience is necessary for moving from one level of expertise to another, but experience is not the equivalent of longevity, seniority, or the simple passage of time. Experience means living through actual situations in such a way that it informs the practitioner's perception and understanding of all subsequent situations (p. 28).

Learning from practice gives experienced practitioners a detailed instruction book. If only we could take this detailed instruction book, boil it down, and then inject it as a liquid into the willing arm of novices. Then voila—an internal compass to guide emerging practitioners through the thicket of working with each and every unique client.

ANTIDOTES FOR TREKKING WITH A CRUDE MAP

Understanding that the classic theory-practice gap is coming can prepare novices for the normalizing reality that the macro theory does not fit the micro level. We all learn this. Be ready for it. And the thrashing is not fun. After all, when you really need a good map, you really needs a good map, whether you are in the wilderness in the great outdoors or the wilderness of an $N=1$ practitioner–client match.

WHERE IS THE FAULT?

After realizing that the practice world of unique situations is different from academic models, novices search for explanation. Earlier I described a variety of them. Two additional ones include disappointment with the training program and disappointment with oneself. Novices often feel an intense disappointment with the adequacy and worth of training in their educational program, whether it is undergraduate or graduate (Rønnestad & Skovholt, 2012; Skovholt & Rønnestad, 1995). Most often, novices focus on training program fault when first feeling this sense of inadequacy. Individuals at this point are almost universally critical of their courses, their professors, or the entire program. It is as if novices are saying "If I was better trained, I wouldn't feel so lost and so incompetent just when I need to perform well!"

Novices often also point the finger of blame in another direction: toward themselves. In this situation, a novice is saying "It is me. I am no good at this and just an imposter in this field. Nothing I try seems to work!" The next description from life as a novice captures the finger pointing at these two fault lines—the inadequacy of one's education and the inadequacy of the self:

> Even after having graduated from an accredited master's program, I didn't learn nearly enough to actually be a school counselor. I sometimes wonder if I really paid enough attention in class or if I read my textbooks too casually. Maybe I just forgot the important concepts that I need to be a helper of children. Yet if I'm asked, I can glibly explain the core conditions necessary for change. I can give a mini-lecture on irrational beliefs and how they impair daily functioning. I can even describe outcome research studies that begin to pinpoint the actual reasons clients do change. Perhaps I studied the theories with the assumption I would be helping insightful clients who know what changes they want. Does the source of this problem lie in my personal shortcomings or in my training?
>
> —*Bandhauer, 1997, p. 7*

The problem is that there is just too much to know, and we really do not know what will be needed at what point. An analogy is with traveling to a foreign country. We pack our suitcases before leaving, hoping to take the right clothes and necessities. Inevitably, we forget some important items. We get anxious and have to compensate in some way. Novice therapists often feel the same. Rodolfa, Kroft, and Reilley (1988) found that, in comparison with professionals, practicum students and interns in psychology experienced significant stress related to a variety of very specific client behaviors that confused them, such as the client's lack of motivation or crying in session. How does one learn how to handle these very specific situations? Bandhauer (1997) responds to this question when describing his development as a counselor:

> I remember someone once telling me that good judgment comes from those experiences brought on by bad judgment. I'm seeking to become a part of the fraternity of wise people who consistently make confident, appropriate decisions. Since wisdom comes from experience, perhaps the confidence I seek must slowly develop over time. To find my way, I must promise to examine

my feelings and reactions to my experiences. When I feel overwhelmed, I must attempt to figure out why. I must try to figure out who owns the problem I'm being asked to solve. I must delve into my experiences to identify what or whom I'm reminded of from the past. Maybe in 10 years wisdom will have arrived (p. 9).

REFLECTIVE EXPERIENCE IS THE LONG-TERM ANSWER

In time and with lots of experience in the work domain, there is a shift from external expertise (the theories of others) to one's own internal expertise (practice-based wisdom and an elaborate set of self-directed procedures). This reflective experience is what guides the long-term practitioner (Rønnestad & Skovholt, 2003; see also the "Themes in Professional Development" section of Chapter 10).

This novice drama is a subset of the larger human drama of trying to avoid the necessary trade of our precious, irreplaceable time on earth for wisdom. Time for wisdom is a cruel but seemingly necessary trade. We humans often seem to object vigorously to this bad bargain—we must give a lot of our life to acquire the experience that leads, we hope, to wisdom. When I was a child, I helped a neighbor who was locked out of his house. As a reward, he gave me a fancy tape dispenser with these words in Norwegian on the side: "Too soon old, too late smart." I kind of understood it, as much as a 14-year-old boy can.

Another example is that of the youngest child in the family who wants desperately to be as old and mature as his or her siblings but can do nothing to speed up the process. Or another: Wouldn't it be wonderful to know the lessons of the last decade without going through the ten years? In reality, building the professional experience base is a long, slow, erratic process (Rønnestad & Skovholt, 2003; Chapter 10).

UNTIL THEN, REDUCE THE TASK

A key for novices is to narrow down the complexity and confusion. As with canoeing, until a person knows a lot of strokes, it is best to just use a few. By focusing on a few things, a few essentials, novices can get some clarity. The great thing about theory and technique is that it tells us what to do and how to do it. Crawford (1988) calls this finding the F-stop, an analogy to adjusting the aperture of a camera to get a maximum adjustment for distance, depth, and light; a way to see the picture most clearly. (Of course, this is a historic analogy because current cameras are mainly point and shoot.)

Almost all training programs in the helping fields, such as counseling, social work, psychology, nursing, and pastoral counseling, have a course for students in basic helping skills. The content of these courses is grounded in the work of Carl Rogers and his classic book, *Client-Centered Therapy* (1951). Rogers has had a tremendous impact on the field and recently was voted the most influential therapist by the readers of *Psychotherapy*

Networker ("The top ten," 2007): "In both the 1982 and the 2006 survey the single most influential psychotherapist—by a landslide—was Carl Rogers" (p. 24). Today there are a number of books in the Rogers tradition used by many students to learn these basic helping skills. These include works by Ivey and Ivey (1999), Brammer and MacDonald (2003), Cormier and Nurius (2003), Egan (2007), Skovholt and Rivers (2007), Okun and Kantrowitz (2008), and Hill (2010). The books present a version of a skills-based approach to doing counseling and therapy work. Based on this Rogers tradition, I will boil this message down to doing ten things:

1. Show interest.
2. Establish a basic agreement, or contract, between you and the client.
3. Listen.
4. Be empathetic.
5. Absorb client affect but not too much.
6. Ask a few good questions.
7. Avoid quick advice.
8. Check with the client for danger to self or others.
9. Try not to get ahead of the client.
10. Go for a good ending including next steps.

Doing these ten things will carry novices a long way in initial client work.

OTHER F-STOP SOLUTIONS

Teyber and McClure (2010) have written a wonderful book, now in its sixth edition, that gives a consistent way to approach clinical work, emphasizing the interpersonal process between client and practitioner. The book has a strong psychodynamic and object relations foundation.

Beck and Beck (1995) present a consistent cognitive-behavioral way to address client problems. Students could use this approach as another way to reduce the complexity and do the F-stop.

The narrative therapy approach (White, 1995) is appealing to many beginning therapists because it presents a coherent and understandable picture of the work of the counselor and therapist. It is also appealing to practitioners because it uses the data of practice—the stories of people's lives—rather than the numbers of empirical research.

The publisher John Wiley & Sons, Inc., has produced a series of treatment planner books that really speak to the beginning practitioner's need for order and direction. At this time, there are over 20 books in the series. They include *The Complete Adult Psychotherapy Planner* by Jongsma and Peterson (2006). These volumes provide lists of diagnostic and treatment hints.

A method called evidence-based practice is very popular now (Hunsley, 2007; Norcross, Beutler, & Levant, 2006). According the American Psychological Association (2005), "Evidence-based practice is the integration of best available research evidence with clinical experience in the context of patient characteristics, culture, and preferences" (p. 1). The problem with the umbrella of evidence-based practice for novices is that it is more an approach about an approach and is not easily absorbed. The complicated nature of evidence-based practice makes it less appealing for novices who cherish elegant simplicity. However, both evidence-based practice and empirically supported treatments are approaches available to novices and the rest of us. In reaction to evidence-based practice being advocated by academic researchers, who claim that the evidence comes from research, another emphasis has developed that focuses on practice, as in the book *Developing and Delivering Practice-Based Evidence* (Barkham, Hardy, & Mellon-Clark, 2010). Evidence-based practice vs. practice-based evidence: this contrast is part of the bigger debate about the source of useful data for counseling and therapy work.

To be popular with emerging practitioners, a method has to help them narrow down the perceptual world while their experience base is being built. In time, novices gradually expand the internalized map of what to do when in the session so it is more inclusive and by definition also more complex.

GLAMORIZED EXPECTATION

A vast deal may be done by those who dare to act.
> —*Jane Austen,* Emma, *cited by Maggio, 1997, p. 176*

I was in the tenth grade, and made some bad choices. Skipping school—I flunked the whole tenth grade. I had a teacher, Mr. Harrison. He just took me under his wing and turned my life around. It was a wonderful thing. I knew right then and there that if he could do that for me, I wanted to be a teacher.
> —*N. Roney in Garvin, 2007, p. B1*

To the extent that you feel inflated as a beginning therapist, you float a bit above ground. I think the origin of "humility" is humans, which is "ground." You are pulled back to the ground . . . becoming less of a god over time.
> —*A veteran practitioner, cited in Dlugos & Friedlander, 2001, p. 301*

Being drawn to working with people often involves the daydream of making a difference in the lives of others. I remember reading as a child about the work of doctors in developing countries—Albert Schweitzer in Africa and Tom Dooley in southeast Asia—and also hearing stories of my uncle Erling, a doctor in rural India. In my mind, all of these stories were about heroic efforts to dramatically reduce the suffering of impoverished people. They were inspiring. I wanted to someday have work of equal worth.

The models we tend to use for inspiration to enter a career field seem to excel at miracles. They may be a teacher who cared so much for us and taught us so much, a nurse who seemed so exceptional, an addictions counselor who helped us quit, or a professor who was so good at the work. Idealized models who seem very competent also feed the idea of glamorized expectations as realistic.

Among those of us drawn to the helping professions, who does not want to enter an occupation where one's efforts produce wondrous results? The dream propels students to study the content of the helping field in an endurance contest of tests, papers, and reports, and reading hundreds of pages of textbooks while filling many notebooks with lecture notes. In the helping professions, novices are highly motivated to find a way to help others.

Without full awareness of the limits to one's good intentions, novices are often more hopeful about the impact of their efforts than is warranted. This overoptimism coexists with fear about one's skill level. The goal is magnificent change. If this occurs, the work is impactful, and a novice is a successful practitioner. The novice may reason: If I am able enough, skilled enough, warm enough, intelligent enough, powerful enough, knowledgeable enough, caring enough, present enough . . . then the other will improve. If the other does not improve, then I am not these things, and my successful entrance into this career field is precarious.

This early novice equation of client improvement equals novice success is less complicated than the seasoned practitioner's equation of client success. For the seasoned practitioner, client success depends on many factors such as readiness, depth of problems, client resources—friends, family, job, money, health—*and* practitioner competence. The more detailed equation for client success buffers seasoned practitioners in self-evaluation.

Who we are as a person enters the equation of our work. Since we are offering ourself to the client, our job is more personal than many. We try to help and please people; this means, for beginners, who want to be liked by clients, the first meeting with a client can be stressful with a need to give a good first impression. Wanting to be liked by the client is often less a factor for the veteran practitioner.

The next first-person account from Pincus illustrates the tie between practitioner self-evaluation and client reaction for the novice:

> Pam was my first client as a professional counselor. I looked forward to meeting her with such unbridled anticipation that I didn't even notice that the air conditioner was broken and the temperature had climbed into the 90s. I fantasized about sitting quietly and listening to Pam with great understanding and much compassion. I just couldn't wait to hear her story.

> Pam was already in my office when I arrived. As I stepped through the door she frowned at me, shaking her head. "Excuse me," she said, "nothing against you, but I'm not talking to anyone but Florence." Florence was her previous counselor who had left our clinic for another job.

I was stunned by Pam's rejection of me. Although I attempted to squelch my feelings, it did not work. I was lost. . . . We sat quietly as I looked at her, waiting for her to make sense of her feelings. I, too, had to come to terms with my own feelings. I was ill-prepared to deal with the assault of my emotions. Despite the pain, I almost wanted to thank Pam for creating this experience for me. If I was going to grow in this field, to find my own way, I had to learn to recognize my interfering feelings and deal with them.

The silence felt more oppressive than the weather. I began to feel anxious, almost faint. . . . My relationship with Pam began to grow. She was speaking to me, even though she was singing the praises of another counselor, and I no longer felt devaluated or rejected.

I continued to see Pam for a while, though somewhat sporadically. Many of our sessions focused on Pam's mother. She told me how her mother gave her to foster care when she was very little because her new stepfather was so abusive. I could see the anguish in Pam's face as she talked about her foster home. Often I wanted to take her in my arms to comfort her. "No one should have had to go through your kind of torment," I said. "You know," she said, "I like you better than Florence." "Why is that?" I asked. "Because you seem to understand me better than she did." I wanted to hug her.

—Pincus, 1997, pp. 59–60*

As a novice, Pincus was thrilled by his client's reaction. However, when clients have other reactions like being angry at the therapist or just not returning for another appointment, the novice can feel quite distressed.

WHAT IS IDEALISTIC? WHAT IS REALISTIC?

In time, the novice becomes more experienced, in part through a "series of humiliations" while doing the work, and develops much clearer, more realistic, more precise, and less glamorous expectations. For example, client readiness, as studied by Prochaska (1999), will be understood as having an important role in client success. In the common factors approach, client readiness and participation is considered a major factor in success (Duncan, Miller, Wampold, & Hubble, 2009).

Realism tends to lower stress. No longer are practitioners able to cure the other quickly and easily. Rather, human change is seen as a complex, often slow process in which

---

*Reprinted from Pincus, S. (1997). Recognizing your emotional vulnerabilities. In J. Kottler (Ed.). *Finding your way as a counselor* (pp. 59–61), Alexandria, VA: American Counseling Association. Reprinted with permission. No further reproduction authorized without written permission from the American Counseling Association.

practitioners play only a part. This recognition helps to reduce practitioner stress. But it takes time to get to a place where "realistic" replaces "idealistic." Only later will novices really comprehend how so many factors, such as readiness by the other, play a role in client/student/patient success. Lange (1988) describes her emerging understanding of readiness:

> [Growth] in my professional development has increased my sensitivity in several areas. First is my appreciation of client readiness to change. No matter how brilliant my insights and strategies, the ability to change rests with clients, who will hear what they need to hear and know what they need to know. What may seem insignificant to me may be the critical incident for a particular client. I am a facilitator and an encourager, but the client decides how and when to create a new identity (p. 109).

In addition to being attracted to a field where one dreams of magnificent work, other factors tend to help inflate and glamorize our expectations. One factor is the many ways that success—and failure too—can be defined. What is success? For example, is a doctor successful if the patient lives? Then how about those doctors who work with high-risk patients with deadly diseases? Right away, with just a few sentences about one occupation, we can see that measuring success within a caring profession can be difficult. When it is hard to measure something, expectations can get glamorized without novices knowing it.

Another factor is the confusion in the literature regarding professional experience and practitioner success. For example, Lambert and Ogles (2004) present mixed data about the impact of professional experience on client improvement. In fact, novices' high expectations fueled by enthusiasm can produce impressive results. This is one of the themes in Chapter 2. Every year, thousands of counselors in training, individuals still in school, help many people. In an analogous study of helping, college professors did as well as trained counselors (Strupp & Hadley, 1978). These results fuel an element of enhanced hope, a trace of glamour attached to the work, and a sense that, if one is really good at the work, big, magical client improvement will occur.

For veteran practitioners, the paradoxical reality is that significant change is possible when one is not so grandiose and unrealistic. For novices, glamorized expectations add to the mountain of elevated stressors. It is just not possible to have a positive impact at each of the thousands of counseling sessions that one has during a career. When novices think, "I want to have an impact in every session," there is pressure and stress.

ANTIDOTES TO GLAMORIZED EXPECTATIONS

Conscientious, serious, and dedicated practitioners continually struggle, throughout their careers, with expectations. Expectations tie directly into how we evaluate the feedback we receive about our work, and feedback is essential to continual growth and improvement. So, the first antidote here is a realization that this topic of expectations never gets really settled.

In time, we do less direct tying of client improvement to our efforts by recognizing that the client is not just a puppet to our efforts. We become more textured in our understanding of the many facets of client change. We can take neither so much credit nor so much blame. This is the good news and the bad news wrapped into reality.

The good news is that we are not that powerful; we do not do soul surgery. Beginners worry whether the words of one sentence will harm a client. Yet when current clients talk about past experience, they seldom talk about the impact of one sentence or another. They are usually vague. I remember one man who said, "Yes, I did have some counseling, first there was a guy and then a woman. I don't remember their names and can't remember what we talked about." Sometimes I start an undergraduate course by asking students to tell me about courses they took two years ago during this term and what they learned. I receive lots of blank looks. I relate this to show how counseling-type activities can be helpful to people but that specific sentences by a counselor usually do not make or break things. Practicum students need not think that this right word or that wrong word will totally heal or totally damage.

As part of managing glamorized expectations, we need to realize that we are often just a blur in people's lives. I do think the deeper perspective is realizing that our efforts eventually fade into the woodwork of the human family—yet we need to work at a highly ethical and high skill level as if things really do matter. It is hard to hold both of these perspectives at the same time.

Some years ago I met an oncology doctor. He worked with stage 4 lung cancer patients, individuals who were on a life course to an early death when he met them and became their doctor. A friend of mine was his patient. I have often thought of this doctor and professional expectations. He seemed excited by the work and fully involved, but he must have, I thought, developed a more elaborate way of thinking of success than the basic physician oath of "keep the patient alive." And so we too, in time, develop more elaborate internal schema of occupational success. Over time, our success schema takes account of the difficulty of the task and involves an extensive formula rather than just a simple equation of my effort equals client success or failure.

At the same time, we can also be inspired by stories like that of Dr. Paul Farmer, who starting going to Haiti while a medical student in the United States. By himself, he performed medical miracles in providing healthcare and training healthcare workers for thousands of impoverished Haitians. I suggest you read about his work in *Mountains beyond Mountains: The Quest of Dr. Paul Farmer, a Man Who Would Cure the World* (Kidder, 2004). It was inspiring to read of his tenacity and achievements in reducing human pain.

BOUNDARIED GENEROSITY

When I first taught, I thought constantly about my classes.

—An experienced high school teacher

The pain stayed with me residually when returning home.

—A novice counselor

What passes in the world for tragedies . . . I hear about them, I see them. I can't be knocked against the wall by each one. I have to construct a coping technique that allows me to survive.

—C. Kleinmaier, cited in Garfield, 1995, p. 6

Teach us to care and not to care.

—A prayer by T. S. Eliot, cited by Orlinsky & Rønnestad, 2005, p. 65

I remember how, during her first year of teaching high school, my mother would come home almost every day in tears.

—Kidder, 2004, p. 67

The word "boundaries" is with us in the helping professions, teaching, and healthcare to help ensure optimal care for our clients, students, and patients. The term is used mostly to describe the not-to-be-crossed line between proper and improper human contact between the practitioner and the client. Although cultural factors can impact boundaries and definitions of "appropriate" and "inappropriate" (Schank & Skovholt, 2006), clear boundaries are an essential part of success in these caring professions. Boundaries are essential in maintaining the integrity of the therapy process!

Although novices often are helped in training and supervision to develop clarity regarding appropriate physical boundaries, less attention is paid to emotional boundaries. The term "emotional boundaries" refers to the internal feelings and accompanying thinking of the helper. Novice therapists and counselors can be very preoccupied with the client's emotional pain. This off-duty penetration of the emotional boundaries is a topic of importance for emerging practitioners, and is discussed in more detail in Chapter 7.

TOO LITTLE OR TOO MUCH EMPATHY?

Although learning to have deep empathy is a standard requirement in the training of the helping professions, having too much empathy can be a problem. In fact, in my own teaching and training, about two out of every ten counseling students expressed difficulty with getting lost in the pain of the other. This wonderful quality of being sensitive can be felt more strongly than is good, in the long run, for practitioners in training.

One factor here seems to be gender. As a group, many females have, through socialization and role expectations, biology, or some combination of these factors, a greater sensitivity to the experience of the other person. This does not mean that all females are more sensitive to others than all males; this is just a general statement about gender.

Some individuals who enter the helping professions grow up with a strong orientation toward the needs of the other. Ironically, often this wonderful attribute of caring deeply for others' needs arises from a less-than-ideal childhood. For example, during my work as a practitioner, I saw a child of a verbally explosive mother who learned to be very sensitive to the mother's needs and wants and responded quickly to them. The child's compass of self-care and other-care was oriented on pleasing the powerful and demanding adult rather than a child's normal developmental focus, on self. This orientation was very adaptive for the child in helping to make an unsafe life safer. This unusual orientation to the needs of the other also can arise when helpers grow up in a family where a member is experiencing difficulty in living (e.g., developmentally delayed, physically ill, chemical dependency, or a tragic and early family death). Here the child learns to put the needs of the other first and gets lots of support for doing so.

These situations can create an unusual orientation to other-care in children who developmentally usually are very self-focused. Children's normal self-focus can be very adaptive because it is like a bank account: Get love and attention in the early years and then, as an adult, withdraw it from the emotional bank in the service of giving to others, as with parenting.

Emerging practitioners with a personal history of a strong other-care focus can find boundaried generosity to be very difficult. They can easily focus so much on the other's needs that their own needs of the self—for protection in order to give later—are abandoned. This is especially true for novices who are filled with enthusiasm and anxiety about helping.

Another factor in the penetration of the practitioner's emotional boundaries is experience level. In some studies of practitioner stress, less experienced practitioners report more stress (Ackerley, Burnell, Holder, & Kurdek, 1988; Farber & Heifetz, 1981; Rodolfa et al., 1988). Ackerley et al. (1988), for example, reported more stress effects for less experienced practitioners in their psychologist sample. Results were measured by the Emotional Exhaustion and Depersonalization subscale of the Maslach Burnout Inventory. Overinvolvement was a variable that accounted for some of the variance on both emotional exhaustion and depersonalization. It produces porous emotional boundaries, resulting in elevated stress.

Novice practitioners who work with acute human problems, such as trauma, often experience difficulty with porous emotional boundaries. Pearlman and MacIan (1995) found that sexual assault counselors with less than two years of trauma work experience had higher overall general distress and more disrupted cognitive schemas regarding issues such as interpersonal trust and safety. This is an extreme example of porous emotional boundaries, one of the factors that contribute to the elevated stress of novice practitioners.

ANTIDOTES TO INSUFFICIENT BOUNDARIED GENEROSITY

Developing a variety of boundaries takes time. This skill involves learning to monitor the self, like a car owner monitoring the car's fluid levels—oil, power steering, transmission, brakes. Practitioners look for a positive interplay between empathic attachment to the other and their own very important self-care needs. Learning to balance other-care and self-care takes time and experience, something novices do not have.

In our sample of master therapists (Skovholt, Jennings, & Mullenbach, 2004), we found that these ten remarkably skilled practitioners developed fences around their work. We called this attribute boundaried generosity. They were not totally selfish but rather they were preservers of the self. Why did they preserve the self? They did so in order to have more to give at another time . . . and another time . . . and another time. Within the professional therapy relationship, there is a commitment, generosity, and energy for the client. Yet there is also clarity about whose work is whose work; there is work for the therapist and work for the client.

Boundaried generosity is not a narcissistic impulse to preserve the self but a necessary occupational skill. After all, as Mary Pipher (2003) wrote: "If you pay attention to the world you see a lot of pain. . . . Francesca was in therapy after a brutal date rape. Sue Anne came because her husband had just killed himself" (p. 53). Master therapists, piloted by boundaried generosity, express compassion within self-developed limits in order to give more of their compassion at a later date.

IMPORTANCE OF COLLEAGUES

I remember when I first started in counseling and mental health work. I worked eight-hour shifts in an inpatient psychiatric hospital. Within the proper confines of confidentiality, some of us would process the experiences with each other after our shifts were over.

Doing this was very helpful for me as a way to reduce the constant thinking about work after my shift was over. After all, we were working with highly distressed patients, and a lot happened during each shift in our intense and eager attempts to help. Group processing of the content of client sessions in meetings, such as formal and informal group supervision, can be a very valuable way to reduce insufficient closure.

This emotional and cognitive preoccupation can be educational. It serves, in fact, to provide the material for reflection, a central method of professional development (Neufeldt, Kavno, & Nelson, 1996; Schön, 1987). However, the task here is to learn how to establish and regulate useful emotional boundaries. Novices, flooded with impressions, images, feelings, ideas, worries, and hopes, often have no established dike to hold all of this back.

Novice emotional boundary establishment often tips either toward porous or rigid. The paradoxical task is to learn to be both present and separate and also to have the ability to strategically attach, detach and reattach. These are difficult, advanced skills. Getting better at them is a part of novice development.

ACUTE NEED FOR POSITIVE MENTORING AND SUPERVISION

Lia, a beginning therapist, has her first session with a client. Coming from the interview she is exhilarated but exhausted—the task facing her seems daunting. After the client presented a series of problems, there was a silence, and Lisa felt pressed to provide *the answer*, or at least guidance toward the answer.

—*Ladany, Friedlander, & Nelson, 2005, p. 3*

Mentors and apprentices are partners in an ancient human dance. . . . It is the dance of the spiraling generations, in which the old empower the young with their experience and the young empower the old with new life, reweaving the fabric of the human community as they touch and turn.

—*Palmer, 1998, p. 25*

Thrown into the tumultuous sea of professional practice, novices eagerly seek safety from the unpredictable, powerful, and frightening forces that seem to quickly envelop the self. Seeking safety while on the high rolling seas, novices hope desperately for a mentor as formal or informal supervisor or professor who will quell the danger and let them practice steering the ship. Here "steering" translates to conducting a counseling procedure, such as a 50-minute session—and then doing it again and again. Ward and House (1998) describe the rough seas for the novice as "increased levels of emotional and cognitive dissonance" (p. 23), which can be translated as "the novice does not know what he or she is doing." This is the inexperience factor. Novices seek help from a wise elder—a mentor, supervisor, or teacher—who knows the ropes through experience and expertise.

In their large international survey study of psychotherapists, Orlinsky and Rønnestad (2005) had a very consistent finding regarding the relative importance of eight different sources of influence on current professional development. They were wondering what was important—seminars, supervision and consultation, direct work with clients, reading books, and other influence areas—among the groups divided by experience. The experience groups are called novice, apprentice, graduate, established, seasoned, and senior. "Experience in therapy with patients" was the most important source of influence for most of the study groups. For the novice group, "getting formal supervision or consultation" was the most important source of influence. This is evidence of the central importance of mentoring and supervision for novices.

Feeling vulnerable, novices want one or more supportive relationships with seasoned practitioners. Novices want and need the mentor to be a certain way: supportive, positive, helpful, consistent, accepting of errors, available, and teaching rather than shaming about specific ways of managing the voyage.

IMPACT OF NEGATIVE MENTOR AND SUPERVISOR EXPERIENCES

When starting a new professional endeavor, having a mentor suddenly seems like a very good idea; just as in life, at times, a person really needs a parent. Yet we do not choose our parents, and we do not have the power to create them to be what we want, when we want them. The saying "The teacher will appear when the student is ready" is an aphorism that, unfortunately, is only sometimes true. I am reminded of the title of an article by Cohen, Morgan, DiLillo, and Flores (2003): "Why Was My Major Professor So Busy? Establishing an Academic Career while Pursuing Applied Work." In this case, the mentor often was unavailable.

The absence of a mentor leaves novices with orphan distress, searching for a way on the high seas without experience. Equally distressing is novice disillusionment with a mentor who has failed to provide what is desperately needed. Examples include the absent, critical, confusing, or convoluted mentor. The terms "orphan stress" and "novice neglect" summarize the fear.

The highly critical mentor as supervisor is one part of Orlinsky and Rønnestad's (2005) double traumatization idea. It occurs when a novice has a 1.) critical supervisor and 2.) clients who have such serious, long-term problems that the novice sees no progress even when working very hard and trying everything known. The novice can easily be overwhelmed by two negative forces interacting. Bad experiences for the fragile novice can be a spirit breaker and damaging. We could use food poisoning as an example. A person may have enjoyed shrimp on many occasions, but the one food poisoning experience is the one that gets remembered. Novices who suffer from such bad experiences may withdraw entirely from the field, although a desperate search for peer support and a positive wise elder can negate the double traumatization effect.

The importance of the mentor, at this point of high vulnerability, can be assessed by asking veteran practitioners of the helping professions to describe the quality of the mentoring they received during their critical period as novices. It is through the positive or negative emotional intensity and the acute recall of events that happened decades earlier that one can ascertain the importance of mentoring for the novice. I remember talking with a licensed psychologist who recalled, with great emotion, her double traumatization experience 15 years earlier. Specific situations will be described, and strong emotions of affection, appreciation, and adoration or anger, criticism, and disappointment will be expressed.

We revisit mentoring for the novice again in Chapter 12.

Here are two retrospective mentor stories, the first positive and the second negative. First, Brinson (1997) writes:

> When I catapulted out of the womb of graduate school . . . it seemed as if I spent much of my time babbling, drooling, crawling and falling on my rear end.

> Still wet behind the ears and suffering the after-effects of that traumatic birth experience, I longed for the support and nurturing of a trusted confidant to help me adjust to this new and exciting profession. This guidance became increasingly necessary for me the more I realized that my graduate experience had not prepared me for the "political" dimensions of the profession. . . .

> Having a mentor made a world of difference in my growth. . . . Not only did I find someone who could provide me with the wisdom, knowledge and experience of many years in the profession, but I found someone who was willing to serve as an advocate on my behalf when I faced certain crossroads in my career. (pp. 165)

Conversely, Walsh (1988) describes a negative experience vividly recalled a decade later. The example again is with the skill area of professional writing in counseling, but it could be from any of many new skill areas that practitioners in the caring professions face.

> After reading my fourth revision, the professor returned the paper, with minor changes, suggesting that it was about time to submit the manuscript for publication. In the same breath he also suggested that his name should be listed first on the manuscript. Nothing more was said, and I left his office in "shock." I had developed the project, I had executed the project, I had written numerous versions (with blood and tears), and I had only had editorial suggestions from him. I was so angry that I never touched the manuscript again. . . . I'm sad that it has taken more than 10 years to write about my first project. Old hurts die hard (p. 88).

ANTIDOTES FOR THE NOVICE MENTOR SEARCH

It facilitates the possibility of positive mentoring if novices try to see the bigger picture, even when doing so is difficult because challenging times of acute need tend to narrow the perceptual field. Mentoring is often an add-on for the mentor with no financial or other material benefit. Novices often request a mentor when they feel the need, not when the mentor can afford an additional time and energy commitment. Sometimes mentees (there must be a better name than this!) are acutely aware that the mentor drops everything else for them. This awareness can add a delight, calmness, and security for mentees.

Understanding the big picture can help novices be appreciative, and that is good because appreciation is one of the benefits for the mentor in the social exchange between the mentor and the novice. And as Palmer said in the quote at the top of this section, there can be great benefit in this ancient dance between the occupationally young and old. Active assertive searching for mentoring in a positive, hopeful way can make it more possible. Often valuable mentors are so committed and engaged in doing good works that they miss the novice's pleas unless they are expressed directly.

Finding a good match is often related to the narrow match—of interests, personality, demographics—needed by novices and the lack of structural or financial considerations built into this need. Orphaned novices or novices with indifferent, incompetent, or hostile mentors suffer an elevated level of stress. Sometimes their clients suffer too. Other novices are more fortunate because they strike mentor gold.

MATURE ADULT AS NOVICE

From being an *adult* to being a *student,* that is the problem; the change in term signals a change in status. The term "adult" is used for anyone who reaches a certain age. It is a term of recognition, respect, and responsibility. "Student" is the term used for those who are not ready and still in preparation. It is first applied to children in preschool and elementary school. It is used for everyone from early childhood to old age, as if there were no differences between them. Do fully responsible, older adults want to be dragged back to the limits of childhood and to be treated as children? Of course not, but this is what the term does in its most brutal form. There are many student terms that indicate adult competence and success, such as graduate student, law student, medical student. Here, though, the topic is about the change for adults who return to school.

The change is from "adult," meaning adequate, to "student," meaning inadequate. These two terms tell the story of people in their 30s, 40s, 50s and beyond who return to school. By this time they have performed competently at many adult roles. Now, as students, there is a loss of status, power, and privilege. Sociologists call this role strain. The clash of roles can be jarring for people. One practitioner, a former mature adult student, described it in this way: "Suddenly any assertion of self was viewed as insubordination, willfulness, negativity" (A. Stillman, personal communication, May 21, 2007).

As a student, there is a trying on of the practitioner self's clothes. Who am I? Am I comfortable in this skin, or unsure? And what skin is it? The mature adult student is in a catch-22: robbed of independence and unable to negotiate for oneself a role that maintains adulthood while adding the student role.

Students who go on in school without large time interruptions usually do not feel this role strain because they're in the groove of being a student and have accommodated to that role.

Some graduate students begin a counseling or therapy training program too early; others begin too late. And timing for school, like so many developmental events, really matters. It is hard to be right on time. I think of it as trying to land an airplane on an aircraft carrier. It is easy to be off with the landing on either end.

A large number of students in our field do enter later in life after doing other things: tryouts with other fields and a variety of adult life experiences. Many students in the helping fields are in their 30s or 40s or older. They may be comfortable with their adult selves. By this time they have performed competently at many adult roles. Now, back at school, they are labeled students. Some career fields, such as math, science, athletics, and music, attract recruits early. Young people get on these paths and get in focus. Other fields seem to attract people after they try out other areas in a sorting-out process. This is often the situation with training in counseling and therapy work. Some try other areas first then come to counselor training. Some build on expertise in an allied field, such as teaching, for a career as a therapy practitioner.

One of the difficulties for the adult student in counseling and therapy is the starting-over again. Remember the first day at a new job? So many of us felt so foolish that first day.

I remember when I was a cab driver. I called in to the dispatcher from my cab with what I thought was the right method, the one used by veteran drivers, only to be greeted by the dispatcher with "Gentlemen, we have a new driver out there today!" How was it so obvious?

Starting the learning curve again at the foolish "I-don't-know-what-I-am-doing" point can be hard. Feeling stupid and incompetent can be thorny, especially for people who have been in working situations where they have felt very competent. The situation has potential for high frustration and insecurity. Many people remain in jobs that have lost their bloom because they do not want to start over and feel foolish and incompetent while on the new learning curve.

Adult novices often have mixed feelings about their teachers, supervisors, and mentors. Margaret Mead (1978) discussed the emergence of a new reality in the evolutionary history of humans of the young teaching the old (e.g., computer and technology skills). The hardwiring of the human brain can make adjusting to the new reality a challenge. Do you really want to have a physician who is a lot younger than you are? Does the adult student want to have a clinical supervisor who is much younger? Sometimes it is not a concern, sometimes it is. The adult novice may have teachers and supervisors who are younger in age or life experience. They may not impress the adult novice with their grasp of adult life skills. Or the adult novice may be struggling with feelings of envy and jealousy or resentment.

Then there is the student culture and peer relations issue. If the novice is in his or her 40s, 50s, or 60s, there is the added strain of being much older than student peers. With the other students who are in their 20s, is the student in her 50s a peer or a mom?

ANTIDOTES FOR THE ILLS OF THE MATURE ADULT
AS STUDENT

The first point that I am going to make is a version of the big-picture, long-term view. In so many life situations, developmental readiness for life tasks and life events is a major factor in success. The overwhelmed new mother at 17 may be comfortable with the challenges of motherhood when 37. Time *does* matter. It gives maturation processes time.

So, a first thing to think about is that going back to school later, rather than at an earlier age, may be the most important ingredient for success for the individual in the new field. The brain keeps developing much later than was thought; many college students, especially beginning ones, may be starting college before their optimal biological period.

Our field is a wisdom field where understanding human experience at a deep level increases our ability level. Age gives wisdom time to develop. All the normative experiences of life—such as being a parent, having a stressful job, seeing a multiyear project through to completion, and managing money responsibilities—are grist for understanding the themes of human life. The loss experiences that come with time—loss of parents, of youth, of beliefs, of innocence about the ugliness of human life and its ability to touch you—and failure experiences give perspective and understanding to human life. Older students can use all of these experiences with clients. Of course, there is no linear relationship between age and wisdom. Life does not work that way. For example, with suffering experiences, some people have a lot of suffering early and are able to reflect on it in a way that illuminates their work as practitioners. Others are not able to capture the maturing effect that suffering can bring.

Mature adults can have an advantage with the learning curve because they have traveled it before in another role, such as teacher or mother. Adult students already have had learning curve cues from a previous route, such as learning to be a teacher—from "I don't know what I am doing" to competence. Adult students have learned that competence takes time. Also, they often are aware of their preferred learning method. Some people learn best through strong use of mentors and supervisors to help select what is important to know and do; others like solitary study and application; and others use an extensive peer support approach. Adult students, through their life experiences, have a better idea of what works for them.

Some adults who are back to the role of being students find that their own personal experience and maturity produces more openness to learning from whoever is teaching—whether the person is younger or older—and an appreciation of the teacher's knowledge and gifts. They may be less defensive about their intellectual ability and, therefore, may find it easier to be open to learning.

In addition, being older makes it easier for adult students to fend off the misuse of power and other damaging behaviors inflected by self-focused professors, supervisors, and other professional gatekeepers.

Yes, shifting from being an *adult* to being a *student* can be a problem. The mature adult is now grouped into the same category—students—with everyone from early childhood to old age. Nevertheless, I suggest that older students try to embrace the wonders of being a student with all the advantages that maturity brings. And may I add that bureaucracies are not very flexible places. Students, of whatever characteristics, are in a funnel. They are placed in the same category and processed through school in the same way regardless of prior status. Also, mature students have the same problem as everyone else: They are in an environment that uses a group approach (classes) to meet individual needs. The group approach is inefficient and wasteful of time and efforts. Some older students start railing against the powerlessness of their role. They usually do not get much of a response. Often it is best to get into school, absorb what you can, graduate, and get the credentials and then rejoin the adult world.

SUMMARY

In this chapter, we have considered many central themes in novice development, such as ambiguity, emotional boundaries, the need for a map/theory to guide oneself, and glamorized expectations. These are all whitecaps in the sea of the novice voyage. For some beginners, the whitecaps are small; for others, they are torrential. I hope that even while your boat is rocking, you will manage to keep going forward.

Next we turn to a topic that is both foundational and hard to grasp: professional identity. It is a very important topic for the novice helper.

REFERENCES

Ackerley, G. D., Burnell, J., Holder, D. C., & Kurdek, L. A. (1988). Burnout among licensed psychologists. *Professional Psychology: Research and Practice, 19,* 624–631.

American Psychological Association. (2005). Policy statement on evidence-based practice in psychology. www.apa.org/practice/ebpstatement.pdf.

Bandhauer, B. (1997). Waiting for wisdom to arrive. In J. Kottler (Ed.), *Finding your way as a counselor* (pp. 7–9). Alexandria, VA: American Counseling Association Press.

Barkham, M., Hardy, G. E., & Mellon-Clark, J. (2010). *Developing and delivering practice-based evidence.* Chichester, UK: Wiley-Blackwell.

Beck, B., & Beck, A. (1995). *Cognitive therapy: Basic and beyond.* New York, NY: Guilford Press.

Benner, P., & Wrubel, J. (1982). Skilled clinical knowledge: The value of perceptual awareness, part 2. *Journal of Nursing Administration, 12,* 28–33.

Bohert, A. C., & Tallman, K. (2010). Clients: The neglected common factor in psychotherapy. In B. L. Duncan, S. D. Miller, B. E. Wampold, & M. A. Hubble (Eds.), *The heart and soul of change.* 2nd ed. (p. 84). Washington, DC: American Psychological Association.

Brammer, L. M., & MacDonald, G. (2003). *The helping relationship: Process and skills* (8th ed.). Boston, MA: Allyn & Bacon.

Brinson, J. (1997). Reach out and touch someone. In J. Kottler (Ed.), *Finding your way as a counselor* (pp. 165–167). Alexandria, VA: American Counseling Association Press.

Cohen, L. M., Morgan, R. D., DiLillo, D., & Flores, L. Y. (2003). Why was my major professor so busy? Establishing an academic career while pursuing applied work. *Professional Psychology: Research and Practice, 34,* 88–94.

Cormier, S., & Nurius, P. S. (2003). *Interviewing and change strategies for helpers* (5th ed.). Boston, MA: Allyn & Bacon.

Crawford, R. (1988). Theory into practice: Finding an F-stop. *Journal of Counseling and Development*, *67*, 127.

Dlugos, R. F., & Friedlander, M. L. (2001). Passionately committed psychotherapists: A qualitative study. *Professional Psychology, 32*, 298–304.

Duncan, B. L., Miller, S. D., Wampold, B. E., & Hubble, M. A. (2009). *The heart and soul of change: What works in therapy.* 2nd ed.. Washington, DC: American Psychological Association.

Egan, G. (2007). *The skilled helper.* Belmont, CA: Thompson.

Eison, J. A. (1985, Aug.). Coming of age in academe: From teaching assistant to faculty member. Paper presented at the annual meeting of the American Psychological Association, Los Angeles.

Farber, B. A., & Heifetz, L. J. (1981). The satisfactions and stresses of psychotherapeutic work: A factor analytic study. *Professional Psychology: Research and Practice, 12*, 621–630.

Garfield, C. (1995). *Sometimes my heart goes numb.* San Francisco, CA: Jossey-Bass.

Garvin, B. (2007, Jan. 15). Ant farm. *St. Paul Pioneer Press*, p. B1.

Grater, H. (1988). I still don't know how to do therapy. *Journal of Counseling and Development, 67*, 129.

Hill, C. E. (2010). *Helping skills: Exploration, insight and action.* Washington, DC: American Psychological Association.

Hubble, M. A., Duncan, B. L., & Miller, S. D. (1999). *The heart and soul of change.* Washington, DC: American Psychology Association.

Hunsley, J. (2007). Addressing key challenges in evidence-based practice in psychology. *Professional Psychology: Research and Practice, 38*, 113–121.

Ivey, A. E., & M. B. Ivey (1999). *Intentional interviewing and counseling.* Pacific Grove, CA: Brooks-Cole.

Jongsma, A. E., & Peterson, L. M. (2006). *The complete adult psychotherapy planner.* Hoboken, NJ: Wiley.

Kidder, T. (2004) *Mountains beyond mountains: The quest of Dr. Paul Farmer, a man who would cure the world.* New York, NY: Random House.

Kidder, T. (2007). *My detachment: A memoir.* New York, NY: Random House.

Ladany, N., Friedlander, M. L., & Nelson, M. L. (2005). *Critical events in psychotherapy supervision.* Washington, DC: American Psychological Association.

Lambert, M. (Ed.). (2004). *Bergin and Garfield's handbook of psychotherapy and behavior change.* Hoboken, NJ: Wiley.

Lambert, M., & Ogles B. (2004). The efficacy and effectiveness of psychotherapy. In M. Lambert (Ed.), *Bergin and Garfield's handbook of psychotherapy and behavior change* (pp. 139–193). Hoboken, NJ: Wiley.

Lange, S. (1988). Critical incidents aren't accidents. *Journal of Counseling and Development, 67*, 109.

Maggio, R. (1997). *Quotations from women on life.* Paramus, NJ: Prentice-Hall.

McCourt, F. (2005). *Teacher man: A memoir.* New York, NY: Scribner.

Mead, M. (1978). *Culture and commitment.* New York, NY: Columbia University Press

Mihoces, G. (2003, Mar. 3). Getting bat to meet ball. *USA Today*, p. 3c.

Neufeldt, S. A., Kavno, M. P., & Nelson, M. L. (1996). A qualitative study of experts' conceptualization of supervisee reflectivity. *Journal of Counseling Psychology, 43*, 3–9.

Norcross, J. C., Beutler, L. E., & Levant, R. (Eds.). (2006). *Evidence-based practice in mental health.* Washington, DC: American Psychological Association.

Okun, B. F., & Kantrowitz, R. E. (2008). *Effective helping: Interviewing and counseling techniques.* Belmont, CA: Thompson.

Orlinsky, D. E., & Rønnestad, M. H. (2005). *How psychotherapists develop: A study of therapeutic work and professional growth.* Washington, DC: American Psychological Association.

Palmer, P. J. (1998*). The courage to teach: Exploring the inner landscape of a teacher's life.* San Francisco, CA: Jossey-Bass.

Pearlman, L. A., & MacIan, P. S. (1995). Vicarious traumatization: An empirical study of the effects of trauma work on trauma therapists. *Professional Psychology: Research and Practice, 26*, 558–565.

Pica, M. (1998). The ambiguous nature of clinical training and its impact on the development of student clinicians. *Psychotherapy, 35*, 361–365.

Pincus, S. (1997). Recognizing your emotional vulnerabilities. In J. Kottler (Ed.), *Finding your way as a counselor* (pp. 59–61). Alexandria, VA: American Counseling Association Press.

Pipher, M. (2003). *Letters to a young therapist.* New York, NY: Basic Books.

Prochaska, J. O. (1999). How do people change, and how can we change to help more people? In M. A. Hubble, B. A. Duncan, & S. M. Miller (Eds.), *The heart and soul of change: What works in therapy* (pp. 227–255). Washington, DC: American Psychological Association.

Rizq, R. (2006). Training and disillusion in counseling psychology: A psychoanalytic perspective. *Psychology and Psychotherapy Theory, Research and Practice, 79,* 613–627.

Rodolfa, E. R., Kroft, W. A., & Reilley, R. R. (1988). Stressors of professionals and trainees at APA-approved counseling and V.A. Medical Center internship sites. *Professional Psychology: Research and Practice, 19,* 43–49.

Rogers, C. (1951). *Client-centered therapy.* Boston, MA: Houghton-Mifflin.

Rønnestad, M. H., & Skovholt, T. M. (1993). Supervision of beginning and advanced graduate students of counseling and psychotherapy. *Journal of Counseling and Development, 71,* 396–405.

Rønnestad, M. H., & Skovholt, T. M. (2003). The journey of the counselor and therapist: Research findings and perspectives on development. *Journal of Career Development, 30,* 1, 5–44.

Rønnestad, M. H., & Skovholt, T. M. (2012) *The developing practitioner: Growth and stagnation of therapists and counselors.* New York: Routledge.

Schank, J., & Skovholt, T. M. (2006). *Ethics in small communities: Challenges and rewards for psychologists.* Washington, DC: American Psychological Association.

Schön, D. (1987). *Educating the reflective practitioner.* San Francisco, CA: Jossey-Bass.

Skovholt, T. M. (2010). *Voices from the field: Defining moments in counselor and therapist development.* New York, NY: Routledge.

Skovholt, T. M., Jennings, L., & Mullenbach, M. (2004). Portrait of the master therapist: The highly-functioning self. In T. M. Skovholt & L. Jennings (Eds.), *Master therapists: Exploring expertise in therapy and counseling* (pp. 125–146). Boston, MA: Allyn & Bacon.

Skovholt, T. [M.], & McCarthy, P. (1988). Critical incidents; Catalysts for counselor development. *Journal of Counseling and Development, 67,* 69–72.

Skovholt, T. [M.], & Rivers, D. (2007). *Helping skills and strategies.* Denver, CO: Love.

Skovholt, T. M., & Rønnestad, M. H. (1995). *The evolving professional self: Stages and themes in therapist and counselor development.* New York, NY: Wiley.

Skovholt, T. M., Rønnestad, M. H., & Jennings, L. (1997). Searching for expertise in counseling, psychotherapy, and professional psychology. *Educational Psychology Review, 9,* 361–369.

Smiley, J. (1991). *A thousand acres.* New York, NY: Ivy Books.

Strupp, H. H., & Hadley, S. W. (1978). Specific vs. non-specific factors in psychotherapy: A controlled study of outcomes. *Archives of General Psychiatry, 36,* 1125–1136.

Teyber, E., & McClure, F. (2010). *Interpersonal processes in psychotherapy: An integrative mode* (6th ed.). Belmont, CA: Brooks-Cole.

Thomas, N. (2010). Healing after tragedy. In M. Trotter-Mathison, J. Koch, S. Sanger, & T. Skovholt, *Voices from the field: Defining moments in counselor and therapist development* (pp. 81–83). New York, NY: Routledge

The top ten: The most influential therapists of the past quarter-century. (2007). *Psychotherapy Networker, 31*(2), 24–36, 68.

Trotter-Mathison, M., Koch, J., Sanger, S., & Skovholt, T. (2010). *Voices from the field: Defining moments in counselor and therapist development.* New York, NY: Routledge.

Walsh, D. (1988). To publish or not to publish: That is the question. *Journal of Counseling and Development, 67,* 88.

Wampold, B. (2010). *The basics of psychotherapy: An introduction to theory and practice.* Washington, DC: American Psychological Association.

Wampold, B. (2001). *The great psychotherapy debate: Models, methods, findings.* Mahwah, NJ: Lawrence Erlbaum.

Ward, C. C., & House, R. M. (1998). Counseling supervision: A reflective model. *Counselor Education and Supervision, 38,* 23–33.

White, M. (1995). Re-authoring lives: Interviews and essays. Adelaide, Australia: Dulwich Center.

Wrenn, G. (1962). The culturally encapsulated counselor. *Harvard Educational Review, 32,* 444–449.

Yalom, I. D. (2002). *The gift of therapy: An open letter to a new generation of therapists and their patients.* New York, NY: Harper Perennial.

4

Who Am I Becoming?

The Unfolding Practitioner Self

Identity achievement is associated with an internal sense of individual uniqueness and direction and accompanied by a social and community validation about the direction one has chosen.

—Newman & Newman, 2007, p. 227

The formation of a professional self can be and often is quite frightening

—Adelson, 1995, p. 35

Without a home, a person can feel like a piece of sagebrush, without roots, blown by the wind. Blown wherever the wind takes one. To an unknown home. Is this the feeling of identity lost? Identity unknown? Identity pre-formed?

At the beginning of any new human role, we walk along a path and cross a bridge from the known and secure of the past to the unknown and insecurity of the future. We usually feel unsure, often very unsure. It is human to feel so unsure. Examples abound: the first date with a new person, landing at the airport of a foreign city, the first day at a new job, the early days of parenting.

In the therapy and counseling professions, novices are trying on new clothes and new ways of being in the world in order to create a practitioner self. I am adapting ideas from Ellwein, Grace, and Comfort (1990) about internal identity development of teachers. This engaging internal work is about creating a practitioner self.

IDENTITY DEVELOPMENT: WHAT DOES IT MEAN?

"Identity" is a term to describe an internal subjective feeling and reality. It is a kind of internal clarity about oneself. It is a coming-into-focus process about the self as a therapist or counselor. When we think of identity development, we think of Erik Erikson (1963).

His eight-stage model of alternatives throughout the life span is both elegant and simple, making it the kind of information readers retain and use later. As you probably remember, the stage alternatives start with Trust versus Mistrust for the infant and end with Integrity versus Despair for the senior person.

Erickson's fifth stage is Identity versus Role Diffusion. In his stages, personal identity development is said to occur in late adolescence. In this way, it differs significantly from professional identity, which occurs at later ages. Yet ideas about personal identity development can be helpful when we think through the issues with professional identity.

Marcia (1980) has provided a helpful framework for understanding identity development. It is a theory for general human identity development, not just practitioner or professional development. For Marcia, both *crisis* and *commitment* are central concepts in the process of identity development. There is a kind of "no pain, no gain" in Marcia's formulation. Marcia has four phases of identity development: diffusion, foreclosure, moratorium, and achievement. Although personal identity development and professional identity development differ, it can be useful to understand and use the personal identity language when developing one's own professional identity. *Diffusion* means a lack of clarity about self and often a lack of internal movement toward self-identity. *Foreclosure* is a kind of buying the external package. It is like putting on the clothes of the UPS delivery person and, presto, one is a UPS delivery person. It is a quick—this is me—without the typical struggles of internal sculpturing in identity development. Foreclosure can be dangerous because having the external identity without the internal work can lead to a later erosion of a solid feeling about the self. *Moratorium* is a time of searching and trying out the self in various values and roles without a commitment one way or another. Finally, *achievement* is when a solid sense of self is felt and experienced (Newman & Newman, 2007). The process of getting to achievement usually involves effort, continual tryouts, dead ends, and redirection. There can be movement between phases, especially between moratorium and achievement. It takes time for the internal sculpturing of identity development. *Yes, it takes time.* This need for time is one facet of identity development that I have seen operating in many, many graduate students in the counseling and therapy fields. The person needs lots of time to try on roles and see if they fit.

I hope it will not confuse you if I suggest another way of thinking of identity development—more as a cycle that both goes round and round and deepens at the same time. It is hard to graph something that is three dimensional—a cycle over time with length, width, and depth. To use an analogy, it is like (1) trying on new clothes to see how they fit, (2) seeing if they reflect me, (3) sensing how others react, (4) all the thinking and talking to others about all of this, and (5) making adjustments to how the clothes reflect me, who I am, and how I am in the world. This is a way of thinking how the practitioner becomes herself or himself.

Identity development may be the most important task when practitioners are in school. It is the work *behind* the work. We think of school as courses taken, papers written, exams taken, and practicum/field placement/internship finished. We do not say to students, "This semester you will work on your professional identity for the equivalent of 15 credits." Yet *without* increased clarity about practitioner identity, students often feel *increased* distress as graduation comes. They may wonder: How can I be a practitioner when it does not seem to be me? As an academic advisor and professor, I have spent many hours helping students sort through their professional identity. I think of it as the most important work I do as an academic advisor. This is true even when it does not appear on an official list of advisor tasks, which include: being the dissertation research advisor, writing reference letters, helping students select courses, and preparing students for preliminary exams. Just as identity development is not a recognized student activity, so too identity development, in a parallel way, is not an official advisor responsibility. Identity work is like that: hard to define and make concrete. The paradox of this kind of quiet work is that it is hard to touch but very important.

As I have said, identity development is time consuming. In our time-pressed human lives, where we worship and celebrate inventions, such as the express train, which save time, identity development is like the old, slow train. We wish for the express. But identity clarity takes time. We need to try on versions of a new self, as with the example of how different new clothes get reactions from others, leading us to decide what it all means to us.

Trying on parts of new identities takes many forms over many novice student days, weeks, and months. With the awkwardness of a new adolescent play-acting in the adult world, the novice is trying to be like an advanced practitioner. As novices, we all go through the same stages, as all of us do as adolescents. A classic method of early counselor/therapist identity development is what we call "imitation of experts" (Rønnestad & Skovholt, 2003, chap. 10). Trying to act, feel, be, and sound like an admired model is a *fast way* to start the overall *slow process* for the emerging self. Admired models may include nationally famous practitioners, our own clinical supervisor, advanced peers, and our own therapist/counselor.

This novice preoccupation with self, and the sense that the practitioner self is on stage, is analogous to the adolescent feeling of being exposed and illuminated while on stage. We fear that others can easily see us as an imposter. Like an adolescent self, the fragile and incomplete practitioner self shifts through a series of moods: elation, fear, relief, frustration, delight, despair, shame, pride, excitement, and self-confidence. This raw mixture of emotions is a predictable outcome when the novice practitioner self steps into the practitioner world.

Identity development is not just a movement from a singular student identity to a singular practitioner identity. It is much more like a whirlwind slowly moving across the landscape; the identity whirlwind moves up and down and in and out. It is filled with parts that interact in chaotic ways. This upheaval is hard, but necessary, as I said earlier. Rønnestad highlights the discomfort and struggles of the identity process in his work on professional development versus stagnation (Rønnestad & Skovholt, in press). There is so much conflicting data to manage: between the academic world and the practice world, between one's view of the ethical self and one's view of the politics of the place; between the personal self and one's idealization of the professional self; between one's own hopes for self and others' hopes for one. All this whirls around as the transition is on: from student to practitioner. This same practitioner identity process occurs in other professions too. Two books portray identity development in the parallel caring fields of medicine and teaching: *Becoming a Doctor* (Gutkind, 2010) and *The Role of Self in Teacher Development* (Lipka & Brinthaupt, 1999).

The novice self is fragile and, therefore, highly reactive to negative feedback while often thrilled with praise. There is not much muscle, and the immune system is stressed. It is important to note that age and experience in allied jobs tends to mute various novice effects. For example, as counseling students, mature adults who have worked as hospital aides tend to have less intense identity roller-coaster stressors than do young counseling students (Skovholt & Rønnestad, 1995).

The next accounts from new student teachers, taken from their diaries (Galluzzo & Kacer, 1991), show the emotional reactivity I am discussing here.

> The students began asking me questions over my head. Questions that I found no material on. I handled it wrongly . . . I was embarrassed and getting worked up. The students laughed at me and that really hurt. (p. 15)

> It was the dullest, driest lesson that was ever recited . . . the students were bored out of their minds . . . I felt like crying. The lesson was over in about a half hour. I thought that it would last two days. Worst of all the students were saying I was boring. That was the worst insult of all. They didn't like me. (p. 16)

> I felt very disgusted and almost indignant toward the kids because they could not grasp the things I was trying to explain. (p. 21)

A senior person perceived as very successful who tells of their earlier struggles can be very reassuring for the novice. Kottler and Carson (2002) have edited a book about this called *Bad Therapy: Master Therapists Share Their Worst Failures.* These accounts are very reassuring to novices. (My only objection to this book is the selection criteria for master therapists. Validity in selection of master therapists is important; writing a lot and being well known have no known correlation with actual practitioner skill.)

As I have said earlier (Chapter 1), one difficulty in the helping professions is that this preoccupation with the self occurs at the same time that novices are preparing for an occupation where the needs of the other—the client—is the work focus. A supportive senior practitioner as mentor can lessen novices' self-protective focus and help keep them open to learning and growing while focusing on the needs of the other. This conflict—sometimes felt and sometimes not felt—between a self-focus and an other-focus is one of the challenges of creating a practitioner self. Those who can do both at the same time have a leg up in the process of internal identity construction. Devoting time to all of the identity development tasks is important because, without a somewhat clear practitioner identity at the end of training, novices often want to stay in school longer, search for another more compatible field, or experience a disorienting, jarring sense of self.

COMPLICATIONS AND RICHNESS OF BICULTURAL IDENTITY DEVELOPMENT

Sometimes novices are trying to sculpt a professional identity while also living within, and between, two cultures. Park (2010) calls her quest "bicultural navigation." She worked at creating a practitioner self while also living in both North American and Korean cultures. She begins her narrative with this:

> I was a second-year doctoral student in a counseling psychology program, completing my practicum at the university counseling center. At the time, I was still recovering from the counterculture shock that I had experienced during my trip back home to Korea. . . . I did not belong to either place. I had no place that I could call home. I had never felt so lonely and lost in my life. (p. 87)

Park goes on to describe how her clinical supervisor was of central importance in helping her find a professional identity while in the rough seas of bicultural living. In fact, Park ends her narrative by describing the positives of the bicultural life for her work as a therapist: "[M]y bicultural experiences afforded me the perceptual acuity that one can obtain only as an outsider" (p. 89). Olson (1988), a white kid from Minnesota, grew up in such a totally Japanese community in Japan that he thought, as a child, that he was Japanese. He described his cultural quest as "bifocality and the space between." He later became a school counselor for international students in Japan and was able to use this bifocality to help clients in their cultural confusion. Another cultural narrative was written by Dixit (2010), who grew up as a first-generation Indian American. Coming from an Indian American family devoted to the physical sciences, Dixit is now, while in graduate school, in the process of creating a practitioner identity as a psychologist. These three examples express the complications—and eventually the benefits—of developing a practitioner identity while also doing the other, more personal bicultural identity work.

TEACHER IDENTITY DEVELOPMENT AS A PARALLEL PROCESS TO THERAPIST/COUNSELOR IDENTITY DEVELOPMENT

Janet Alsup, a professor at Purdue University, did an intensive study of teacher identity development (2006). She asked the question: How does a college student, wanting to be a teacher, actually become a teacher? She did not mean the techniques of teaching, such as lesson plans, wearing proper teacher clothes, or what is euphemistically called classroom management (i.e., how to keep kids from throwing paper airplanes, spitballs, or other assorted objects that are intended to defy gravity).

Instead, she asked the deeper question of how a person who internally feels like a student makes the transition to internally feeling like a teacher. How does this professional identity process happen? This is not just an academic question. If we cannot make the internal transition, then we cannot successfully cross the bridge to the new world. We will feel like an alien.

Over two years, while working as a professor in teacher education, Alsup interviewed six college students who were training to be teachers. The interviews produced 1,100 pages of transcript data, which she combined with other material for her analysis. Her own experience of the college student–to–teacher transition, her seven years as a high school teacher, and her extensive reading of the professional literature gave Professor Alsup the context to understand the results.

Like many research projects, Alsup started with her own personal experience. After majoring in education in college, she began as a 22-year-old teacher in New Bloomfield, Missouri. This is a small town, and one I have visited. The optimistic name of New Bloomfield is not matched by the reality of a big, bursting place of blooming fields. But it may still be a wonderful place to live. There, Alsup tried to be a teacher without having a strong, internalized identity as a teacher. She wrote:

> As the school year progressed, the students began to take advantage of my fledgling professional identity. . . . [B]oys broke apart ink pens, smeared the ink on the bottom of their shoes and proceeded to walk around the room leaving large, blue footprints. . . . [Even with more experience,] I continued to struggle toward a professional identity. I vacillated among teacher personas. The first few years, I chose between alternative tactics: either the strict, no-nonsense teacher or the "teacher as friend." Both of these situated identities had good days and challenging days, but each only offered a fragment of a full professional identity.
> —*Alsup, 2006, p. 3*

She goes on to say:

> I struggled with how to become a teacher; I always felt as if I was simply playing a role. . . . I now believe that success as a teacher . . . is attached to a sense of professional identity.
> —*Alsup, 2006, p. 36*

When Alsup did this intensive study of the college student–to–teacher transition, she asked many questions: How does this change occur? What makes it possible? How is this process derailed? She concluded that the central factor in becoming a successful teacher is the development of a strong new professional identity. She said this is much more than knowing how to do the tasks and techniques of teaching.

For some, the coming-into-focus process goes on long enough for clarity about the self to develop. For others, professional identity development does not occur sufficiently for a coherent identity to emerge. Alsup (2006) found this with teachers too. This does not necessarily represent failure; often it is more fruitful for a person to shift, take a moratorium, and seek other ways to find occupational meaning. Three of the six students in the Alsup study who were in college to be teachers were not able to bridge the tensions and make the complex connections between different identities: student to teacher, personal to professional. Their own sense of themselves did not fit with their internal schema of a competent teacher. And when a person does not fit with his or her own idea of an identity, a crisis can emerge. What should I do? The result in Alsup's research is understandable—three of the six decided not to become teachers.

PROCESS OF INTERNAL SCULPTURING

Alsup (2006) uses the term "borderline discourse" to describe a central process in identity formation. "Discourse" is a fancy word for talking, and "borderline" here means the area between one's identity as a student and one's identity as a professional. Alsup is referring to the internal and external, full of confusion and reflection, conversations that students have with each other, their professors, and their supervisors about shifting sense of self from student to professional. These are activities and conversations between aspects of the self that move the individual toward a deeper and more secure professional identity. I call it "internal sculpturing."

The cohort model of education where students in professional training go through school together facilitates this need for constant, pertinent conversations with classmates. This model involves metacognition, or critical reflection between contrasting identity positions and personal and professional realities. This produces upheaval. We can think of it as a giant remodeling project where there is order at the beginning and order at the end with chaos in the middle. The middle is an in-between stage with parts of our past identity coexisting with our future identity in the present. Alsup (2006) describes a productive tension or cognitive dissonance between different identities. This tension is important: "The more borderline discourse they [the student teachers] expressed, the greater their likelihood of becoming teachers" (p. 37). For therapist development, this is a fancy way to say that you should talk to your school friends to sort things out about becoming a therapist/counselor.

PERSONAL IDENTITY AS A FOUNDATION FOR PROFESSIONAL IDENTITY

The more clearly we feel our personal identity—who we are as a person, what we believe, how we think, feel, and behave—the more time and energy we can devote to the molding of the professional self. In her research, Alsup (2006) concluded that for professional identity to emerge, "only the preschool teachers who had a strong sense of their personal identity and its connections or disconnections with their professional identity were able to successfully transition into the profession" (p. 25). Here we have a key to practitioner self-identity development: An already strong sense of personal identity can give stability and energy to the professional identity process. Although there are different issues and routes for different people on the identity path, some things are easier for some than for others. Age usually helps because older people have been doing the internal sculpturing for a longer period of time. Usually 40-year-old novice practitioners can do the practitioner identity development work more quickly than 23-year-olds. I remember one woman, who was a graduate student in counseling when she was 23, tell me years later after she graduated, "I had to grow up and become a psychologist at the same time. That was a lot."

At 23, a person is often doing active personal internal construction work: Who am I? What do I want? How do others see me? What are my natural strengths and my values? This is the personal identity work. And there is also the practitioner identity work at the same time, and it often feels that answers must come quickly. This hurry up feeling with identity development can be expressed with the cute saying: "Not long ago I couldn't spell psychologist, now I am one."

Recently, I had a student in a class who was studying to be a counselor. He had returned to school after retiring as the owner of a small store. While operating the store, he had lots of time for personal identity work and the thinking and imagining of a new career as part of the "Who am I?" question. (Early in my career, Jim Morgan and I [1977] wrote about this imagining of our futures in an article titled "Using inner experience: Fantasy and daydreams in career counseling.")

Please do not misunderstand me when I discuss advantages of being older in terms of identity development. I am not criticizing novice practitioners who enter our field when they are in their 20s. I am an alumnus of that group. I remember my supervisor at the University of New Hampshire saying that I was good at the work but kind of young. Age 26 has wonderful advantages over 62 just as 62 does over 26. And 34 over 43 and 43 over 34. And 19 over 91 and 91 over 19. Take what God gives you and work on the developmental tasks of that stage.

I end this section by mentioning a personal note: When I was 48 and my father was 84, we had a picture together with me standing on my head next to him. I suggest you try it with one of your parents when, and if, you have matching years. There are not many years when we can get these alignments just right.

OVERLAP BETWEEN PERSONAL IDENTITY AND PROFESSIONAL IDENTITY IN THERAPY AND COUNSELING CAREERS

One of the most confusing aspects of identity development for novice practitioners is the boundary between the personal self and the professional self. Students preparing for professional roles in helping, healing, and teaching are often encouraged to act more professionally; that is, to erase the personal. When novices are told to "act professionally," "professional" is understood to be different and more formal than the normal way people live and conduct themselves. A student in a therapy/counseling practicum who is suppressing her natural bountiful sense of humor while in the session is an example of this. Yet in the longer period of practitioner development, it is the merging of the personal and the professional that gives the individual vitality and uniqueness. Professional identity is not a staid cookie-cutter form of teacher, counselor, doctor, lawyer, engineer, or inventor. Alsup (2006), when acknowledging the work of Britzman (1991) on teacher identity development, said "this suppression of personal identity is only a sham, a facade, because personal subjectivities and ideologies do not disappear; they simply remain, and even fester as sites of tension and discomfort" (p. 41). As I mentioned earlier, in Chapter 10 of this book, Helge Rønnestad and I discuss connections between personal identity and professional identity.

TRY-OUT EXPERIENCES HELP DEVELOP PRACTITIONER IDENTITY

I advise students against sectarianism and suggest a therapeutic pluralism in which effective interventions are drawn from several different therapy approaches.

—Yalom, 2002, p. xv

It is important to have many try-out experiences. Each provides clay for the molding of the practitioner self. It is valuable for newer practitioners to have a wide variety of practicum and internship experiences that differ in terms of populations (children, adolescents, and adults), problems (anxiety, depression, anger, and more), and procedures (cognitive, interpersonal theory, and more).

A standard reason for different placements relates to skill development. Equally important is the trying on of the new practitioner self in various places. For example, one psychology student first had a placement in academic advising, then later at a phone counseling smoking cessation program. This was followed by a community therapy placement with low-income adults. All were valuable try-out experiences for these questions: Is this me? Do I fit with the other practitioners here? Am I any good at this?

Early in my career as a psychologist, I was trying out some behavior counseling methods. Someone said, "You must be a behaviorist." I was distressed by the idea, as such an identity was negative for me, and I withdrew from any endorsement of that kind of identity. Another person would like this identity connection. This is an example of how identity is sculpted.

Although the practice world produces very positive and valuable experience for the slow development of practitioner expertise, it is also the context, as I mentioned earlier, for the "series of humiliations" experienced by the rookie in the practice world. For me, the early "series of humiliations" involved trying really hard and feeling that I had failed in helping the client; having a client not return after we had, I thought, just begun;

using a technique I read about in a journal article and getting no response; trying to learn how to use classroom technology while 150 University of Florida undergraduates sat in a lecture hall waiting and waiting and waiting; and having a teen I was interviewing as a consultant—in front of the staff—listen to me for a few seconds and then get up saying "Go to hell!" and leave suddenly. Actually, this last one was a morale booster for the staff, who must have thought: "If the consultant can't do better than that, we must be doing fine!" It kept them going all year. The series of humiliations is a private feeling of futility. But the negative experiences, just like positive experiences, provide clay for the molding of the practitioner's self.

TALKING IT OUT HELPS DEVELOP OUR PRACTITIONER IDENTITY

As I discussed earlier, talking out identity issues is important.

A practicum class can be a very good way to discuss identity concerns. Individual meetings with supervisors or professors can also be valuable. As useful as anything is the constant talking with other novices. Alsup (2006) highlighted how the more internal changes and transitions come from discussions with others and discussions with the self about who I am and who I am becoming:

> [T]his professional identity formation happens through a new teacher's participation in various genres of discourse. . . . Such discourse, as it becomes more complex and sophisticated, results in a more effective physical and emotional embodiment of teacher identity as well as increased intellectual competence. (p. 27)

The ongoing student narrative is often between contrasting identity strains and the blurring and bending of positions. Alsup (2006) quotes developmental psychologist Jerome Bruner as saying: "I have argued that it is through narrative that we create and re-create selfhood, that self is a product of our telling. . . .[I]f we lacked the capacity to make stories about ourselves, there would be no such thing as selfhood" (p. 40).

Often progress occurs mostly through frequent conversations with peers and friends after try-out experiences. Alsup (2006) said the graduate school environment is not focused on student identity formation as much as on intellectual and cognitive knowledge. This often leaves students to do their own identity work, which is unfortunate because the personal narrative that helps produce identity can be facilitated within formal education if faculty make a concerted effort to do so. I am reminded of Parker Palmer's (1998) book, *The Courage to Teach*, with its focus on more internal character traits as essential parts of teacher development.

My experience is that in the more prestigious research universities, the faculty members focus on research, writing, and grants and devote less effort to helping students with their own personal narratives. (After all, there are only 24 hours in a day.) This is one of the ironies of graduate education: the negative correlation between the prestige of the program and the time faculty spend with students. In my experience, those applicants who flock to high-prestige universities are unaware about the environment they are about to enter. They want to go to the places where the faculty are famous without realizing that faculty members are famous because they spend time on activities that are very taxing but do not involve high contact with students about professional identity. This, of course, does not always happen; many professors are very committed to their students' development and help in various ways (e.g., interaction in research teams, teaching together as instructor and assistant, and mentoring about therapy practice).

SUMMARY

Who am I becoming? This is a central question for the emerging practitioner. And one that needs—gradually over time—answers. Novices are molding the practitioner self so that an energized transition to a professional person can occur. We can think of it as a kind of birth: Gradually the baby emerges after so much internal work to become a human being.

REFERENCES

Adelson, M. J. (1995). Clinical supervision of therapists with difficult-to-treat patients. *Bulletin of the Menninger Clinic, 59,* 32–52.

Alsup, J. (2006). *Teacher identity discourses: Negotiating personal and professional spaces.* Mahwah, NJ: Lawrence Erlbaum.

Britzman, D. P. (1991). *Practice makes practice: A critical study of learning to teach.* Albany, NY: State University of New York Press.

Dixit, V. N. (2010). The gap. In M. Trotter-Mathison, J. Koch, S. Sanger, & T. Skovholt. *Voices from the field: Defining moments in counselor and therapist development* (pp. 89–92). New York: Routledge.

Eliot, T. S. (1942). *Little Gidding.* London, UK: Farber and Farber.

Ellwein, M. C., Grace, M. E., & Comfort, R. E. (1990). Talking about instruction. Student teacher's reflections on success and failure in the classroom. *Journal of Teacher Education,* 41(4), 3–14.

Erikson, E. H. (1963). *Childhood and society.* New York, NY: Norton.

Galluzzo, G. R., & Kacer, B. A. (1991). The best and worst of high school teaching, AERA Annual convention, Chicago.

Gee, J. P. (1999). *An introduction to discourse analysis: Theory and method.* London, UK: Routledge.

Gutkind, L. (Ed.). (2010) *Becoming a doctor.* New York, NY: Norton.

Kottler, J. A., & Carson, J. (Eds.). (2002). *Bad therapy: Master therapists share their worst failures.* New York, NY: Brunner-Routledge.

Lipka, R. P., & Brinthaupt, T. M. (Eds.). (1999). *The role of self in teacher development.* Albany, NY: State University of New York Press.

Marcia, J. E. (1980). Identity in adolescence. In J. Adelson (Ed.), *Handbook of adolescent psychology* (pp. 159–187). New York, NY: Wiley.

Morgan, J., & Skovholt, T. M. (1977). Using inner experience: Fantasy and daydreams in career counseling. *Journal of Counseling Psychology, 24,* 391–397.

Newman, B. M., & Newman, P. R. (2007). *Theories of human development.* Mahwah, NJ: Lawrence Erlbaum.

Olson, T. (1988). Bifocality and the space between. *Journal of Counseling and Development, 67,* 92.

Palmer, P. (1998). *The courage to teach: Exploring the inner landscape of a teacher's life.* San Francisco, CA: Jossey-Bass.

Park, J. (2010). Paradoxical empowerment: Finding a voice in bicultural navigation. In M. Trotter-Mathison, J. Koch, S. Sanger, & T. Skovholt, *Voices from the field: Defining moments in counselor and therapist development* (pp. 87–89). New York: Routledge.

Rønnestad, M. H., & Skovholt, T. M. (2012). *The developing practitioner: Growth and stagnation of therapists and counselors.* New York: Routledge.

Rønnestad, M. H., & Skovholt, T. M. (2003). The journey of the counselor and therapist: Research findings and perspectives on development. *Journal of Career Development, 30,* 1, 5–44.

Yalom, I. D. (2002). *The gift of therapy: An open letter to a new generation of therapists and their patients.* New York, NY: Harper Perennial.

5

Developing Habits of Culturally Competent Practice

Michael Goh, Thomas M. Skovholt, Ava Yang, and Michael Starkey

The development of therapists and counselors from novice to expert and the development of cultural competence share a common path (Goh, 2005). Cultural competence is foundational to practitioner expertise.

Emotional stress and mental health care have disadvantaged racial and ethnic minorities (Sue & Torino, 2005; Sue et al., 2007). To become a competent and ethical practitioner, it is important to understand the limitations of traditional western models of counseling. The 1973 Vail Conference resulted in recommendations, among other things, that psychologists in training: (1) be exposed to "multicultural contexts"; (2) be prepared for professional roles in a wider variety of target groups; and (3) maintain a balance between professional acculturation and retention of their group's cultural identity and sensitivity to other cultural groups (Ponterotto & Casas, 1991). As a product of the problem of training that focuses only on one culture (Sue & Sue, 2008), cultural competence guidelines and counselor responsibility in working with culture and cultural values are now described and outlined in the *Guidelines on Multicultural Education, Training, Research, Practice, and Organizational Change for Psychologists* published by the American Psychological Association (APA; 2003). These guidelines have come to serve an omnipresent, multiuse framework for minority mental health and have played a defining role in the efforts to train culturally competent counselors and psychologists.

IMPORTANCE OF CULTURALLY COMPETENT PRACTICE

Counselors and therapists usually enjoy being with individuals and families and journeying with them through the myriad stories and circumstances that require help. Given the growing diversity in many communities, these stories and circumstances should make these helping encounters even more engaging. However, layers of diversity can make clients' lives seem confusing and complex.

Ethnic minorities will numerically outnumber whites by the year 2050 (Sue & Torino, 2005). Therefore, courses and experiences in diversity are of paramount importance for students of counseling and psychotherapy. But beyond ethnic diversity, this chapter embraces a broad definition of "culture" as embodied in the APA guidelines for multicultural practice. In the same spirit of these guidelines, we believe that habits of cultural competence described in this chapter will be helpful in clinical interactions not just with ethnic minorities but also with other forms of diversity, such as social and economic class, gender, age, religion, sexual orientation, ability, and national origin.

THREE STUDIES

In this chapter, we present findings from three studies that suggest habits that can help all of us, as practitioners, move toward cultural competence.

Study 1: Lessons from Multicultural Master Therapists

How does a therapist achieve cultural competence? An elusive question, perhaps. However, if we can answer it, we will be able to not only improve current practice but also help future generations of therapists and counselors address a growing need to help clients of diversity.

In the first study (Goh, Starkey, Jennings, & Skovholt, 2007), we sought to add clarity to the definition of the term "cultural competence" and how counselors and therapists develop it. There is a substantial advantage to studying this topic through qualitative means. Since multicultural counseling expertise is such a rich and complex topic, selectively extracting themes from qualitative research provided us with the flexibility to understand the concept of cultural competence on many different levels. Questions in our minds, when starting this study, were: Who could help us understand this construct? Who were the practitioners who best demonstrated culturally sensitive counseling and psychotherapy? We decided to obtain a sample of the best of the best—the masters if you will—of culturally competent counseling and psychotherapy.

The multicultural master therapists in this study were one male and six females. Three of the therapists identified as Asian American, two identified as African American, and one identified as white. The amount of counseling and psychotherapy experience ranged from 6 to 35 years (M = 19 years). Three participants are licensed as psychologists at the PhD level, one is licensed as a psychologist at the PsyD level, one is licensed as a psychologist at the MA level, and one is licensed as a marriage and family therapist at the MA level. Exploratory qualitative studies of this nature often have smaller sample sizes, as this one had.

What these multicultural master therapists helped us understand was that culturally competent therapy and counseling is not only about technique; it is rather a combination of several attributes. From the sample group, we learned that:

1. It is important to have a repertoire of helping responses when working with people from different backgrounds, not only to have culturally specific knowledge.
2. It is important to understand the different customs and mores of the client, not simply be aware of them.
3. It is important to understand our own biases and prejudices and to be sensitive so that culture is of maximal value to the *person* of the therapist. It must matter, on a very deep level, to each of us.

The next list is a compilation of what the multicultural master therapists in this study taught us. These are highly interdependent constructs (see Table 5.1 for thematic structure of the seven domains). Culturally competent counselors and therapists:

1. Possess a strong sense of cultural identity.
2. Are avid cultural learners.
3. Possess specific attributes that contribute to cultural competence.
4. Possess a finely tuned self-awareness.
5. Are relational experts.
6. Evidence cross-cultural strategizing.
7. Believe training in culturally specific knowledge is important.

We describe each of these seven characteristics.

Table 5.1   Themes from the Multicultural Master Therapist Study

Domain A: Expert Multicultural Therapists Possess a Strong Sense of Cultural Identity

Theme 1: Expert multicultural therapists' own cultural identity is an important part of being culturally competent.

Theme 2: Expert multicultural therapists are sensitive to microaggressive behavior and its deleterious effects.

Theme 3: Expert multicultural therapists are sensitive to their clients' experience of oppression because they have experienced it.

Domain B: Expert Multicultural Therapists Are Avid Cultural Learners

Theme 4: Expert multicultural therapists' cultural competence is not gained through simple experience of working in the field; rather, it is based on a desire to become culturally competent.

(continued)

Table 5.1   *(continued)*

Theme 5: Expert multicultural therapists continuously expose themselves to diversity.

Theme 6: Expert multicultural therapists are always challenging themselves to grow and learn.

Theme 7: Expert multicultural therapists are fervent learners of their own culture and the culture of others.

Theme 8: Expert multicultural therapists are ever curious and concerned about other people and their experience.

Theme 9: Expert multicultural therapists are open to diverse worldviews.

Domain C: Expert Multicultural Therapists Possess Specific Attributes

Theme 10: Expert multicultural therapists do not simply tolerate differences; rather, they appreciate cultural differences.

Theme 11: Expert multicultural therapists are compassionate.

Theme 12: Expert multicultural therapists are genuine.

Theme 13: Expert multicultural therapists are committed to becoming culturally competent.

Theme 14: Expert multicultural therapists persevere, as the development of cultural competence is a long, arduous road.

Theme 15: Expert multicultural therapists are courageous in dealing with their own culture and that of other people.

Domain D: Expert Multicultural Therapists Possess a Finely Tuned Self-Awareness

Theme 16: Expert multicultural therapists are keenly self-aware through self-reflection.

Theme 17: Expert multicultural therapists' work with diverse populations is largely based on intuition.

Theme 18: Expert multicultural therapists know their limits: They know that they cannot work with everyone.

Theme 19: Expert multicultural therapists do not impose their values onto the client.

Theme 20: Expert multicultural therapists are humble but self-assured in what they do.

Theme 21: Expert multicultural therapists are not afraid to admit mistakes.

Domain E: Expert Multicultural Therapists Are Relational Experts

Theme 22: Expert multicultural therapists continuously process the therapeutic relationship in treatment, as they recognize that the collaborative therapeutic relationship is of utmost importance when working with people from different cultures.

Theme 23: Expert multicultural therapists are able to empathize extensively with people from many different backgrounds.

Theme 24: Expert multicultural therapists learn from their clients.

Theme 25: Expert multicultural therapists use self-disclosure to enhance the therapeutic relationship.

(continued)

Domain F: Expert Multicultural Therapists Evidence Cross-Cultural Strategizing

Theme 26: Expert multicultural therapists have the ability to navigate within many different worldviews and have the flexibility to understand their clients in context.

Theme 27: Ordinary therapy disregards culture and maintains a homogeneous perspective on human nature.

Theme 28: Expert multicultural therapists pay attention to culture in therapy, which expedites therapy and makes it more effective.

Theme 29: Expert multicultural therapists raise other people's awareness of cross-cultural issues.

Theme 30: Expert multicultural therapists think about culture and its effects with every client.

Theme 31: Expert multicultural therapists have their own values but are willing to put these aside in order to understand their clients' worldviews.

Theme 32: Expert multicultural therapists know when they are working well with a client from a different culture.

Domain G: Expert Multicultural Therapists Think Training in Culturally Specific Knowledge Is Important

Theme 33: Expert multicultural therapists described good training as key to developing cultural competence.

Theme 34: Expert multicultural therapists have the ability to relate to people from many different backgrounds.

Theme 35: Expert multicultural therapists have some knowledge of different cultures and have skill in working with people from many different backgrounds.

Cultural Identity

The most important tool in the therapist's toolbox is the therapist's self (Yalom, 2002). Therefore, it is vitally important to continually—early in one's career and in later years—try to understand our own developmental history, cultural background, family history, and relational history if we are to be very helpful to our clients. The multicultural master therapists taught us that if we are to be culturally competent, we need to explore our own cultural background; we need to do that work ourselves. Expert therapists spoke about the importance of having a strong cultural identity in order to connect with clients. As one therapist explained, having done the work of exploring his own culture helps him in this process.

> [H]aving been through [exploring my own culture] and continuing to go through that process, I think at this stage of my life it's pretty integrated. I think that's informed my ability to be able to enter the world of the other and help and try to understand my clients and how they see themselves.
>
> —*Goh et al., 2007, p. 14*

If we understand where our values originated, where we learned to make sense of the world, and how culture uniquely affects us, then we more fully understand how central culture is to how a person thinks about, interprets, and makes sense of the world. Of course, counselors and therapists have always sought to understand themselves. The newer emphasis on cultural competence gives us more language to use in this understanding

Avid Cultural Learning

We do not develop expertise by simple exposure to a particular activity. Just because we have done something hundreds, maybe thousands, of times does not mean that we are experts at that particular activity. Cooking is an example: We cook everyday to feed ourselves. Does that mean a person is going to work as the executive chef at a high-end New York restaurant? The same principle applies to culturally competent therapy. Just because a therapist has worked with dozens of clients from diverse backgrounds does not make him or her an expert in multicultural therapy and counseling. Experience is a definite advantage and prerequisite, but it is not sufficient. There is not a simple progression from cross-cultural therapeutic experiences to cultural competence. As one participant reported, the depth of cultural exploration is far more important to becoming culturally competent than simple experience.

> My first reaction is not the years, it's the mileage . . . it's the depth of experience. I know some people who are young in age and young in practice who are more culturally competent than people who have been practicing for 40 years.
> —*Goh et al., 2007, p. 17*

The master multicultural therapists we studied suggested that there needs to be a desire to become culturally competent. More important, they emphasized the ability to learn how to learn. They indicated that this skill is especially important when working with people from different cultures. One respondent indicated that once this process is started and continues to be fostered, it cannot be undone.

> You need to learn how to learn—that is what creates cultural competence: having the ability to learn how to learn. Once you have learned how to learn, you won't unlearn that process. It's the same process but a change of venue, a change of cultural experience, change the group you're in, but you learn how to learn and there are some key things you teach students.
> —*Goh et al., 2007, p. 18*

Practitioners must continuously expose themselves to diversity. There are, of course, many ways to look through a window into another life. Cultural immersion is one. Other options include attending cultural events; reading widely; volunteering in diverse communities; watching foreign movies; being adventurous with food; studying abroad; and traveling abroad in a manner that maximizes diverse social, cultural, language, and religious encounters. With an active process, a person seeks out opportunities to open the self up to diversity to learn different things about other cultures. The natural by-product of this openness and exploration is sensitivity to clients' worldviews, how they make sense of the world, what cultural elements have shaped their experience. This sense of curiosity and openness about other people and their worldviews is paramount in the development of cultural competence—it helps us appreciate the many ways human beings think, feel, and make sense of the world.

Therapist Attributes

In our interactions with them, the multicultural master therapists seemed to possess these traits: compassion, genuineness, commitment, perseverance, and courage. This may be a seemingly obvious list of traits for any counselor or therapist. Yet think of the implications these traits have for competent cross-cultural therapy. If we are compassionate, we become more attuned to how the client suffers and how culture helps explain that suffering, and we become more helpful by understanding that person's suffering. The committed therapist constantly wants to become more culturally competent, perseveres when the examination of his or her own biases becomes difficult, and has the courage to challenge self and the profession to become culturally competent. One respondent captures the difficult and painful journey toward cultural competence:

> So, to me it was hard to come by because it was a painful journey—painful! But you know what, it was worth it because now I see that all of us belong and psychology's role in helping everyone belong and heal, I believe in the field of psychology and our ability to use our power to help people get there. I believe in it. And all of us who are in this field are gifts if we use our power, our knowledge, and our spirits to help others. Everybody has a potential and a reason for existence and that's why we do it. We help people heal, to be well, as we were divinely created to be.
>
> —*Goh et al., 2007, pp. 25–26*

Finely Tuned Self-Awareness

One of the great privileges of being a therapist is the consistent immersion into the experience of the other. We encounter ideas, values, and behaviors that are different from ours, even some with which we disagree, find repugnant, and perhaps abhor. Our own culture delineates what is considered right and wrong, normal and aberrant; therefore, it is exceedingly important to understand our own values, biases, and limitations when working with people from different backgrounds. This awareness helps us to understand our clients' stories, our reactions to hearing those stories, and, at times, limits to our understanding. This awareness is gained through intense introspection and personal therapy. Reading, attending seminars, and other activities designed to expose oneself to diversity are helpful, but awareness requires the extra step of thoughtful introspection. With gained awareness comes many realizations regarding our own limits, including the realization that, as a practitioner, you cannot help everyone, that another therapist might be better for a particular client.

Relational Expertise

Another concept we learned from the multicultural master therapists was the importance of the therapeutic relationship. The culturally competent therapist is always concerned with the operation of the therapeutic interaction. Early in graduate school, we learn that the therapeutic relationship is one key to good client outcome (Teyber & McClure, 2005; Yalom, 2002). When working with people from different backgrounds, one indication of cultural competence is the strength of the therapeutic relationship. Key components that help with the creation and maintenance of a strong therapeutic bond are the ability to empathize extensively with people from many different backgrounds, the openness to learn from one's clients, and the comfort in using self-disclosure in treatment if culturally appropriate. Said one respondent:

> I think the therapeutic relationship is very important. And I think that most people don't think about it on a deeper level. And I don't think you think about it when you're working with patients. . . . I think the therapeutic relationship encapsulates culturally competent work. If [what you are doing is] culturally competent, culturally sensitive, then the therapeutic relationship will develop.
>
> —*Goh et al., 2007, p. 33*

Cross-Cultural Strategizing

Cross-cultural strategizing occurs when therapists evidence a continual process of evaluating themselves in different cultural circumstances and being aware of the impact of their behavior on others (Earley & Mosakowski, 2004). A key word here is navigation. The multicultural master therapists showed an ability to navigate many different worldviews. One respondent described the skill of navigation in this way:

> I think one piece of it is the ability to navigate within another person's culture of origin, so their cultural worldview, understanding aspects of the culture— behaviors, roles, mores, those kinds of things. So, not necessarily that you're an

expert of that but you know how to navigate through it and . . . I really want to underscore that part because fortunately I think it's shifting but there's been a lot of . . . misunderstanding about cultural competence meaning "cultural expert." Knowledge of culture does not make you culturally competent; in fact, I've had many instances where I feel like it's done the opposite in that the person's desire to be the expert of the culture makes them uniquely monocultural and only able to understand culture from their view of that culture, so not what it's like for person A, B, and C to experience growing up in that culture or to live with that worldview.

—*Goh et al., 2007, p. 37*

This does not mean that culturally competent therapists are experts in culturally specific knowledge; rather, it means that they have the flexibility to understand the client in context. This means that the culturally competent therapist is always paying attention to culture in therapy, how it affects the work, how it affects the interaction, and how important culture is to a good client outcome. The therapist knows that culture is key when working with all clients and constantly pays attention to it.

Culturally Specific Knowledge

Much has been said in these pages about the person of the therapist and the honing of the self necessary to become culturally competent. However, the multicultural master therapists made it clear that good training in culturally specific knowledge is also key. They read books, attended conferences, surrounded themselves with people who talk about culture, and experienced strong training in cross-cultural domains. It is difficult to understand another person's cultural background entirely, but having culturally specific knowledge is important.

The multicultural master therapists we interviewed taught us many important lessons about cultural competence. What we learned from them aligned well with the multicultural competencies that Sue and Sue (2008) outline. Sue and Sue state that in order to be helpful with a diverse clientele, culturally competent counselors and therapists must possess several attributes, including:

- Cultural awareness (awareness of one's own values, biases, and assumptions).
- Racial cultural knowledge (gaining knowledge about other cultural groups related to life experience, cultural heritage, and historical background).
- Racial cultural skills (counselors must have a wide range of helping mechanisms to be helpful with minority populations).

Next we introduce the results and implications of a second study.

Study 2: Developmental Model of Intercultural Sensitivity and Some Exemplars

In a study by Goh and Yang (2007), a group of students and mental health practitioners were identified as having an extraordinary ethnorelativist worldview. Individuals with an ethnorelative worldview are more likely to generate attitudes, knowledge, and behaviors that lead to more culturally appropriate responses in diverse situations. In other words, individuals in our sample were mindful and behaviorally adept at navigating culturally contrasting and complex situations.

Individuals in this sample produced high scores on the Intercultural Development Inventory (IDI; Hammer, Bennett, & Wiseman, 2003). The IDI measures intercultural sensitivity as conceptualized in Bennett's (1993) Developmental Model of Intercultural Sensitivity (DMIS). The DMIS is a framework for explaining the reactions of people to cultural differences. According to the DMIS, to be interculturally sensitive is to be able to recognize and adapt to culturally diverse situations. Sensitivity in this manner is considered a marker of effective cross-cultural practitioners.

Goh and Yang (2007) offered cultural competence training and the IDI to a group of 425 therapists and counselors. Of the group, only 5% (20 counselors) had an IDI profile that reflected a culturally sensitive worldview toward cultural differences. Each was invited to share personal insights into how he or she developed cross-cultural sensitivity. Sixteen of these 20 therapists and counselors (including some graduate students in counseling) participated in in-depth interviews to elicit their personal, clinical, and worldview characteristics as well as their conceptualization and practice of culturally competent psychotherapy. It was the authors' belief that by studying such exemplars, we would glean the essence of what sets these therapists apart from others in intercultural competent practice. This captured essence can serve to advance efforts in training interculturally competent counselors and psychologists.

Themes Gleaned from the Culturally Competent Exemplars

Data were analyzed using inductive analysis and modified consensual qualitative research (CQR; McCarthy Veach, Bartels, & LeRoy, 2001) from which 18 themes (Table 5.2) emerged. They are briefly summarized in this section. These counselors had a fluid conceptualization of intercultural competence and sensitivity. Many of them held a lifelong and unrelenting view toward continually searching out diverse experiences in order to learn. Most did not have one definition or a single approach to understanding intercultural competence and sensitivity. In this study, respondents described a desire to be surrounded by, to learn about, and to learn from other cultures. They sought opportunities and were drawn to experiences that involved interactions with individuals and groups from other cultures.

Table 5.2   Themes from the DMIS Exemplars Study

Theme 1: A multitude of cultural experiences

Theme 2: Understanding of own privilege

Theme 3: Culture consciousness

Theme 4: Family of origin influences

Theme 5: Yearning for more cultural experiences

Theme 6: Being cognitively lithe and adaptable

Theme 7: Means to cultural competence

Theme 8: Suspension of judgment

Theme 9: Appreciating human universality and uniqueness

Theme 10: Practice as opportunity for continuous exposure to cultural differences

Theme 11: Comfort with complex ambiguities

Theme 12: Social justice

Theme 13: Cultural identity as an essential tool in therapy

Theme 14: Constantly evaluating one's clinical work

Theme 15: Tripartite process of cultural competence

Theme 16: Mastery of basic counseling skills

Theme 17: Being intentional about developing cultural skills

Theme 18: Comfortable with self

For example, one participant said:

> [W]hen all the refugee kids came . . . I was invited to participate in the programs there, that was when I first met people who were different . . . you know, the large group were very different. And immediately, almost immediately, it was quite . . . I don't know how to explain it . . . there was an interest. Interest isn't the right word, but I was abducted by the power of the experience, of their experiences having come from [different countries]. . . I love meeting new people and asking them about their culture and even white people, it's not as thrilling to me most of the time as other people . . . like where did you grow up and what was that like, kind of questions, but getting specific.
>
> *—Goh & Yang, 2007, pp. 15–16*

All of the 16 who were interviewed noted having interactions with cultures other than their own. Many spoke of having personal (familial) experiences with culture and diversity at a young age as well as exposure to culture and diversity through educational and work experiences. Both positive and negative experiences contributed to a clearer awareness of the existence of cultures and helped pique their interest to continue to be involved in cultural diversity in order to foster social justice.

These counselors developed intercultural competence and sensitivity through practice and by continually seeking opportunities to interact with individuals and groups from backgrounds and cultures other than their own. They viewed their work in counseling as an opportunity to do so. These counselors were aware of how their cultural identity impacted work with clients by being alert to clients' verbal and nonverbal responses in cross-cultural situations. They felt that awareness, knowledge, and mastery of basic counseling skills were important but that being a culturally competent therapist required more attributes than these basics. A culturally competent therapist had, they told us, a deliberateness that sets him or her apart from others. Such a therapist:

- Has strong social skills (i.e., reading cues).
- Is willing to continue to learn.
- Has a genuine interest in learning about others.
- Is comfortable with self.
- Has courage, energy, and a tolerance for pain and discomfort.
- Is not afraid to ask questions.
- Is comfortable with ambiguity.

Respondents in this study felt that their definitions of intercultural competence and sensitivity are constantly evolving and that developing competence takes a lifetime. About this, one participant said:

> I know that the kind of the didactic training that I've had is really important in introducing me to the idea in the first place that there could be certain things for intercultural sensitivity. And I don't think it doesn't mean I wasn't at all interculturally sensitive before, but it gives me more of a concrete framework. And I think that kind of textbook training is really important, but beyond that I know the only way that I've learned . . . how to do that, how to define intercultural sensitivity is through experience. And . . . one job in particular has given me new eyes . . . being forced to work with people who are very different from myself . . . so , . . . about 70% are African-American, probably 25% are homeless and then there's this big kind of drug-using culture and . . . just the culture of severe mental illness is a bit of it . . . so that comes into play. And that has really forced me to kind of stretch how I look at things.
>
> —*Goh & Yang, 2007, p. 16*

Becoming a Culturally Competent Therapist

One resounding theme among our sample of culturally competent exemplars is their breadth of personal experiences with others who are culturally different (i.e., exposure at a familial level, study abroad, intercultural friendships, etc). The second resounding theme is self-awareness. The interviews with the exemplars suggested to us that culturally competent therapists:

- Are aware of transference and countertransference.
- Recognize that racism and injustices exist.
- Have courage, energy, a tolerance for pain and discomfort.
- Are not afraid to ask questions.
- Are comfortable with ambiguity.

One said:

> I think there's got to be some kind of long-term commitment. It's not just you're in your professional life that you're aware of cultural differences, you're being culturally sensitive. I truly believe it's something because who you are as a counselor is who you are everyday. And you might not be using the same mind-set in every interaction or I know I can be very attuned and sensitive when I'm counseling and I don't always practice those in my private life and I have to practice it but I do think, particularly, being a counselor is knowing yourself and when you're talking about cultural differences, intercultural sensitivity and competence, the way you think about the world and all your personal biases and all your beliefs and associations are things that are triggered every single day, so you have to be aware of them . . . it's a kind of a commitment to a lifestyle and working towards change in your world.
>
> —*Goh & Yang, 2007, p. 24*

We believe that experiential learning can facilitate the development of cultural competence. The exemplary therapists in our IDI study taught us many cultural learning strategies that we would describe as experiential learning activities. Cross-cultural expert Paige (2004) suggests similar ideas with these ways to maximize cross-cultural experiential learning:

- When you travel, aim for cultural immersion experiences beyond the comfortable tourist experience.
- Read books outside of your repertoire of cultural knowledge.
- Actively seek and engage with individuals/groups from diverse cultures.
- Actively experiment with cultural foods and languages.
- Develop awareness of how your own cultural identity impacts your work as a counselor.
- Take a lifelong journey toward understanding your own prejudices and stereotypes.
- Appreciate human universality and uniqueness.
- Find what inspires you to seek social justice.
- Learn ways to advocate for social justice.

- Understand whether and how oppression manifests itself in our society.
- Constantly evaluate your own interpersonal skills and effectiveness.
- Pause often to reflect about how well you are doing all of the above.

Study 3: Experts in Appreciating Cultural Diversity

The three studies of experts we are reviewing here all offer insights into the parameters of cultural competence. The third study is a dissertation research project completed by Laura Jarrett (2003). She was very interested in interviewing individuals who showed a great zeal and talent for living and working in a multicultural world, those who had high cultural tolerance (Sullivan, Shamir, Walsh, & Roberts, 1985). Jarrett wondered: Who are the experts who thrive in a world of cultural diversity?

Jarrett did not want to examine negative qualities, such as bigotry, racism, discrimination, racial hatred, prejudice, and cultural rigidity. In her dissertation, she described the classic work on prejudice by Allport (1979) and the writing of many others on these negative constructs. Rather, she wanted to examine positive qualities and study culturally appreciative individuals, which she did.

In terms of method, first Jarrett (2003) asked members of a 14-person civic organization devoted to diversity issues to nominate anyone in the organization who was highly appreciative of cultural differences. Nine of the 14 individuals were nominated at least seven times, and that number of nominations was used as the nomination criteria. At the same time, all members of the organization were given the IDI (Hammer et al., 2003). To be included in the study, participants had to show a significant level of intercultural sensitivity on the IDI by scoring at stage 4 or higher on the six-stage scale. All nine individuals who met the criteria for being appreciative of cultural differences and who had seven peer nominations also had a high IDI score. Each of the nine individuals agreed to an hourlong face-to-face taped interview with the researcher. The focus of the interview was the participant's history with cultural differences—their life experiences and the development of their attitudes. Then, within weeks, Jarrett conducted a second interview focused on the participant's current life, experiences with cultural differences, and current beliefs and attitudes.

Using a standard methodology from qualitative interview research described by Patton (2002), Jarrett analyzed the interview data. In the analysis, she found about 1,000 meaningful units of text. This led to a preliminary portrait of the culturally appreciative person. Jarrett then sent this preliminary description to the participants for their reactions. Six of the nine responded, and their feedback was used to modify the results. For the final results, 30 themes were grouped under 6 categories (see Table 5.3). The categories are: influential experiences; reactions to cross-cultural experiences; defining characteristics; core values and beliefs; struggles; and recommendations for interpersonal peace. Jarrett (personal communication, March 9, 2010) said that her participants, as a composite, described cross-cultural experiences as fun and fascinating as well as invaluable in understanding others. Although cross-cultural experiences increased the participants' comfort in new cultural situations, they could also be very challenging and stressful.

Table 5.3 Categories and Themes from the Experts in Appreciating Cultural Diversity Study

---

Category 1: Influential Experiences

    Theme 1: I was exposed to other cultures early on, by my parents and others, who generally set an example of acceptance and respect.

    Theme 2: Throughout life, I have interacted with a wide variety of culturally different people.

    Theme 3: I have experienced lots of homogeneity.

    Theme 4: I have personally felt the pain of not fitting in.

Category 2: Reactions to Cross-Cultural Experiences

    Theme 1: Cross-cultural experiences are fun!

    Theme 2: Cross-cultural experiences are fascinating.

    Theme 3: Cross-cultural experiences are invaluable: I get to learn and better understand others.

    Theme 4: Cross-cultural experiences increase my comfort being uncomfortable in new cultural situations.

    Theme 5: Cross-cultural experiences are sometimes really hard.

Category 3: Defining Characteristics

    Theme 1: Empathetic

    Theme 2: Nonjudgmental

    Theme 3: Committed to making a more tolerant human world

    Theme 4: Reflective about human experience: my own and others

    Theme 5: Acutely observant of human similarity and difference

    Theme 6: Disturbed by instances of unfair treatment

    Theme 7: Seek diversity and avoid homogeneity

    Theme 8: Strong human connectedness

    Theme 9: Intensely curious

Category 4: Core Values and Beliefs

    Theme 1: Everyone has value and worth.

    Theme 2: We're all part of the human community.

    Theme 3: Human cultural diversity is a positive though challenging reality.

Category 5: Struggles

    Theme 1: I too struggle to set my biases aside and be accepting.

    Theme 2: I have to constantly push myself to grow and learn.

    Theme 3: How do I pick my battles? When I do speak up, and when not?

    Theme 4: I struggle to clarify my own values and beliefs.

(continued)

Table 5.3 *(continued)*

Category 6: Recommendations for Interpersonal Peace
Theme 1: Getting to know people different from you is critical.
Theme 2: Relating to others should include hearing and respecting them, not judging.
Theme 3: Talking about some cultural topics, though difficult, is important for increasing our understanding of each other.
Theme 4: Recognizing that at a deep, profound human level we are both incredibly alike and very different.
Theme 5: We must challenge ourselves and others to change and grow.

Source: Jarrett, 2003.

Jarrett (2003) described her participants as very aware of the human cultural world around them—very reflective about the meaning of human experiences, empathetic toward others, upset about human injustice when they witnessed it or heard about it, and committed to a more tolerant human world. Overall, the research participants viewed human cultural diversity as both a positive and a challenging human reality. The challenging part meant that conflict—both interpersonal and intrapersonal—came with the territory of actively participating in a multicultural world.

These peer-nominated experts in cross-cultural living and understanding described their own struggles—to recognize other worldviews, to keep pushing themselves to grow and develop, to clarify their own values and beliefs. It seems that even cultural experts have to keep working at it.

Regarding recommendations for better cultural appreciation skills, the research participants of the Jarrett (2003) study made a number of suggestions. Several are discussed next.

Seek Out People of Difference

For example, one research participant said:

> [M]y experience is that although it's scary and it's a little difficult at first, . . . over time it becomes easier and easier and pretty soon . . . it just seems like something clicks. And all of a sudden, instead of always walking in and feeling uncomfortable in situations where you might be the racial minority, you don't anymore. There's a little barbeque place that opened down here. . . . Sometimes you'll walk in and people will wonder, "What's that white guy doing here?" But if you don't act weird, and it's not making you feel weird, then right away they sense "he's ok" and then people are friendly.
>
> —*Jarrett, 2003, p. 102*

For other research participants, seeking diversity was not hard because diversity found them at an early age. One research participant commented:

To begin with, I was born in a diversity in that both of my parents were deaf. And the deaf community is a separate kind of culture . . . so I grew up in the deaf culture. I probably signed before I talked.

—Jarrett, 2003, p. 93

Talk About Some Cultural Topics

Although it is difficult, talking about sensitive cultural topics is important for increasing our understanding of each other. In order to be an effective cross-cultural communicator, one participant said a person has to have:

The ability to . . . be open and to receive and not prejudge and to still have a certain sense of, a very strong sense of, your own identity. Your own historic background, where you come from—it's crucial. But at the same time, to be able to be open to looking at the world in a different way. But not losing that core of who you are. It is still there, but I still appreciate and understand other ways of being, seeing the world in a different way.

—Jarrett, 2003, p. 107

Some research participants discussed traveling as an excellent way to talk more about cultural topics. One noted:

For some reason I always knew that at some point in my life I needed to travel and see some parts of the world. It was very, very important to do that.

—Jarrett, 2003, p. 95

Challenge Ourselves and Others to Change and Grow

For these research participants, new experience was often fun and exciting. They said things like:

[I am] incredibly fascinated and enjoy learning about other cultures.

—Jarrett, 2003, p. 100

Others talked of the agony—while getting the benefits—of challenging oneself with differences.

I was tortured by trying to straddle: trying to be a [law firm] partner and yet being one of the other people, non-partner staff. And being their voice . . . that's what I started priding myself on, taking these people who had no voice at the partner table and giving them a voice. And it meant butting heads with my partners. And it meant pointing out the differences between my partners and me and it meant making me feel like I didn't fit in. But it was still something that I felt essential to do.

—Jarrett, 2003, p. 109

Now using the data from all three of these studies, we will make recommendations for training programs and for the novice therapist or counselor.

RECOMMENDATIONS FOR TRAINING PROGRAMS

Within counseling training programs, Kim and Lyons (2003) identified experiential activities and games as two teaching strategies for multicultural counseling training. They also suggest the use of films, role-plays, and training videos; performing cross-cultural interviews; writing cultural autobiographies; studying a second language; and conducting values clarification work. Teaching strategies rooted in gaming and simulation in combination with didactic teaching methods traditionally found in most multicultural counseling courses can be used to instill and enhance counseling students' multicultural counseling competencies within the divisions of awareness, knowledge, and skills. Experiential activities can provide trainees with opportunities to observe and practice the skills that they have read about in the literature and listened to in instructional seminars, all the while providing a space to sensitize them to previous behaviors of which they have been unaware. Simulations allow trainees to confront feelings of powerlessness and offer opportunities to deal with dissonant rules not otherwise extant in their geographical community. These simulations are analogous to many examples of racism, oppression, power, stereotyping, sexism, and conflict that exist in society.

We believe that these classroom activities merely set the foundation for developing culturally competent habits for practice and that more impactful experience takes place in practicum and internships. We encourage students to seek out training sites that will immerse them with culturally diverse clients and environments as well as to contract with supervisors to pay attention to their cross-cultural skill development. Naturally, for such experiences to exist, training programs may have to dedicate energy toward having a good selection of culturally diverse practice sites.

RECOMMENDATIONS FOR NOVICE PRACTITIONERS

Earlier we made a variety of suggestions about ways we can develop cultural competence. Here we summarize some of these ideas:

1. *Experience! Experience! Experience!* Whether cultural competence is consistent with the theory of cultural intelligence or the developmental model of intercultural sensitivity, unless we expose ourselves to a myriad of culturally diverse experiences, we will have no opportunity to reflect and learn from those experiences.

2. *Self-reflection is an indispensable tool.* Culturally competent habits do not develop simply by attending events. They grow from thinking and feeling about the experiences, thinking and feeling about how we behaved and reacted during those experiences, thinking and feeling about the meaning that experiences have for us, and, subsequently, considering ways we may want to learn and change our behaviors for such situations in the future.

3. *Seek out opportunities for practice.* We often learn best by doing. Working at practicum and internship sites with diverse clientele naturally creates new opportunities for learning. Choosing practicums and internships that are geographically and characteristically different from our usual world pushes our cultural learning.

4. *Find good supervisors.* It is especially helpful to have supervisors and mentors who will tell us when our cultural skills need improvement. But it is even better when they model for us how they work with culturally and ethnically diverse clients. Good supervisors help conceptualize cases with multicultural lenses and with cultural understanding about how different cultures explain health and healing.

5. *The world at our doorstep.* It is instructive to pay attention to the diversity in our own communities. With the increasing diversity in the demographics of the United States and constant immigration, new cultural experiences are nearer than most of us imagine. Shopping and dining in these communities and participating in their festivals and celebrations often are good ways to introduce and immerse ourselves in new cultural learning. In these experiences, it is important to pay attention to similarities and differences, the diversity within, and to observe other layers of diversity, such as gender, age, class, sexual orientation, and religion.

6. *Participate in the virtual world through cyberspace.* Internet technology, Internet books, and video rentals are contemporary examples of a borderless world. Cyberspace and social networking Web sites make it possible to visit cultures and people virtually through audio and video means. Watching with friends allows for discussion and reflection.

7. *Attend conferences.* Attending professional association conferences is both an intellectually stimulating experience and a cultural immersion experience. Conferences provide a multitude of papers, symposia, posters, and special addresses that broaden our understanding of the cultural issues that present in therapy. Film sessions at the APA annual conventions present outstanding and thought-provoking documentaries that highlight cultural issues. Certain conferences focus on cultural issues. The APA National Multicultural Conference and Summit and the Columbia University Teachers College Winter Roundtable on Cultural Psychology and Education are two good examples. Organization divisions with specific foci are good sources of multicultural information; these include APA Division 45, the Society for the Psychological Study of Ethnic Minority Issues; APA Division 44, the Society for the Psychological Study of

Lesbian, Gay, Bisexual, and Transgender Issues; and the American Counseling Association's Association for Multicultural Counseling and Development.

8. *Network.* A wonderful by-product of attending conferences is the forging of important professional friendships. These relationships are critical for growth-engendering dialogues, research partnerships, and collegial support. Often these informal gatherings and "napkin brainstorm scribbles" are the sources of new ideas and cowriting opportunities. In this age of multiple social media tools, it is not difficult to maintain and strengthen these relationships outside of conference meetings.

9. *Find mentors.* As we meet new people at professional meetings, in the workplace, or the community where we live, it is vital that we seek out a mentor or mentors who are willing to stand with us and help us and cheer our accountability as we develop habits of cultural competence. The lives of the individuals who were interviewed in the three studies were peppered with mentors who were willing to both inspire and challenge them toward new cultural learning and to help make sense of culturally complex situations.

10. *Read.* It is important to read widely. Academic journals that focus on cultural issues include: *Cultural Diversity and Ethnic Minority Psychology, International Journal for the Advancement of Counseling, Journal of Homosexuality, Journal of Multicultural Counseling and Development, Psychology of Men and Masculinity,* and *Psychology of Religion and Spirituality.* But the literature that populates bookstores and libraries, both fiction and nonfiction, is filled with real and poignant stories and phenomena that truly enrich us. Books have a wonderful way of creating such explorations. Below is a short list of recommended books that can transport readers into rich and evocative cultural worlds.

SUGGESTED READINGS

Beah, I. (2008). *A long way gone: Memoirs of a boy soldier.* New York, NY: Farrar, Straus.

Carter, S. (1994). *The culture of disbelief: How American law and politics trivialize religious devotion.* New York, NY: Random House.

Chabon, M. (2000). *The amazing adventures of Kavalier and Clay: A novel.* New York, NY: Picador.

Conley, D. (2000). *Honky.* New York, NY: Vintage Books.

Corwin, M. (2001). *And still we rise.* New York, NY: Harper.

Diamant, A. (1998). *The red tent.* New York, NY: Picador.

Ehrenreich, B. (2001). *Nickel and dimed: On (not) getting by in America.* New York, NY: Henry Holt.

Forrest, K. (2002). *Curious wine.* Los Angeles, CA: Alyson.

Garrod, A., & Davis, J. (1999). *Crossing customs: International students write on U.S. college life and culture.* New York, NY: Taylor and Francis.

Guthrie, R. V. (2004). *Even the rat was white: A historical view of psychology* (2nd ed.). Boston, MA: Pearson.

Lahiri, J. (1999). *Interpreter of maladies.* New York, NY: Mariner Books.

Lahiri, J. (2004). *The namesake.* New York, NY: Mariner Books.

Linde, P. R. (2002). *Of spirits and madness: An American psychiatrist in Africa.* New York, NY: McGraw-Hill.

MacLeod, J. (1995). *Ain't no makin' it: Aspirations and attainment in a low-income neighborhood.* Boulder, CO: Westview Press.

Morrison, T. (2004). *Beloved.* New York, NY: Vintage.

Mortenson, G., & Relin, D. O. (2007). *Three cups of tea: One man's mission to promote peace . . . one school at a time.* New York, NY: Penguin.

Nerburn, K. (1994). *Neither wolf nor dog.* Novato, CA: New World Library.

Pipher, M. (2002). *The middle of everywhere: The world's refugees come to our town.* New York, NY: Harcourt.

Richburg, K. B. (1998). *Out of America: A Black man confronts Africa.* San Diego, CA: Harvest.

Rushdie, S. (1980). *Midnight's children: A novel.* New York, NY: Penguin.

Sue, D. W. (2003). *Overcoming our racism: The journey to liberation.* Hoboken, NJ: Wiley.

Sue, D. W. (2010). *Microaggressions in everyday life: Race, gender, and sexual orientation.* Hoboken, NJ: Wiley.

Sue, D. W. et al. (2007). Racial microaggressions in everyday life. *American Psychologist, 62*(4), 271–286.

Suskind, R. (1998). *A hope in the unseen: An American odyssey from the inner city to the Ivy League.* New York, NY: Broadway Books.

Takaki, R. (1993). *A different mirror: A history of multicultural America.* Boston, MA: Little, Brown.

Urrea, L. A. (2004). *The devil's highway: A true story.* New York, NY: Little, Brown.

Watters, E. (2010). *Crazy like us: The globalization of the American psyche.* New York, NY: Free Press.

Zinn, H. (2003). *A people's history of the United States: 1492–present.* New York, NY: HarperCollins.

REFERENCES

Allport, G. W. (1979). *The nature of prejudice* (25th anniversary ed.). New York, NY: Addison-Wesley.

American Psychological Association. (2003). Guidelines on multicultural education, training, research, practice, and organizational change for psychologists. *American Psychologist, 58* (5), 377–402.

Bennett, J. M. (1993). Towards ethnorelativism: A developmental model of intercultural sensitivity. In R. M. Paige (Ed.), *Education for the intercultural experience* (pp. 109–135). Yarmouth, ME: Intercultural Press.

Earley, P. C., & Mosakowski, E. (2004). Cultural intelligence. *Harvard Business Review, 82,* 139–146.

Goh, M. (2005). Cultural competence and master therapists: An inextricable relationship. *Journal of Mental Health Counseling, 27,* 71–81.

Goh, M., Starkey, M., Jennings, L., & Skovholt, T. M. (2007). In search of cultural competence in mental health practice: A study of expert multicultural therapists. Paper presented at the 115th annual convention of the American Psychological Association, San Francisco, California.

Goh, M., & Yang, A. (2007). The developmental model of intercultural sensitivity: A study of culturally competent exemplars. Paper presented at the 115th annual convention of the American Psychological Association, San Francisco, California.

Hammer, M. R., Bennett, M. J., & Wiseman, R. (2003). Measuring intercultural sensitivity: The Intercultural Development Inventory. *International Journal of Intercultural Relations, 27,* 421–443.

Jarrett, L. M. (2003). The nature of appreciation: The psychological experience of appreciating human cultural diversity. (Unpublished dissertation.) University of Minnesota.

Kim, B. S. K., & Lyons, H. Z. (2003). Experiential activities and multicultural counseling competence training. *Journal of Counseling and Development, 81,* 400–408.

McCarthy Veach, P., Bartels, D. M., & LeRoy, B. S. (2001). Ethical and professional challenges posed by patients with genetic concerns: A report of focus group discussions with genetic counselors, physicians, and nurses. *Journal of Genetic Counseling, 10,* 97–120.

Paige, M. R. (2004, June). The intercultural in teaching and learning: A developmental perspective. Paper presented at a university-wide seminar on the intercultural in teaching and learning, University of South Australia, Adelaide.

Patton, M.Q. (2002). *Qualitative Research and Evaluation Methods.* Thousand Oaks, CA: Sage.

Ponterotto, J., & Casas, J. (1991). *Handbook of racial/ethnic minority counseling research.* Springfield, IL: Charles C. Thomas.

Sue, D. W., & Sue, D. (2008). *Counseling the culturally diverse: Theory and practice (5th ed.).* New York, NY: John Wiley & Sons.

Sue, D. W., & Torino, G. C. (2005). Racial-cultural competence: Awareness, knowledge, and skills. In R. T. Carter (Ed.), *Racial-cultural psychology and counseling* (vol. 2, pp. 3–18). Hoboken, NJ: Wiley.

Sue, D. W., et al. (2007). Racial microaggressions in everyday life. *American Psychologist, 62*(4), 271–286.

Sullivan, J. L., Shamir, M., Walsh, P., & Roberts, N. S. (1985). *Political tolerance in context: Support for unpopular minorities in Israel, New Zealand, and the United States.* Boulder, CO: Westview Press.

Teyber, E., & McClure, F. (2005). *Interpersonal process in therapy: An integrative model.* Belmont, CA: Thomson Brooks/Cole.

Yalom, I. D. (2002). *The gift of therapy.* New York, NY: Harper Collins.

6

Issues, Concerns, and Tips as Antidotes to Novice Stress

This chapter focuses on a variety of very practical but very real topics that concern novices when beginning to see clients as practicum students or interns.

WHEN THE CLIENT DOES NOT COME BACK

"Why didn't she come back?" the student therapist asks this tensely and follows with "What did I do wrong?" This lament may be expressed privately, to peers or to the supervisor. It is an important novice question and one that often has no clear answer.

This happened with my first client in my first graduate school practicum. The client came to the first interview. I thought it went well, but he did not return for the next appointment. That sinking feeling! The did-not-return factor has a special impact when early novices have little, or no, history of practicum success and the equation of client satisfaction = novice success seems to be the only way to think about the work.

Wanting a clear answer and not getting one is one more part of the curse of ambiguity. Why is there no clear answer? Think of your last dental visit. Did you go to the dentist with the idea of giving the dentist feedback about his or her performance? Counseling clients have the same mind-set. They are there to get help, not to give feedback. That is the implicit and explicit contract between you and clients. The contract dictates so much of the behavior of the two parties. Add confidentiality to the equation, and the feedback loop narrows even more.

The level of distress about clients not returning can be reduced if novices have more than enough clients or few other no-shows. It also helps if the agency supervisor normalizes the situation by saying something like "We expect this here." Distress increases if novice practicum students need hours for graduation and things are slow at the practicum site. Even more distress occurs when a novice has a lot more no-shows in practicum than other classmates are having.

A major reason clients do not return is the mismatch of expectations between the practitioner and the client. Among other reasons, no-shows increase when:

- Clients do not want to attend sessions but are forced to do so.
- The counselor lays out a more ambitious agenda than the client wants.
- The client, for many possible reasons, feels uncomfortable with the therapist.
- Other life events take priority.
- The client experiences some emotional relief and is satisfied.

Here are some examples of such situations. (Note: These are not real clients but rather hypothetical examples.)

- Pete is arrested and told by his attorney to go to counseling because the judge will like that. After his court appearance, Pete does not return for his next appointment.
- Alicia appears at her first appointment very distressed by her husband's behavior toward her. The practicum therapist is very concerned about Alicia and suggests at the end of the appointment that she leave the home and immediately seek a divorce. Alicia appreciates the concern but later is overwhelmed by the losses involved if she ends her marriage. She cancels her next appointment.
- Jennifer called for a counseling appointment and was seen that day. She was very emotional in the session when she told the novice counselor about her boyfriend's sudden lack of interest in her. When the session ended, she was very thankful for the help and made another appointment. After the first session, the novice counselor spent time trying to understand the relationships between all the topics Jennifer discussed and thinking of what to explore in the next meeting. Over the next days, Jennifer felt better, forgot her next appointment, and did not even think of calling to reschedule.

As I said, many things can lead to the client not returning. There may be a mismatch between the goals of the client and the practitioner. Clients may not want to return because they judge, after the first meeting, that the therapist was not helpful, competent, or some mix of these—these are reasons that most frighten novices. Clients also may not return because they do not want to address painful or embarrassing topics again. There are other reasons too. Sometimes the practitioner reminds the new client of someone in his or her past; it could be a positive association, or it could be a negative one. The connection between the past and present may be in or outside of the client's awareness. When the association is negative (i.e., the therapist reminds a client of an older sister who was mean, a parent who disappeared, or a lying lover), the therapeutic bond may be weakened, or even stillborn, with premature termination a result.

Other life events also can take precedence. Having a test the next day, wanting to play softball that night, a sick child, no transportation, not wanting to pay a copayment, falling asleep—these are all reasons why people miss their counseling appointments. Life events of one kind or another get in the way. One novice in our research had a client say: "I can't come to counseling tonight. I have too much on my mind" (Skovholt & Rønnestad, 1995, p. 40). This really upset the novice practitioner.

Sol Garfield (1969), a leading psychotherapy researcher, asked the no-show question early in his career while a psychology intern at a Veterans Administration hospital. He discovered, to his relief, that almost all cases at that hospital ended after one or just a few sessions. This was directly opposite the very popular, at the time, psychodynamic approach that held that many sessions were necessary for a cure. Garfield, as a novice, was surprised and relieved to get the actual data. By understanding this reality, he could avoid two common novice thoughts when things are not going well: "What is wrong with me?" and "Why didn't they, in the training program, teach me so I could be successful?"

No-shows and premature termination are stressors for novices. They are parts of the novice burden that are easily activated until more experience and a fuller definition of success buffer the stress effect.

The work of Michael Lambert (Ogles and Hayes, 2010) has been very valuable in giving therapists feedback about client reactions to therapy. His OQ-45 now translated into 15 languages gives quick feedback about client progress or deterioration. Such a feedback measure helps the counselor answer questions about "What happened in that session?"

ALL THIS INTROSPECTION IS STIRRING UP MY INNER WORLD

Psychology is a popular college major in the United States and many other countries. Why? Is it because young people are interested in learning advanced abstract theories and research methods? Usually the answer to this question is no. Is it because it is a broad major that can lead to many different career routes? Yes. Is it because students are attracted to a topic—psychology—that promises to help them understand themselves? Yes. As undergraduates are taught qualitative research methods, they are quietly, and with each other, applying other methods—psychologizing and introspection—to their own lives. This deeply reflective process of psychologizing introspection is defined as thinking and reflecting about psychological ideas, interpersonal events, and internal feelings.

A parallel process occurs in training programs in the counseling and therapy professions. Here students take courses in statistics and research design. In these courses, they are never introduced to that other central research method they use: psychologizing and introspection.

Why are students not introduced to this central research method? The reason goes back to the split between science and practice. Scientists who teach these courses do not consider introspection a legitimate and valid way of understanding data. Conversely, practitioners apply abstract ideas to their clients' lives and their own personal lives to see if they fit and illuminate. Practitioners find this method valuable. We consider some of these epistemology issues in more detail in later chapters too.

Students in counseling and therapy training programs, caught between the worlds of science and practice, routinely take the ideas taught to them in class and apply them to their personal lives to see how they fit. Do the ideas illuminate their personal or family development? Do the ideas help them understand their intimate partner? Do the ideas help them understand their own personal feelings?

The practicum experience adds a layer of psychologizing and introspection for students in counseling and therapy. The lives of the clients that novices see in practicum are new data sources. Supervision about novices' work as counselors also provides fuel for the introspection fire. The intense personal encounters of counseling and therapy stir up beginning practitioners. There is much to think about, to feel, to ponder. Perhaps realizing that the intense introspecting and psychologizing is a natural part of training, that it is a universal phenomenon, makes it easier to understand why the novice is so reflective.

FEELING INCOMPETENT

A big part of frustration of the novice is always feeling like you're doing inferior work and wanting to be better than you perceive yourself to be.
—*Julie Heideman Murphy, personal communication, February 28, 2007*

Conscientious, considerate, and compassionate individuals enter the helping professions. They have a long history of doing well in school and of doing good deeds for others. Suddenly they are in practicum and ready for all of their efforts over the years to show in positive and productive ways. However, as Julie said above, often there is a lot of frustration. Novices feel more incompetent than competent. This felt frustration can be very, very agonizing for new helping professionals.

Does this describe you? If it does, I suggest that you think about an area of your life where you went from feeling unskilled to being confident and proud of your skills. It can be helpful to think of an area where you started with no skill or knowledge and then, in time, blossomed into a skillful, knowledgeable person. When I ask graduate students in the helping fields about this process, they mention many topics. Examples include playing the piano, public speaking, learning to be alone in a foreign country, cooking, and hitting a baseball. For each student in each of these areas, there was a period of not knowing, followed by early tryout experiences, often in the form of lessons. Gradually through practice and the influence of teachers and mentors, the skill–knowledge level went up. All of these areas took time to develop. The path to competence takes time, encouragement, practice, feedback, teaching, and more refinement.

I remember reading the life story of a Chinese dancer (Cunxin, 2003). It is also a movie, *Mao's Last Dancer.* Li Cunxin grew up in a very poor village in rural China. At age 11, he was chosen for a ballet dance troupe in Beijing. At the dance school, he lived in a dormitory with the other selected children. Defying great odds, in time he became one of the most talented ballet dancers in the world. How did he do it? The development of expertise often means having the right teachers at the right time. For Li Cunxin, this included teacher Xiao. To become an expert, there must be some natural skill, a strong will, intense practice beyond what others do, and a gradually emerging view of self as skilled.

When you the reader are wondering whether you have the skills and ability to become a competent practitioner, remember other areas in which you have gone from no ability to a high level of skill. It may be in an area mentioned earlier. The process of developing expertise was probably similar to what you are now going through in counseling and therapy training. It is a process; it takes time. When you recognize the parallels, I hope you can feel a shot of confidence: "If I can do _____, then I can also use much of my own learning process to become a good practitioner in counseling and therapy."

OPTIMAL SUPPORT–CHALLENGE BALANCE PROPELS POSITIVE CHANGE

I ask busy people to slow down and people with stagnating lives to get something cooking. . . . The trick is finding the step size that propels people forward but allows them to succeed with each move.

—*Pipher, 2003, pp. 38, 43*

We can understand how to grow as a person, and as a practitioner, via the simple but profound formula of a balance between *support*—encouragement and manageable tasks—and *challenge*—being pushed by others and trying things that are hard to do. This term, "support–challenge balance," is a popular one that is used to capture human motivation and development.

As you work with your clients, think of the support–challenge balance and try to pace the work. The goal is a little forward movement. Here are some examples of client growth and development:

- More maturity
- Fewer intense distress emotions
- More optimism
- Better life skills
- Closer relationships

Getting to these goals depends on a balance between support and challenge. And it often means slow and uneven progress. In my view, human failure often relates to going too fast at a task. This leads to being disappointed in the result, which leads to a feeling of being dispirited, which leads to giving up. It is better to go slow, have success, and keep going . . . and going . . . and going. For example, often in baseball and softball, going for the home run leads to more strikeouts, but trying to make contact with the ball leads to more success.

Figure 6.1 Support–Challenge Balance

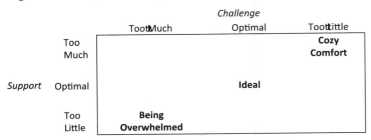

Think about your own growth as a practitioner. How is your support–challenge balance? Too much support from supervisors, classmates, and professors does not always stretch us, but too much challenge can overwhelm us. We can all recall times when we had too much challenge. I remember as a college student having so many final exams in a row that the studying and test taking became overwhelming. What are your examples? We can also all recall times when the task was not challenging enough.

As a novice, think of the support–challenge balance. At one end (see Figure 6.1.), we have Being Overwhelmed and at the other end, we have Cozy Comfort. Neither produces optimal novice growth. Being Overwhelmed may reflect the experience of novice practitioners who have highly distressed clients who show little improvement and an absent supervisor. This combination is difficult for novices because they face the responsibility of helping people in need without the ability to do it combined with no experts to help. I call this lack of help from a supervisor or mentor orphan distress.

And then there is Cozy Comfort. Cozy Comfort occurs when the challenge level is much lower than the support level. Some novices are permitted to do their practicum at the same site where they have worked or been a graduate assistant. They may have worked for a considerable time at the site and already accelerated up the learning curve. The supervisor may be highly supportive but not push the novice to learn new skills. The supervision meetings become a love fest replete with constant supervisor support and positive validation. This lack of challenge does not provide an optimal environment for development.

Neither end produces optimal human development. Think support–challenge balance for your own professional development and also for your work with your clients.

DEFINING SUCCESS IN THERAPY AND COUNSELING SEEMS LIKE CHASING A MIRAGE

What is success? With so many jobs, success and failure are clearly outlined. For example, bridge construction either produces a bridge that works, or gravity wins. The outcome is clear. A marathon race with professional runners is like that too. Many compete, and there is one winner. There is success and lack of success. In other parts of life, there are examples of clear winners and losers too. The March Madness college basketball tournament is like that: fun, excitement, an unknown outcome, and then a winner. How about the reality TV shows? Winning is success.

Here are other examples from real life. Bricklayers, tree trimmers, and cooks see the results of their work. They can count what they have done: 40 bricks laid, 10 trees trimmed, 7 dinners made. My favorite is painting a room. The wall is green and then, with paint, it is blue or some version thereof. There is effort and success.

In the professions where human interaction is at the core, definitions of success are more complex. For example, in the caring professions such as counseling, advising, teaching, doctoring, nursing, and ministering, the definition of success is confusing and unclear. The human interaction element produces definitions of success on multiple levels. Simple definitions just do not work very well in many situations. The client's readiness and motivation for change is one factor. Another is that success often involves internal changes (i.e., more self-efficacy, less anxiety) that are hard to measure.

One semester I taught an introductory college course for struggling first-year undergraduate students and a seminar for new doctoral students. The first group had a long history of mixed (very good, mediocre, and very bad) experiences in school and with teachers. It was hard for them to be motivated for school, and they brought little enthusiasm to the classroom. As much as anything, for them, in their lives, teachers were punitive agents. The second group, the doctoral students, acted like hungry animals going after food. They were chasing after learning like dogs chase bones. They were highly motivated, had a long history of great experiences as students, and related very positively with teachers.

It is natural to think that teaching the doctoral students was more difficult. The prestige system in higher education works this way, meaning that being an instructor for a higher level course bestows more prestige because it is considered more difficult. For me, the experience was the opposite. Teaching the first-year college students who had highly ambivalent feelings about school, teachers, and themselves as students was much harder for me. I do not know how to compare how successful I was in the two courses. They were so different. It is easy to say I was more successful teaching the doctoral course. All the students there read the material, wrote great papers, and got As. This did not happen with the first-year students. The teacher evaluations were positive in both courses, but more positive in the advanced course. Was I successful in the two courses? I do not know. Perhaps I did a better job in the course with the lower evaluations because the students started at a more negative level toward school. Perhaps I was not successful in either class. Student evaluations only measure student reactions. How about other things, such as a newfound ability, or not, to question the epistemology of knowledge? The inspiration they got from an admired peer in the class? A level of learning they discovered only many years later? This all leads us to the big question in the caring professions: What is success?

For novice practitioners, success often is linked directly to the supervisor's evaluation. That does not solve the problem of finding clear, unambiguous scientific grounded measures of occupational success because supervisors are only human and subjective in their judgments. Supervisors have a lot of power, because they can define the ambiguity of the therapy and counseling situation in one way or another. The same data from the work between the practicum counselor and the client can produce these two supervisor reactions: "Yes, the client didn't change much, but she had a lot of problems before she came to you" and "Yes, the client didn't change much, and if you would have been more aware of what she was saying, she could have made more progress." So, success for novices often is defined by the supervisor. Luckily, most supervisors have had training in supervision and are positively oriented to novice development.

A second way of defining success relates to client reactions. Beginning counselors treasure expressions of appreciation by clients. A client's obvious improvement in anxiety, depression, or anger is another way novices can celebrate success.

Yet these two definitions of success—supervisor reaction and client reaction and affective improvement—are not absolute; both have limitations. There are so many qualifications regarding the definition of success. How motivated and ready is the client? Was the client sent by others? Did the person come in voluntarily, or was attendance mandated by the court? Is the problem very serious and long term, or is it more situational (i.e., is it heart disease or the common cold?). Is success in couples counseling when the client stays married or gets divorced? Is success staying in school and getting a high grade-point average or dropping out of school to do something else? If clients refer their friends to the practitioner, is that a sign that the therapist really helps, or is it a sign that the therapist was just very supportive? Is success when the client comes to all planned sessions or stops early?

Getting comfortable with the complexity of defining success is part of the work and is an issue for novices on the voyage. How can someone reach the goal when the goal is elusive? This dilemma is part of what is challenging about the therapy professions.

EXPERIENCING THE CLIENT'S PAIN AND SUFFERING

For me the hardest work is being present when couples decide to divorce. Absorbing all of their pain absolutely wastes me.

—Pipher, 2003, p. 75

Our work in therapy and counseling is an invitation to share in the suffering of others. This is in contrast to others sharing our suffering. The first is good practice; the second is unethical practice. There is a very big difference.

In our work, it is a privilege to sit with clients and hear and absorb their fears, anxiety, anger, despair, grief, confusion, doubt, and anguish. The pain is usually about something that has happened to them: a loss or disappointment. Some of the losses I have heard about include the suicide of a parent, the betrayal of a spouse, the failing of doctoral exams, the rage of a chemically dependent partner, the indifference of a parent, a rejection by a highly sought and selective school program, and a client's pain-filled and advanced illness. I have heard the anguish of clients wishing to be dead; intense, unbearable anxiety; a stunning realization that their intimate partner has suddenly died; a deep feeling of being ugly and unwanted; a sexual assault by a trusted friend; and the recognition that after decades of service, a client's employer indifferently discarded him.

Many times with loss or anguish, the practitioner must sit with the painful and stillborn emotions that fill the room. Often all choices for the client involve significant loss, as in "can't leave this job and, *equally as much*, can't stay with it." Massive life discouragement may radiate from the client.

Entering the suffering room is a major part of the experience of novice counselors and therapists. Sitting with pain is usually not new, because novice practitioners often have sat with distressed friends or family members. Those early life experiences of being a helper are a major draw for the work. Now it is the same yet also different. The novice is in a professional role and now sitting in the sacred professional space of the counseling office. Learning to take in the affect of the client—not too much, not too little—and learning what to do with it is a topic I address in other parts of this book such as Chapters 1 and 7.

Being able to share in such important personal feelings is an honor and a privilege. Sharing the pain—something people often want to avoid—paradoxically gives our work so much of its meaning and richness. We have no need to read novels or watch movies to experience the depth, width, courage, despair, and richness of human life. To be valuable to the other, we need only to listen quietly and deeply.

HIGH-SPEED MOVIE

For novices, sitting in the session can be like sitting in a movie where the picture and sound are coming in double speed. It is all coming fast. If we think of a roller coaster as a way to capture the intense and rapidly changing emotions of the early days of practice, the high-speed movie can capture the cognitive confusion of early practice. There is so much screaming for our attention. As one of my friends said during our early training days, "Ignorance is bliss." For novices, all the courses, theoretical ideas, and practice techniques have blasted through the ignorance and the bliss is gone. As the saying goes, "The more we know, the more we are aware that we do not know."

The high-speed cognitive overload occurs because everything seems important. For any of us, when everything all seems important, our attention is pulled here and then there. Novices would like to say "Stop the movie, I have to think if that is important." Unfortunately, the session, just like a movie, does not stop.

In class, novices have learned theories, techniques, and methods that reduce the needed focus. However, once in session, it gets muddled. Is it important to think of x or y or z? Should I pay attention to what the client says, how it is said, or when it is said? The list multiplies regarding important things. Novices are acting highly responsible and, therefore, want to respond to all that is important. How do they know what is important?

When novices watch a video session of a famous practitioner, it looks easier because the novices are just following along, like following the trail blazer on a clearly defined trail. Blazing the trail through a patch of dense woods is different. It involves many decisions and lots of data.

In sports there is a saying that, with experience, the game slows down. The player actually experiences the game as slowing down. This is very useful because a quarterback, for example, has all kinds of data coming at him and needs to make split-second decisions. When the game is slower, the sense of time increases.

What actually is happening? What happens is that the quarterback, through much experience, learned what is more important and what is less important. So, instead of 50 equally important pieces of data, the quarterback has 10 very important pieces of data, 10 of no importance, and 30 in the middle. Paying most attention to the 10 that are very important produces a feeling of things slowing down.

In research on common factors of experts across different fields (Chi, Glaser, & Farr, 1988), the authors state that experts know what is important and what is less important. Experts, compared to novices, pay attention to certain pieces of information and not to others. The attentional focus is one factor that counts the most for success. This happens with counselors and therapists too. On an intake interview, the experienced practitioner may pay attention to a few factors, such as establishing rapport, assessing the client's distress level, trying to understand the client's expectation for length and commitment to counseling, and a few history facts. Paying attention to just some of the data slows down the movie.

Learning what is important is one of the rewards of experience. If experienced practitioners still are struggling with what is important, then they have not used previous experience to learn, grow, and understand the task more completely. There has been insufficient reflected experience.

Unless novices are able to get an injection of hundreds of hours of experience, as I have pointed out in other chapters, the sorting through of what counts and what does not count goes on for a considerable time. The payoff of the interview slowing down is the reward for time spent on the task.

Figuring out what is important goes on in many areas of life. For example, students learn how to be better students. This often means that they learn what is important and what is unimportant in a class. Students, for example, learn the art of listening to subtle cues from the instructor, such as voice pitch, as to what is important for the upcoming test.

I remember as a college student underlining the sociology text very diligently. Unfortunately, as I looked at the book years later, I saw that I had underlined almost every line! In time we all learn to read a book much faster and pick out the important points.

The same occurs in therapy and counseling. With experience, we recognize that some of what occurs in each session is important for success and some of what goes on is less important. The high-speed movie has slowed down. After lots of therapy experience, it will for you too. Until then, there will be times when you will be overwhelmed by so much information—verbal, nonverbal, direct, indirect. Like a high-speed movie.

THIS IS NOT A ROLE-PLAY—THIS IS REAL! THIS IS EXCITING! THIS IS A SESSION!

What a thrill: Your first session with your first practicum client is over. If it went well, you are so relieved, so happy. I remember recently when this happened with one of my students. She was so excited. The session had gone really well.

There is so much preparation for the first practice experiences—so many years of academic preparation. It is like other firsts in our personal lives: climbing on a horse for the first time and surviving, performing at a concert, giving a speech, being in the starting lineup for a first varsity basketball game, driving a car at night, reciting answers when first called on in a law school class, doing a first physical exam as a medical student. And the relief and excitement when it goes well!

Sometimes, for some counselors, the very first time does not go well. And that can be very difficult. This situation has its own emotional low just as the first session that goes well has its own emotional high.

Novices have already invested so much of themselves. They have taken so many risks. Students often ask themselves, "Do I have what it takes, or am I an imposter in this profession?" At that moment when the client leaves and the session has gone well, time stands still. There is a feeling of "YES, I did it, and I can do it!"

NOT GETTING HELP

We all know the famous song from the guys from Liverpool, the one about help and needing somebody. Entering a new profession we often are less self-assured. May I suggest you hum the words of that song to yourself as we start this section.

The precarious nature of the emerging practitioner's journey jumps out in unexpected ways at unexpected times. The pattern of practice is abstract and unique. No one before has ever said exactly what a client says, so you do not know how to reply. So much of our work consists of unique, never-before-experienced interactions between two people who have never had this unique encounter. How can research or theory help this? Here are examples of the uniqueness of each interaction with each therapist–client set and the novices' need for expert consultation/supervision while in early practicum. I am imagining possible inner dialogues of you, the reader, as novice practitioner when you and the client are in session.

It seems the client is experiencing a kind of frozen grief, but is that right? Should I say it to her now? If so, in what way? Then what?

Is the client motivated? For what? He was forced to come by the probation office. How does that factor into our work? Should I bring it up or wait? Should I ask him what he wants to concentrate on or put out an agenda and get his reaction?

The client suddenly says this will be the last meeting. He is a traditional guy, and this therapy is difficult for him for the typical reasons—he feels shame about needing help and expressing weakness, letting someone care for him is unsettling, he is uncomfortable with crying in public, he doesn't know how to put feelings into words, he is only here because he was forced to do it. Should I accept his reluctance to continue? Is that the most respectful position? What about the motivational interviewing perspective (Miller & Rollnick, 2002) of actively engaging the client?

These are just three examples of how we as novices, and often later in our careers too, feel that we need help in answering our many questions.

Here is an example from early in my career. Right after receiving my master's in counseling, I was working as a counselor in New England. I had good supervision, but then it seemed to disappear. Maybe it was because I suddenly needed help. A client started having suicidal thoughts and continued to have them over a number of sessions. I tried to do all the right things for suicide prevention, but I was getting more and more scared. I had a lot of other clients, and then I started having chest pains. The doctor said I did not have heart disease and that it was probably stress. Suddenly the work was so hard and I needed help from a supervisor, a mentor, colleagues, a wise elder or perhaps all of them. Help did come, the client got better, and my chest pains went away. But it seemed to take forever.

For novices, the need for help can arise suddenly. Sometimes help, such as a supervisor, shows up in a timely fashion in the right form; sometimes it does not. Sometimes some help shows; something often is better than nothing. Let us hope that when you as novice therapist cry out for help, help will arrive.

SUMMARY

Issues, concerns, and tips—these have been the focus of this chapter. Some related topics and themes are covered in other chapters.

In Chapter 7, we turn to the need to care for the self while we care for others. Burnout prevention and resiliency development are important parts of the novice journey. Caring for the self makes it possible to continue to make professional attachments with people in need and to do it over and over again and, by so doing, help so many people along the way.

REFERENCES

Chi, M.T.H., Glaser, R., & Farr, M. (Eds.). (1988). *The nature of expertise*. Hillsdale, NJ: Lawrence Erlbaum.

Cunxin, L. (2003). *Mao's last dance*r. New York, NY: Penguin

Ellwein, M. C., Grace, M. E., & Comfort, R. E. (1990). Talking about instruction: Student teachers' reflection on success and failure in the classroom. *Journal of Teacher Education, 41*(4), 3–14.

Garfield, S. L. (1969). Applicants for psychotherapy and the problem of early termination. *Community Mental Health Journal, 5*(1), 70–75.

Miller, W. R., & Rollnick, S. (2002). *Motivational interviewing: Preparing people for change*. New York, NY: Guilford Press.

Ogles, B. M., & Hayes, J. A. (2010). Michael J. Lambert: Building confidence in psychotherapy. In L. G. Castonguay, J. C. Muran, L. Angus, J. A. Hayes, N. Ladany, & T. Anderson., *Bringing psychotherapy research to life* (pp. 141–151). Washington, DC: American Psychological Association.

Pipher, M. (2003). *Letters to a young therapist*. New York, NY: Basic Books.

Rønnestad, M. H., & Skovholt, T. M. (in press). *The developing practitioner*. New York, NY: Routledge.

Skovholt, T. M., & Rønnestad, M. H. (1995). *The evolving professional self: Stages and themes in therapist and counselor development*. New York, NY: Wiley.

7

Becoming a Resilient Practitioner

This chapter focuses on ways to be highly engaged with one's clinical work even when the work can, at times, feel exhausting and overwhelming. In the past, training in the caring professions, such as therapy and counseling, did not include this topic. Novices were left to figure out how to avoid burnout and emotional depletion on their own. Often the end result was not pretty. Today we can help novice practitioners address issues early so that resilient practitioners can emerge. It is exciting for me to be writing about this topic for a novice audience.

First, I suggest that you as the reader take the inventory at the end of this chapter to give yourself some ideas and information about yourself and your resiliency.

INTRODUCTION

How does the opera singer take care of the voice?
The baseball pitcher, the arm?
The woodcutter, the ax?
The photographer, the eyes?
The ballerina, the legs and feet?
The practitioner, the self?

CARING FOR OURSELVES

In the caring professions such as therapy and counseling, ourselves are our central professional instrument. We must preserve the self in order to be able to use it for the other. That is what we do in the caring professions. In the "high-touch" (compared to the "high-tech") career fields, the interpersonal realm is in the spotlight.

> The demand to be attuned, to be interested, to be energetic for the other—the other who is often in misery, anger, defiance, or hopelessness—and to continue to do it over and over again, defines the work of the therapy practitioner.
>
> —*Skovholt, Goh, Upidi, & Grier, 2004, p. 18*

The catalyst for growth of the client is the intense reaching out by the practitioner in the one-way caring relationship. It is our self that we give. For example, this focus on the relationship is clear in the title of a book edited by Norcross (2002): *Psychotherapy Relationships that Work.*

Before I discuss the perils of burnout and secondary traumatic stress and then make a case for practitioners to assertively practice resiliency development and self-care, I want to note that many helping practitioners report high work satisfaction and lower work stress. For example, Rosenberg and Pace (2006) found a low to moderate level of burnout in a sample of marriage and family therapists. In an excellent study on empathy and nurses, Bradham (2008) found that most of the hospital nurses in her sample did not currently score high on burnout. So, although burnout and related difficulties such as secondary traumatic stress and compassion fatigue do affect practitioners in the caring professions, they are not plagues that grab all with intensity and deadly effects. In fact, the point of this whole chapter is to help novices inoculate themselves so that high work satisfaction is constant throughout their careers.

How does one become a resilient practitioner? What exactly does the term "resilient practitioner" mean? I hope this chapter will help readers in their own quests to avoid the exhaustion, disillusionment, and burnout that has reached out and grabbed many others in the caring professions. Don't let it snatch you!

In the next pages, I provide 11 essential tasks for practitioners in therapy and counseling (and related professions too). I think of these 11 tasks as creating a shield against the forces that pull energy from practitioners and take away the power of the therapeutic relationship to energize the client.

ESSENTIAL RESILIENT PRACTITIONER TASKS

Task 1: Lose One's Innocence About the Need to Assertively Develop Resiliency and Self-Care Skills

Self-care is not being self-centered but rather a way to increase intellectual and emotional commitment to the work.

—*Susan Neufeldt, psychologist and clinical supervisor, personal communication, July 16, 2007*

Being a therapist is largely about giving. It requires the giving of our full and undivided attention to our clients, providing support and encouragement, and demonstrating patience and unconditional acceptance. While being there for our clients is rewarding, it also demands a lot of energy and can take an emotional toll.

—*Nicole Park, doctoral counseling student, personal communication, May 10, 2012*

Right now you [my supervisee] are working with several traumatized clients and I encourage you to go see the cranes as a way to relax.

—Pipher, 2003, p. 52

High mental well-being was associated with enhanced [practitioner] empathy.

—Shanafelt et al., 2005, p. 559

How do you develop self-care skills when you have never felt the exhaustion and feelings of being overwhelmed that can attack the therapy and counseling practitioner? For beginning novices, work has not become exhausting, just as marathon runners are not exhausted at mile 1. Is this what it means to be innocent about the precarious nature of the work? How do people know they have to save something if they have never lost it?

In the past, often there were no words or terms to warn us and prepare us. This is true for many topics: What was once no recognition evolved to a clear recognition of danger and the need for self-care (e.g., sunscreen, brushing and flossing, saving over decades for retirement). For work as a helping practitioner, the first big warning word was "burnout." Herbert Freudenburger (1974) made a great contribution when he first used the term. He described the eroding effects on mental health practitioners in a high work stress community center in New York City. He told how counselors and advocates gave, gave, and gave of themselves and eventually ended up depleted and unable to function competently. We now have many other warning words, including: emotional depletion, secondary trauma, compassion fatigue, and vicarious traumatization. Yet the reality of burnout is also hard to describe precisely. Bradham (2008) articulated this imprecision when she wrote about nurses she interviewed:

The picture of burnout is not always clear. It is like looking at a Monet watercolor, an impressionistic view, where from a distance an overall picture is formed, but up close the painting looks like a lot of fuzzy little dots of color, seemingly unrelated to one another. This fuzziness makes it difficult to clearly remember, much less clearly describe the experience of burnout. It is as if the nurse is too close to herself to be able to see the full picture. With the distance of time, some of the nurses were able to see that they had experienced burnout. (p. 177)

When I went to graduate school, we had no concepts like burnout prevention, self-care, or practitioner resiliency development. Now we do. Now there is recognition that the work can be very difficult and leave us empty and unable to function. Next I describe some studies that can help us lose our innocence about the need to actively work on being resilient. Radeke and Mahoney (2000) found that 28% of their sample of therapists were emotionally exhausted, and 80% were emotionally depleted. A study of psychiatrists found that two-thirds had moderate to high levels of emotional exhaustion and a low level of personal accomplishment (Kumar, Fischer, Robinson, Hatcher, & Bhagat, 2007). As noted earlier, Bradham (2008) found that nurses who were generally not burned out also reported patterns of episodic burnout over their work life.

There are no magical, quick answers for being a therapist for people with posttraumatic stress disorder, intense grief, panic attacks, abuse and addictions. Often therapists have to work very hard, absorb pain, and see only slow progress. The job of a helping professional is difficult because we have to be empathetic with people and often hear the horrible and tragic events in their lives. What happens to a person who gives seven hours of empathy in a row to a series of horrifying and tragic stories from people? Therapists work in relative isolation due to the nature and the confidentiality of the work. It can be difficult to be so sensitive and caring.

In the years after Freudenberger (1974) first used the term "burnout," many books have addressed this topic (e.g., Baker, 2003; Larson, 1993; Norcross & Guy, 2007, Rothschild & Rand, 2006; Skovholt & Trotter-Mathison, 2011; and Wicks, 2008). The book titles shout out the concern and can help remove our innocence: *A Perilous Calling: The Hazards of Psychotherapy Practice* by Sussman (1995); *Secondary Traumatic Stress: Self-Care Issues for Clinicians, Researchers, and Educators* by Stamm (1995); *Sometimes My Heart Goes Numb* by Garfield (1995), and *When Helping Starts to Hurt: A New Look at Burnout among Psychotherapists* by Grosch and Olsen (1994).

Must we really put time into self-care and resiliency development? Some years ago, an old wise professor told me that it works like this. "A person can go a long time but eventually a work-only life leads to blowing a tire." When he said that to me, I grew afraid and had an image of a car going very fast, blowing a tire, then flipping over and over with the driver inside. This is what a practitioner told me happened to him after he worked and worked over many years. His body shut down and said "No more!"

It is hard to take in this message. When human need spills out from all corners of our awareness, how can we, as therapists and counselors, focus on ourselves? Doing so seems to be the height of selfishness. But then we remember the airplane message: Put the oxygen mask on yourself first, then help another. The message from international aid organizations to famine workers is similar: You will lose your job helping starving people if you don't take time yourself to eat.

Erosion of our ability to do the work can come in many forms. Two kinds of erosion are meaning burnout and caring burnout. Meaning burnout can arrive in different ways: The work is no longer interesting, not much client progress seems to occur, and original motivations for the work have been satisfied. Caring burnout is the erosion of our ability to attach with the next person in need. We are each wired to attend to our own sensory data for our own welfare. The focus on the other—like swimming upstream—is unnatural. It is hard work. At some point, people lose the ability to care for the other. This is caring burnout. Either meaning burnout or caring burnout damages the practitioner's ability to do essential work.

Awareness of the need for self-care is important. Those in other careers realize that they must care for their instrument—the opera singer's voice; the pitcher's arm; the woodcutter's ax; the eyes of the photographer; and the toes, feet, ankles, and legs of the ballerina. How about us?

In life, it is important to first take good care of yourself. If you don't, you can't take care of others.

—My mother, Elvera Meyer Skovholt, August 1994

Still true.

—At age 93, 2002

I want you to watch the ballgame tonight.
—Instructions to the family while in hospice two days before her death, 2004

An important task for us in the helping and caring fields to realize is that in order to fully give of ourselves, we must also protect ourselves. This paradoxical style of giving and protecting at the same time is a characteristic of master therapists as expressed in the term "boundaried generosity" (Skovholt & Jennings, 2004).

We offer the other—the client, the patient, the student, the adviser—our "underside of the turtle," the part of us that can connect, that can feel, that is exposed, because the hard shell side cannot be proficient in the work. Giving of ourselves is our chief instrument for client recovery, development, mental health, and transformation.

Many practitioners in the helping fields have discovered their own need for self-care after they have collapsed in one way or another. They may have acquired the disease of sadness of the soul after being enveloped in too much client tragedy. They may have collapsed physically and developed a disease. They may have developed the classical burnout symptom of cynicism and bitterness toward those they were trying to serve: clients, patients, students, advisees. At that point, they became useless and incompetent in the work because a big part of what we do is to engage the other's capacity for self-development, healing, learning, changing. We need to offer hope and possibility to the other, who is often demoralized (Frank & Frank, 1991).

As a first essential resilient practitioner task, we must lose our innocence about the need for assertive self-care.

Task 2: Develop Abundant Sources of Positive Energy

Many of the patients [military veterans] who fill the day are bereft, angry, broken. Their experiences are gruesome, their distress lasting and the process of recovery exhausting. The repeated stories of battle and loss can leave the most professional therapist numb and angry.

—Carey, Cave, & Alvarez, 2009, p. 1

Hope is oxygen to someone who is suffocating on despair.

—Carr, 2008, p. 50

I have worked on the topic of burnout prevention and self-care for many years. Over time, I have concluded that this task of developing abundant sources of positive energy is the most important one for long-term practitioner resiliency.

The work is hard. It takes a lot out of us. Taking in all the carbon dioxide of human need and giving off oxygen is draining and sometimes exhausting. Attaching to the other in need with our underside of the turtle is important but also leaves us vulnerable. So, it is natural to work to reduce the sources of career stress. Yet this alone is not enough.

We need to have energy to give it away. Beginners sometimes can live off excitement and anxiety. But over time, people cannot live just on adrenaline. This is especially true when we talk about long-term practitioner vitality. One or more gushing wells of positive energy is essential.

Which well(s)? Where? How large? More than one? The specifics do not matter as much as the bottom line of energy generation. Different practitioners have different wells. The key is to have a place, people, an activity, a pet, a set of beliefs and principles, and so on, that provides high satisfaction, pleasure, deep purpose. The idea is to provide the opposite affect of that which inhabits the lives of our clients when we work with them: clinging despair, acute sadness, numbing boredom, heightened apathy, terrifying fear, escalating rage, cloaking shame, ingrained selfishness, and more. When we form professional attachments, we connect with our feeling side, the part that gives us an accurate assessment of the other's life. This valuable work is hard. To do it, we need energy, lots of it, and lots of positive emotions and satisfaction too.

Our abundant sources of positive energy give us tingling excitement, bubbling joy, layered contentment, throbbing pleasure, enveloping quiet, pulsed elation, peaceful happiness, intense thrill, spectacular wonder, and more. What gives you these positive reactions? In the workshops, classes, and talks I have given on professional resiliency, I have heard of many different sources of this energy. For some, vacations are especially renewing. Others have hobbies or activities that are satisfying. I know three people—a social worker, a psychologist, and a chaplain —who find great renewal in fishing. I know two others who collect rocks; the rocks are always there, need no nurturing, and are concrete objects that can be felt and counted. This is different from the ambiguity of the helping work. Then there is the quilter who goes into a pleasure trance when quilting. Deep spiritual meaning does it for some. Telling lots of jokes and being playful is the key for one counselor. For others, it is a white-hot intense romance that does not cool but continues month after month and year after year. Receiving love from others is, of course, a great human source of energy.

The common ingredient across all of the possibilities is the presence of a well of energy that gushes out into the person's life when engaging in the personal interaction, activity, distraction, hobby, spiritual presence, or other source that is so positive for the practitioner.

Task 3: Relish the Joy and Meaning of the Work as a Positive Energy Source

Far and away the best prize that life offers is the chance to work hard at work worth doing.

—President Theodore Roosevelt, 1903

Of all the possible sources for positive energy, feeling that one's work is meaningful for the growth and development of humanity is one of the most important. Our work in the helping professions, although often very difficult, must also be a source of joy and meaning. What are the components of this work-related joy and meaning?

Privilege of Living in the Intensity of the Human Drama

Being a practitioner in the helping professions gives the helper a ringside seat to the human drama of lives lived, choices made, pain felt, triumphs achieved, hope expired, confusion exposed, and more. Practitioners experience novels, movies, and, even more so, artificial attempts like reality TV shows, as secondhand when the fullness of life is right there in the interview room.

It has been an enormous privilege for me to be in close space with those in the client role who have wrestled with the great themes in human life, such as:

- Loving (e.g., an exhausted, despairing mother who keeps trying to help a sullen son who is failing in high school, a husband who learns to forgive his betraying wife)
- Leaving (e.g., an intimate partner, a geographic location, a set of cherished values, an unfulfilling but salaried career)
- Wrestling with the choice of going on or stopping (e.g., to achieve success as an artist, to keep a body going that is racked with pain, to try for medical school)
- Reconnecting with another (e.g., a father succeeds after great effort in connecting with a daughter, the effect of past trauma gets muted when a woman earnestly works to love a new man)
- Facing failure (e.g., going bankrupt, not passing a major graduate school exam)
- Experiencing drenching grief (e.g., the sudden death of one's mother, sudden abandonment by one's lover)
- Mastering a new skill (a walled-off man learning to express emotions of vulnerability rather than using anger as the vehicle of all feelings, a couple becoming more tender and accepting with each other)
- And so many other very human experiences

Theologian Krista Tippett (2007) expresses a version of being vividly alive. She told of living in fear-drenched East Berlin near the Berlin Wall during the Cold War.

I was learning the exhilarating intensity that can accompany human catastrophe. I struggle not to glory it now in memory. But it was teaching me about the human condition. It was pressing me to question definitions of power and meaning. (p. 36)

Within the therapy and counseling relationship, practitioners are able to experience this exhilarating intensity about human life. We are fortunate to witness its profound nature. Sometimes we are an instrument for positive significant alterations in the developmental arc of the other. And when any of the trilogy of distress emotions— anxiety, depression, anger— decrease for the client, it can give us an intense level of satisfaction.

Another Level of Meaning for Practitioners

As a species, we are aware that others die. Are we aware of our own mortality? Of course. Higher cognitive functioning produces the awareness of our own mortality. Yet this awareness gets blunted too. In his Pulitzer Prize–winning book, *The Denial of Death,* Ernest Becker (1973) states, as his major premise, that enormous human activity is consumed by efforts to deny death as an essential reality. He says a full awareness of death is terrifying and unbearable.

To make it worse, we can say that we not only die but we are also forgotten. I remember a few years ago, standing on the sidewalk in a small city and glancing into a nearby cemetery. No one was there. No one was visiting. I had an unsettling realization that the flow of human life goes on and no one visits the cemeteries. Sometimes the forgetting takes a few years. You don't agree? How often do you think of your great-grandparents?

Many human religious and spiritual practices have answers to the fear of death expressed by Becker. For example, the concept of eternal life is a central belief of Protestant, Catholic, and Greek Orthodox approaches within Christianity.

Are there other ways we can find immortality? There is, of course, the passing on of DNA as a parent. One other way I suggest is what I call "species immortality." By this I mean that our efforts can help propel the species forward into the future. In this way, we also go forward.

We in the helping professions live into the future with our species immortality work. When we do our work, we are giving "oxygen" so others can live. Here are examples:

- Teaching a child to read
- Helping a college student avert suicide
- Assisting in reducing conflict between a husband and wife
- Intensively trying to reduce the effect of addiction in the life of a young man of promise

- Helping a teenager learn to distinguish between the positive search for independence and a fiery self-destructive defiance toward parents
- Grieving with a 35-year-old woman who has miscarried

This is all species immortality work—work that can produce enveloping satisfaction and meaning in our lives. When abundant meaning no longer comes to us from the work, we can suffer from already-mentioned meaning burnout, a potentially debilitating condition in our quest to be highly engaged practitioners.

Here are some of my favorite quotes on the meaning making we get from our work:

This is the true joy in life, the being used for a purpose recognized by yourself as a mighty one; the being thoroughly worn out before you are thrown on the scrap heap; the being a force of Nature instead of a feverish selfish little clod of ailments and grievances complaining that the world will not devote itself to making you happy.

> —*George Bernard Shaw; cited in Larson, 1993, p. 2*

The reward of teaching is knowing that your life made a difference.

> —*Ayers, 1993, p. 24*

What do we live for, if it is not to make life less difficult to each other?

> —*George Eliot [Mary Ann Evans], 1956*

Task 4: Search for Empathy Balance

The pain stayed with me residually when returning home.

> —*A novice counselor*

Empathy Balance

The term "empathy balance" describes the dynamic between entering the world of the other, a kind of diving into the ocean of the other, and living in one's own phenomenological world. Finding this balance is a major task for helping professionals. Serious professional errors can occur with excess in either direction. Too little empathy removes the human caring, which is the central gift of these professions. Too much empathy for the other leads to practitioners losing themselves, which can reduce professional and personal effectiveness. Closely related to this losing of the self in the other, the sign of an excess of other focus, is the concept of codependency.

Too Little or Too Much Empathy?

In my own teaching and training, about 20% of the students express difficulty with getting lost in the pain of the other. The internal experience of this empathetic entering of the other's world has been explored in depth by Rothschild and Rand (2006).

Some students in the helping fields have been emotionally attuned to the needs of others ever since they were young. They may have been in a kind of informal practicum for many years, long before formal practicum in school. There can be many developmental roots for such a caring-for-others orientation. For example, the helper's cultural background, such as a religious community, may have been very focused on meeting the suffering needs of others.

Sometimes this ability to focus on the needs of the other comes out of the helper's own childhood, where the child received attention and praise for being very considerate and caring toward others. This caring for others can be very helpful as the child grows and becomes a mature adult. Yet excessive caring puts the child at risk of losing the self.

The early life of the helping professional can create an unusual orientation to other-care for children who developmentally would usually be very self-focused. As I said in an earlier chapter, the normal self-focus of children can be very adaptive because it is like a bank account: Get love and attention in the early years and then, as an adult, withdraw it in the service of giving to others, as with parenting.

In *Drama of the Gifted Child*, Alice Miller (1997) offered a detailed explanation of the developmental events in the early life of many in the helping professions. She wrote:

> The therapist's sensibility, empathy, responsiveness, and powerful "antennae" indicate that as a child, he [*sic*] probably used to fulfill other people's needs and to repress his own. (p. 19)

In this quote, Miller is expressing a paradox that often affects the professional helper—skills learned for survival and attention as a child can be both adaptive and harmful when an adult.

Empathy balance is aligned with an understanding of human personality needing a "self" pole and a "relations with others" pole. Blatt (2008) expresses these two dimensions of relatedness and self-definition in his book *Polarities of Experience*. Another term that encompasses the two poles is the concept of individuation. Writing about psychological individuation—or becoming your own person—other researchers describe a two-sided process of aloneness and connection. For example, by Grotevant and Cooper's (1986) definition of the individuation process includes both the "qualities of individuality and connectedness" (p. 89).

Figure 7.1 depicts empathy balance in action in the actual work environment of the therapy meeting.

A challenge for therapists is to be empathetically present in the life of the client, to be empathetically present with themselves, and to be observing both of these expressions of the self. We do this by shifting back and forth, as the figure indicates.

Figure 7.1 Optimal Empathy Balance in the Client Meeting

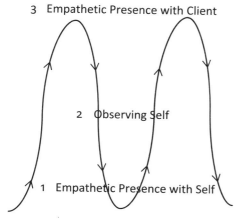

3 Empathetic Presence with Client

2 Observing Self

1 Empathetic Presence with Self

Empathetic Presence with the Client

Being present with the client in a caring, empathetic way—feeling the other person's reality and understanding his or her thoughts and behavior—is essential to the work. Being able to have our self merge with the other is part of being a highly effective practitioner. However, if we do only this, we can get swept away in their life and lose a sense of ourselves as separate. Getting really lost in the other fits with the definition of codependency, where there is a loss of the self and the needs of the self. This stance is dangerous to a person's long-term well-being. To use perhaps a silly example, how well does the chicken do with no feathers?

Empathetic Presence with the Self

We are not our clients. Our clients' suffering is not our suffering. We have our own lives, our own human suffering as well as our own joy and confusion. Cutting myself does not stop a client's bleeding. It is important that we have an empathetic presence, an emotional acceptance, for ourselves as part of being vibrant and energetic as people, because being vibrant and energetic people is a good base for effective client work.

Yet too much focus on the self is dangerous. The work is not about us. A practitioner with an excessive self-focus is ineffective in the caring professions. This phrase explains the concept: The work is about caring. At its extreme, a self-focus cannot produce effective therapy for the client.

Observing Self

"Metacognition" is a term that means thinking about thinking. It is important that we observe the situation we are in with clients. We need to understand the other, our own reactions, and the interplay between the two of us. All of this information gives us some hints of how to respond and help clients. No wonder the work is tiring; there is a lot to pay attention to.

More on Empathy Balance

A valuable skill for practitioners is the ability able to make continual shifts between an empathetic focus on the other while not losing touch with the self. An excessive emotional merging with the other is a symptom of co-dependency, to use a term from the addictions field. This focus on the other and a focus on the self and stopping at the observing self is engrossing activity. Think of this capacity to go back and forth as a way to pick up oxygen from the self and deliver it to the other and then switch back. The switching back is accompanied with the carbon dioxide (the suffering feelings, thoughts, and behaviors of the other). The carbon dioxide is deposited and replaced with oxygen when visiting the self. This empathetic presence with the self is crucial for self-renewal. See Figure 7.1 again to see this flow. This capacity to shift is, in my view, a defining feature of resilient practitioners—they can inoculate the self against the diseases and infections that can ravage them. These diseases go by a variety of names: (here is the list again!) secondary traumatic stress, vicarious traumatization, emotional depletion, and the classic term—burnout. Figure 7.1 shows part of the prevention formula of how to be involved but not be damaged by the work.

Empathy balance can be understood using concepts from Rønnestad (1996) who has described, as we outline in Chapter 10, three different practitioner styles of relating to the emotional, cognitive, and behavioral expressions of the client. According to Rønnestad, practitioners use these styles to process and regulate the intense data of practice where clients express the pain of their lives. I am discussing these ways of responding to the intense data of the therapy session in this chapter because they can help us understand empathy balance.

Premature Closure

Premature closure is a style of stopping the material before it is fully felt and visualized. Practitioners use premature closure when they feel overwhelmed, especially by the painful struggles clients are describing. This closure may protect practitioners from feeling things, just as a hard shell protects the turtle. But it is done at a high cost. Clients deeply value our ability to feel their pain. It is part of the central gift we give them. Also, assessment comes most accurately not from tests and instruments, but from our feeling the other's suffering. Premature closure is a maladaptive method often used without full awareness by practitioners. Rønnestad calls it a pre- and unconscious defensive maneuver (Rønnestad & Skovholt, 1991). This is similar to the ideas of Firestone and Catlett (1999), who describe an intimacy style where a person uses emotional cutoffs, ending contact with the other, when the interpersonal world is too threatening.

Insufficient Closure

> Cognitively, [insufficient closure] refers to an inability to stop thinking about the client's problems or one's own reactions to them. Emotionally, it refers to continually feeling the disturbing emotions produced in the session. Relationally, it refers to an inadequate regulation of professional boundaries, and behaviorally, expressions may be a variety of counter-therapeutic actions.
>
> —*Skovholt & Rønnestad, 2003, p. 50*

Thinking of the interaction with the other when outside of work is a form of insufficient closure. It is a common experience for novices and for experienced practitioners as well. Practitioners experience insufficient closure as an invasion by the client into their inner world that practitioners are unable to stop. Practitioners can feel the invasion in the body, in the thought processes, or in the behavior. This invasion into the practitioner's personal self can be a major early stressor for the beginning practitioner. Constant highly stressful anxious ruminating drains the energy from novices.

Functional Closure

Functional closure involves a kind of empathy balance where the focus is on the other at times but especially on the self when practitioners are off duty. Thinking about and feeling the content from the client session later can be helpful. This use of reflecting on our work can be a very positive way to learn. Creative solutions can come from off-duty reflection—the so-called aha! experience in the shower. The issue is the duration, severity, and intensity of the feeling and thinking about client situations.

One of the marks of highly experienced practitioners is being able to turn off the data and go on with their lives. Functional closure means learning both to use the reflection process and how to turn it off. Learning the art of functional closure takes time—the novice period is a good time to start learning this skill.

Learning and Practicing Empathy Balance

Regulating empathy balance is an important developmental skill for novices to hone. This kind of regulation is not easy to achieve, especially for all the dedicated, sensitive individuals in the helping professions. This is especially true for novices who are filled with enthusiasm and anxiety about helping. Regulating empathy balance often is a work in progress. We can easily focus so much on the other that we abandon the needs of the self—which are vital for protection in order to give later.

Many practitioners are able to find the often-thin line between the needs of the other and the needs of the self and succeed in both. Resilient practitioners change their focus over the course of a day, week, month, year. For example, responding to a client emergency, the practitioner is totally focused on the needs of the other. Later, there is a self-care element. Perhaps during one week, effort tilts in one direction. Later, there is a tilt in the other direction. The self-care/other-care equilibrium is dynamic and shifting.

Antidotes to Insufficient Empathy Balance

The helping professions and the public are best served by individuals who have a strong impulse to help others. Then, in order to survive and thrive, these helpers need to learn how to both help the other and protect the self. Developing empathy balance takes time. It involves learning to constantly monitor the self, just as a car owner monitors the car's fluid levels: oil, power steering, transmission, brakes. We must look for a positive interplay between empathic attachment to the other and our own very important self-care needs. How much does worry and preoccupation outside of the session really improve the work? How much of it just depletes practitioners? These are important but often difficult questions for practitioners, especially beginners.

I have emphasized the following point many times in this book because it is so central to the therapist experience. The point! Novices, flooded with impressions, images, feelings, ideas, worries, and hopes, often have no established dike to hold back all of the affective content. Novice emotional boundary establishment often tips either toward porous or rigid. The paradoxical task is to learn to be both present and separate and also to be able to strategically attach, detach, and reattach. These are difficult, advanced skills. Getting better at them is a part of novice development.

Task 5: Develop Sustaining Measures of Success and Satisfaction

Sometimes our efforts make no difference.
Sometimes they do.
Occasionally we know the results.
Often we don't.
Our impact can be felt later . . . or much later.
Our efforts are very tiny in the infinity of time and space.

Practitioners usually accept the ambiguity of results after they wrestle with the self in a struggle of confusion, asking such questions as:

Is my practitioner self any good?
How do I know?

Novices hunger for positive feedback from peers, supervisors, and clients.
Some novices and experienced practitioners hate the ambiguity and quit.
Others force concrete results and, therefore, limit their work like a dancer who can perform only one structured dance.

It is better to learn to accept the existential reality of not knowing; once we do, we recognize that the client does not need to put energy into pleasing us.

The paradox is that when we accept the powerlessness of our efforts, we can sometimes be very helpful guests in the life of the other.

If the outcome comes quickly and is easy, that means the problem is not very big. And since all people are problem solvers, for simple things they do not need us. People who welcome us into their lives as their professional helpers come to us when they have difficulties that fester, unsolved.

We are told in this profession to be realistic, not so idealistic, yet who wants realistic if it means embracing failure, mediocrity, and being unsuccessful? Realistic is not a word that I warm up to. I did not get into the helping professions for "realistic" results. Did you? I got into the work to have an impact, to transform lives. There is so much in the human world that needs fixing; how can we accept so little change as good enough? It is as if we are being asked to accept "the banality of evil" (Arendt, 1994) as a fine outcome in this human community where there is so much suffering.

Realistic versus idealistic is a gut-wrenching topic for helping professionals. No one wants to accept limits to the work when starting out. Getting to a point of accepting less than the ideal is so difficult. Yet there is the crushing feeling of failure, of emptiness, of despair when we demand the ideal and end up with so much less. Many have left the work at this point—when they cannot accept the less-than-ideal outcome. Consider these examples of caring professionals watching poor results right in front of them:

- The teacher with the student who cannot pass the test
- The physician who watches the patient die without being able to prevent it
- The counselor who cannot reduce the client's constant debilitating anxiety

On this topic, how do these words from Tippett (2007) resonate with you?

> Sometimes in this world the best you can do is plant the seed, attend patiently and reverently to a reality you cannot change quickly or even in your lifetime, be present to suffering you cannot banish. (p. 58)

Why, why, why must it be this way? One reason is because our work is a dance between two or more people. It would be great if the work of the practitioner is to do a version of taking a can of spray paint and painting the other—as if the person was a passive wall—with the paint. That way we could have control of outcome. And so many of the theories, methods, and techniques are set up this way: to maximize practitioner control. "I will do something to you and you will feel better, learn easier, get along better, and so on."

People are not that malleable, and it is good that they are not. In my hundreds of hours of clinical work during 30-plus years, I have told clients some things that could have really helped them when they were in deep trouble. Sometimes they rejected the ideas, brushing them away as if they were flies landing on their skin. I am a guest in the life of clients, and they have no obligation to accept my ideas. Would you want no

Table 7.1 How Much Control Does the Practitioner Have Over the Outcome in These Dimensions?

Client/Student/Patient positive change and/or appreciation	Limited
Supervisor/Work peers' support and/or appreciation	Limited
Expert knowledge	Yes
Presence and process: The Cycle of Caring	Yes

freedom to make your own choices? Of course not. It is the same with your clients. This dimension of the client's right for self-determination is a central issue in our need sometimes to embrace "realistic" when we want "ideal."

One way to view success is to consider multiple outcome measures. Of course, most of all we want the client to do well. We want our supervisor to think we are skilled. However, as I have mentioned, we have limited control over these dimensions. We can concentrate on being an expert in the content area and doing the Cycle of Caring well (as described in detail in Chapter 12).

Part of the ambiguity of success is the fact that so much of the work lacks closure. As Wicks (2008) says: "Let us not pretend it does not hurt when a client abruptly ends treatment" (p. 19). I call the disappearance of clients ambiguous professional loss. As I have mentioned, clients do not continue for many reasons: They reached a plateau; got a lot from the counseling; cannot afford the fee; had different, but unexpressed goals, from us; forgot about the appointment because they have better things to do; and many others.

It is important that we embrace the small, often unseen, victories. The small victories are to be cherished and celebrated—sometimes that is all there is. An important task is for us, as resilient practitioners, to find measures of success that can sustain us. We must learn to embrace the ambiguity of success and hope for idealistic outcomes while being sustained by realistic ones.

Yes—embrace the small victories. That is one of the secrets of resilient practitioners.

Task 6: Create a Greenhouse at Work

Practitioners in the helping professions reach out to the human need around them. They instinctively hope that they will have a very positive and supportive work environment. Sometimes we do have wonderful administrators, supervisors, and bosses who provide a positive atmosphere for our work. They are so valuable because they provide a strong structure while we reach out and concentrate on our work. However, sometimes our work environment is toxic.

When practitioners who express caring toward their clients do not receive great inspired leadership from administrators, supervisors, and colleagues, they sometimes passively wait and hope, wait and hope, wait and hope. And then get discouraged, lonely, cynical, and drained of the energy needed for the work.

Maslach and Leiter (1997) document the importance of a positive environment for our work. What elements in the work environment make a difference for helping practitioners? One is a sense of control. This finding is common in the occupational stress research. For example, Ben-Zur and Keren (2007) found that perception of control is important for burnout prevention with helping professionals. Studying nurses, Hochwalder (2007) found that empowerment, a kind of control, lowered burnout. Murdoch and Eagles (2007) reported that 93% of a sample of psychiatrists found a program called stress-busting to be helpful; it involved problem solving and venting about work. These studies highlight the importance of the work environment for practitioner resilience.

I have used the metaphor of a greenhouse as a way for us in the helping professions to think about an ideal work environment. Why a greenhouse? Plants thrive in a greenhouse because the environment is set for growth. We too need to work in a greenhouse in order to maximize our potential. Great managers and directors in the human services create a greenhouse for practitioners. Unfortunately, in many situations, no greenhouse is provided, and we practitioners wait for it. The play *Waiting for Godot* by Samuel Beckett is about the perils of waiting. Two men wait and wait and wait . . . and then the curtain comes down. Sometimes we have to create our own greenhouse. Table 7.2 highlights the differences between positive and negative environments.

Table 7.2   Differences between a Greenhouse and a Stressful Environment

Wonderful Work "Greenhouse"	Stressful Work Environment
Trust and respect between peers	Lack of trust and disrespect between peers
Appropriately playful, fun, and supportive atmosphere; a sense of community	Tense, critical, low-support workplace, breakdown of community
Place for all to develop professionally	Atmosphere of professional complacency
Have choices/control	Lack of choices and control
Sustainable workload	Work overload
Recognition and reward	Insufficient reward
Fair performance standards	Unfair performance standards
Meaningful work	Lack of meaning

Source: Modified from Maslach & Leiter (1997, p. 149).

Importance of Good Peer and Supervisor Relationships for Practitioner Resiliency

Throughout this book I have discussed the importance of peers, supervisors, and mentors, especially in the first years of the journey on the practitioner path. Here is more on that topic. Talking to school and work friends about the work can be very valuable. Trusting and respecting each other makes it possible to share real dilemmas that we face.

I am happy when I hear counseling practicum students mention the meeting room and meeting times they share with other practicum students, often from a variety of training programs. Those peer conversations are filled with useful social comparison information.

Throughout this book, I discuss the use of reflection as a way to learn and grow (Schön, 1983). This talking about work with friends, colleagues, and peers is another place for the value of reflection. However, the task here is to learn how to find empathy balance. Rich, positive clinical supervision in an individual or group format is also part of the greenhouse at work. The processing of the content can be a very valuable way to reduce insufficient closure.

Often we are not handed an ideal greenhouse in which to grow. Perhaps we find no greenhouse at all. I remember one work environment, where I worked for many years, that had hardly any greenhouse effects. It was a frightening place to work because it had so many negative features. Seeing so many burned out senior staff members mobilized me to actively seek ways to be continually energetic about work. I suggest that you actively work to make a greenhouse for yourself at work if none exists.

Task 7: Connect with Your Own Spirituality

The mystery of life, clocked so guileless in day and night, makes the search for God the enduring human drama. We know so little, we feel so much. We have only the shape of our lives, experienced in the cycle of light and dark, to guide us toward meaning.

—*Hampl, 1995, p. xxvi*

In the vast majority of studies, religious people report higher well-being than their non-religious counterparts.

—*Diener and Biswas-Diener, 2008, p. 114*

[P]ositive emotions and the experience of spiritual contact—of getting in touch with the divine, regardless of your definition—are intimately related. When people attend church services, sing hymns, pray, and engage in other religious activities, they often feel a surge of positive emotions. In fact, the experience of spirituality may be an emotional one, inseparable from good feelings.

—*Diener and Biswas-Diener, 2008, p. 124*

Spirituality/religion is such a big, individual, and divisive topic that I am inclined not to include it at all. But that is not the way to address a big topic. So here we go.

One concern at the heart of spiritual and religious questions concerns our future after death. Earlier in this chapter, I discussed the classic book, *The Denial of Death*, by Becker (1973), where he proposes that death is the great human fear, outshining all others. The reality of death is a profound truth, and practitioners in the caring professions often deal with profound truth in their work with clients. The evangelical religious leader Rick Warren has written an immensely popular book, *The Purpose Driven Life* (2007), that puts death in a Christian context of good work now and then life after death. In contrast, Irv Yalom (2008), in *Staring at the Sun: Overcoming the Terror of Death*, offers a secular humanist method of coping with death when the afterlife does not exist. These are contrasting styles of relating to spiritual questions.

I suggest that practitioners connect with their own spirituality, however they define it. The searching process can open up channels for emotional and spiritual connections with the infinite and the religious. Having a relationship with God, or whatever terms you use, can enrich our lives and help us put so much in perspective.

A spiritual/religious life is an important part of how many resilient practitioners sustain the self. For example, one special education teacher told me that her religious life gave her the strength for a long career in the field. This sense of "something beyond" takes many different shapes for people in our global community of 7 billion people. For me, a religious sense of the infinite and a feeling of God's presence can bring peace, contentment, and happiness. Many people find one set of rituals necessary for a religious experience. For me, it has been different. I have celebrated the sacred and spiritual with Muslims in Turkey, Buddhists in Thailand, Catholics at the Vatican, Jews when my father was a resident of a Jewish nursing home, and Lutherans at my grandfather's church in Norway. I have also experienced the power of the Christian God in the beautiful wilderness of Minnesota's canoe country.

An active spiritual/religious life acknowledges the reality described by Becker (1973): Death is terrifying, and facing the reality directly through a spiritual/religious life is one way of acknowledging this reality. Also, an active spiritual/religious quest addresses the central mysteries of life: What is the meaning of life? Is there an active divine presence? What is God's plan for my life? Are people basically good or evil? How can I achieve forgiveness, atonement, and peace? What moral rules should govern my life? Is there eternal life?

Practitioners in the helping fields are actively present in the drama of human tragedy, disappointment, and pain. We witness all kinds of difficult and painful things. Recently I was visiting with a psychologist who works with brain-damaged veterans. The soldiers went within days from being wounded by roadside bombs to Walter Reed Army Medical Center to our local veterans' hospital. How does this psychologist understand the level of pain and tragedy of her clients? An active spiritual/religious life can help practitioners search for meaning and understanding of these painful human realities seen on a daily basis at work. For example, it can be important to ask questions, such as: How can I understand this kind of suffering? Are there spiritual ways for me to know how a spiritual/religious force permits acute human pain and suffering?

In summary, for many practitioners, an active spiritual/religious life seems an important source of their wellness and resiliency. For some, it is the primary source of their positive energy for the work.

Task 8: Finding Balance to the Imbalance of Too Many One-Way Caring Relationships in One's Personal Life

As in the Mahalia Jackson song "Sometimes I Feel Like a Motherless Child," the motherless child is vulnerable and unable to defend him- or herself. Helping professionals sometimes have this experience in their personal lives. They respond to the needs of others and, without knowing it, they end up caring for others at work and caring for others in personal lives. Of course, caring for others in our own personal lives is often an honor and a privilege. I am here discussing one-way caring relationships as the predominant or only type of relationship in the person's life. When all the energy goes out and little comes back, how can practitioners energize themselves for the rigors of work?

For the helper of others, and for a motherless child, sometimes the alarm bell of concern for oneself goes off. When it does, there can be great anxiety. And when it never goes off, there can be *even more* danger. Novices in the helping professions, like fawns grazing while a predator approaches, must learn danger signals and protect themselves. *Helpers* in the *helping professions* are *helpers* of others. That is who we are, that is what we do. What if the person being helped is very focused on the self and does not reciprocate? And does not know that the equation is uneven? This is fine and as it should be in professional relationships with clients. The one-way helping relationship is what gives the professional helping of others so much of its value. Of course, we do need to protect ourselves from being harmed physically or emotionally by clients, or from being used by clients. Earlier I discussed the concepts of empathy balance and boundaried generosity, concepts that are important here.

We need to have limits at work. When do you refer a client who is often a no-show? How about one who will not do homework assignments? Or another who is irresponsible about paying for services? These are important work dilemmas, but it is in our personal lives where the danger of one-way caring can be significant.

I am hesitant to use words like "narcissistic" in professional work, let alone in describing what we could call dangerous others in the personal lives of helpers. Yet "narcissistic" seems to capture the force I am warning against. The word communicates a powerful personal force. It is when the person looks at the mirror and sees only self needs.

The developmental history of narcissism often involves a childhood where there was insufficient affection and attention. So, for a narcissistic person, instead of an adulthood where more maturity is sought, with "maturity" defined as being able to go progressively farther beyond the self, adulthood is a prolonged childhood where attention and external validation are constantly sought. Such a person often has very low empathy for the other and his or her needs. Narcissistic injury and narcissistic rage (Masterson, 1990) occur when this external validation does not come, when the person is not admired enough, listened to enough, followed enough. A constant need for external validation leaves little room for giving to and caring for others.

Learning to Recognize the Danger of Unequal Personal Relationships

It is easy for the helper of others to get ensnared in relationships where the equality equation tilts to unequal. It may occur in friendships, with colleagues, community members, or a romantic partner. This situation does not happen with like-minded givers where thoughtfulness, kindness, and mutual caring is back and forth like a ping-pong ball over the net and across the table. This back-and-forth is captured with the word "bid," as in I bid for your attention and you bid for mine. In positive two-ways relationships, both individuals make bids to the other and get responses; it goes back and forth. The bid-and-response sequence is the oxygen of romance and other positive relationships. No response to one's bids in personal life is a yellow flag for the person.

The helper's impulse is to give to others. Consequently, it can be hard for novices to learn to protect themselves, to even recognize the *need* to protect themselves from being used. It is important for helpers to learn to recognize this danger. It often comes as a vague feeling of being used by the other. Excessive amounts of giving in relationships where there should be more equality depletes us. And being depleted is dangerous because our work demands so much energy from us. One simple rule is to make sure that friendships are give-and-take; if the other person talks about his or her life struggles and problems, we talk about our struggles and problems. Without give-and-take, the interpersonal exchange is not friendship, it is work.

Being aware of the danger of one-way caring relationships in one's personal life is an important task for novice resiliency development.

Task 9: Max Out the Body as a Source for Positive Energy

Self-care presentations, books, and articles often focus on this topic of physical health-related activities, practices, and habits. Since we have all been exposed to so many messages regarding the importance of our physical healthcare, I am not going to focus on this topic. That does not mean these practices are not important. Our vitality depends on assertively working on our own health.

Top Five Body Energy Sources

Intense Exercise

Physical exercise serves as a natural physiological barrier against the physiological stress of vicarious traumatization and compassion fatigue.

This intense activity can be a tremendously beneficial factor for those in the helping professions. Weight training seems to have some of the same effects. Stretching is, of course, valuable but does not seem to reduce the distress emotions—anxiety, depression, and anger—to the same degree. Some yoga programs provide all three components.

Sleeping Well

Sleep is really important. Significant periods of insomnia produce elevated levels of the distress emotions, whereas significant sleep reduces their levels. It is important to practice good sleep hygiene, such as by going to sleep at the same time every day, performing a ritual to prepare the body to sleep, and reducing the noise of technology and instant communication around sleep time.

Nutritious Eating

Again, we all hear so many messages about healthy eating that I will not focus on this here. We all know, and sometimes practice, good habits, such as having breakfast, thinking organic, watching our sugar intake, and avoiding caffeine highs as a way to fuel the body.

Meditation and Relaxation

Mindfulness-based meditation, yoga, and similar practices are used by many people in the helping fields to reduce the insidious effects of stress. Consistent practice adds great value. Being able to relax one's body through a relaxation method can be valuable to practitioners while in the intensity of a session. It is both relaxing and empowering to be able to relax the body in the middle of client work.

Love and Affection

I am surrounded by an extremely caring, loving, and supportive nuclear family.
—*Counseling practitioner in resiliency workshop, June 2008*

Popular songs come and go, but their themes are constant. And one constant is the power of love and affection and the pain of its withdrawal. Being deeply in love is a wonderful-beyond-wonderful human experience! When we see, at the zoo or in books, the grooming behavior of other primates, our genetic cousins, we can get a sense of the importance of affection and personal touch. In our own lives, affection and touch are important. Of course, this most often happens in intimate relationships, in families, and with friends. Dogs, cats, and other pets provide some of the wonder of touch too, for some practitioners.

Task 10: Long-Term Continual Focus on the Development of the Self

Working on developing the self is analogous to what happens when pruning a tree.

The pruning stresses the tree, but the longer-term effect is growth and vitality. Our "pruning effect" can occur with both the professional and the personal self producing energy for the work and for life. Remember that it is energy that the resilient practitioner needs; not for just today but for all the todays of tomorrow.

Concerning professional development, engaged practitioners often are energized by both the process and outcome of development. To use an analogy with athletes, this is like saying that they are energized *by working out* and also energized *as a result of developing skills because they worked out.* This double source of energy—the process and the outcome—produces vitality for master therapists. Creating an ongoing professional development process leads to exciting growth.

When in school, the professional development process is highly structured. The practitioner self gets a workout when one is an active student in the helping professions. School is often very intense, and professional growth is propelled forward. After graduation, therapists are in charge of their own growth. With the Minnesota master therapist sample, three relevant characteristics for ongoing development are being insatiably curious, being voracious learners, and having an intense will to grow (Skovholt & Jennings, 2004; Jennings, Skovholt, Goh, & Lin, 2012).

Sometimes professional development is not straightforward but rather like a loop or a roller coaster. A feeling of success can, for example, get progressively stronger or it may start strong, dip, and then get strong again. There can be sudden bursts of insight, as with a critical incident or defining moment for the individual. Moving to a new work domain can bring a feeling of going backward—more performance anxiety, more turning to others for help.

This "trying the new," one of the important skills to nurture, is about career risk taking and trying out new skills. It is hard to put ourselves in new situations. Yet when we stop putting ourselves in new situations, we can stagnate. And part of stagnation is cynicism and general negativity because the work can get boring and less fulfilling. This is the price for not taking risks and trying out new things. Novices seldom are bored because novelty and its cousin, performance-related anxiety, often are present. Yet, in time, the familiar can get old and boring; no longer is there novelty to provide energy and vitality for the work with your clients. So, as novices, think about new development as an ongoing, career-long process.

In our personal lives, there are many ways to work on developing the self. One is to use the gift of a method we offer to others—counseling/therapy. This is a way to accelerate the growth process and can be useful to all. In addition to learning about the self and working on what we call issues, new practitioners often learn a lot from the modeling of their own therapists. In fact, more than one new therapist in our research study (Rønnestad and Skovholt, 2003) has commented about how much of their early practice behaviors came predominantly from doing what their own therapist was doing with them.

One personal goal can be summed up as trying to get closer to personal maturity. The word "maturity" is both a common word and an elusive concept. It is common in that it is widely used, but it is elusive because it is so hard both to define and to consistently attain. Related concepts are character and wisdom. At all life stages, there are challenges to maturity. I think of the life cycle as consisting of constant challenges and having the form of the bell-shape curve. First, it is a challenge for the infant to cope and thrive even when an adult is fully responsible. Then in time, over years, the challenge is to take care of the self. This often leads to taking care of ourselves and taking care of a few others at work and at home. Next in the life cycle we are challenged to take care of even more people, in addition to ourselves, at work and at home. Maturity is a challenge here, as at all other times. Then often we shift to taking care of fewer people at work and at home in addition to ourselves. In time, the challenge is to take care of just ourselves. Finally, the challenge is to take care of ourselves while others have responsibility for us too. This is the 90-year life cycle in a bell curve form of dependency, independence, responsibility, less responsibility, and then eventually dependency. There are challenges during each phase. Becoming more mature while managing these challenges enhances practitioners' sense of self-efficacy and reduces potentially debilitating levels of guilt and shame. Maturity involves expanding the self when contraction is a natural response, just as it is with our muscles. Firestone, Firestone, and Catlett (2003) write of the human tendency to be more protective and defensive:

> Most of us reject or manipulate our environments to evade emotional interactions that would contradict our earlier conceptions of reality. This phenomena may be the single most limiting factor for all psychotherapies [and counseling methods]. . . .
>
> Psychological defenses predispose an inward, self-protective lifestyle that is the basis of a core resistance to change or improvement in one's life circumstance. (p. xii)

Firestone et al. (2003) describe challenges to maturity when they tell us to open up to others even at a deeper level that the existential message is that with every hello there is always a good-bye, sometime, someplace. One of the important tasks related to maturity is our own grief work. For all the attachments we obtain—people, positions, things, ideas—we have a corresponding number of losses. Developing an active grief method is important because the word "grief" is not something for the dead. Grief work is the route we use to keep living and making new attachments. It is important for practitioners to be good at this work in their own lives as a source of vitality and as a method they can teach their clients.

Doing our own therapy, working on our own spirituality, honing our ethical sense, and living according to higher values—these are all ways to seek maturity.

Working on developing the self is a source of energy. Just the process of self-awareness—which includes the use of feedback to improve and the constant risk taking involved in trying out new behaviors, emotional reactions, and thinking patterns—produces energy. As I have said, with the development of the self, the process of doing the work and the outcome of the work both produce professional resiliency. The classic Rogers (1961) book is called *On Becoming a Person*. In it, the becoming is the idea.

Mary Mullenbach has made a valuable contribution with her study of burnout prevention and self-care strategies of expert practitioners (Mullenbach & Skovholt, 2011, pp. 219–243). She started with a sample of ten expert practitioners and investigated their methods of renewal. Table 7.3 collects her overall categories and themes.

Table 7.3   Burnout Prevention and Self-Care Strategies of Expert Practitioners
Category A: Professional Stressors
Participants are stressed by issues that challenge their competency.
A frozen therapy process is highly stressful for participants.
Breaches in peer relationships are stressful.
Intrapersonal crises negatively impact the professional role.
Category B: Emergence of the Expert Practitioner
Participants learned role limits and boundaries.
Over time, participants experienced less performance anxiety.
With experience, participants moved from theory to use of self.
Participants view attachment and separation as a natural process.
Participants understand human suffering at a profound level.
Category C: Creating a Positive Work Structure
Mentor and peer support was critical at the novice phase.
Participants have ongoing and enriching peer relationships.
Multiple roles are a protective factor.
Participants create health-promoting work environments.
Category D: Protective Factors
Participants directly engage highly stressful professional dilemmas.
Participants confront and resolve personal issues.
Highly engaged learning is a powerful source of renewal.
Category E: Nurturing Self Through Solitude and Relationships
Participants foster professional stability by nurturing a personal life.
Participants invest in a broad array of restorative activities.
Participants construct fortifying personal relationships.
Participants value an internal focus.

Source: From Skovholt, T. (2001). *The Resilient Practitioner,* originally published by Boston: Allyn & Bacon. Copyright Thomas Skovholt. Published in Mullenbach and Skovholt, 2011.

Task 11: Have Fun and Be Playful

The world of play favors exuberance, license, abandon. Shenanigans are allowed, strategies can be tried, selves can be revisited. In the self-enclosed world of play, there is no hunger. It is its own goal which it reaches in a richly satisfying way.

—Ackerman, 1999, p. 6

Over the last thirty years I've watched a lot of pain flow under the bridge. By now, I have a Ph.D. in human suffering.

—Pipher, 2003, p. xvi

One of our gifts to our clients is our courageous willingness to enter and join them in their emotional world. This world—at least the one they show us—is not filled with mirth, laughter, and foolishness. No, it is filled with worry, despair, fear, anger, insignificance, failure, anxiety, humiliation, and betrayal.

For career-long vitality, we need emotional balance. We need laughter, play, exuberance, delightful escape, zest, and fun. The world of play helps make our world of work possible. Therapists and counselors are usually earnest, pensive, responsible, hardworking, conscientious, and serious. These are all good traits, except not all the time. Consider the saying "All work and no play makes Jack a dull boy." Perhaps a better word for practitioners is "dulled" rather than "dull." The onslaught of negative affect that arrives via client meetings can dull us. With all work and seriousness, the recharging potential of fun and play gets lost.

There are many fun and play options. The method is not critical; the doing it is. One method is just being playful, fun, frivolous, and mischievous. Telling jokes and reading the comics are other examples. Computer games are very engrossing for many people. Another is a hobby, such as gardening. Collections are a good choice for practitioners— they are concrete, countable, and easily enjoyed. Escape reading is popular with some practitioners, as is visiting with friends. Having lunch together after shopping is lots of fun for some. In *Deep Play*, Diane Ackerman (1999) travels through multiple examples: scuba diving, mountain climbing, wearing a mask, studying animals in the wild, and visiting exotic sites.

Watching sports, and going to concerts, shows, or movies counts too. I know of one woman who dresses in the colors of her favorite hockey team, including face paint, and goes into a patriotic self-hypnotic frenzy while watching a game. During that time, the toxins of the week just roll away. My minister as I was growing up, a straitlaced, serious Christian man caring for a whole flock, would turn beet red screaming at the referees while watching college basketball. Then he was back to work the next day and the serious work of ministry.

Then there is vacation and recreation as re-creation. Related terms are: time off, break, holiday, escape, rest, retreat, goofing off. Taking a vacation is an often-cited method of renewal by practitioners in resiliency workshops.

Running on empty can work for a while, but not forever. Play is a valuable energy source for the work.

SUMMARY

Becoming and being a resilient practitioner is about wellness. Our own wellness is necessary so we can marshal the enormous energy necessary for the work with our clients. Here are two examples of practitioners from the broader caring professions, a nurse and a physician, who show the need for practitioner resiliency.

With dignity and grace, Kelly Johnson (2009) tells of her immersion as a nurse with traumatic spinal cord injury patients. It started with a first patient; a 15-year-old boy told her how he became paralyzed playing football. She continues her article on secondary traumatic stress as an issue for nurses by writing: "Since that time I have listened to and cared for literally thousands of families with similar tragic stories" (p. 1). This listening to stories is the core of the caring professions, including, of course, therapy and counseling. It is of enormous value to individuals who are suffering to have a practitioner care for them by listening intensively to them. Doing this is highly respectful to clients and serves to mobilize their self-healing properties. It is also very important as a source of knowledge about clients and, in this way, offers possible useful avenues for intervention.

Here is another example. Each year, forensic pediatrician Toni Laskey and colleagues see 500 to 700 children where there is suspected physical and/or sexual abuse. About the work, she says:

> Anybody that doesn't let it get to them isn't putting their heart into it... If my work can somehow make a difference in how a child is cared for, that's my greatest hope.
> —*Smith, 2007, p. 55*

I end this chapter on resiliency development and burnout prevention by reminding you of the inventory following, and then asking you to engage in an imagery exercise.

SKOVHOLT PRACTITIONER PROFESSIONAL RESILIENCY AND SELF-CARE INVENTORY

The purpose of the inventory is to provide self-reflection for practitioners and students in the caring professions. Practitioner here refers to individuals in the caring professions—such as the helping professions, teaching, and health care. Examples are psychologist, counselor, social worker, academic advisor, K-12 teacher, college professor, clergy, human resources specialist, physician, registered nurse, dentist, and family law attorney.

Questions are addressed to both active practitioners and also students in training programs. There is no total number that is considered best. In fact, some of the questions are not relevant to some professionals or students who fill out this inventory. The inventory is intended to help decrease stress, not increase it!

The checklist consists of four sub-scales: Professional Vitality, Personal Vitality, Professional Stress and Personal Stress.

1=Strongly Disagree, 2=Disagree, 3=Undecided, 4=Agree, 5=Strongly Agree

Professional Vitality   **Circle Your Response**

1. I find my work as a practitioner or as a student to be meaningful 1 2 3 4 5

2. I view self-care as an ongoing part of my professional work/student life 1 2 3 4 5

3. I am interested in making positive attachments with my clients/students/patients 1 2 3 4 5

4. I have the energy to make these positive attachments with my clients/students/patients 1 2 3 4 5

5. The director/chair at my site/school is dedicated to practitioner welfare 1 2 3 4 5

6. On the dimension of control of my work/schooling, I am closer to high control than low control 1 2 3 4 5

7. On the dimension of demands at my work/schooling, I have reasonable demands rather than excessive demands from others 1 2 3 4 5

8. My work environment is like a greenhouse—where everything grows—because the conditions are such that I feel supported in my professional work 1 2 3 4 5

Subscale Score for Professional Vitality (Possible score is 8-40)

Personal Vitality

9. I have plenty of humor and laughter in my life 1 2 3 4 5
10. I have a strong code of values/ethics that gives me a sense of direction and integrity.. 1 2 3 4 5
11. I feel loved by intimate others.. 1 2 3 4 5
12. I have positive/close friendships.. 1 2 3 4 5
13. I am physically active and receive the benefits of exercise 1 2 3 4 5
14. My financial life (expenses, savings, and spending) is in balance 1 2 3 4 5
15. I have lots of fun in my life 1 2 3 4 5
16. I have one or more abundant sources of high energy for my life (examples—other people, pleasurable hobby, enjoyable pet, the natural world, a favorite activity) 1 2 3 4 5
17. To balance the ambiguity of work in the caring professions, I have some concrete activities in my life that I enjoy where results are clear cut (e.g. a rock collection, painting walls, growing tomatoes, washing the car) 1 2 3 4 5
18. My eating habits are good for my body 1 2 3 4 5
19. My sleep pattern is restorative 1 2 3 4 5

Subscale Score for Personal Vitality (Possible score is 10-55)

Professional Stress

20. There are many contradictory messages about both practicing self-care and meeting expectations of being a highly competent practitioner/student. I am working to find a way through these contradictory messages 1 2 3 4 5
21. Overall, I have been able to find a satisfactory level of "boundaried generosity" (defined as having both limits and giving of oneself) in my work with clients/students/patients 1 2 3 4 5

22. Witnessing human suffering is central in the caring professions (e.g., client grief, student failure, patient physical pain). I am able to be very present to this suffering, but not be overwhelmed by it or experience too much of what is called 'sadness of the soul' 1 2 3 4 5

23. I have found a way to have high standards for my work yet avoid unreachable perfectionism 1 2 3 4 5

24. My work is intrinsically pleasurable most of the time 1 2 3 4 5

25. Although judging success in the caring professions is often confusing, I have been able to find useful ways to judge my own professional success 1 2 3 4 5

26. I have at least one very positive relationship with a clinical supervisor/mentor/teacher 1 2 3 4 5

27. I am excited to learn new ideas—methods—theories—techniques in my field 1 2 3 4 5

28. The level of conflict between staff/faculty at my organization is low 1 2 3 4 5

Subscale Score for Professional Stress (Possible score is 8-40)

Personal Stress

29. There are different ways that I can get away from stress and relax (examples—TV, meditating, reading for fun, watching sports) 1 2 3 4 5

30. My personal life does not have an excessive number of one-way caring relationships where I am the caring one 1 2 3 4 5

31. My level of physical pain/disability is tolerable 1 2 3 4 5

32. My family relations are satisfying 1 2 3 4 5

33. I derive strength from my religious/spiritual practices and beliefs 1 2 3 4 5

34. I am not facing major betrayal in my personal life 1 2 3 4 5

35. I have a supportive community where I feel connected 1 2 3 4 5

36. I am able to cope with significant losses in my life 1 2 3 4 5

37. I have time for reflective activities such as journaling-expressive writing or solitude.. 1 2 3 4 5

38. When I feel the need, I am able to get help for myself 1 2 3 4 5

Subscale Score for Personal Stress (Possible score is 10-50)

Total Score for the Four Subscales (Possible score is 38-195)

There are a total of 38 questions in the Skovholt Professional Resiliency and Self-Care Inventory. All are scored in a positive direction with 0 low and 5 high. As stated earlier, the scoring system is a method for self-reflection by practitioners and students in the caring professions. There is no total number that is considered best. In fact, some of the questions are not relevant to some professionals or students who fill out this inventory. The inventory is intended to help decrease stress, not increase it!

As a way to consider professional resiliency and self-care in your career work, consider these questions. First, scan the questions and focus on your high answers, those with 4 and 5 responses. What do you conclude? Write here.

_____

_____

_____

_____

Then focus on your low answers, those with 1 and 2 responses. What do you conclude? Write here.

_____

_____

_____

_____

Then look across the four categories of Professional Vitality, Personal Vitality, Professional Stress, and Personal Stress. Are they in balance? If not in balance, what remedies could you consider? Write here.

_____

_____

_____

_____

Finally, consider the different topics covered in the inventory, your answers, and the comments you made for future self-reflection, clinical supervision, and discussion with others. Best wishes!

Tom Skovholt

Resilient Practitioner Imagery Exercise

Imagine looking ahead and seeing your favorite tree. Visualize it as vibrant, very healthy, strong and beautiful. The health of the tree permits it to take in enormous amounts of carbon dioxide and give off reams of life-giving oxygen.

Just like you and others in the helping professions.

To give its gift of oxygen, the tree must be nurtured.

Just like you.

The tree must have lots of sunlight, plenty of rain, and rich soil.

Just like you.

The tree must ward off big pests that may suddenly appear and eat its leaves. It must also defend itself against stealth pests, those little ones that are very difficult to see.

Imagine what happens to the tree without sun, without rain, without rich soil. It is not a pretty picture. Without nurturance, the tree shrivels up and, in time, can no longer take in toxic carbon dioxide and give off oxygen. Its valuable place in our world is lost. No longer can it nurture human life by taking in carbon dioxide.

The same is true for all of us in the helping professions, in education, and in healthcare—the caring fields. Self-care is not about selfishness but is rather the food and drink for the practitioner who is on the vigorous hike to higher-level competence in helping to enrich the lives of others.

Burnout means we are no longer able to do the Cycle of Caring and that means we can no longer be competent in this work. Our oxygen is essential, for the other (client, student, patient, advisee, supervisee) who is overwhelmed by carbon dioxide. That giving of oxygen is the meaning of the term "helping professions."

Think again of your favorite tree.

Thomas Skovholt, © 2001

REFERENCES

Ackerman, D. (1999). *Deep play*. New York, NY: Random House.

Arendt, H. (1994). *Eichmann in Jerusalem*. New York, NY: Penguin Classics.

Ayers, W. (1993). *To teach: The journey of a teacher*. New York, NY: Teachers College Press.

Baker, E. (2003). *Caring for ourselves: A therapist's guide to personal and professional well-being*. Washington, DC: American Psychological Association.

Becker, E. (1973). *The denial of death*. New York: Simon & Schuster.

Ben-Zur, H., & Keren, M.(2007). Burnout, social support, and coping at work among social workers, psychologists, and nurses: The role of challenge/control appraisals. *Social Work in Health Care, 45,* 63–82.

Blatt, S. J. (2008). *Polarities of experience: Related and self-definition in personality development, psychopathology and the therapeutic process*. Washington, DC: American Psychological Association.

Bradham, K.M. (2008). Empathy and burnout in nurses. (Unpublished doctoral dissertation.) Institute for Clinical Social Work, Chicago.

Carey, B., Cave, D., & Alvarez, L. (2009, November 8). A military therapist's world: Long hours, filled with pain. *New York Times*, p.1.

Carr, D. (2008, July 20). Me and my girls. *New York Times Magazine*.

Diener, E., & Biswas-Diener (2008). *Happiness: Unlocking the mysteries of psychological wealth*. Hoboken, NJ: Wiley.

Eliot, G. (1874). *Middlemarch*. Edinburgh, Scotland: William Blackwood & Sons.

Firestone, R. W., & Catlett, J. (1999). *Fear of intimacy*. Washington, DC: American Psychological Association.

Firestone, R. W., Firestone. L., & Catlett, J. (2003). *Creating a life of meaning and compassion: The wisdom of psychotherapy*. Washington, DC: American Psychological Association.

Frank, J. D., & Frank, J. B. (1991). *Persuasion and healing* (3rd ed.). Baltimore, MD: Johns Hopkins University Press.

Freudenberger, H. (1974). Staff burnout. *Journal of Social Work, 30,* 159–165.

Garfield, C. (1995). *Sometimes my heart goes numb*. San Francisco, CA: Jossey-Bass.

Grosch, W. N., & Olsen, D. C. (1994). *When helping starts to hurt: A new look at burnout among psychotherapists*. New York, NY: Norton.

Grotevant, H. D., & Cooper, C. R. (1986). Individuation in family relationships. *Human development, 29,* 82–100.

Hampl, P. (1995). *Burning bright: An anthology of sacred poetry*. New York, NY: Ballantine Books.

Hochwalder, J. (2007). The psychosocial work environment and burnout among Swedish registered and assistant nurses: The main, mediating, and moderating role of empowerment. *Nursing & Health Sciences, 9,* 205–211.

Jennings, L., Skovholt, T. M., Goh, M., & Lin, F. (2012). Master therapists: Explorations of expertise. In M. H. Rønnestad and T. M. Skovholt, *The developing practitioner: Growth and stagnation of therapists and counselors* (pp. 213–246). New York, New York: Routledge.

Johnson, K. (2009, Summer). Healthcare providers caring for others: High risk for secondary traumatic stress. *Caring for Our Future: Nursing at the Children's Hospital*, pp. 1, 13.

Kumar, S., Fischer, J., Robinson, E., Hatcher, S., & Bhagat, R. N. (2007). Burnout and job satisfaction in New Zealand psychiatrists: A national study. *International Journal of Social Psychiatry, 53,* 306–316.

Larson, D. G. (1993). *The helper's journey*. Champaign, IL: Research Press.

Maslach, C., & Leiter, M. P. (1997). *The truth about burnout*. San Francisco, CA: Jossey-Bass.

Masterson, J. (1990). *The search for the real self: Unmasking the personality disorders of our age*. New York, NY: Free Press.

Miller, A. (1997). *The drama of the gifted child: The search for the true self*. New York, NY: Basic Books.

Mullenbach, M., & Skovholt, T. M. (2011). Burnout prevention and self-care strategies of expert practitioners. In T. M. Skovholt & M. Trotter-Mathison (Eds.). *The resilient practitioner: Burnout prevention and self-care strategies for counselors, therapists, teachers and health professionals* (2nd ed., pp. 219–243). New York, NY: Routledge.

Murdoch, J. M., & Eagles, J. M. (2007). "Stress-busting" groups for consultant psychiatrists. *Psychiatric Bulletin, 31,* 128–131.

Norcross, J. (Ed.) (2002). *Psychotherapy relationships that work: Therapist contributions and responsiveness to patients.* New York, NY: Oxford University Press.

Norcross, J. C., & Guy, J. D. (2007). *Learning to leave it at the office: A guide to psychotherapist self-care.* New York, NY: Guilford Press.

Pipher, M. (2003). *Letters to a young therapist.* New York, NY: Basic Books.

Radeke, J. T., & Mahoney, M. J. (2000). Comparing the personal lives of psychotherapists and research psychologists. *Professional Psychology: Research and Practice, 31,* 82–84.

Research findings and perspectives on development. *Journal of Career Development, 30,* 1, 5–44.

Rippe, J. M. (2008). *Your plan for a balanced life.* Nashville, TN: Thomas Nelson.

Rogers, C. (1961). *On becoming a person.* Boston, MA: Houghton-Mifflin.

Rønnestad, M. H. (October, 1996). *Strains and challenges in the therapeutic work.* Paper presented at the XIX Nordic Psychology Conference, Stockholm, Sweden.

Rønnestad, M. H., & Skovholt, T. M. (2003). The journey of the counselor and therapist: Rønnestad, M. H., & Skovholt, T. M. (1991). En modell for profesjonell utvikling og stagnasjon hos terapeuter og rådgivere. *Tidsskrift for Norsk Psykologforening* [A model of the professional development and stagnation of therapists and counselors. *Journal of the Norwegian Psychological Association*], *28,* 555–567.

Roosevelt, T. (1903, September). *Square deal.* Speech given at New York State Agricultural Association, Syracuse, NY.

Rosenberg, T., & Pace, M. (2006). Burnout among mental health professionals: Special considerations for the marriage and family therapist. *Journal of Marital & Family Therapy, 32,* 8–99.

Rothschild, B., & Rand, M. (2006). *Help for the helper: The psychophysiology of compassion fatigue and vicarious trauma.* New York, NY: Norton.

Schön, D. A. (1983). *The reflective practitioner.* New York, NY: Basic Books.

Shanafelt, T. D. et al. (2005). Relationship between increased personal well-being and enhanced empathy among internal medicine residents. *Journal of General Internal Medicine, 20,* 559–564.

Skovholt, T. M., Goh, M., Upidi, S., and Grier, T. (2004). The resilient multicultural practitioner. *California Psychologist, 37*(6), 18–19.

Skovholt, T. M., and Jennings, L. (2004). *Master therapists: Exploring expertise in therapy and counseling.* Boston: Allyn & Bacon.

Skovholt, T. M., & Rønnestad, M. H. (2003). Struggles of the novice counselor and therapist. *Journal of Career Development, 30*(1), 44–58.

Skovholt, T. M., & Trotter-Mathison, M. (2011). *The resilient practitioner: Burnout prevention and self-care strategies for counselors, therapists, teachers and health professionals* (2nd ed.). New York, NY: Routledge.

Smith, D. (2007). For the children. *Missou, 95*(3), 55.

Stamm, B. H. (Ed.) (1995). *Secondary traumatic stress: Self-care issues for clinicians, researchers, and educators.* Lutherville, MD: Sidran Press.

Sussman, M. B. (Ed.). (1995). *A perilous calling: The hazards of psychotherapy practice.* New York, NY: Wiley.

Tippett, K. (2007). *Speaking of faith.* New York, NY: Penguin.

Warren, R. (2007). *The purpose driven life: What on earth am I here for?* Grand Rapids, MI: Zondervan.

Wicks, R. J. (2008). *The resilient clinician.* New York, NY: Oxford University Press.

Yalom, I. D. (2008). *Staring at the sun: Overcoming the terror of death.* San Francisco, CA: Jossey-Bass.

8

The Cycle of Caring

Thomas M. Skovholt and Michelle Trotter-Mathisen

Winter is necessary for the bursting of spring, which leads to the radiance of summer, which unfolds into the gorgeous colors of fall, which brings on the quiet beauty of the snows of winter. This cycle of the seasons, and its beauty and its energy and its excitement, is reflected in the life of the therapy and counseling practitioner in the Cycle of Caring. In this chapter, we introduce this concept to you.

CARING AS CENTRAL IN THERAPY AND COUNSELING CAREERS

Care is a state composed of the recognition of another, a fellow human being like one's self ; identification of one's self with the pain or joy of the other; of guilt, pity and the awareness that we all stand on the base of a common humanity from which we all stem.

—*May, 1969, p. 284*

When teachers discover what is dormant in themselves . . . they become more perceptive about what is dormant in their students—and become better teachers as a result. People who have had a great teacher almost always say, "That teacher saw something in me that I was unable to see in myself."

—*Palmer, 2004, pp. 82*

Earlier versions of this chapter appeared in T. Skovholt, (2001), "The Resilient Practitioner: Burnout Prevention and Self-Care Strategies for Therapists, Counselors, Teachers and Health Care Professionals." Copyright © T. Skovholt; and T. M. Skovholt and M. Trotter-Mathisen (2011), *The Resilient Practitioner: Burnout Prevention and Self-Care Strategies for Therapists, Counselors, Teachers and Health Care Professionals* (New York: Routledge). Permission granted by Routledge.

The essential ingredient that makes psychotherapy effective and successful...is human involvement and struggle. It is the willingness of the therapist to extend himself or herself.

—*Peck, 1978, p. 173*

It is better to know the patient who has the disease than it is to know the disease which the patient has.

—*Hippocrates, 460 BC–377 BC*

In a world where technological innovation is illuminated in splendor and applause, it seems much too simple to say that something more basic is of equal importance. Yet in the counseling, therapy, and related fields, the research evidence overwhelmingly points to the power of human caring as the essential among essentials.

In one study, we asked people to describe in two words the teacher they *most liked* when a student. Others were asked to describe their *best* teacher (Skovholt & D'Rozario, 2000). Each person in this sample of 171 individuals gave us two words for a total of 342 words. The favorite word chosen did not describe how brilliant or well educated the teacher was, the prestige of the teacher's university training, the methods of teacher education that the teacher learned or practiced, or the teacher's physical attractiveness. The most popular word described whether the student felt cherished by the teacher in a personal way. The overwhelmingly popular word used to describe the most-liked or best teacher was "caring." Themes were created from the words in this study, with the strongest theme being *caring and understanding.* For this theme, these words—*caring, understanding, kind, patient, concerned, helpful,* and *loving*—were stitched together to highlight the importance of the connection that the teacher makes with the student.

Since this study in 2000, we have asked others in resiliency workshops and classes about their favorite teacher and have come up with similar results. For example, Tom asked the favorite teacher question to 14 doctoral students in a Midwestern program in professional psychology. He asked the students to use three words to describe their favorite teacher. Their answers were consistent with other results, and again, "caring" was the most popular word.

Right now, we ask that you think about your favorite teacher. What were her or his most amazing traits? You may not be consistent with the results just presented. Your answer is your own. In a fundamental way, your favorite teacher probably altered you. It may have been in your own view of your ability. Maybe your favorite teacher opened up a new field of study or way of understanding the world. Most people have some feeling of connection with their favorite teacher. Most describe the teacher as knowing about them personally and being concerned about them as a student. When there is a combination of your teacher being very knowledgeable in the content area, highly skilled in teaching the content, deeply committed to your welfare, and passionately caring for you as a person—there is a favorite teacher! Without the personal caring, the other factors usually lose their powerful effect.

Reflecting on your favorite teacher:
What were his or her most amazing traits? (List your responses in the oval.)

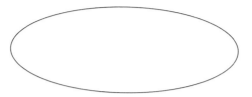

How did these traits help you succeed in school?

_____

_____
_____
_____
_____

Examining factors in student achievement, Klem and Connell (2004) found that teachers' support and caring were central to student success and participation.

> [T]eacher support is important to student engagement in school as reported by students and teachers. Students who perceive teachers as creating a caring, well-structured learning environment in which expectations are high, clear, and fair are more likely to report engagement in school. (p. 270)

Mayeroff (1990) describes the benefits of caring this way: "Perhaps few things are more encouraging to another than to realize that his growth evokes admiration, a spontaneous delight or joy, in the one who cares for him" (p. 56).

The process seems to work as described by psychiatrist Scott Peck (1978) when illuminating the crucial importance of parental love for the child. He wrote:

> [W]hen children know that they are valued, when they truly feel valued in the deepest parts of themselves, then they feel valuable. The feeling of being valuable—"I am a valuable person"—is essential to mental health and is a cornerstone of self-discipline. (p. 24)

Here, this idea of the capacity for self-discipline, an essential skill for student success, may help us understand why teacher caring is valued so highly by students.

As additional evidence, let us mention how caring, defined as love, is the bedrock, central element in the parent–child bond. And think of popular songs on the radio. No matter what song, singer, country, year, or decade, they often speak of one kind of caring—romantic love—usually found or broken.

Our premise is that caring is the essential quality that must be *maintained* in career fields like therapy and counseling, where there is high level of need and high levels of personal connection. Here, the inability to care is a dangerous signal of burnout, ineffectiveness, and incompetence. The inability to care, therefore, must be strongly guarded against during one's career.

Over and over again with clients, the practitioner must engage in a mini-cycle of closeness and then some level of grief with the ending of an often-intense professional connection. Let us now turn to the four parts of the Cycle of Caring: empathic attachment, active involvement, felt separation, and re-creation. (See Figure 8.1.)

One essence of practice in the therapy and counseling fields is to be a highly skilled relationship maker who constantly attaches, is involved, separates well, then steps away from the professional intensity . . . then does it again with a new person. We could, in fact, say this is the essence of the work; it is a very concise summary of a long career.

In a major contribution in understanding human development, Bowlby described these processes in the classic books *Attachment* (1969), *Separation* (1973), and *Loss* (1980). This practitioner's work mirrors the larger human drama of connection and disconnection between people. This process continues over and over in interaction with those we try to help:

Empathic Attachment Phase → Active Involvement Phase → Felt Separation → Re-creation Phase → Empathic Attachment Phase…and on and on

Making positive attachments, being engaged, and making positive separations with others in need is a core professional skill for practitioners in the caring professions.

Figure 8.1   Cycle of Caring

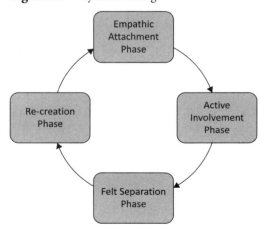

How many helping contacts does the social worker have before noon on Monday? How many student-teachers-parents consults does the school counselor have each day? How many therapy clients does the marriage and family therapist see each week? How many students does the academic advisor work with each month? How many clients does the addiction counselor see in group work per year? How many suddenly fired clients does the outplacement counselor have per decade? How many suicide-surviving families does the grief therapist have during a career?

How does the worker do this over and over again? How is this done well? Person after person—attach, be involved, then separate, re-create, attach, be involved, separate, re-create day after day, week after week, month after month, year after year. Long-term social workers, counselors, therapists, and other helpers work for 30 to 40 years. They make attachments, involvements, and separations over and over again. Hundreds of them! Thousands of them!

It is the endless Cycle of Caring, with distinct phases that makes up the life of the practitioner. Each of the phases—attachment, involvement, separation, re-creation—is important in itself, and each is discussed separately. However, it is also important to focus on the Cycle of Caring as a whole and the need for competent practitioners to be skilled at all phases of the cycle. It is not easy to be skilled at each phase because they are distinct and call for different practitioner attributes. Attachment demands an emotional connection and openness to the experience of the other. Involvement demands the content skills of the practitioner and the energy to do the work. Separation paradoxically demands the opposite of attachment. To remove oneself is the opposite of connecting oneself. It reminds us of the saying about the tasks of parenting: "roots and wings." Parents who make roots often find it hard to give wings because of their emotional connection to their sons and daughters. Giving wings is easy for the parent who never develops deep roots, although the child usually suffers in such a situation. The same dilemma confronts the practitioner, yet, as with good parenting, the challenge is to be good at both attachment (roots) and separation (wings). The last phase of re-creation can be hard for a variety of reasons. We want extremely responsible and conscientious individuals to enter the caring professions because of the ethics of caring for vulnerable people. Yet, being highly meticulous and diligent as a person does not easily translate to the re-creation phase. This is the letting-go, resting, having-fun part of the cycle, which is necessary to actively attach again. Sustainability is possible when the practitioner actively engages in all four phases of the Cycle of Caring.

Some individuals are extremely good at involvement but less skilled at attachment or separation. Teachers who focus on specialized content (e.g., high school physics) may have this orientation. The specialized content or skills may be the focus for the individual's work (e.g., critical care nursing, psychological assessment), and the emotional connection–disconnection may be less a focus. However, the emotional dimension at the active involvement phase is important for ideal results in all the helping fields. Now for a discussion of each phase.

EMPATHETIC ATTACHMENT PHASE

The therapeutic value of empathy continues to receive strong support.
—*Bachelor & Horvath, 1999, p. 142*

Attaching, connecting, bonding—these are key terms that describe the emotional oxygen-giving link between the practitioner and the client. Attachment theory, described by Bowlby (1988), is considered the most important conceptual work in understanding how a child becomes emotionally secure and able to be close to others. Pistole (2003) and Pistole and Fitch (2008) have provided rich applications of attachment theory to the caring professions.

The literature in the counseling and psychotherapy field supports the power of the human relationship dimensions in this work. In a 72-page literature review on the counseling relationship, Sexton and Whiston (1994) state in the line of their abstract: "The quality of the counseling relationship has consistently been found to have the most significant impact on successful client outcome" (p. 6). They go on to say:

> The success of any therapeutic endeavor depends on the participants establishing an open, trusting, collaborative relationship or alliance.... Research has shown that failure to form such an alliance is strongly associated with client noncompliance with treatment plans...premature termination...as well as poor outcome. (p. 7)

The importance of the therapeutic alliance is emphasized further by Strauss et al. (2006). They assert:

> The strength of the alliance early in therapy is one factor that influences treatment engagement, retention, and outcomes. Ruptures in the alliance also occur and can be therapeutic or can be associated with early dropouts and worse outcomes, if not handled properly. (p. 337)

In a review of the literature on the working alliance, Castonguay, Constantino, and Grosse Holtforth (2006) report that one of the most notable findings that emerged from their review of the research was that the "alliance correlates positively with therapeutic change across a variety of treatment modalities and clinical issues" (p. 272). Lambert, Garfield, and Bergin (2004) speak to what is now called "common factors" (others use the term "therapeutic factors") as the core of that which promotes positive change regardless of a therapist's theoretical method.

> [T]he humanistic, phenomenological perspective, suggests that the common factor is a caring relationship characterized by warmth, support, attention,

understanding, and acceptance. These ingredients are said to have direct healing properties somewhat like the effects of good nutrition or solar radiation, which strengthen the organism and stimulate growth. The therapeutic relationship is thus seen as a "condition" that leads to the dropping of defenses and the reintegration of conflicted aspects of thought, feeling, and action that makes growth or the healthful blossoming of self possible.

—*Lambert, Garfield, & Bergin, 2004, p. 811*

ATTACHING WITH OUR "UNDERSIDE OF THE TURTLE" SIDE

What is the nature of this attachment process? How is this important but difficult task done well? To do this well, we often need to attach with our caring side; Tom calls this the underside of the turtle versus the hard shell. With the hard shell, we cannot get hurt, but we cannot attach very well either. So we must continually present our soft side and attach with it. And we must do this with individuals who are often struggling with emotional, intellectual, spiritual, or physical needs. Learning an optimal level of attachment—in which the practitioner experiences the world of the other but is not overwhelmed—is an essential professional skill, and a complex one. Learning how to regulate and modulate the level of emotional attachment in the curative relational process takes time. It is a paradoxical skill—learning how to be emotionally involved yet emotionally distant, united but separate. Baker (2003) described this as self/other differentiation and discussed how this is an important part of practitioner self-care.

Often the job of the therapist or counselor is to establish a good relationship with individuals who cannot relate well or are highly distressed. For example, some children who are socially rejected often believe that others with good intentions actually want to harm them (Dodge & Feldman, 1990). The helper often must relate to people who have psychological or physical complaints and want things to be figured out for them *or* want answers to their questions *or* are confused or lacking in confidence *or* are hostile or depressed. Often the person is highly distressed, in pain, or feels unsuccessful. There may be a loss or struggle of some kind. For example, Harmon, Hawkins, Lambert, Slade, and Whipple (2005) presume that

some clients, because of their interpersonal histories, find it difficult to establish a trusting relationship with a therapist, and that these clients are especially sensitive to therapist characteristics and actions that spark memories of past painful experiences. (p. 177)

Mallinckrodt and Wei (2005) suggest that

continuing struggle [by the practitioner] to build a more secure therapeutic attachment productive working alliance results in a corrective emotional

experience that the client, equipped with new social competencies, can generalize to other relationships. (p. 358)

To be effective, helping practitioners are expected to be able to attach successfully
with highly distressed individuals. As shown by Mallinckrodt's research, being
highly skilled at creating positive human relationships is an essential occupational
trait.

The responsibility for competent, ethical, professional relationship-making lies with
the practitioner, not the client. The client may be very depressed or angry; may feel
stupid and ashamed about academic challenges; may be struggling with the sacred; may
have a serious physical illness. The practitioner must step forward and create a positive
human connection so that the power of the healing work can occur. To do the job well,
the practitioner must absorb so much from the other, especially in the more emotionally
demanding fields, such as psychotherapy.

Learning how to attach with the caring side—the underside of the turtle versus
the hard shell—is a part of all degree training programs in the helping professions. For
example, school counselors, social workers, adolescent therapists, elementary teachers,
nurses, physicians, and clergy are all taught professional relationship skills and how
to be empathetic with their clients. Practitioners spend hours trying to learn the attachment skills of attending, intense listening, emotional sensitivity, and nonverbal
understanding. Accurately absorbing the reality of the other, caring about the other,
and feeling the feelings of the other are essential in this skill of empathic attachment.
Practitioners in training learn metaphors for helping, such as "the ocean," a visual
way of thinking about immersing the self in the world of the other, an empathic immersion. For some individuals in the caring professions, learning to be empathic is
difficult. These individuals often leave this work while in training, voluntarily or upon
request, because of an inadequate ability to connect and, just as likely, because of a
lack of interest in committing such a huge amount of their emotional energy to the
work of connecting.

OPTIMAL ATTACHMENT

What do clients recall when they look back, years later, on their experience in therapy?
More often than not, they remember the positive support. The focus in training in
the therapy and counseling professions is on teaching the student practitioner to care
enough by use of verbal and nonverbal attending behavior. Often, in reality, the problem for many in the helping fields is caring too much—excessively feeling the distress
emotions of the other, such as sadness, fear, shame, anxiety, and despair, and replaying
the "movie" of the other's life over and over again in one's own mind. The practitioner
can be engulfed by the other's pain and even experience vicarious traumatization, a
process described in Chapter 7. Learning an optimal level of attachment, in which the

practitioner experiences the world of the other but is not overwhelmed, takes much training, practice, and supervision. It is an essential professional skill and a complex one. Learning how to regulate and modulate the level of emotional attachment takes time. It is a paradoxical skill—learning how to be emotionally involved yet emotionally distant, united but separate. The demand to be attuned, to be interested, to be energetic for the other—the other who is often in misery, anger, defiance, or hopelessness—and to continue to do it over and over again with client after client is taxing, as well as a skill that is part of a larger role of deeply rewarding work.

Novices in the caring professions are especially vulnerable to being overwhelmed by the realities of others. Learning physical boundaries, such as with touching between practitioner and client or student or patient, is important. Learning the skills involving emotional boundaries can be even more difficult. For example, a school social worker asked, "When a student or family is really upset and there are no easy answers, I keep trying, and then I take it home with me. How can I leave it at the office?" (I. Smith, personal communication, February 21, 1996.) Is this optimal attachment? Sometimes it is, sometimes it is not. Being able to know an optimal level and artfully perform the sequence of attach-involve-separate-recreate and begin it all anew is a core characteristic of a skilled practitioner.

Larson (1993) suggests "detached concern" as an optimal style of involvement and writes that it is "the state of being emotionally involved while simultaneously maintaining a certain emotional distance" (p. 38). Writing about family functioning, Olson (2000) describes the optimal level of family functioning as a midpoint between enmeshed and disengaged on one dimension and chaotic and rigid on another dimension (see Figure 8.2). Perhaps this can also be a guide to practitioner attachment.

DIFFICULTY IN ATTACHING

The task of attaching to the other is especially hard when the client, for example, does not have the skills for positive attachment. Forming optimal, positive professional attachments over and over is often difficult for practitioners or those in training who have

Figure 8.2   Levels of Family Learning

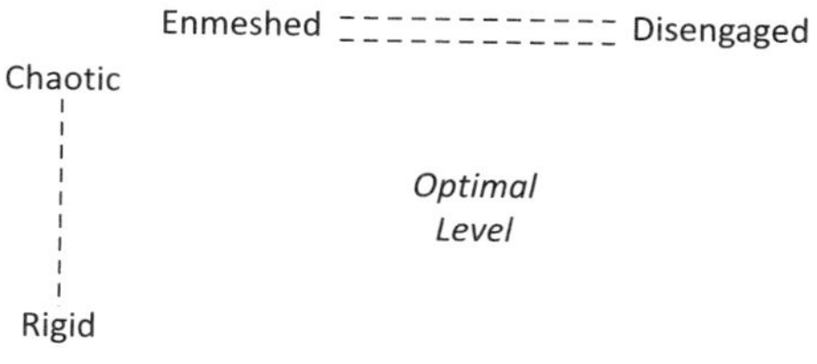

Source: From "Circumplex Model of Marital and Family Functioning," by D. H. Olson, 2000. *Journal of Family Therapy,* 22(2), p. 151.

had serious attachment distress in their personal lives. If the practitioner had intense stress in his or her primary attachments in childhood or adolescence, such as a very distressed relationship with a parent, forming consistent, optimal professional attachments in later life can be difficult. To paraphrase Freud, sometimes the child is the parent of the adult, which means that childhood events can profoundly affect adult life. Other attachment distress examples include losses such as a major geographic move and its effects, such as culture shock.

In *Fear of Intimacy*, Firestone and Catlett (1999) make a compelling case for the impact of early life experiences on later life capacity for intimacy. For example, the authors argue that the child can be strongly affected by the same-sex parent's modeling of intimacy/nonintimacy behavior. Unless the child, when an adult, consciously addresses the fear of closeness, the internalized early life messages can overwhelm any other reality and produce an extreme reaction of fear and avoidance.

As an extension, personal life attachment behavior can have a direct bearing on the practitioner's professional attachment style. The effect on professional attachment may mean that the practitioner either attaches too deeply, is unable to attach sufficiently to understand clients, students, or patients or make them feel cared about, or expresses an inconsistent attachment style with one person or across a number of clients, students, or patients. The inconsistency can seriously affect the quality of the professional relationship and, therefore, the possible benefits for the other. As mentioned earlier, Pistole and Fitch (2008) provide a valuable perspective in their application of attachment theory to counseling work.

The skill of professional attachment is complex. It is more than just trying to help. For optimal effectiveness, there must be a profound understanding of the other.

ACTIVE INVOLVEMENT PHASE

By far the most common and important way in which we can exercise our attention is by listening.... How difficult it is to listen well. Listening well is an exercise of attention and by necessity hard work.... There are times when I shudder at the enormity of what I am doing when I accept another patient.

—*Peck, 1978, pp. 121, 141*

Trust in the other to grow and in my own ability to care gives me courage to go into the unknown.... And clearly, the greater the sense of going into the unknown, the more courage is called for in caring.

—*Mayeroff, 1990, pp. 34–35*

The active involvement phase is the work phase for the practitioner. One's content area expertise, i.e., counseling with adolescents, rises up as a dominant part of this phase. It is important to know the research and theory related to the content area. A central question becomes: Does the practitioner know how to assess the problem and make things better? The active involvement phase demands the continuous attachment of the practitioner to the client. The consistent, sustained work for the other makes up this phase of the cycle. An analogy is with the work of parenting, in which the long phase of active involvement follows the early days of birthing and attachment. The consistent caring for one's child over the days, weeks, months, years, and decades is one indicator of positive parenting.

The practitioner's consistent emotional caring is part of the active involvement phase. The time period for this phase varies greatly. It could be months of counseling appointments or one session or some other variation on length of involvement. A classic period is the mental health counselor's contract for ten sessions. In essence, it is the time between the professional attachment and the professional separation.

SEPARATING WELL PHASE

With every hello there is a goodbye.

—*S. Larson, junior high school teacher*

Parting is such sweet sorrow.

— *Shakespeare,* Romeo and Juliet, *Act 2, Scene 2*

All counseling relationships must eventually end.

—*Goodyear, 1981, p. 347*

From terminations that are highly satisfying to those that are downright disturbing, the provider's emotional experience receives scant, if any, attention.

—*Davis, 2008, p. 173*

We know much less about the practitioner's experience with professional separations than with the empathetic attachment phase. In personal life, attachments and separations are connected, as in the accepted thesis that the quality of previous attachments and separations predicts future attachments and separations. If so, do professional separations take on as much importance as professional attachments? Perhaps the ability to separate well, to be energized paradoxically by the professional loss process, is a key attribute for the relationship-building elements of long-term professional vitality in the helping and related professions.

How then do highly competent practitioners separate? Teachers of children give hints of their attachment when they speak of their students as "my kids." Are there, in fact, elements of loss and grief in this professional separation process? Are there elements of a grief process that operate positively and enable the practitioner to attach again to another client, student, or patient? Some examples of the dynamics of professional attachment and separation are presented next.

I (Tom) remember teaching college undergraduates in the academic quarter system of ten weeks. Three quarters a year and then summer session. I would often have a group of 30 students—living, feeling, thinking, acting human beings with names, faces, hopes, fears, and dreams. Especially after the fall quarter was over, I would struggle to learn the new names, and the students may have thought I was indifferent to them for one reason or another. In time, I came to understand that during each academic quarter, I was still struggling with the loss of the classes that I had the quarter before and was still "possessed" by those classes. It was a kind of emotional, retroactive inhibition. A class can, after all, be a living group, a living organism that, all of a sudden with the final test, disappears and dies forever. It would usually take until the sixth or seventh week of the new quarter for my grief (Is that the right word for this loss? Do we even have language to describe the loss of professional attachments?) to wane, and my embarrassment—for not knowing the student's names—to grow. Then I would learn the names, only to have the whole process repeat itself the following quarter. It took a long time for me to understand this attachment and loss process. I assume that the undergraduates knew nothing of it. Students just hoped to be treated well, learn something, get a good grade, and move on. Students are appropriately focused on themselves and seem to have little awareness of the teacher's inner struggles, the kind Palmer (1998) discusses in *The Courage to Teach*.

A colleague working as a residence hall director in the past spoke of a similar loss reaction. For years, he experienced a three-week depression in June when the resident assistants and students left the dorm. The dormitory, teeming with people to whom he was professionally attached, suddenly was empty. He expected to be relieved and elated. Instead, he felt lost. For years, he did not really understand his reaction.

An internship training director described her struggles, when a student in training, with professional separation (S. Renninger, personal communication, February 1995):

> The more clients that I see, and the more clients that I terminate with, the more I am aware that this is a process of loss. I believe it is currently affecting my professional work as I am increasingly having difficulty getting close to my clients. I find myself hardening and retreating behind my "expertise."... I believe that this year I feel the losses more than ever before, and I think it is connected to the brief therapy I am providing. I saw most of my clients at my past therapy site for the entire year. We had time to connect and time to terminate over a period of several sessions.

Do highly experienced, highly competent practitioners—experts in attachment, involvement, separation and re-creation, experience the separation process in a way that permits them to attach again? Is there a way to do this that distinguishes positive professional separations from negative professional separations in terms of the ability to attach again? Is there a pattern of attachment, involvement, separation, and re-creation that continues, cycle after cycle, and produces good, ongoing professional attachments, involvements, separations, re-creations for proficient practitioners? As authors of this chapter, our suggestion is that an optimal level of other-care versus self-care correlates highly with proficient professional attachments for counselors and therapists.

The concepts of anticipating grief and honoring the loss can facilitate the separation. "Anticipating grief" is defined as the internal preparation a person does, often without much conscious awareness, in preparing psychologically for change in life. Examples include the death of a loved one after a long, slow illness, the end of school and graduation, or a long-planned geographic move. Practitioners know that the cycle of Empathic Attachment → Active Involvement → Felt Separation → Re-creation with clients is contained within the boundaries of the professional relationship, yet it still can be very challenging. Doing the cycle well means internally preparing for the change that is part of the separating well phase.

Davis (2008) discusses five kinds of termination in mental health work with clients. She describes the five kinds as prospective, flexible, complex, oblique, and unprofessional. She also says that "termination may be likened to a pilot's task of landing an aircraft" (p. 1). Using her metaphor of landing a plane, we will provide some examples. Prospective termination consists of a long planning process by practitioner and client, talking about the trip during the descent and a smooth landing. The plane stops, and they both get out and go their own ways. This is a positive process for the practitioner and tends to energize the practitioner to enter the Cycle of Caring again.

Flexible termination lacks the long planning process. Suddenly, it is time to land the plane as, for example, the client announces in midsession, "I think this will be my last visit."

The practitioner, as pilot, then shifts the focus to termination, and together they do the separating well phase work together. Again, an ending that gives energy to the practitioner.

Complex termination does not have a smooth landing. The plane gets to the runway and stops, but it is often a harrowing event for both practitioner as pilot and client as passenger. External events may force termination, such as a college internship training site where both graduate student clinician and student client stop when the school year ends. Other examples involve a conflicted therapy relationship that slowly gets worse or a stalled therapy process with either practitioner or client not satisfied. Then it ends perhaps by the client not returning for the next appointment. Complex termination can deplete the practitioner for the next Cycle of Caring.

Oblique termination can be likened to the client as passenger jumping from the rear of the plane via a parachute while the pilot is guiding the plane unaware that the passenger has left.

This happens when the client cancels an appointment and disappears while the practitioner was thinking that the work was going well and that they were in midstream. This situation can be depleting for the practitioner.

This lack of closure for the practitioner is a kind stressful experience we call ambiguous professional loss. Ambiguous loss (Boss, 1999) is often stressful for a person because the factors of loss are unclear—is a missing-in-action soldier returning or not? For us in the caring fields, ambiguous professional loss occurs during all those times when things end without an ending in our work with clients, students, practitioners, and patients.

Back to the pilot metaphor and the last kind of termination in the group of five by Davis (2008). Unprofessional termination occurs when the practitioner acts in an unprofessional manner and the helping relationship ends. The metaphor is that the plane crashes because of pilot error. There are many reasons for pilot error, but none is acceptable for the passenger, just as unprofessional conduct by the practitioner, for whatever reason, is never acceptable.

The varieties of termination offered by Davis are all part of the ending process in helping relationships; all human relationships have a beginning and an end. A good termination is positive for both parties. Honoring the loss means building in a time and energy commitment for the separation. This is not idle practitioner work. Practitioners need to do professional attachments again, and soon. Doing separations well permits new attachments to emerge.

Grieving is important. Why? Grief work is for living; it makes intensity in living possible. That is why it is so important. Do not misunderstand. We are not suggesting that every practitioner, after only a short contact with a client, for example, engages in a long mourning ceremony. Professional grieving of the loss reflects the depth of the attachment and involvement, just as in one's personal life; therefore, more contact with the other leads to more time and energy for honoring the loss. For example, a nursing home nurse may go to the funeral of a resident that she cared for over a long period. An elementary teacher may devote the last days of the school year to honoring the loss of her students and of the class as a living, breathing group that will never reappear in the same way. She may engage in a series of good-bye and transition activities to help the children and herself. A therapist or counselor often relishes the chance to spend all of a last session with a client reviewing progress made, talking about goals for the client, and saying good-bye. So often there is no acknowledged ending for the therapy or counseling relationship (i.e., the client calls the office to cancel a next appointment because she feels better), and the practitioner has to do the ending internally without the client present.

Some practitioners develop separation rituals for themselves. These may involve internal thought processes (i.e., thinking about the work with the individual in a certain way) or external events (e.g., a ritualistic walk within one's office area). Using one's own creativity and imagination here can be useful. One academic advisor, writing about her ritual, said:

> It is helpful to think of ways I can say goodbye and separate in ways that leave me feeling renewed and ready for new connections with clients. My own ritual

is to picture each client as a great novel, one that I have the pleasure of reading as I become engrossed in the character's life. But always I know that I am merely a page-turner, a facilitator, an active reader who both affects and is affected by the humanness of the words on the page. Upon termination, I envision closing "the book," my access to the client's life, and place it on an important shelf in my mind.

—J. Langer, personal communication, July 1998

RE-CREATION PHASE

The re-creation phase is the fourth phase of the Cycle of Caring. It is the getting-away-from-the-work phase, the "off button" phase, as opposed to the three previous "on button" phases. It is as important as the three other phases—empathetic attachment, active involvement, and felt separation—because, without an off button, eventually there will not be any "on button" phases.

Consider the simple light switch. Let us imagine that the light switch is attached to a solar panel that collects energy from the sun only when the light is off. When the light is off, energy is generated. Then when the light switch is turned on, there is illumination. And not just dim illumination; rather, strong, intense illumination. It is the illumination of the highly caring practitioner deeply devoted to the other, the one in need of help-assistance-guidance-teaching-healing.

The re-creation phase can be understood using many different words that start with the letter *r*. These include: renewal, rest, refurbishment, repair, restoration, renovation, restitution, return. Other terms include having fun, having lots of fun!, being playful, having a break, time out, and goofing off. We like to use the word "re-creation" because it communicates the paradox of the serious purposefulness of the fun. Recreation is about the re-creation of the self. And that is important because it is the practitioner's self that is essential for the curative factors of the working alliance. Restoration is necessary for growth.

Practitioners vary in the quality and quantity of their time off, their restoration. Some are good at this activity, a kind of self-care. Others never seem to get to it. And that eventually is dangerous. Sustainability in offering the Cycle of Caring over and over again demands involvement in this phase as well as the other three.

SUMMARY

I have learned one important thing in my life—how to begin again.
—Sam Keen (cited by Goodyear, 1981, p. 347)

All four phases in the Cycle of Caring are important, just as the great seasonal differences in northern climates depend on each other. For example, in our state of Minnesota, winter is necessary for the bursting of spring, which leads to the radiance of summer, which unfolds into the gorgeous colors of fall, which bring on the quiet beauty of the snows of winter. . . and it goes on and on. Sustaining oneself, being vital, and being active as a therapist or counselor means being fully present for the other. But how does the practitioner maintain such a presence for person after person? How does the practitioner empathically attach with the underside of the turtle side, get involved in working with the client, end the work in a felt and positive way, then take a break only to start again with another and then another? Being able to do this well is a central focus of the practitioner's work. The exact nature of the cycle differs across career fields within the helping professions and the nature of the contact within these occupations. Yet, whatever the differences, the principle of proficiency with the endless Cycle of Caring remains a measure of a successful practitioner.

The Cycle of Caring is one definition of the essence of the helping professions. It is what practitioners do over and over again thousands of times. This is noble and courageous work and so valuable too when it is done well. May you learn to be highly talented and skilled at the art and science form of the Cycle of Caring.

REFERENCES

Bachelor, A., & Horvath, A. (1999). The therapeutic relationship. In M. A. Hubble, B. L. Duncan, & S. D. Miller (Eds.), *The heart and soul of change: What works in therapy* (pp. 133–178). Washington, DC: American Psychological Association.

Baker, E. (2003). *Caring for ourselves: A therapist's guide to personal and professional well-being.* Washington, DC: American Psychological Association.

Boss, P. (1999). *Ambiguous loss: Learning to live with unresolved grief.* Cambridge, MA: Harvard University Press.

Bowlby, J. (1969). *Attachment.* New York, NY: Basic Books.

Bowlby, J. (1973). *Separation: Anxiety and anger.* New York, NY: Basic Books.

Bowlby, J. (1980). *Loss: Sadness and depression.* New York, NY: Basic Books.

Bowlby, J. (1988). *A secure base: Parent–child attachment and healthy human development.* New York, NY: Basic Books.

Castonguay, L. G., Constantino, M. J., & Grosse Holtforth, M. (2006). The working alliance: Where are we and where should we go? *Psy-chotherapy: Theory, Research, Practice, Training, 43*(3), 271–279.

Davis, D. D. (2008). *Terminating therapy.* Hoboken, NJ: Wiley.

Dodge, K. A., & Feldman, E. (1990). Issues in social cognition and sociometric status. In S. R. Asher & J. D. Coie (Eds.), *Peer rejection in childhood* (pp. 119–155). New York, NY: Cambridge University Press.

Firestone, R. W., & Catlett, J. (1999). *Fear of intimacy.* Washington, DC: American Psychological Association.

Goodyear, R. (1981). Termination as a loss experience for the counselor. *Personnel and Guidance Journal, 59,* 347–350.

Harmon, C., Hawkins, E. J., Lambert, M. J., Slade, K., & Whipple, J. (2005). Improving outcomes for poorly responding clients: The use of clinical supports tools and feedback to clients. *Journal of Clinical Psychology, 61*(2), 175–185.

Klem, A. M., & Connell, J. P. (2004). Relationships matter: Linking teacher support to student engagement achievement. *Journal of School Health, 74*(7), 262–273.

Lambert, M. J., Garfield, S. L., & Bergin, A. E. (2004). Overview, trends, and future issues. In M. J. Lambert (Ed.), *Handbook of psychotherapy and behavior change* (pp. 805–821). Hoboken, NJ: Wiley.

Larson, D. G. (1993). *The helper's journey*. Champaign, IL: Research Press.

Maclay, E. (1977). *Green winter: Celebrations of later life*. New York, NY: Readers Digest Press.

Mallinckrodt, B. (2000). Attachment, social competencies, and interpersonal process in psychotherapy. *Psychotherapy Research, 10,* 239–266.

Mallinckrodt, B., & Wei, M. (2005). Attachment, social competencies, social support, and psychological distress. *Journal of Counseling Psychology, 52,* 358–367.

May, R. (1969). *Love and will*. New York, NY: Norton.

Mayeroff, M. (1990). *On caring*. New York, NY: Harper Perennial.

Olson, D. H. (2000). Circumplex model of marital and family functioning. *Journal of Family Therapy, 22*(2), 144–167.

Palmer, P. J. (2004). *A hidden wholeness: The journey toward an undivided life*. San Francisco, CA: Wiley.

Palmer, P. J. (1998). *The courage to teach: Exploring the inner landscape of a teacher's life*. San Francisco, CA: Jossey-Bass.

Peck, M. S. (1978). *The road less traveled: A new psychology of love, traditional values and spiritual growth*. New York, NY: Simon & Schuster.

Pistole, C. M. (2003). Linking work, love, individual, and family issues in counseling: An attachment theory perspective. In P. Erdman & T. Caffery (Eds.), *Attachment and family systems: Conceptual, empirical, and therapeutic relatedness* (pp. 117–137). New York, NY: Brunner-Routledge.

Pistole, M.C., & Fitch, J.C. (2008). Attachment theory in supervision: A critical incident experience. *Counselor Education and Supervision, 47,* 193–205.

Sexton, T. L., & Whiston, S. C. (1994). The status of the counseling relationship: An empirical review, theoretical implications, and research directions. *Counseling Psychologist, 22*(1), 6–78.

Skovholt, T. M., & D'Rozario, V. (2000). Portraits of outstanding and inadequate teachers in Singapore: The impact of emotional intelligence. *Teaching & Learning, 40*(1), 9–17.

Strauss, J. L. et al. (2006). Early alliance, alliance ruptures, and symptom change in a nonrandomized trial of cognitive therapy for avoidant and obsessive-compulsive personality disorders. *Journal of Consulting and Clinical Psychology, 74*(2), 337–345.

9

The Practitioner's Learning Triangle

Practice, Research/Theory, and Personal Life

Thomas M. Skovholt and
Michael Starkey

Art and science are two extremes of the polarity from subjectivity to objectivity, a dimension which permeates all human enterprises. . . . [P]sychotherapy manifests this duality in many ways, and the artistry of master therapists shows in their ability selectively to blend the subjective with the objective, their art with their science. . . . [Some] therapeutic goals (e.g., adjustment, symptom reduction) are well served by objective means, but life-changing psychotherapy requires major attention to the subjective.

—*Bugental, 1987, p. ix*

I now walk into the wild.

—*Chris McCandless, cited in Krakauer, 1996, p. 3*

Armed with a .22 caliber rifle, a 10-pound bag of rice, a rudimentary map, and an assortment of books, Christopher McCandless waved good-bye to the last person he would ever see and walked into the Alaskan wilderness (Krakauer, 1996). A final picture, taken just before he walked into the wild, shows the young adventurer, rifle perched on his shoulder, smiling wide. He looks proud, almost giddy. The Alaska Range looms in the background, the ground is still covered with snow; indeed, this is pristine nature, perfect innocence. There are no fences, no roads, no power lines, no houses, and no people. This is exactly what McCandless envisioned. He sought to live off the land, experiencing life unencumbered by materialism and socially recognized successes. Most important,

An earlier version of this chapter appeared as T. M. Skovholt and M. T. Starkey (2010), "The Three Legs of the Practitioner's Learning Stool: Practice, Research/Theory, and Personal Life," *Journal of Contemporary Psychotherapy, 40*(3), 125–130.

though, McCandless was searching for answers. Who am I? How do I fit in? Why do I live? These questions brought him to the brink of the wild, the basin of the unknown (Krakauer, 1996).

At first, the landscape exhilarated McCandless. The crisp mountain air, cool in the morning, filled his young lungs with life. It is easy to imagine McCandless hiking through unmarked, tangled woods as a frontiersman, thinking to himself that he was the first to ever discover this land. Crossing semifrozen rivers, following instinct instead of paths, losing himself deeper in the wild, everything was new, exciting. When he first arrived—still April—the nights were cold, the days short, but these were minor inconveniences compared to his experience of unadulterated freedom.

He eventually stumbled on an abandoned bus and decided to call it home. It contained a stove, a protective roof, and a mattress. This was his only reminder of the technological world he left behind.

After a few months living in the bus, McCandless decided that he was finished with his voyage, so he packed up his belongings and began his walk out. However, in July, the semifrozen river he crossed months prior was now raging and impassable, and the softly flowing river of April now posed a major problem (Krakauer, 1996). An attempt to cross would probably cost the novice swimmer his life. He was left with one choice: return to the bus. His already lean body became leaner, he began to run out of food, his only way out was blocked, and the exhilaration he experienced at the beginning of his journey likely transformed into dread.

McCandless spent his last days trapped in the wilderness keeping journal entries and self-portraits as a record of his physical and mental deterioration. His words soon became desperate: "[I]n weakest condition of life. Death looms as serious threat. Too weak to walk out, have literally become trapped in the wild" (Krakauer, 1996, p. 195). Thirteen days after penning these words, an emaciated young man from Annandale, Virginia, crawled into his sleeping bag, closed his eyes, and never woke up.

Alaskans, as well as Krakauer (1996) and his readers, have speculated about what brought the demise of the young adventurer. Many agree: McCandless was extraordinarily ill prepared to deal with the Alaskan wilderness. He thought he could survive with his few trifles. And he did—for 112 days, alone—a feat most people could not replicate. But he was trapped and had no idea how to escape.

Some Alaskans wrote to Krakauer admonishing McCandless's disrespect for the wild, stating that his arrogance is what ultimately caused his death. If he had respected the Alaskan wilderness, McCandless may have prepared more effectively for his journey. Instead, he relied on his survival instinct, his years as a vagabond, and his keen sense of survival. His personal experiences, while important, were not enough. A topographical map and a compass would probably have saved his life. According to Krakauer (1996), there were a number of alternate routes out of the place where McCandless found himself trapped. Thirty miles east lay a major highway; 16 miles south was a Denali National Park road used daily by hundreds of tourists; and half a mile downstream was a cable that traversed a gorge over the river he found impenetrable months earlier.

In what ways does McCandless's story relate to the novice therapist or counselor? Like the Alaskan wilderness, our clients' lives need to be navigated with care. Their tales are like the woods McCandless found so exhilarating: tangled, pathless, and without guide. Arriving at this place is certainly exciting, but the shadow of uncertainty is a constant companion. Therefore, we need guides to help us travel the unknown. But what knowledge bases can we rely on to help us successfully travel the unknown? What tools serve as our guides through the briars and overgrown trails that are our clients' lives? How do we know how to help those who seek our services? The answers to these questions will be examined in the pages that follow.

PURPOSE OF THIS CHAPTER

Our hope for this chapter is to introduce readers to the many guides that serve as our knowledge base in the helping professions. To what sources do practitioners turn for their ideas? The academic culture suggests it should be science; the practitioner culture suggests reflection on practice; candid discussion with practitioners suggests that the therapist's personal life is the richest source of knowledge. In this chapter, we argue that practitioner expertise is like a three-legged learning triangle with each of the foregoing areas essential to optimal functioning.

INTENSE SEARCH FOR ANSWERS

As practitioners, we are driven by an intense search for answers to ease client pain. The goal is to find definitive answers that really work, like the proverbial hot knife cutting through butter.

In time, this search for certainty shares the stage with a reluctant accepting of uncertainty. Eventually, we begin to realize that the circle of not knowing grows as fast as the circle of knowing and that ambiguity is part of the fabric of the counseling and therapy professions. Really knowing is like a mirage on the highway: Just when a person gets close, it goes ahead on the highway—a frustrating realization for advancing graduate students and young professionals. In any given therapeutic hour, so much is said, not said, nonverbally communicated. Therapists have the daunting task of encoding information, making sense out of it, and giving it back to the client in a way that, we hope, helps. Reed (2006, p. 20) lists 33 variables as active in the counseling/therapy session. When 33 variables are interacting, there are 1,089 possibilities in each therapy/counseling session. The work is confusing, and at times the ambiguity is frightening.

This paradoxical quest, the intense search for answers while accepting the swampy reality of human complexity, is a lifelong journey. How wonderful it would be to think that therapy is the application of the treatment to the client—a kind of spray-painting the other. Then all we need to do is learn a method, a school, a technique, an empirically supported treatment, a manualized approach, and apply it. Unfortunately, clients are not like a rock that we can spray-paint but rather living, thinking human beings who are very much a part of the two-person dance of therapy. But it is very hard to accept uncertainty. As Yalom (1995) states: "The unexplained—especially the fearful unexplained—cannot be tolerated for long. . . . Giving a name to chaotic, unruly forces provides us with a sense of mastery or control" (p. 84). Even so, the chaotic is exciting: With it comes a sense of newness, of something to be discovered. But heed this warning: That is what got McCandless lost. He followed the siren call of the wild and was consumed by it, unprepared to deal with its reality.

The hallmark feature of counseling and psychotherapy is ambiguity. Our work lacks a certain precision craved by practitioners and persistently sought by researchers. How do we manage the ambiguity, the uncertainty, and negotiate the convoluted material presented to us by our clients so we do not find ourselves lost? The first task is the career-long process of looking for certainty while reluctantly accepting the world of uncertainty. The second task, a more formidable one, indeed, is the acquisition of wisdom.

DEVELOPMENT OF PERSONAL WISDOM

A group of master therapists taught us (Jennings & Skovholt, 1999; Skovholt, Jennings, & Mullenbach, 2004; Chapter 12 in this book) that it is the therapist's personal qualities that really carry the freight. These elite therapists embodied a mixture of cognitive characteristics (e.g., a voracious appetite for learning), relational characteristics (e.g., a proficient ability to intensively engage clients), and emotional characteristics (e.g., a fine-tuned self-awareness), which all help maintain their equilibrium in times of extreme uncertainty. We concluded that excelling as a practitioner mainly involves developing, at a very high level, as a person. This idea fits with Bruce Wampold's (2007) research: "[T]here is little evidence, after decades of clinical trials with children and adults, that for any diagnosis, one treatment has been shown to be demonstrably superior to another" (pp. 866–867). He goes on to say: "There is increasing evidence that it is the therapist and not the treatment per se that is responsible for therapeutic change" (p. 868).

Learning a technique takes a few hours. Becoming a wise person takes years. Here we define wisdom as Bales and Staudinger (2000) do: "[W]isdom [is] an expertise in the conduct and meaning of life . . . knowledge and judgment about the essence of the human condition and the ways and means of planning, managing, and understanding a good life" (p. 124). This second task—becoming a more mature and wiser human being—is an elusive, slippery, and hard-to-catch goal. Continuing education to become wiser and more mature becomes lifelong.

These two tasks—striving toward personal maturity and wisdom and searching for certainty while accepting uncertainty—fit well with descriptions of master therapists. Here is one description:

Somebody that's accepting. Somebody that's smart. Somebody that's interesting, curious, stays informed. Somebody who takes care of themselves, so that they have some energy to give. Somebody who has that blend of being compassionate and empathetic, but also challenging. Somebody who's available. . . . Somebody that's wise. . . . Kindness, humility is a good word. . . . Willing to listen and grow, I'm thinking, an ability to see uniqueness

—*Jennings, 1996, pp. 111–112*

The development of expertise and the drive toward mastery begins with these two premises: that our field is uncertain and that greater wisdom as a person allows the mature therapist to understand and embrace this uncertainty and do good work. An obvious question ensues, though: How does the therapist accept uncertainty and develop personal wisdom? Shouldn't there be some guide for the practitioner, some rough map that at least shows us bits of the terrain? We assert that there are guides, at least three of them, that help practitioners navigate the search, traverse the terrain, and come out alive.

LEARNING TRIANGLE AS EPISTEMOLOGY

What sources of knowledge are acceptable for practitioner development on the way to mastery? Where do practitioners get their best ideas for the highly complex and difficult counseling and therapy enterprise? What epistemology—practitioner experience, personal life, or academic research—can we use? And which are acceptable?

The practitioner culture suggests that reflection on the craft is the most important source of influence. The academic research culture suggests that science is the best source of knowledge for practice. Candid discussion with practitioners, and a perusal of their writings, tells us that personal life is also a rich source of guidance and knowledge. Great tension exists in the profession about the use of these three knowledge bases. Each on its own provides us with rich data, but each, when used exclusively, is not necessarily sufficient to understand the complex nature of our clients' lives.

We suggest that all three strong parts of the practitioner's learning triangle—professional experience, academic research, and personal life—are necessary for intellectual strength and balance. Wampold (2007) says that psychotherapy walks a tightrope between the accepted world of science and medicine and the less accepted world of the religious, spiritual, and cultural. We propose a tightrope that legitimizes all three sides of the learning triangle.

For example, a study of the ten most influential therapists over the last 25 years—Rogers, Beck, Minuchin, Yalom, Satir, Ellis, Bowen, Jung, Erickson, and Gottman ("The Top Ten," 2007)—reveals the importance of each of these legs for practitioner development. The biographies, combined as one, describe these therapists as weaving together, so naturally, the science, the practice, and the personal that it seems like the traditional gold standard for understanding human behavior. While the scientific method is imperative, these stories illustrate the equal importance of the therapist's personal life and practice life. Also, Goldfield's (2001) edited book of the professional development of 15 well-known practitioners captures the rich, multilayer, multisource, long-term development of experienced practitioners.

PROFESSIONAL PRACTICE AS ONE SIDE OF THE LEARNING TRIANGLE

My patients have been . . . my richest source of learning, and I am indebted to them.

—May, 1972, p. 15

You [my clients], each of you, have been my teachers and my companions. I cherish our time together. . . . Let this book bespeak my caring and salute to you.
—Bugental, 1976, pp. xvii–xviii

In the largest international study of practitioners, interaction with clients was rated the number-one source of professional development (Orlinsky & Rønnestad, 2005). These practitioners said their own hundreds and hundreds of hours of practice was the central fountain of their own continuing education. Sitting with clients who try to make sense of their innermost experiences, to try and relate and integrate their pain is an extraordinary privilege and it is nearly impossible to be unaffected by listening to their tales. To try to quantify some of these experiences is a daunting task and likely an impossible one, so it is no wonder that experienced therapists rate their clients as their number-one source of knowledge. Being with clients and trying to help them heal their most vulnerable wounds offers us a real-life laboratory into how clients' problems develop. As much as the research method would like to capture the "main" way in which pathology develops, working with clients clues us in to the staggering variability of the human condition, and working with this ambiguity can be a tall order indeed. Practitioners in the helping, teaching, and healing fields use the interaction with the other as an intense learning laboratory; in fact, the expertise literature tells us that professional experience is considered essential for expertise (Chi, Glass, & Farr, 1988).

Most psychology professors use their own experience as instructors, rather than the scholarship on teaching, to guide their own teaching style and method (Thomas Brothen, teaching award winner in psychology; personal communication, September 3, 2007). This is testimony to the power of professional experience as a guide to competence. For example, learning to judge client readiness comes out of interaction with many, many clients.

Many therapists who write books dedicate their books to their clients. Why? Perhaps the answer lies in the fact that the most learning they have encountered has been from those with whom they have worked intimately, who taught them so much about the human condition and what it means to be alive. How do we learn from our clients? Shouldn't learning be reserved for the classroom, from teachers who are qualified to indoctrinate us? The classroom can teach us only so much. We work with human beings who are incredibly variable. We do not work with inert objects that can more easily be understood in the laboratory. We need to understand how we humans are put together, what tears us down, and how to heal that. Such understanding comes partially from books, but much of it comes from the intense interactions between counseling and therapy, and learning from that dynamic.

In graduate school, we are so often exposed to how working with clients "should" be. For example, empirically supported treatments come from the idea that empirical research should guide practice. Sounds good, right? How could it be negative to base what we do on science? Yet, when working with clients, we learn about the limitations of the scientific method. We work with single cases, not large numbers of people chosen very narrowly for a study. The stories that they bring to us are so wrought with pain, hardship, joy, wonder, and awe that often we are overwhelmed with the material we are presented. This is where the large map—the research method—is handy but not completely useful. Yet human judgment error makes data from one's own clinical work less than ideal when used alone, which is why the other two legs of the triangle become so imperative.

Lebow (2006) reports that his colleagues who were part of both research and practice cultures stated that they used research findings sparsely in their practice. Does this mean that research should be abandoned altogether and that we should let practitioners do as they please? Not at all. However, this finding indicates that practitioners either need to be more accepting of study results findings, or researchers need to start performing research that is more relevant to the practice of psychotherapy.

We encourage readers to seek out many different training opportunities and opportunities to receive quality supervision. The life of a beginning therapist is wrought by hardship, and often frustrating and confusing due to the uncertainty of the therapeutic interaction. Rather than fighting therapeutic ambiguity, learn to embrace the cognitive complexity of the process and the various walks we couragously take as we enter our client's personal labyrinths.

ACADEMIC RESEARCH AS ONE SIDE OF THE LEARNING TRIANGLE

Thanks in large part to researchers' responses to Eysenck's charge [that psychotherapy is ineffective] we now know, generally speaking, that psychotherapy does indeed help people.

—Clarkin & Levy, 2004, p. 194

There is less need to discuss the academic research leg because in the empirical research world that dominates university life, this is the high-prestige knowledge source. Graduate programs ask inexperienced students to abandon earlier ways of helping and adopt a more objective way of working with clients (Rønnestad & Skovholt, 2003). It is assumed at this point in the educational process that the many who have gone before and contributed original research or scholarly work should be emulated. This is a valuable way of learning how to do something. Learn what others have done, do the same, and you will, it is hoped, have the same results.

The traditional scientist practitioner model teaches students to be connoisseurs of research, to learn what works with whom and why. We are taught to be skeptical of the research findings so that we, in our own research, can find more effective ways of helping people. Some programs have even adopted treatment approaches in which practitioners are asked to formulate a diagnosis, choose a manualized treatment for that diagnosis, and follow therapeutic guidelines outlined in that manual in order to be of greatest help to the client (Chambless & Hollon, 1998). Faced with convoluted clinical material, psychological researchers help give names, and thus control, to ambiguous concepts.

Indeed, research on counseling and psychotherapy helps us navigate the equivocal nature of what clients bring to the therapeutic interaction. Research has taught us many things in psychology and has helped answer the difficult questions posed by prominent psychologists. For example, as quoted previously, Hans Eysenck (1952, cited in Clarkin & Levy, 2004) challenged the psychotherapeutic nation by declaring that psychotherapy was about as beneficial as receiving no treatment. In fact, in his research, he found that people who engaged in psychoanalysis actually had worse cure rates than people not treated. His finding spawned thousands of research studies demonstrating the positive efficacy of counseling and psychotherapy. A comprehensive summary of these studies can be found in the esteemed *Bergin and Garfield's Handbook of Psychotherapy and Behavior Change* (Lambert, 2004). Readers of the book find themselves immersed in a sea of good, objective data stating that psychotherapy works, and it sometimes works quite well.

These early pioneers who carved out the roads we travel are invaluable forebears. Studies completed by brilliant researchers finding a way to operationalize very complex psychic phenomena have stood the test of time and have provided both researchers and practitioners valuable tools for future trends in this field.

Many studies found in *Bergin and Garfield's Handbook of Psychotherapy and Behavior Change* (Lambert, 2004) examined disorder-based psychotherapies. The wisdom behind these approaches is clear: The practitioner, a skilled diagnostician, chooses a treatment approach that has been shown—in the research lab—to be effective in working with a particular disorder. Interestingly, though, the more research that is completed, the more controversy about what works is stirred up. For example, the work of Wampold (2001) informs us that there are factors common to all treatment approaches that seem to predict outcome better than the individual treatments themselves. While we are quite sure that gradual exposure to a feared stimulus will reduce anxiety in the majority of clients (a behaviorist approach), the other more complex phenomena of the therapeutic interaction are not so easily parceled out in regard to individual therapeutic approaches. In fact, Wampold (2001) found that there is not a single therapeutic intervention that provides the most meaningful and lasting benefit to clients.

In a way, research gives us a rough map of how to work with clients. Human beings share many similarities, and things that work with one person are likely to translate into working with another person. But because clients live in a world dominated by subjectivity, the generalizability of research findings is unclear at best.

Unfortunately, from the practitioner side, there are limitations with this leg. The academic terms of "impact factor" and "citation index" sound like they relate directly to practice. They do not. These are terms academics use to judge each other in the small circle world of research. The fact that there is no "practitioner impact factor" reduces the usefulness of the specific research for practitioners. Alan Kazdin (2004) discusses this when he writes: "The limitations of contemporary research related to how therapy is studied greatly restrict the extent to which the results from therapy research are likely to be generalizable to clinical practice" (p. 560). Thus, a balance of the three sides form the complete fiber of being for the practitioner's learning triangle.

Here are some suggestions to increase your knowledge base in this area: Develop a strong grasp of statistics and research methods. Read empirical articles in professional journals. Conduct your own research studies.

PERSONAL LIFE AS ONE SIDE OF THE LEARNING TRIANGLE

The only way to really know and understand the client's dark, hopeless place is by visiting that place in yourself. Then, as a therapist, you can really understand and be effective in the work with the client.

—*Therapist Jane Brodie, personal communication, September 27, 2007*

Indeed, most of my deeply held beliefs about therapy, and my areas of keenest psychological interest, have arisen from personal experience.

—*Yalom, 1989, p. 31*

Living our lives as human beings is a powerful source of knowledge. The education is ubiquitous and ongoing; there is richness to our personal lives. We have had to make sense out of a world with no guidebook, a potentially dangerous world filled with wonder, awe, pain, and loss. Most of the best lessons in developmental psychology concern our own experience of going through life. The intense series of attachments and losses and more attachments—to people, ideas, places, values—that comprise human life teach us so much that we can use to help our clients in their struggles.

The personal world of loss and recovery is of great value to practitioners because this is the expertise area that their clients need. Many counseling and therapy clients make the pilgrimage to the practitioner's office because of loss. Scientific research and theory on many topics can be of use, but the practitioner, to really understand, must know and feel loss and suffering either directly or vicariously on an emotional level. (See, e.g., *The Year of Magical Thinking* [Didion, 2006] for an important discussion of this topic.) Practitioners need to know the schema of grief: what it is, how it is expressed, how to enter it, and how to be helpful in the healing process.

The personal-life leg of the stool also relates to our motives for the work. Derald Wing Sue (2005) writes: "I will never forget that incident [of racial harassment as a child]. It taught me several important lessons in life that have remained with me to this day and form the basis of my professional work" (p. 75). He also offers young therapists this advice: "Strive to integrate both your professional and personal journeys. If you are able to do that, the dichotomous distinction we often make between work and personal life becomes less an either/or choice and more a manifestation of your total being" (p. 82).

Applicants for graduate school in the caring professions often come for very personal reasons. The next statements echo the importance of the personal life of the aspiring practitioner.

"Addiction research is of interest. I went through treatment."
"I want to study ethnic identity because I am a person of color."
"I am a 23-year-old female and am interested in eating disorders."
"We had family problems and couples work is of interest."
"My own personal counseling really helped me. That is why I want to study psychology."

Existential psychologists tell us that being informed by an existential lens lets us know that we, the therapists, are also involved in existence, are also affected by our existential situation, and are not immune to life's harsh realities. To be most effective with clients, we need to realize and accept our humanness. Not only does doing this help us as therapists to connect with our clients; it also provides our clients with a sense of universality in which they can understand that therapists are human and are affected by the exigencies of the human condition.

Furr and Carroll (2003), in a study of graduate counseling students' critical incidents, found that many involved important relationships outside of academic life. These incidents—not surprisingly—greatly influenced their academic lives.

Personal life is a powerful knowledge source and an important leg of the practitioner stool. Yet the impact of our own emotional life can distort as well as illuminate; thus, the research and practice legs offset the subtle distortions that may bubble up from this epistemological pool. To increase your personal knowledge base, consider these suggestions:

- *Engage in your own psychotherapy.* An expansion of personal knowledge will benefit the novice and experienced practitioner alike along the path to mastery. Seasoned therapists rate their own therapy as an important source of learning how to perform psychotherapy.
- *Realize that you are not immune to the harsh existential realities of this life.* Doing so will foster empathy, make it easier to relate to clients, and help with the creation of the ultimately important therapeutic relationship.

THREE SIDES OF THE TRIANGLE MAKE A WHOLE

In both the 1982 and the 2006 survey the single most influential psychotherapist—by a landslide—was Carl Rogers.

—*"The Top Ten,"* 2007, p.26

Beginning therapists reading about performing therapy and the rewards of practice often itch to get out and practice and replicate what they have read, observed, and even fantasized about. When they finally face the reality of the therapy room, however, they often feel frustration, confusion, and anxiety about what to do.

Each side of the learning triangle offers insight and instruction to the practitioner. One of the major prerequisites for optimal functioning as a therapist is a sense of openness to learning. Closing oneself from any of the three sides of the learning triangle ultimately robs oneself of important learning. The triangle is no longer a triangle but just one or two disconnected sides. The absence of a side makes the triangle unstable—it can no longer provide the foundation for the fascinating and exciting work of therapy.

Carl Rogers used all three sides of the triangle in his work. Perhaps that was the key to his success. Without his active work as a practitioner—especially in Rochester and at the University of Chicago—his conceptual style would not have blossomed. Practitioner work was essential. Without his active reflection in his own life, his work would have had less depth. (See Rogers, 1961, and his reflection of turning age 85 (1989).) If he had not used the research methods that he had first learned in agriculture, he would not have made the extensive tape recordings that were essential to his professional development.

SUMMARY

Our clients' lives are venerable forests that need to be navigated with great care. We hope that the navigational tools outlined in this chapter will guide you throughout your career. Chris McCandless did not respect the Alaskan wild, and it cost him his life. It is important for us to be as prepared as possible when working with clients. The three sides of the practitioner learning triangle provide clinicians with a framework on how to navigate the woods of our clients' lives. While each side is imperfect standing alone, these three epistemological sources, when taken together and reflected on deeply, provide us with a much-needed guide. We can never predict what will happen in any particular clinical situation, but having knowledge from each of the epistemological sides of the triangle provides a welcome guide that prevents us from getting lost in the wild.

REFERENCES

Bales, P. B., & Staudinger, U. M. (2000). Wisdom: A metaheuristic (pragmatic) to orchestrate mind and virtue toward excellence. *American Psychologist, 55,* 122–136.

Bugental, J.F.T. (1976). *The search for existential identity.* San Francisco, CA: Jossey-Bass.

Bugental, J.F.T. (1987). *The art of the psychotherapist.* New York, NY: Norton.

Chambless, D. L., & Hollon, S.D. (1998). Defining empirically supported therapies. *Journal of Consulting and Clinical Psychology, 66,* 7–18.

Chi, M.T.H., Glass, R., & Farr, M. J. (Eds.) (1988). *The nature of expertise.* Hillsdale, NJ: Lawrence Erlbaum.

Clarkin, J. F., & Levy, K. N. (2004). The influence of client variables on psychotherapy. In M. J. Lambert (Ed.), *Bergin and Garfield's handbook of psychotherapy and behavior change* (5th ed.) (pp. 194–226). Hoboken, NJ: Wiley.

Didion, J. (2006). *The year of magical thinking.* New York, NY: Vintage.

Furr, S. R., & Carroll, J.J. (2003). Critical incidents in student counselor development. *Journal of Counseling and Development, 81,* 483–489.

Goldfried, M. R. (Ed.). (2001). *How therapists change: Personal and professional reflections.* Washington, DC: American Psychological Association.

Jennings, L. (1996). Personal characteristics of master therapists. (Unpublished doctoral dissertation.) University of Minnesota.

Jennings, L., & Skovholt, T. M. (1999). The cognitive, emotional, and relational characteristics of master therapists. *Journal of Counseling Psychology, 46,* 3–11.

Kazdin, A. E. (2004). Psychotherapy for children and adolescents. In M. J. Lambert (Ed.), *Bergin and Garfield's handbook of psychotherapy and behavior change* (5th ed.) (pp. 543–589). Hoboken, NJ: Wiley.

Krakauer, J. (1996). *Into the wild.* New York, NY: Anchor Books.

Lambert, M. J. (Ed.) (2004). *Bergin and Garfield's handbook of psychotherapy and behavior change* (5th ed.). Hoboken, NJ: Wiley.

Lebow, J. (2006). *Research for the psychotherapist.* New York, NY: Routledge.

May, R. (1972). *Power and innocence.* New York, NY: Delta.

Orlinsky, D. E., & Rønnestad, M. H. (2005). *How psychotherapists develop: A study of therapeutic work and professional growth.* Washington, DC: American Psychological Association.

Reed, G. M. (2006). What qualifies as evidence of effective practice? In J. C. Norcross, L. E. Beutler, & R. F. Levant (Eds.), *Evidence-based mental health* (pp. 13–23). Washington, DC: American Psychological Association.

Rogers, C. (1961). *On becoming a person.* Boston: Houghton Mifflin.

Rogers, C. (1989). On reaching 85. In H. Kirschenbaum and V. L. Henderson (Eds.), *The Carl

Rogers Reader. Boston, MA: Houghton Mifflin, pp. 56–58.

Rønnestad, M. H., & Skovholt, T. M. (2003). The journey of the counselor and therapist: Research findings and perspectives on development. *Journal of Career Development, 30,* (1), 5–44.

Skovholt, T. M., Jennings, L., & Mullenbach, M. (2004). Portrait of the master therapist: The highly-functioning self. In T. M. Skovholt & L. Jennings (Eds.), *Master therapists: Exploring expertise in therapy and counseling* (pp. 125–146). Boston, MA: Allyn & Bacon.

Sue, D. W. (2005). The continuing journey to multicultural competence. In R. K. Coyle & Bemak (Eds.), *Journeys to professional excellence: Lessons from leading counselor educators and practitioners* (pp. 73–84). Alexandria, VA: American Counseling Association.

The top ten (2007): The most influential therapists of the past quarter-century. *Psychotherapy Networker, 31* (2), 24-36, 68.

Wampold, B. (2001). *The great psychotherapy debate.* Mahwah, NJ: Lawrence Erlbaum.

Wampold, B. (2007). Psychotherapy: The humanistic (and effective) treatment. *American Psychologist, 62,* 857–873.

Yalom, I. D. (1989). *Love's executioner.* New York, NY: Basic Books.

Yalom, I. D. (1995). *The theory and practice of group psychotherapy* (4th ed.) New York, NY: Basic Books.

10

Path Toward Mastery

Phases and Themes of Development

Thomas M. Skovholt and
Michael H. Rønnestad

INTRODUCTION TO THE PRACTITIONER'S PATH

Important questions for the novice are: How do I learn to be a good practitioner? What steps have good practitioners taken in their careers? What did they focus on? What mistakes did they make? What mistakes did they avoid? How hard did they work at it? How long did it take? These are exciting and engaging questions for the novice.

We asked the same questions for ourselves when we were graduate students and embarking on careers in the helping professions, specifically counseling and clinical psychology. How do I learn to do this? Am I going to be good enough? Will my supervisors approve of my work? What if my clients deteriorate? How will I react if a client becomes suicidal? Will I know enough to help people with so many different human problems? Later we combined our own career worries and concerns with our positions as faculty members to ask some of these questions in a formal research study.

Unlike many researchers and psychologists in the helping professions, we were fortunate to receive graduate training in career development theory and research. Although Freud admonished that the happy person was one who was satisfied in both love and

---

This chapter is an expanded version of other writings including: T. M. Skovholt and M. H. Rønnestad (1995), *The Evolving Professional Self* (New York, NY: Wiley); T. M. Skovholt and M. H. Rønnestad (2001), "The Long Textured Path from Novice to Senior Practitioner," in T. M. Skovholt, *The Resilient Practitioner: Burnout Prevention and Self-Care Strategies for Therapists, Counselors, Teachers, and Health Professionals* (pp. 25–54) (Boston, MA: Allyn & Bacon); M. H. Rønnestad and T. M. Skovholt (2003), "The Journey of the Counselor and Therapist: Research Findings and Perspectives on Development," *Journal of Career Development, 30*, 5–44; and T. M. Skovholt and M. Trotter-Mathison (2011), *The Resilient Practitioner: Burnout Prevention and Self-Care Strategies for Therapists, Counselors, Teachers, and Health Professionals* (2nd ed., pp. 39–77) (New York, NY: Routledge).

work, most of the helping professions (psychiatry, social work, marriage and family therapy, psychiatric nursing, and clinical psychology) focus on love without corresponding research and practice focus on work. Our academic doctoral advisors (Joseph Johnston and Norman Gysbers) were experts in career psychology and career development. We were fortunate to be able to use their early career development formulations as part of our research questions regarding effective therapists and counselors.

The research we present here on phases and themes of development is built on different building blocks: our own hopes and efforts to become efficient therapists and counselors; our academic positions as researchers; our exposure to career development theory through our advisors and graduate training; the rich theory in the science of psychology and related fields; our exposure in the 1980s to qualitative research through European psychology and Rønnestad's position at the University of Oslo when these methods were not yet endorsed in American psychology; and, as important as any of these factors, our friendship, which began in graduate school and continues to this day.

At a meeting in April 1985, we decided to begin a research project on therapist and counselor development. We can trace our many-years research collaboration to this meeting, when we suddenly realized that we had both been writing about the same research questions. We decided to begin a large study on this topic. We spent five years collecting data before we knew if we had anything of value. The process was very exciting but also very unnerving, as we were embarking on a long and unknown journey. We felt like the great Nordic polar explorers Amundsen and Nansen. There were many struggles—we did not know if we would ever have worthwhile results; we lived 4,025 miles apart, so collaboration was more difficult than if we lived close to each other; we had very little research funding. There were many questions as we were embarking on this large study, questions similar to the uncertainties and doubt of beginning counselors or therapy students. We also had the other emotions that beginning students have in abundance: enthusiasm and excitement.

Since that time we have engaged in a number of joint and separate research projects. In addition, valuable data has come to us from our interactions with others in the field. We have learned from our experiences as teachers, practitioners, colleagues, supervisors, and workshop presenters over these many years. Students, clients, colleagues, supervisees, and workshop participants have been so instructive in giving us feedback that has improved our ways of thinking and our writing about professional development. Our thanks to them!

Next we present the results of our qualitative research study of 100 participants. Details of the specific research method can be found most recently in Rønnestad and Skovholt (2003, 2012) and in Skovholt and Rønnestad (1995).

PHASES OF THERAPIST/COUNSELOR DEVELOPMENT

Phase 1: Pretraining Phase

Central in the pretraining phase is being untrained in therapy or counseling yet engaged in the process of trying to help another person feel better, make decisions, understand the self, or improve relations with others. The person is most often a helper to others as a friend, family member, colleague, mentor, classmate, or someone in the neighborhood. In past descriptions we used the term "lay helper" for this phase.

Helping usually occurs within the person's social network, with geographic proximity being a key of who interacts with whom. Increasingly today, physical closeness is being replaced by access to each other via technology and social networks.

As discussed first in Chapter 1, professionals in therapy and counseling often report that early in life—during childhood and adolescence—they give emotional support to others. This was often the learning period for the essential therapist/counselor skill of affective attunement. It also was often the time when boundaries of who should help whom in a family could get blurred (i.e., child helping the parent).

Helpers in the pretraining phase use their own personal life experiences as the source for knowing what to suggest. Decisions are based on a kind of internal cognitive schema of their own personal experiences with life. There is a naturalness, a simplicity, and an unexamined quality in the attempt to transfer, or project, personal methods of coping to the other person. It is a kind of "based on my life, here is what to do" approach. And as much as the friend's life offers useful help, then the lay helper approach is useful in helping another person. But it also has limits because the friend's helping method and solution, based on his or her own life, may not be a glove that fits. Helping at the pretraining phase is a lay helper–type style that often involves a combination of listening, fairly rapid problem identification, specific advice concerning the problem, and then encouragement to the person to follow this course.

Pretraining helpers often are guided by a sense of sympathy for the other person. Continual emotional support is the main ingredient offered by lay helpers. Sometimes they get too involved in the other's problems, and sometimes lay helpers are too emotionally removed. A major aspect of professional training in the caring professions is learning how to be emotionally engaged but not engulfed by the distress of the other. Pretraining, by definition, means that this extensive training is lacking.

Overall, the sympathetic friend role enables lay helpers to have a conceptual system based on common sense and personal epistemology of life experience, worldview, perceptual and value biases, and mode of functioning. For example, when told of confusion and distress from not knowing whether to leave a romantic relationship, a lay helper may be highly directive by saying, for example: "He isn't worth it. You will be better off without him," or "Stick it out. You will be happy that you did."

At this phase, there is usually less self-awareness regarding the concerns that students in professional training programs have, such as "Am I doing this right?" or "Am I any good at this work?" Here, there is a more relaxed, commonsense approach to both the work method and evaluation of success.

Phase 2: Beginning Student Phase

Going from the known helping role of friend to professional therapist or counselor is both exciting and unnerving. All of a sudden, there is so much new data. Of course, this is not true for all. Some helpers have been psychology majors, have been in the helping role before, and may be older and have lots of life experience. All these buffer the intensity of the new. In general, professional elders (professors/supervisors/mentors/personal therapists), their own personal lives, theories/research, clients, peers/colleagues, and the social/cultural environment provide lots and lots of new data for beginning students.

The task is to move from the known role of lay helper to the unknown role of professional. This change becomes most real—and intensely felt—when, in time, students start seeing clients. They often feel a chasm between the world of theory and the world of practice. Without realizing it, students in practicum are joining the anxiety of other practitioner-oriented students (e.g., medical students, teachers in training, nurses, lawyers, physical therapists) in courageously trying to cross from the clarity of theory to the confusion of practice. For example, Sarikaya, Cinaver, and Karac (2006) report on the anxiety of medical students in clinical training. One counseling student expressed his self-doubt and sentiment by asking: "Could I really pull it off?"

Professors and supervisors have a major impact on beginning students, as do peers. Entering a new world makes people vulnerable and unsure; naturally they seek the support and encouragement of others, overtly or directly, and it is appreciated. Without the strong protective layers of years of professional experience, real or perceived criticism (by professors, supervisors, peers, clients) stings beginning students.

The first client meetings for beginning students are memorable. One female in our study said the big issue was: "How does it feel to be sitting with a person and being the professional responsible for improvement?" Reflecting the anxiety of meeting clients and the confusion of human interaction, another said; "At times I was so busy thinking about the instructions given in class and textbooks, I barely heard the client." Anxiety is the most common affective reaction for beginners, and it often interferes with their natural ability to listen, process, respond, and remember. Senior practitioners, by contrast, can fluidly respond and have a clear memory of key aspects of the session. Oh, how beginners would like the results that come from hundreds and hundreds of hours of experience without the pain and agony of getting there!

Positive feedback—especially from professors, supervisors, peers, and clients—helps. Negative feedback from clients often brings reactivity from the beginning students in the helping role, as does a negative supervisor response. Jennings (2010) reports on the nightmare of early supervisor negativity and how he overcame it.

All the complexity of the early client sessions lead to an urgent search for a theory method that clarifies the complexity and gives direction. Novices typically avoid complex models because they demand the opposite of what they desperately need: a system that they can quickly master and that gives them the confidence to go ahead. Books that offer checklists and easy-to-grasp methods are popular with novices but shunned by veteran practitioners.

Models to emulate (e.g., a veteran who is a group cofacilitator with the beginning student, one's own therapist, experts demonstrating on video) speed up the learning process. One research participant at this phase said: "I learned more about therapy when I was in therapy." (Note: All quotes are from Skovholt and Rønnestad, 1995.) In this situation, novices are like dry sponges hitting a patch of water—learning is soaked up. As one research participant expressed it: "I wanted to absorb from counselors I observed." Hundreds of students in training over the past 40 years have watched the classic *Three Approaches to Psychotherapy* films (the Gloria films) with Rogers, Perls, and Ellis. Students want to know how experts act, think, and feel in clinical practice. This seeking after and watching of models early in professional development happens across many careers, not just the counseling and therapy fields. It is often a very intense, empowering experience. Bela Fleck, now an expert at the banjo, writes of a powerful, early experience:

> I remember seeing jazz great Chick Corea when I was seventeen. There was a moment of revelation when I realized that all the notes he was playing had to exist on my banjo. I went home and stayed up most of the night, figuring out the scales, modes, and arpeggios for myself, mapping out the banjo fingerboard in my own way.
>
> —*Fleck, 2008, p. 80*

It should be emphasized that students usually are not passively modeling the complete behavior of any one expert. Rather, they actively choose to copy parts of the behavior, appearance, style, and viewpoint of various experts. Sometimes beginning students shut off the learning process and become "true believer[s]," to use the term from Eric Hoffer (1951). Hoffer's true believers hold a narrow set of principles to explain all the relevant data. There is no room for doubt, uncertainty, or multiple realities.

At times, new students do not seem to have enough new ideas. Then suddenly they can have too many. Through these sudden shifts of too many and too few, it is important for students to remain open. An open stance helps people move down the path of development. A more restrictive stance can produce temporary comfort, but it leads to stagnation on the developmental path. Maintaining openness, which also implies tolerating confusion and bewilderment, can be difficult to do in the high-achievement and perfectionist academic culture. The option of a more closed stance with energy devoted to impression management can be appealing to students who want very much to appear as if they know what they are doing.

Student affect vacillates with the immediate challenge faced and current feedback received. MacFarlane (2011) summarizes the counselor-in-training roller coaster this way: "Graduate education poses a wonderful opportunity and a difficult struggle for those who seek to become therapists" (p. 6).

Clinical supervision is a site for student anxiety became of the seemingly incompatible demands of being open about one's shortcomings while also being evaluated by the supervisor. A great working alliance with the supervisor can overcome this stressful situation. Crook Lyon and Potkar (2010) have demonstrated the counterproductivity that may result from a poor supervision relationship.

The initial excitement of being in school can turn to disappointment and frustration, feelings most often voiced to peers. Without the life vest of an all-encompassing method to use in practicum with clients (and what method ever works that well while confronting human complexity?), rather than being more prepared for the work, students feel more vulnerable. One of our research participants expressed it this way: "The intensity of the anger comes from the next set of challenges. The person must perform at a consistent level and often feels unprepared" (p. 35). Faced with this reality, the central task here—being open to professional complexity while finding safety in temporary solutions (different theoretical and technique anchors)—continues as students enter the next phase.

Phase 3: Advanced Student Phase

For the advanced student phase, we focus on the end of training and the intense "practicing the art" part of being a student. Terms for this phase are: internship, practicum, clerkship, and field placement. The central task at this phase is to function at a basic professional level.

Still focused on passing through the gates of the professional gatekeepers of the therapy/counseling profession, advanced students often are cautious, careful, and conservative in approach. Less formality and more individuality in style come in time in the years after graduation. When working as interns, people show playfulness and humor sparingly.

For what are these students responsible? That is a continual intern question. Often these interns have high internalized performance standards, which lead to a tendency toward excessive and misunderstood responsibility. A male intern at this phase said: "I do a good job of letting myself feel responsible for everything" (p. 46). Another said: "Now I'm less intense, less responsible for solutions, trust my intuition more and have better clinical judgment" (p. 46), while a third expressed it this way: "I thought I could and should help everybody" (p. 46).

Advanced students have two natural reference points: those coming behind and those ahead. They are reassured when seeing the work of beginners and feeling that they are beyond that point. As one intern said: "I have gone from being petrified to being comfortable" (p. 43). Another, supervising beginning students, told us: "It was a concrete realization of what I had learned. It was really valuable. The contrast between them and me helped me see my own style and how far I had come in my development" (p. 44).

If, however, the evaluation lens turns 180 degrees toward advanced professionals, their views of their competence alter; now they feel ill prepared for the challenges ahead. Along with this appraisal is a hope for more support and guidance from seniors and peers.

Clinical supervision is an affect-loaded experience for interns. In one study ($N = 204$), 84% of supervisees withheld information from their supervisors during their most recent supervision meeting (Mehr, Ladany, & Caskie, 2010). So much is at stake, and the task of trying to be open and avoid impression management while being evaluated presents a tremendous challenge for interns. All of this to do while also meeting the many challenges of seeing and trying to help clients!

Interns' reaction to supervision can vary greatly on an evaluation continuum of wonderful to awful. Here is a positive reaction from one of our sample: "I always got what I needed to do, to do what I needed to do." Another said: "Supervisors are important to me both as role models and in helping me identify how my personality influences my work both as a resource and as a hindrance" (p. 48). The clinical supervisor's influence can be even more positive for interns. In her article "Silence," Melanie Nuszkowski (2010) expresses the intensity of a positive supervision experience at the advanced student phase:

> We sat in silence, and then we processed all that occurred during those seemingly quiet moments. Through this supervision experience, I learned the incredible skill of being with and using silence. I believe that this skill has been the most essential element in enhancing the supervisory and therapeutic services that I have the honor of providing. Years after this supervisory experience, I reflect on it, wondering what ingredients contributed to the immense personal and professional growth that occurred during the year after the silence. . . . I recall trying to capture my experience and adequately express my thanks to my supervisor for this gift. The words are still difficult to find. (pp. 100–101)

Sometimes the supervision relationship is ambivalent for interns—they want to function autonomously while, at the same time, they still are being evaluated, reaching out for help and sometimes needing it too. It is a kind of professional adolescence with a push-pull toward senior gatekeepers.

Nonconfirming supervision experiences grab supervisees' attention and focus—the interns have risked so much to go this far into professional training. And high personal standards for performance also play a part. Interns have an expectation of supervisor expertise. When this expectation is not met, there is often disappointment. Reflecting back on her internship, a female said: "I wanted to believe that supervisors knew more than I did. It was disappointing to discover that they didn't" (p. 44).

In addition, modeling by more senior practitioners, not just one's supervisor, continues as a highly influential learning process. For novices, carefully observing those with credentials function professionally is like watching a three-dimensional movie rather than reading a book. Affect, behavior, and cognition, interpersonal relating, ethical nuances, conceptualizing cases, and so much more are on display when watching more experienced practitioners. All of this modeling continues, as with phase 2, to be part of the learning process. Interns have gone through several acquisition, application, and validation sequences with models and are now actively selecting and rejecting model components. "The extreme trust I had in experienced counselors as people to copy is not so true now because I have seen so many different styles," said one female intern (p. 47). From supervisors, a male intern said, "I take what I like" (p. 48). A female said it was her own therapist who served as the most influential model for her. Rejecting some models, another female said, "My God, I don't want to be like that" (p. 48).

Interns have an eagerness to observe senior practitioners at work, an eagerness often not matched by opportunity. One female intern said: "I wanted more opportunities to observe senior practitioners work" (p. 48). Another said: "I had very little opportunity to observe experienced practitioners, even after repeated requests of a supervisor. The only model of an experienced person I had was the Gloria films. Supervisors and experienced people were unwilling to demonstrate skills" (p. 48).

Students' individual assessment of their graduate program is usually most negative at this phase. This assessment contrasts sharply with the anticipation that accompanies their entrance into the program and the appreciation that they may feel long after receiving the degree. There may be a reality base for this criticism; graduate programs and individual faculty members often are less than adequate. However, the criticism also appears to have a developmental base. The program and faculty have failed to provide the ingredients for interns to feel adequate for the professional tasks coming soon after graduation. Years later, the people will realize that training programs cannot prepare one for everything. In the ambiguous work world of human psychology, it is necessary to be out in the real world and the school of hard knocks. The 10,000-hour rule for expertise development, that one needs 10,000 hours in a domain, is notable here (Gladwell, 2008).

Students' Theoretical Stance

From our interviews of 20 beginning and 20 advanced students, we sorted out and analyzed the ways that students relate to theoretical methods, at least at the time of our interviews. We identified four distinctly different orientations:

1. No conceptual attachment (which we also called laissez-faire orientation to theory)
2. "One theory, open" (which indicates preference for one theory but with openness to others)
3. Multiple serial attachments (which indicates a serial monogamy type orientation)
4. True believer (which indicates a strong belief in one theory *in combination with* active rejection of others)

Choices 2 (one theory open) and 3 (multiple attachments) seemed to us to be the most valuable for the continually searching process that is part of professional development.

Moving to the next phase involves a constant reorientation to role. One postintern commented:

When I was an intern I felt that I was to be in control and powerful. That made me feel responsible. Later it was different. My anxiety went down, I gave up some of the control and I felt less responsible. That helped me see client improvement as depending on more than me. (p. 48)

Now on to the first postgraduation phase.

Phase 4: Novice Professional Phase

The novice professional phase encompasses the early after-graduation professional years. A wide variety of professional and personal experiences have already occurred, and the individuals are developing a professional experience base. Yet currently they are experiencing many new challenges, and many lie in the future. Full credentialing and licensure may still be years ahead.

Euphoria and dread are bookend emotions for those entering this phase. New professionals are celebrating the end of being a student, and that can be a joyful reality. The culture for students often produces the combination of low control and high demand. As this is the combination that defines high work stress, its end is welcome. Graduates often throw their hats in the air at the graduation ceremony to symbolize this new freedom. Of course, having a job lined up at graduation makes this transition so much more positive.

Just as euphoria is an emotion that can possess new graduates, so is dread. They are now entering the professional world—perhaps prepared, perhaps not— for all the challenges that lie ahead. When a lack of preparation is deeply felt, dread is an accurate emotional reality. Often, though, there is a more muted, worrisome response. Lack of awareness of what lies ahead often buffers us as humans as we go forward. For example, at weddings, there is a lot of crying. The older audience members—knowing from experience that the future is uncertain—cry, in part in appreciation for the couple's willingness to go forward, even without guarantees. The task for novice professionals is to go forward, as in Danish philosopher Kierkegaard's "leap of faith" (Hong & Hong, 1983).

Next we further discuss the bookend emotions of euphoria and dread and so many emotions that lie between these extremes. And we discuss the themes of this phase of confirmation, disillusionment, and exploration.

Confirmation

There is often a honeymoon start for new professionals with positive emotions and optimism fueling them forward. We call this a confirmation of one's training period. Having a graduate degree and the recognition that comes with it, and often positive pride about the ranking of one's university, training program, and professors—all of these factors fuel people to feel confirmation about their competence. There can be an eagerness to test out new skills—skills honed during hours and hours of effort while students in class and in practicum.

The crack in the experience of confirmation relates to the word "commencement." As said in an earlier chapter, although the work is often used to describe the end, as in "commencement ceremony," commencement is defined in the dictionary as the beginning. Novice professionals often feel this beginning—or need to continue to develop professionally—when in the new work environment. Things can quickly feel different. Holahan (1988) captured the sudden loss of the support structure when he described moving from being a university counseling center intern to being a staff member.

> I saw myself on internship as one of five prized children who had our narcissistic strivings mirrored by a supportive group of elder sibling and parental objects. With few exceptions, jobs well done were quickly met with words of encouragement and reinforcement. . . . As a new senior staff member the prized child status lasted about 1 week. I was welcomed, oriented, and then expected to go about my job. (p. 120)

Disillusionment

As a new PhD counselor, Matt Hanson (2010) recalls how he, when at this phase, prepared so much to help a client with her grief only to have the client's focus veer in a different direction. He wrote about how his client taught him new lessons:

> Julia and others have clearly shown me (more deeply than I knew at that point in my professional development) that one of the few things that's predictable about the process of therapy is how uncertain and unpredictable it's likely to be. . . . I think I've come to expect the unexpected. (p. 181)

The realization that there is so much new to learn, and so much previously learned to now unlearn, can be exciting, but often can be just as disillusioning. Widick, Knefelkamp and Parker (1980) call this a "loss of old signposts and the experience of being lost and alone in a chaotic world" (p. 94).

In our sample group, we have plenty of examples of this disillusionment experience for novice professionals. There is so much hope and promise that all the effort, expense, commitment, delayed gratification, and learning from school would be enough! Some quotes now:

One female looked back and said:

> I realized that graduate training had real gaps. There was much I had to cover that was not offered in graduate school. I remember writing letters to the director of the program, pointing out things that should have been addressed. (p. 59)

Another said: "Having less guidance from professors and supervisors was scary" (p. 52). Lack of client progress can fuel disillusionment. A male therapist described his reactions this way:

I used to think that my doubts about me and my despair would go away with the degree. . . . Now people look at me, call me doctor and want more and expect more. But what am I going after? It is a disorienting process because I don't know any more now except that there are more expectations. It is great to be done, but what do I really want to be? Where did I really want to go? I didn't expect the formal training would lead to feeling adequate until I felt inadequate and then realized how much I expected to know by now. My professional training was over and I lacked so much. (p. 51)

Another, with colorful language, talked of his early professional days and said:

There were days when everything I touched turned into horseshit. Whatever made me think I could do it or that it worked, it was a sham; people were paying me to make money off their pain. (p. 53)

The struggles can be reduced through peer support. One female said, "If there weren't good peers around, the feelings would have been much harder to handle. (p.53)

Exploration

The catalyst for exploration is, in part, the disillusionment that we have already discussed. Exploration takes place outward to new skills and inward to new values. For example, counselor educator Amanda Purnell (2010) describes her first experience teaching as a time she tried so hard to be a great instructor for new counseling students, yet realized that "I had failed them" with her teaching techniques (p. 189). This realization led her to explore better ways to teach. In our research interviews, we remember interviewing a new PhD psychologist who had become so competent in cognitive-behavioral therapy yet now was starting over with psychoanalytic training. For him, the new efforts were part of being more congruent with who he was—the shedding and adding were part of the sculpting of the new identity.

As part of the exploration process and new identity development, people often feel a more honed sense of boundary regulation. A male at this phase said:

I was a pretty personal therapist with clients when I started out in the business. They would call me in a time of crisis or need. They had my home phone number. That isn't working anymore because my case load is big and difficult. Now calls are screened and I use an answering machine. I had to change it because I was getting "fried" and mad at clients and things like that. But it is tough saying no to people in tremendous distress; I feel guilty when I don't respond to demands, exhausted when I do. (p. 55)

Two strong sources of influence at this phase are reflection—the ongoing processing of experience and the meaning from it—and the use of peers. About the second, a female at this phase said:

> I find my colleagues to be my best resource. I tap people with similar as well as divergent theoretical orientations. We even have a "when therapy fails" group to help sort out what happens when we're ineffective. (p. 61)

Now on to the experienced professional phase, which comprises the longest time period of the six phases.

Phase 5: Experienced Professional Phase

The experienced professional phase is the longest one, stretching over many years. This period usually contains the high point of responsible, productive adult work over the career-long developmental arc. However, this is not always the case. Since therapy and counseling is partially a wisdom field, highly productive work may continue during the most senior years.

About wisdom, David Brooks (2011), the influential *New York Times* columnist, wrote:

> Wisdom doesn't consist of knowing specific facts or possessing knowledge of a field. It consists of knowing how to treat knowledge: being confident but not too confident; adventurous but grounded. It is a willingness to confront counter-evidence and to have a feel for the vast spaces beyond what's known. (pp. 168–169)

This phase, of the experienced professional, and the next, of the senior professional, are times when practitioners can exhibit this kind of wisdom. Knowing a lot and being cognitively, affectively, and behaviorally flexible come from lots of reflective experience, according to expertise researchers Ericsson, Charness, Hoffman, and Feltovich (2006), and as popularized by Gladwell (2008). Experienced professionals have an elaborate web of cognitive schemas—the product of hours and hours of experience in therapy, counseling, supervision, consultation, teaching, and related activities—that guide their professional work. This was expressed so well by one of our participants, who said:

> With a new client I think about cases I've had. I think about how they have gone. Themes come in a case and this stimulates a memory in me. The memory is in the form of a collection of vignettes, stories and scripts. It isn't fully conscious but new cases do kick off the memory—the memory of how things went before provide a foundation to begin the current case. Interestingly, most of the stories come from the early days of my practice; they are the most embedded. Later cases don't stand out as much except if I was proved wrong

or something dramatic happened. Then my thinking changes and my memory changes. (p. 77)

Personal life and professional life affect each other. For example, one participant said: "You learn a lot from your kids just like you learn a lot from your clients" (p. 65). Another talked of her divorce being the most difficult experience of her life. She found that it forced her to see herself as separate person and not a daughter or wife in relation to others. She said: "It really shocked me to my core. I had to tap into some dark places and look at things about me" (p. 65).

There is a stronger level of confidence based on experience in the domain. For example, a female said: "Nothing completely floors me anymore. In the past, I took it to mean there was something wrong with me if things were novel or new" (p. 64).

By this time, therapists/counselors have created a work role that is congruent with their identity and perceptions of self in terms of personality characteristics such as ethical values and attitudes. When there is a strong person–environmental fit, people usually feel authentic in the work world. The urge to find a great fit between the work environment and personality of the self is expressed clearly by Holland's (1997) well-researched vocational psychology theory.

By this phase, an integration and consolidation process has occurred whereby people have "thrown out the clutter," and therapists/counselors have built consistency and coherence across the personal and professional self. When asked to identify a method, practitioners at this phase may say they are cognitive-behavioral therapists, existentialists, family systems counselors, or some other well-known method. There is great professional pressure to identify with a well-known method—one that is a legacy method, empirically validated or evidence based. We believe this has merit but leaves out the power of professional experience and personal life in sculpting method. In his study of great college teachers, Bain (2004) found similarities between his subjects but also expressions of uniqueness. He says:

[T]he great Dutch artist [Rembrandt] could not be Picasso any more than the Spanish painter could replicate his predecessor; each had to find his own genius. So too must teachers adjust every idea to who they are and what they teach. (p. 21)

This uniqueness factor is also clear in reading the Lisle (1987) biography of the great American painter Georgia O'Keeffe. This uniqueness of the individual is what we are describing with therapists at the experienced professional phase and their process, as we said, of throwing out the clutter. One of our favorite quotes regarding this point is this by a female practitioner:

I learned all the rules and so I came to a point—after lots of effort—where I knew the rules very well. Gradually I modified the rules. Then I began to use the rules to let me go where I wanted to go. Lately I haven't been talking so much in terms of rules. (p. 66)

By now practitioners typically are good at regulating involvement and identification with clients. A male therapist said: "I have a better sense of personal boundaries and blame myself less if things don't work out well." (p. 85). Another said: "When the session is over I can leave it there" (p. 93). Finding balance between involvement with client suffering and then letting go is a difficult skill. This is expressed when counselors/therapists are able to be totally absorbed in client work but then can end many workdays more refreshed and stimulated than exhausted and depleted. Learning this skill, what in the studies of master therapists we called "boundaried generosity" (Skovholt, Jennings, & Mullenbach, 2004), is crucial for the long-term close involvement with human suffering that is central to the work of therapists. Yet we do not want to paint a rosy, easy picture of the work, for as one research participant said at this phase: "Practice is still difficult... because difficult clients are still draining" (p. 64).

Paralleling improved regulation of professional boundaries, experienced professionals have learned how to separate the professional role from roles such as that of a friend, parent, or spouse. One female reflected back to her graduate school years, when this was more of a problem. Laughing, she said that her daughter gave her useful feedback when she said: "Mother, will you quit being a damn social worker and just be my mother!" (p. 69).

One of the major findings of our research concerns the multiple sources of influence in the development of therapists/counselors. Look at this list:

Theories/research
Clients
Professional elders (professor/supervisors/mentors/therapists)
Peers/colleagues
One's own personal life
The social/cultural environment

When beginning students are hit by data from all of these sources, they often feel overwhelmed—like the proverbial example of trying to drink water from a fire hose. All of these influences continue through the practitioner's life, although there are shifts in influence.

One of the most notable shifts at this phase is the withdrawal of active professional elders. Experienced professionals are no longer students, so professors are gone from their primary role; these professionals typically are no longer in individual clinical supervision, so the supervisor is gone; mentors are not so present, and therapists are less present for practitioners in this phase.

Death, distance, and changes in relationships have reduced the presence of seniors in the personal and professional lives of experienced professionals. For example, experienced professional phase psychologist Salina Renninger (2010) recalled how, as a beginning counselor, she lost her strongest source of support, her mother. At the time of her mother's sudden illness and death, Renninger asked: "Could I survive without my mom? How could I continue to believe that love, joy and connection would be steady for me when something I thought was unshakeable was so suddenly taken? How could I trust the world to hold me steady?" (p. 200).

Although professional and personal seniors disappear, they also *do not* disappear from the lives of experienced phase practitioners. Often the senior person gets internalized, and his or her influence continues that way during later phases. One of our informants, for example, clearly described this internalization process when he talked about his supervisor, John, from 20 years earlier. He said: "I have been running around in my mind words, phrases, quotes that I periodically pull back to . . . and sometimes I say to myself, How would John handle this situation?" (p. 79). The more experienced practitioners in our sample group often recalled with great fondness and appreciation these "internalized mentors."

About learning and development, there is a newer realization at this phase that "not much is new." One person said: "I've recently stopped going to workshops. They seemed to be geared to 'Freshman English' and to be old stuff. For example, assertiveness training was done long ago under a different label. I'm especially uninterested in workshops on new little techniques" (p. 78).

Now on to the final phase in our six-phase model.

Phase 6: Senior Professional Phase

Practitioners at the senior professional phase can be both like each other and also quite different. The likeness comes from being in the same field for decades and doing similar work, defined as nurturing human development by use of psychological-type ideas. Differences are expressed through the individuality of the healer at work. Just as we understand that artists and teachers have their own style, so do therapists and counselors.

Age and multiple years of professional experience give perspective on the human journey that a younger person just does not have. For example, one senior practitioner in our sample said: "Doing a lot of living is a great help. I remember, in my 30s I had a client in his 50s who wanted a divorce. I thought why bother at that age? Then, in my 50s I finally understood when I got a divorce" (p. 91).

Acceptance of the self is a predominant affect. Said a male at this phase: "I think I am more myself than I have ever been" (p. 87). Another male told us: "If I can do three out of four things well, I concentrate on those things. I used to work on the one of four, but not now" (p. 87).

For many, there is a nourishing of the self as it is. It means slow growth in new assumptions, techniques, and style with an overall focus not on newness but on maintenance and prizing what has been developed by the individual. A sense of occupational power and competence is often balanced with the limits of one's work. About limits, a female at this phase said: "I used to be afraid that I might make a terrible mistake and ruin someone's life forever and now I feel you can't do that, you're not that powerful" (p. 90).

Although many at this age have settled down, others at the senior level are very energized by new challenges. For example, Spokane (2010) writes how his work shifted dramatically at age 60; he became more vibrant because of this very meaningful new direction. Also, Romano (2010), late in his career, was captivated by first-time challenges of international crisis work in psychology. These two examples demonstrate that it is not accurate to paint this phase with a broad brush, "acceptance of what is," combined with a withdrawal from work into retirement.

Some, but not all, senior professionals welcome the chance to guide younger practitioners and students in the therapy and counseling professions. From our research on therapist and counselor development, we conclude that being the receiver (as supervisee, student, mentee, advisee) has about twice the growth potential as being the giver (as supervisor, teacher/professor, mentor, advisor) across hundreds of individuals during the six phases of professional development. This is, of course, a generalization, and there are, as with any broad description of human development, many exceptions. However, listening carefully to individuals in all the receiver roles and all the giver roles during interviews over many years has led us to this conclusion. We base it on our assessment of the way individuals discuss the value of various activities.

As we stated, some seniors take on this role with individuals at earlier phases.

One male, describing the transition to senior status, said: "Suddenly I was seen by others as a leader, but I didn't see it that way. I didn't feel I belonged" (p. 80). Another was excited by supervising younger interns and said: "They get brighter all the time: I feel that I learn as much from the interns as I teach them. They have become my teacher" (p. 92).

We interviewed the most experienced group in our sample twice, average age 64 and average age 74. These interviews were engrossing and compelling. We heard of older adults who were actively engaged in work and outside of work. It seemed their natural curiosity, ability to learn, and interpersonal skills led to engagement in life. Yet we also heard of the unrelenting impact of time never stopping and stories of distress, concerns about failing health of self and family members, of reduced energy, limitations in activities and accomplishments. Old age was not enthusiastically endorsed as the golden age. One male therapist said: "I think the golden age is not best by any means. As far as I can tell, being old and wise is not better than being young and innocent and energetic" (Rønnestad & Skovholt, 2001, p. 183).

As expressed in phase 5, there were more comments about the recycled nature of knowledge—something beginners would not understand or sense. Our favorite quote on this topic is this one:

> By the time a person reaches the end of one's work life, he/she has seen the wheel reinvented so many times, has seen fashions in therapy/counselling change back and forth. Old ideas emerge under new names and it can be frustrating to the senior therapist to see people make a big fuss about something he/she has known about for years. This contributes to cynicism for the person. (p. 95)

At the senior level, there is often a major internal battle between the utility of the internal schema of hundreds and hundreds of hours of clinical experiences and the boredom of it all. Boredom can come from seeing the same problems over and over again and feeling that therapists/counselors, as cultural anthropologists, have been there too many times. Boredom can also relate to pervasive exhaustion due to surrounding themselves with human hopelessness and suffering for many decades.

Conversely, being highly engaged in the work often is related to seeing the individuality and uniqueness of each client. When this happens, practitioners can, as Yalom (2002) says, create a new therapy with each client. Helen Roehlke worked as a psychologist and clinical supervisor at the University of Missouri for 40 years. When asked about this issue of boredom for the senior practitioner, she told us: "I never got bored—every person is different" (personal communication, June 21, 2007). For a description of Roehlke's career-long engagement, see Flores (2008).

Our favorite quote from all our research interviews in the 100-person Minnesota study is this one from a senior person (age 63) who expressed the joy of using her elaborate internal schema of professional experience. We end the phase descriptions with this joyful description by this highly experienced practitioner:

> With diminishing anxiety, I became less and less afraid of my client and with that came an ease for me in using my own wide repertoire of skills and procedures. They became more available to me when I needed them. And during those moments it became remarkable to me that someone would have the willingness to share their private world with me and that my work with them would bring very positive results for them. This brought a sense of intense pleasure to me. (p. 96)

THEMES IN PROFESSIONAL DEVELOPMENT

We have just presented our research using phases. There are advantages and disadvantages to phase descriptions. One advantage is that we often think of breaking up human life into phases (i.e., sophomore year in school, junior year in school). One disadvantage is that the phase concept seems to communicate breaks between time periods (although not as much as the stage concept does); however, in real life, change is more gradual, as with seasons. To combat the disadvantages of using phases, we have also organized the content according to themes, which comprise this section of the chapter. Here is our research expressed through 14 themes of professional development. We have used an outline format in this version of the themes. A more complete version can be found in Rønnestad and Skovholt (2003) and Rønnestad and Skovholt (2012, in press).

Theme 1. Professional development involves an increasingly higher-order integration of the professional self and the personal self.

- Increasing consistency between therapist's personality and theoretical allegiance.
- Increased congruence through selection and formulation of professional roles.
- Relates to clients with an increased ability to differentiate responsibilities and to know what self and the client contribute to the working relationship.
- Progressively more able to relate in a professionally connected way to clients.

Theme 2. The focus of functioning shifts dramatically over time from internal to external to internal.
- *Pretraining.* The conventional mode:
  - Individual operates from a commonsense base of helping.
  - Some characteristics of conventional helping in our culture are:
    - To define the problem quickly.
    - To provide strong emotional support.
    - To provide sympathy rather than empathy.
    - To give advice based on own experience.
- *Training.* The external and rigid mode:
  - Attention shifts toward the theoretical bodies of knowledge and toward professionally based conceptions of methods and techniques.
  - Student functioning becomes increasingly more externally driven with students suppressing personally characteristic ways of functioning.
  - Use of humor typically disappears for the student counselors/therapists to reappear with the professional self-confidence of experienced counselors/therapists.
- *Posttraining/experienced.* The internal and flexible mode:
  - There is a gradual shift toward a renewed internal focus with internally directed shedding and adding to the practitioner self.

Theme 3. Continuous reflection is a prerequisite for optimal learning and professional development at all levels of experience.
- The ability and willingness to reflect on one's professional experiences in general, and on challenges and hardships in particular, is a prerequisite to avoid the slow erosion of skills. Stagnation comes from not learning from experience, when task work does not increase competence.

Theme 4. An intense commitment to learn propels the developmental process.
- Commitment to learn and willingness within ethical boundaries to take risks and to be open to new learning are building blocks of increased professional functioning.

Theme 5. The cognitive map changes: Beginning practitioners rely on external expertise; seasoned practitioners rely on internal expertise.
- Ideas of how to proceed in the work changes from external to internal.

- The intense demand to observe models of professionally defined expert behavior and for favoring instructive and didactic supervision declines dramatically over time.
- There is a marked shift toward a self-directed preference for what to learn and how to learn.

Theme 6. Professional development is a long, slow, continuous process that can also be erratic.
- Professional development is generally experienced as a continual increase in a sense of competence and mastery.
- This process may at any point in time be barely noticeable, but retrospectively it appears substantial. There are also sudden bursts and recycling loops.

Theme 7. Professional development is a lifelong process
- There is an increased sense of competence, improved ability to handle challenges, and more skill in regulating responsibilities as the practitioner has more and more meaningful experiences.

Theme 8. Many beginning practitioners experience much anxiety in their professional work. Over time, most master their anxiety.
- Anxiety levels diminish markedly.
- "In time you are no longer afraid of your clients."

Theme 9. Clients serve as a major source of influence and as primary teachers.
- Interacting with clients is a powerful source of learning and development.
- Client reactions to counselor/therapist behaviors and attitudes continually influence practitioners.
- Although clients provide valuable feedback for practitioners at all levels of experience, inexperienced practitioners are particularly receptive and often vulnerable to client feedback.

Theme 10. Personal life influences professional functioning and development throughout the professional life span.
- Experiences in childhood, adolescence, and adulthood impact professional functioning and development.
- These experiences influence professional life and functioning in various ways, such as selection of work role and theoretical orientation, therapeutic style and focus, attitude toward colleagues, experienced hardships, and ways of coping in practice.
- Adversities and crises in adult personal life exert an immediate negative influence on professional functioning, yet often the long-term consequences are positive for work as a practitioner.

Theme 11. Interpersonal sources of influence propel professional development more than do impersonal sources of influence.
- Meaningful contact with people is the catalyst for growth.
- Clients, professional elders (i.e., supervisors, personal therapists, professors, mentors), professional peers, friends, family members, and, later in one's career, younger colleagues are impactful.
- Interacting with clients is the most impactful source of influence for professional development.
- Supervision and personal therapy were rated second and third, and personal life frequently was ranked fourth, in a large international study.

Theme 12. New members of the field have strong affective reactions to professional elders and graduate training.
- Students in training continually scrutinize and evaluate professors, teachers, and supervisors. Students want to learn from and model seniors they see as competent.
- Strong admiration is expressed for those more advanced in the profession who possess behaviors or personal characteristics that are perceived as highly positive, such as intellectual brilliance, strong therapeutic skills, outstanding supervision ability, unusual emotional support for beginners, and the modeling of professional values in personal life.
- Negative reactions to professional elders were just as common and just as intense.
  - Devaluation seems to occur at the same intensity level as idealization.
- Professional elders are devalued if they possess behaviors perceived as highly negative.
  - Examples include supervisors who are perceived as unfairly critical, or professors who teach counseling but seem unable to practice it.
- Most therapists and counselors experience some disillusionment regarding their graduate education and training.
- Good supervision seems to buffer against student confusion when first interacting with clients and stress.

Theme 13. Extensive experience with suffering contributes to heightened recognition, acceptance, and appreciation of human variability.
- Insight, introspection, and reflection contribute to the development of wisdom and the seeing of great human variability in coping with life challenges.

Theme 14. For practitioners, there is realignment from self as hero to client as hero.
- Increased experience with a large variety of clients and experiences of failures and successes over the years contribute to a gradual shift in understanding the change process.
- There is movement from therapist/counselor power to client power.

SUMMARY

In this chapter, we have described the results of our research study of counselors and therapists. Over the years, we have modified our results based on new data sources. However, the results discussed in this chapter are essentially consistent with our earliest formulations, which were cited on the first page of this chapter. We hope these ideas can be of use to you, the novice practitioner, as you are engaged with the exciting process of professional development. Now on to the next chapter!

REFERENCES

Bain, K. (2004). *What the best college teachers do.* Cambridge, MA: Harvard University Press.

Brooks, D. (2011). *The social animal: The hidden sources of love, character and achievement.* New York, NY: Random House.

Crook Lyon, R. E., & Potkar, K. A. (2010). The supervisory relationship. In N. Ladany & L. J. Bradley (Eds.) *Counselor supervision* (pp. 15–56). New York, NY: Routledge.

Ericsson, K. A., Charness, N., Hoffman, R. R., & Feltovich, P. J. (2006). *The Cambridge handbook of expertise and expert performance.* New York, NY: Cambridge University Press.

Fleck, B. (2008). Doing things my own way. In J. Allison and D. Gediman (Eds.), *This I believe II: More personal philosophies of remarkable men and women* (pp. 97–81). New York, NY: Henry Holt.

Flores, L. (2008). Roehlke, H. J. (1931). In F.T.L. Leong, E. M. Altmaier, & B. D. Johnson (Eds.), *Encyclopedia of counseling* (pp. 375–378). Thousand Oaks, CA: Sage.

Gladwell, M. (2008). *Outliers: The story of success.* Boston, MA: Little, Brown.

Hanson, M. R. (2010). Expecting the unexpected. In M. Trotter-Mathison, J. M. Koch, S. Sanger, & T. M. Skovholt (Eds.), *Voices from the field: Defining moments in counselor and therapist development* (pp. 180–182). New York: Routledge.

Hoffer, E. (1951). *The true believer.* New York, NY: New American Library.

Holahan, W. (1988). From intern to senior staff: Movement toward self-nurturance. *Journal of Counseling and Development, 67,* 120.

Holland, J. L. (1997). *Making vocational choices: A theory of vocational personalities and work environments.* Lutz, FL: Psychological Assessment Resources.

Hong, H. V. & Hong, E. H. (1983). *Kierkegaard's writing, VI: Fear and trembling/repetition.* Princeton, NJ: Princeton University Press.

Jennings, L. (2010). Practicum pain, professional gain. In M. Trotter-Mathison, J. M. Koch, S. Sanger, & T. M. Skovholt (Eds.). *Voices from the field: Defining moments in counselor and therapist development* (pp. 50–52). New York, NY: Routledge.

Lisle, L. (1987). *Portrait of an artist: A biography of Georgia O'Keeffe.* Albuquerque, NM: University of New Mexico Press.

MacFarlane, I. M. (2011). "Anxiety's effect on the experience of supervision of graduate student counselors in training." Unpublished paper. University of Minnesota.

Mathison, J. M. Koch, S. Sanger, & T. Skovholt (Eds.) *Voices from the field: Defining moments in counselor and therapist development* (pp. 180–182). New York, NY: Routledge.

Mehr, K. E., Ladany, N., & Caskie, G. I. L. (2010). Trainee nondisclosure in supervision: What are they not telling you? *Counselling and Psychotherapy Research, 10,* 103–113.

Nuszkowski, M. A. (2010). Silence. In M. Trotter-Mathison, J. M. Koch, S. Sanger, & T. M. Skovholt (Eds.), *Voices from the field: Defining moments in counselor and therapist development* (pp. 100–102). New York, NY: Routledge.

Purnell, A. l. (2010). On becoming a teacher. In M. Trotter-Mathison, J. M. Koch, S. Sanger, & T. M. Skovholt (Eds.), *Voices from the field: Defining moments in counselor and therapist development* (pp. 188–190). New York, NY: Routledge.

Renninger, S. (2010). How could I trust the world to hold me steady? In M. Trotter-Mathison, J. M. Koch, S. Sanger, & T. M. Skovholt (Eds.),

Voices from the field: Defining moments in counselor and therapist development (pp. 200–201). New York, NY: Routledge.

Romano, J. L. (2010). The 2004 tsunami: An American psychologist and disaster recovery in Thailand. In: M. Trotter-Mathison, J. M. Koch, S. Sanger, & T. M. Skovholt (Eds.), *Voices from the field: Defining moments in counselor and therapist development* (pp. 221–224). New York, NY: Routledge.

Rønnestad, M. H., & Skovholt, T. M. (2012). *The developing practitioner:* Growth and Stagnation of Therapists and Counselors, New York, NY: Routledge.

Rønnestad, M. H., & Skovholt, T. M. (2001). Learning arenas for professional development: Retrospective accounts of senior psychotherapists. *Professional Psychology: Research and Practice, 32,* 181–187.

Rønnestad, M. H., & Skovholt, T. M. (2003). The journey of the counselor and therapist: Research findings and perspectives on development. *Journal of Career Development, 30,* 5–44.

Sarikaya, O., Cinaver, M., & Karac, S. (2006). The anxieties of medical students related to clinical training. *International Journal of Clinical Practice, 60,* 1414–1418.

Skovholt, T. M., Jennings, L., & Mullenbach, M. (2004). Portrait of the master therapist: Developmental model of the highly-functioning self. In T. M. Skovholt & L. Jennings (Eds.), *Master therapists: Exploring expertise in therapy and counselling* (pp. 125–146). Boston, MA: Allyn & Bacon.

Skovholt, T. M., & Rønnestad, M. H (1995). *The evolving professional self.* New York, NY: Wiley.

Spokane, A. R. (2010). At 60, I finally found what I was put on this planet to do! In: M. Trotter-Mathison, J. M. Koch, S. Sanger, & T. M. Skovholt (Eds.). *Voices from the field: Defining moments in counselor and therapist development* (pp. 251–254). New York, NY: Routledge.

Widick, C., Knefelkamp, L., & Parker, C. A. (1980). Student development. In U. Delworth & G. R. Hansen (Eds.), *Student services* (pp. 75–116). San Francisco, CA: Jossey-Bass.

Yalom, I. D. (2002). *The gift of therapy: An open letter to a new generation of therapists and their patients.* New York, NY: Harper Perennial.

11

Practitioner Mastery and Expertise

Thomas M. Skovholt, Mark Vaughan, and Len Jennings

The difference between expert performers and normal adults reflect a lifelong period of deliberate effort to improve performance in a specific domain.
— From the classic study by Ericsson et al. (1993) on the key to expertise being demanding, focused work over a long period of time. Cited by Colvin, 2010, p. 63

PURPOSE OF THIS CHAPTER

This chapter is about a goal that many novices envision for their own future—to somehow get to mastery, to no longer feel afraid of all the new situations that come with each new client, to sometime finally arrive! The chapter provides a map of mastery so that novices can have an idea of the path from being a beginner to being an expert. And here is the key: Knowing the big picture and the end point helps us actually get there. David Campbell (2007) has a catchy title for his self-help career planning book: *If You Don't Know Where You're Going, You'll Probably End Up Somewhere Else.* If we know about expertise and mastery, then each of us has a better chance of ending up there.

GENERAL CHARACTERISTICS OF EXPERTS

Is there such a thing as a description of an expertise in general that corresponds to Charles Spearman's (1927) idea of G as a general factor in intelligence? Is there a way to define E as a general factor like G?

Perhaps there is. In 1988, Chi, Glaser, and Farr published a book titled *The Nature of Expertise.* Reviewing research on experts across a variety of areas (including chess players, cab drivers, restaurant servers, etc.), Glaser and Chi (1988) outlined seven characteristics of experts.

1. Experts tend to excel mainly in their own domain.
2. Experts perceive larger, more meaningful patterns in their chosen domain.
3. Experts are faster than novices in performing domain skills.
4. Experts have superior memory.
5. Experts see and represent a problem in their domain at a deeper (more principled) level.
6. Experts spend a great deal of time analyzing a problem qualitatively
7. Experts have strong self-monitoring skills.

1. Experts Tend to Excel Mainly in Their Own Domain

We tend to think that an expert in one area is an expert in everything. George Foreman was a great boxer; therefore, buy his grill for grilling. Meryl Streep is a giant talent on the screen. Does that make her a great author of children's books too?

In reality, of all the research conducted to date, little evidence has been uncovered that suggests that an expert in one domain can easily achieve expertise in a very different arena. Most research, in fact, indicates the opposite; an example comes from a study by Voss and Post (1988) in which chemistry experts were asked to solve political science problems. Results showed that the chemists were no better than novices in their analysis of these problems because the chemists' main focus when discussing political science was on very concrete issues rather than detailed abstract issues that they typically used in their everyday work in chemistry (Skovholt, Hansen, Jennings, & Grier, 2004). Glaser and Chi (1988) suggest that the reason for this lack of transfer from one area to another is because expertise in a particular domain is the result of years of study and exposure in that domain, which subsequently yields a high degree of specialized knowledge.

Experts develop complex cognitive representations within a domain—a kind of mental schema or picture—which subsequently allows them immediate access so they can integrate information for a situation or task (Feltovich, Prietula, & Ericsson, 2006). Physics experts represent problems in complex abstract terms relative to major physics principles; expert medical diagnosticians organize their hypotheses around major pathological issues relevant to each particular case; expert taxi drivers are capable of identifying alternative routes to a particular destination while novices tend to rely heavily on well-known routes. The expert performance in each of these areas comes only after extensive time dedicated to study and practice within the particular domain.

2. Experts Perceive Larger, More Meaningful Patterns in Their Chosen Domain

The phenomenon of "chunking" (putting relevant information together) as described of expertise in chess suggests that experts organize data into larger, more meaningful chunks, which have a profound impact on their capacity for short-term working memory and allow for more effective and efficient processing of relevant information. This ability can be especially useful in counseling and psychological therapy fields, where the natural confusion and uncertainty of the work is better accomplished by practitioners who are able to identify meaningful patterns and profiles that are more likely to be overlooked by novices (Skovholt et al., 2004). As cited in a chapter on expertise by Feltovich et al. (2006), research exploring this same phenomenon has identified its influence in the comparative performances of experts and novices in the fields of architecture, radiology, and computer programming.

3. Experts Are Faster Than Novices in Performing Domain Skills

A domain is an area of expertise for those with extensive experience. The family law attorney, the marathon runner, the bathroom tile specialist, the addictions counselor, the mother of five, and the high school math teacher, all have a domain of expertise.

This greater fluency of task completion, however, is dependent on the particular task. Proficiency and speed in completing manual labor tasks, such as typing or factory work, are highly correlated with the amount of time spent performing the task in a practical setting. For example, based on extensive work experience in the domain, one of the present authors (Mark Vaughan) believes that expert printers generally can complete setup tasks more proficiently and more accurately than novices, thereby producing consistently high-quality work in a much shorter time span. This speed is a direct result of:

- The number of years spent both learning and engaging in the craft
- Experience in machine adjustment
- Knowledge of the qualities and characteristics of various ink types
- Ability to identify and resolve various problems in an efficient manner with significant reduction of trial-and-error techniques

In scientific and technical fields, doing the work more quickly than novices is the result of being able to represent the problem in larger, more meaningful patterns. Novices tend to see more isolated parts of the problem that may not be connected to each other (Skovholt et al., 2004). Expert counselors have acquired, over hundreds of hours of work, cognitive skills that allow them immediate access to knowledge that is relevant to the task at hand; novice counselors, however, lack this internal integration of information and therefore must rely on externally available information, such as textbook theories or tips from clinical supervisors to make decisions on how to proceed (Feltovich et al., 2006). Colvin (2010) explains:

Expert psychological counselors sort statements from patients according to the factors most relevant for choosing therapy, while novice counselors sort by superficial detail. (p. 96)

Feltovich et al. (2006) describe what can be called *weak* methods of problem resolution, ones that do not consider the content of the domain when assessing a situation. Novices need external guidance because they have weak methods of problem resolution. This need for external guidance is expressed in the helping professions by novice practitioners' strong interest in explicit treatment manuals and very specific methods, methods veteran practitioners eschew.

The expert way of doing the work consists of rich knowledge of the area and a thorough understanding of operations that will lead to a successful resolution. The novices' weaker methods utilize only general, superficial information; in contrast, domain experts implement strong methods that rely on more integrated knowledge (Feltovich et al., 2006). We say this not, of course, as a criticism of novices—everyone goes through this professional time period of great uncertainty. Rather, we want to emphasize the importance of a lot of reflective practice in the ambiguous world of the helping professions. This difference between the novice and expert is discussed under Theme 5 in Chapter 10: The cognitive map changes: Beginning practitioners rely on external expertise; seasoned practitioners rely on internal expertise.

Slowly and continually, and then more and more, internal expertise replaces external expertise. This is a very exciting change in the lives of practitioners. Yet sometimes practitioners do not recognize the shift, because it is usually slow and incremental. Also, expertise in the people-oriented professions is often described as coming from empirical research and theoretical work developed by others, rather than one's own professional experience. And, yes, expertise does come from these latter sources, but the expertise is mediated more and more by the rich professional experiences of the practitioner. In fact, the American Psychological Association's (2005) definition of evidence-based practice now has a stronger emphasis on the practitioner's clinical expertise than did previous versions of the definition. Over years of practice, experience-based generalizations and accumulated wisdom become more important than research and global theory developed by others, because expertise entails a "rich structure of domain specific knowledge" (Glaser & Chi, 1988, p. xxi).

The *good news* is that internalization of expertise leads to being faster in doing the work—the experienced cab driver immediately knows how to get to a particular street address while the beginner must consult the Global Positioning System, ask the dispatcher, or use conventional routes. In counseling and therapy work, this internalization of expertise results in less anxious practitioners because they have more sense of control and self-efficacy. In the occupational stress literature, lack of control is a strong predictor of more stress.

The *bad news* is that developing expertise takes so much time. Ten thousand hours is a number used as a benchmark for expertise for all complex tasks. Another number is ten years, which came out of a study of the years of work necessary to become exceptional at chess (Colvin, 2010). It is thought that it takes about ten years to get 10,000 hours of doing the core work. In his book—*Outliers: The Story of Success*, Gladwell (2008) quotes the neurologist Daniel Levitin as saying:

The emerging picture . . . is that ten thousand hours of practice is required to achieve the level of mastery associated with being a world-class expert—-in anything. In study after study, of composers, basketball players, fiction writers, ice skaters, concert pianists, chess players, master criminals and what have you, this number comes up again and again. Of course, this does not address why some people get more out of their practice sessions than others do. But no one has yet found a case in which true world-class expertise was accomplished in less time. It seems that it takes the brain this long to assimilate all that it needs to know to achieve true mastery.

—*cited in Gladwell, 2008, p. 40*

As Gladwell (2008) says, "Ten thousand hours is an *enormous* amount of time" (p. 42).

The Wish for an Expertise Injection

As also stated in other places in this book, Tom has often wished that he had an expertise injection that he could give to graduate students starting their first practicum in counseling and therapy. It would take away so much of the roller-coaster emotions that beginners have in seeing their first clients. It would take away so much of the anxiety, insecurity, confusion, and preoccupation that possess beginners. Unfortunately, no injection can replicate the complete internal schema of each person who is a therapist or counselor with 10,000 hours of experience.

Often, the large amount of experience is accumulated in an intensity of activity. "Mozart became Mozart by working furiously hard" (A. Ross, cited by Colvin, 2010, p. 19). Here is another example from music. After leaving his small Minnesota hometown for college, Bob Dylan went to Minneapolis to go to the University of Minnesota. Instead of going to class, he played music—*all the time*. A few years later, he moved to New York, lived wherever he could, and played music *all the time* (Sounes, 2002). As Gladwell (2008) notes in *Outliers*, as a college student, in the days before personal computers and laptops, Sun Microsystems cofounder Billy Joy would stay up all night, night after night, programming at the college mainframe computer. Bill Gates did the same. Each was working on a complex task, hour after hour. Gladwell (2008) discusses the Beatles and their key to success being the eight-hour—day after day— gigs they did in Hamburg, Germany. Gladwell quotes John Lennon as saying: "We got better and more confident. We couldn't help it with all the experience playing all night long" (p. 49).

Jackie Stiles is a basketball legend who holds the National College Athletic Association record for most career points at 3,393. As a junior in high school, Jackie scored 61 points in 17 minutes of the season's opening game. She is another example of the intense, long-term effort needed for excellence. In college, she practiced and practiced her shot and did not quit until she made hundreds of shots (Stewart, 2002).

Graduate students can relate to this idea of working hard. A key to graduate school is, simply put, working hard for a long period of time.

Related to this concept of lots of experience changing the person's way of working is the idea that knowledge changes and practitioners go from being receivers of ideas to producers of ideas. To help explain this concept, we mention a model of knowing developed by Belenky, Clinchy, Goldberger, and Tarule (1986), based on Perry's (1970) model of cognitive meaning and development. (This work was also discussed in Chapter 10 of this book.) Beginning practitioners, as new students, seem to fit the entry level:

> While received knowers can be very open to take in what others have to offer, they have very little confidence in their own ability to speak. Believing that truth comes from others, they still their own voices to hear the voices of others. (Belenky et al., 1986, p. 37)

Senior practitioners seem to fit the highest level.

> All knowledge is constructed, and the knower is an intimate part of the known. . . . To see that all knowledge is a construction and that truth is a matter of the context in which it is embedded is to greatly expand the possibilities of how to think about anything . . . theories become not truth but models for approximate experience. (Belenky et al., 1986, pp. 137–139)

This model of ways of knowing is another way of looking at the impact of many years of work as a practitioner and how this movement from external expertise to internal expertise profoundly affects the practitioner's functioning.

4. Experts Have Superior Memory

It seems that the memory structure of experts permits them to be more efficient at recall. The more a skill is practiced, the less attention needs to be paid to the conscious performance of it, which frees up memory capacity that can be focused on other, perhaps more important yet not quite as salient, elements of a problem (Skovholt et al., 2004). The automaticity of these overpracticed skills and their unconscious successful completion allow experts to apply significant amounts of energy to other valuable cognitive tasks, such as retrieving relevant information from long-term memory, examining its relevance to the current problem, and performing the executive mental functions related to weighing options and making decisions (Skovholt et al., 2004). Feltovich et al. (2006) articulate this capacity by stating; "[A]utomaticity is central to the development of expertise, and practice is the means to automaticity" (p. 53).

5. Experts See and Represent a Problem in Their Domain at a Deeper (More Principled) Level

When trying to understand a problem and how to respond to it, experts tend to assess it from a more meaningful perspective, one that is more conducive to seeing solutions embedded in the problem itself; in contrast, novice analyses are based more on more obvious features (Skovholt et al., 2004). Relevant to this concept is the research cited by Feltovich et al. (2006), which examined the performance of individuals with varying levels of experience in bridge. In these studies, players were briefly presented representations of bridge deals and then requested to reproduce the hands. Experts tended to reproduce the hands based on suit, whereas novices were more apt to recall the cards by order of rank—an organization that is not pertinent to the tactical characteristics of the game.

6. Experts Spend a Great Deal of Time Analyzing a Problem Qualitatively

Research has suggested that experts strive more than novices to form an enhanced appreciation of the problem by devoting greater amounts of study when first faced with a problem before attempting to solve it. Experts examine the problem from multiple perspectives and compare it to previous situations before implementing a solution (Glaser & Chi, 1988). The research of Hill and Ridley (2001) in the field of diagnostic psychology provides an example. While examining the performance of mental health clinicians, they found that those individuals who reached their diagnostic assessments late in the process of therapy were more accurate than those who arrived at their conclusions earlier. Unlike novices who do not have the experience base on which to form a diagnostic picture, and who must rely strictly on theoretical knowledge learned in the classroom, expert clinicians use these very complex delineations as the basis from which to develop their final diagnoses.

As we try to understand expertise and its development, we must remember that there is much conflicting data about whether more professional experience does produce more expertise. Consider the Spengler et al. (2009a) meta-analysis of clinical judgment ability. The authors found significantly more experience did not produce better outcome !

Paige and Simon (1966) found that, when facing a potential problem, experts quickly establish complex mental representations of its fundamental aspects from which they accurately define and assess its critical elements. This process of identifying the most salient qualities of the problem facilitates both rapid conceptualization of the situation and identification of solutions that seem to be interlaced within the problem itself. The result is a drastic reduction in the time spent on disproportionate or unjustifiable solutions (as cited in Skovholt et al., 2004).

In a chapter by Scardamalia and Bereiter (1991) on literate expertise, the authors found that, as compared to novices, expert writers generally apply more effort in the planning and problem-solving stages of a task. Experts tend to take more time to begin writing the first sentence and take far longer to complete a simple essay than those with less experience. In addition to these findings, the researchers also discovered that experts take time after successful problem resolution seemingly extracting knowledge from the experience that they can generalize to other similar problems in the future. Scardamalia and Bereiter hypothesize that nonexperts often fail to learn from their experiences because they do not apply this strategy.

7. Experts Have Strong Self-Monitoring Skills

Strong self-monitoring skills are the final characteristic of expertise as defined by Glaser and Chi (1988). Experts tend to have a good grasp of the limits of their knowledge regarding a specific problem. They also seem better able to assess the difficulty of the problem. Although when faced with a problem, experts generally spend more time in the beginning stages analyzing it from multiple angles, their strategies ultimately lead to greater time savings. You may wonder, How does that work? It seems that experts spend less time pursuing solutions that ultimately are ineffective and end up as dead ends. Because they are aware of the limits of their knowledge, experts take appropriate steps to obtain the information necessary to make an intelligent choice among possible solutions. For example, in tasks of reading, it was found that experts take much longer to read a text; in effect, they backtrack during points of difficulty to pick up missing information. It is suggested that experts engage in these practices simply because they set for themselves the higher goal of profound comprehension and integration of new knowledge with old (Scardamalia & Bereiter, 1991).

Summary of the Seven Characteristics

Chi et al. (1988) provided a valuable overview of expertise in general in their aptly named book, *The Nature of Expertise*. Together, these seven attributes form what we could call an *E* factor for expertise, similar to the previously mentioned Spearman *G* factor in intelligence.

STAGES OF EXPERTISE

In a 1986 book, two brothers, one a philosopher and the other a computer scientist, collaborated in an argument against a computer model at the time. Hubert and Stuart Dreyfus insisted that the expertise of human beings was intrinsically different from that of expert computer systems. By design, historically computers process information in a serial fashion, one piece at a time, and are not able to learn or actively discard the rules they are intended to follow. Computers cannot act intuitively or think in holistic terms. As Dennett (1991) states: "It seems that no mere machine, no matter how accurately it mimicked the brain processes of the human wine taster, would be capable of appreciating a wine, or a Beethoven sonata, or a basketball game" (p. 31).

Conversely, human beings process an enormous amount of bits of information at the same time, a capability that is imperative for daily functioning. Imagine the simple act of crossing the street if we were capable of processing only one piece of information at a time. While concentrating solely on moving our legs one at a time in a smooth fashion to travel from one side of the street to the other, we would not be able to either see or hear the car that is about to hit us when we step off the curb. It is precisely because we process information in parallel that we are able to learn new skills, develop new talents, and accurately assess each new situation as it is presented to us. For example, expert professional baseball pitchers, winners of such awards as the annual Cy Young award, must be able to fluidly and simultaneously process multiple pieces of information (base runner positions, defensive positions of teammates, and batter tendencies) in order to determine the best type of pitch to throw. Only then can pitchers focus at the deeper level and deliver the pitch consistently. This ability—to learn not only the mechanics of a particular skill but to reflect on what we know and then also to know what is needed to progress to the next level—is uniquely human. While some species of animal have demonstrated varying degrees of cognitive ability (e.g. apes, African gray parrots, crows, and even octopi) (Morell, 2008), only humans have developed the inimitable ability to self-reflect, to know *that* they know, to know *what* they know, and to *design* future learning so that their progress will continue along the most beneficial path.

The Dreyfus brothers (1986) suggest that humans progress through five stages of development toward expertise: the novice, the advanced beginner, competent, proficient, and expert. Their model proposes that individuals at the beginning stages process information in an "objective and context free" manner and gradually progress to a state where their decisions are based more on rich "subjective contextual cues."

Dreyfus and Dreyfus (1986) describe novices as people who are somewhat more apt than those with experience to adhere to the rules blindly, giving little regard to the overall circumstances; in effect, they are unable to see the forest for the trees. Beginners, strongly motivated by a desire to "do a good job," do not have the ability to consider the situation from multiple perspectives and consequently make decisions based on surface-level information and judge their own performance by how closely they follow the rules.

The use of rules operates paradoxically as people try to become more expert. While the rules allow novices to successfully complete tasks and accumulate experience, progress dictates that novices sometimes use these rules less rigidly in order to progress beyond the basic ability level. This need to put aside the procedures—the rules that people have used to get where they are—is very difficult for some. For example, some people have excelled in school because they followed the teacher's assignments perfectly and did exactly what they were told to do, at a very high level. Here is the problem: What if moving up the path of expertise demands a rebellion against the strict structure one has been given? What if increased competence demands novel forms? Sometimes people have to put aside what they have learned in order to develop further. Some individuals are great at following rules for beginners but really struggle at putting them aside.

We remember a beloved professor at the University of Minnesota, Jim Rest, who would tell the new doctoral students that getting A's was important in order to get into the doctoral program. Rest said that, after getting into the program, grades were not so important. There were other ways to develop at the next level. However, Rest found that many doctoral students could not let go of the school structure of excelling in the narrow structure of classes. They felt most comfortable following the rules they knew over many years as students.

In the application of psychological theories of counseling, for example, novices may adhere very closely to techniques and methodologies that have been learned in classes without considering the gap between theory and practice. The complex contextual information of the actual work with a real client can change everything. It is experience, supervision and training, and the application of those unique human qualities of reflection and self-monitoring that move people through this initial stage of development to the next: the advanced beginner.

As advanced beginners, therapists are better equipped to consider the rich contextual information available in the counseling setting and integrate it with the academic theories that form the foundation of their own developing approach to counseling (Fook, Ryan, & Hawkins, 1997, as cited in Skovholt et al., 2004). In defining characteristics of the master therapist, Jennings and Skovholt (1999) posit that an essential factor in this developmental process relates to the "cognitive processes that help organize and access that knowledge base" (p. 4). It is these developing cognitive processes that make it possible for less experienced people to become increasingly more comfortable with uncertainty and to begin assessing situations more accurately.

The Competent Stage is defined by the development of hierarchical decision-making skills (Dreyfus & Dreyfus, 1986). Unlike novices who make decisions from limited, objective, and context-free information, those in the Competent Stage can make better-informed, effective decisions, holistic decisions that are based on an ability to see the forest, not just a collection of individual trees. During this stage, self-reflection begins to take a more prominent role in the aspiring experts' expanding world of mental representations. In this way, through an increasingly intimate relationship with ambiguity, those in this stage begin to respond more efficiently in crucial conditions (Feltovich et al., 2006). They begin to carefully examine the diversity of their accumulated academic knowledge and practical experience and to creatively determine which factors are most pertinent to the work with clients.

In the Proficient Stage, people's development of intuition—a skill based on hundreds and hundreds of hours of professional experience—approaches the level of experts. Dreyfus and Dreyfus (1986) characterize this stage as one in which individuals develop a higher skill of expertise marked by the rapid and fluid behavior representative of expert problem solving. It is suggested that persons in this stage evaluate problems as holistic patterns without reducing them to their constituent elements. Here, practitioners are able to grasp, seemingly without effort, holistic patterns that represent the most important part of the situation. Dreyfus and Dreyfus argue that computer programs, regardless of the efficiency of processing or the complexity of programming, will never develop the deeper understanding capabilities of the human being. This reflective aptitude is the exclusive realm of human cognition. The complex schemata of talented practitioners allow recognition of more subtle features of a situation simultaneously with the rapid and accurate assessment of problem conditions.

What really is "knowledge," a word we use over and over again? Holyoak (1991) described knowledge as a collection of successful problem resolutions that are stored in memory and characterize the cognitive rules that, when implemented in similar situations, will lead to the continuing development of even more efficient solutions for the future.

The evolution of these production rules is the direct result of hundreds of hours of experience in the domain and the distinctly human ability to reflect on what we know and then make decisions that continually enhance and expand our base of knowledge. Expertise, and the effective use of metacognition, involves determining what information is useful and what is tangential to the situation at hand (Feltovich et al., 2006).

The final stage of Dreyfus and Dreyfus (1986), expertise, represents the evolution of individuals through the accumulation of knowledge and experience of all previous stages. This stage represents the persistence of the lessons from all other stages. It is a phase in which increased emphasis is placed on critical self-reflection, and is marked by what Skovholt and Rønnestad (1995) referred to as "wisdom." When individuals reach this stage, knowledge gained through school and practical experience has become fully integrated with motivation, intuition, and a significant accrual of tacit knowledge (the knowledge of internal reflection). Feltovich et al. (2006) describe this as "unencumbered elegance"—experts can perform so efficiently to adapt to various conditions through the effective application of finely developed metacognitive skills.

NOVICE VERSUS EXPERT DIFFERENCES

One way to think of novice versus expert differences in counseling and therapy is to imagine looking at a movie screen. On the screen is the client addressing the practitioner in the first session. The client starts talking, and continues describing more and more elements of his or her life. The novice looks overwhelmed—the client's words keep coming—and so much of the content seems important. Just as the novice begins conceptualizing one problem area, the client starts on a different topic. So much is coming at the novice and so much seems of possible importance. The situation often is exhausting and frightening for the novice.

In contrast, experts have been in a first interview with a new client hundreds of times. They have developed a schema of what really matters in the first interview and what is secondary or of even less importance. The experts are not trying to grasp everything because a lot of it is not important to the work of the first interview. So, as the data come at the experts, they feel less urgency to get everything. Therefore, the work is less exhausting. In such a situation, the experts' high experience makes the work more pleasurable. (Note, however, that clear novice advantages also exist. See Chapter 2 of this book.)

Sometimes novices enter the people-oriented professions with considerable prior experience in human services, teaching, healthcare, or a related field where interpersonal skills are central to the work. Others begin as counseling/therapy novices with little relevant work experience. Younger, less experienced novices usually feel the next description most acutely.

Beginning as novices with only theoretical and methodological knowledge, practitioners in training are immersed into a practical experiential world like clothes being thrown into a washing machine. Suddenly, and inevitably, there are situations of increasing difficulty. Valuable experience is gained through this immersion. Client reaction and client outcome tend to vary, as do the application, many times, of hit-and-miss solutions.

Experience can be golden if new practitioners are able, with each success or failure, to store the information in memory in order to use it in disentangling future ambiguity. The phenomenon of ambiguity compels these practitioners to learn and know more, lest they give up due to intolerable frustration.

This sense of intolerable frustration can lead to routes that reduce the distress but ultimately are not as productive for practitioner development. Navigating through failures (real or imagined) is essential to the progress of individuals if the goal is expertise. As Skovholt and Rønnestad (1995) point out, a common crisis occurs when a theoretical approach employed by aspiring therapists does not lead to significant improvements in the client's symptoms. Because the therapists have worked hard to master these techniques, the lack of improvement leads them to search for the cause of the failure. "The quality of this search affects whether stagnation or development is likely to occur" (p. 130).

As ambiguity, by nature, increases in relation to problem complexity, it is the tacit knowledge, the knowledge from practice obtained through perceived success and failure as a practitioner, that becomes the most constructive element in maturity through each phase of development. *Tacit knowledge*, a term coined by Polanyi (2002) in the 1950s, describes the kind of knowledge that one acquires by extensive practice. Here is an example: As a driver enters a busy intersection while driving a car, multiple concerns of various levels of importance shift. How to describe in writing the process of driving through an intersection is very difficult. Watching a skilled driver is a better method, because by doing so one can pick up many verbal and nonverbal contextual cues.

As people move closer to the attainment of expertise, ambiguity can still be present. Readers may be distressed to read this and think: "Just as I get better, things get more confusing!" Actually, the process is more like this: As you get better and feel more competent, you can let things be as ambiguous as they are in reality. You do not need to put them in clear boxes. Problems become more easily resolved because people are better equipped to accurately interpret all contributing variables and, therefore, engage less and less in unproductive blind-alley solutions.

CARL SAGAN AS EXAMPLE OF AN EXPERT

Carl Sagan became a famous teacher of science topics on television. At the age of 5, he attended the World's Fair with his parents and was immediately enchanted by the romance of science. From that moment, his life consisted of a never-ending series of questions, most of which began simply as "Why?" or "How?" He was fascinated by the thought that the twinkling lights of the night sky were actually suns burning at tremendous distances from earth. This reality staggered his imagination. He was intrigued by the idea of evolution, that all creatures had progressed from a common origin to the multiplicity of life-forms that currently populate the earth: It gave him a profound sense of humility. He questioned whether, with the billions of possible planetary systems within our galaxy, we are alone in the universe. He questioned everything and pursued answers for the rest of his life. He made a career of asking questions, with the understanding that the most he could hope for was a successive improvement in his understanding with each new answer.

He knew that regardless of how far he traveled; of the nature or quantity of his questions; of his perseverance; of his age, creativity, intelligence, or wisdom, he might never arrive at the final, ultimate truth. Undaunted by this realization, however, the prospects for his future exhilarated him. He recognized the exciting prospect of infinite knowledge, and his life became a marriage between skepticism and wonder (Sagan, 1996).

Sagan was aware that with each new discovery, his knowledge increased and that each of these incremental increases served as the step to a new understanding of the world. This incremental progress motivated him and kept him excited about what new discoveries would be made tomorrow, next month, or next year. He was never content to accept that his current understanding was complete but always sought to learn more, to increase his knowledge and thereby his wisdom.

Considered an expert by many of his contemporaries, Sagan knew that this status was contingent on his ability to continually accommodate new information, thereby evolving his understanding and positioning himself to better help others in their understanding of the universe. Rather than becoming discouraged by the ambiguity inherent in the scientific endeavor, he was motivated by it; for him it presented a world of never-ending possibilities! He knew that inherent in the nature of the novice was an absence of domain-specific knowledge and experience. He knew also that successful attainment of expertise would depend as much on willingness and ability to learn and adopt the theories and principles specific to a field of study as it would on certain underlying innate qualities.

This process can be conceptualized as a sort of cognitive scaffolding (Feltovich et al., 2006) in which knowledge builds on itself, with previous experiences providing support for new information, which in turn supports and strengthens the very knowledge that gave it birth. Implicit in this concept is the understanding that something will inevitably be missing at every level of the scaffold, and that becoming proficient in any domain will require persistent pursuit of additional information. There is a scaffolding of implicit knowledge interwoven throughout the scaffold that essentially holds it together. People's ability to sustain motivation over extended periods of time as they strive to integrate past domain-specific knowledge with information gained through the experience and resolution of more recent problems is critical.

Sagan's endeavor was satisfying, and fulfilled him throughout his life. Quite possibly, this trait, the intrigue of ambiguity and what Skovholt, Jennings, and Mullenbach (2004) describe as the voracious learner, is part of what separates aspiring experts from the ordinary.

MASTER THERAPIST STUDIES

The aim of a skilled performance is achieved by the observation of a set of rules which are not known as such to the person following them.

—*Polanyi, 2002, p. 49*

[I]t appears that "common factors" and the individual therapist account for dramatically more of the variance in therapy outcome than do the particular treatments.

—*Lichtenberg & Wampold, 2002, p. 310*

The observation from Polanyi highlights one difficulty in studying high-level performance. Sometimes experts cannot describe their own expertise because it is so much a part of them. Yet, given this difficulty, the study of master therapists is important!

In 1995, Len Jennings began what we believe to be the first research-based study of therapy and counseling master practitioners.* (We use the words "master" and "expert" interchangeably.) Until recently, over many decades in the therapy and counseling professions, expertise was closely related to how well practitioners were able to adhere to a specific theoretical approach. For example, the goal was to be more Rogerian than Rogers, or at least as close to the master as possible. Graduate courses, workshops, and clinical supervision were all oriented to learning and following a method. To this end, dissertations were written on how closely people were able to follow the master using

---

*Some of the material in this section was originally published in T. M. Skovholt, L. Jennings, and M. Mullenbach (2004), "Portrait of the Master Therapist: The Highly-Functioning Self," in T. M. Skovholt and L. Jennings (Eds.), *Master Therapists: Exploring Expertise in Therapy and Counseling* (pp. 125–146). Boston, MA: Allyn & Bacon.

scales to measure qualities such as empathy. Tom and his classmates, including Helge Rønnestad in the 1970s, wrote such dissertations. In those days, individual practitioners were vehicles in the delivery of a method. Now, in 2012, there is a new view of therapy and counseling expertise: The method is the vehicle for the delivery of the therapist.

When Jennings began his study, he used a peer-nomination approach to find ten master practitioners. Two other studies by Mary Mullenbach and Michael Sullivan were done on the same sample group. The methods for all three of these studies can be found in Skovholt and Jennings (2004). One of the strengths of these studies was the use of a competence measure to assess mastery. Usually, in the history of this profession, there was an equation between fame (e.g., Ellis) and mastery without a more research-based indication of expertise. For example, Skovholt and Jennings (2009) review a book where fame is used as the criterion for mastery. However, just because a person can write a book about a method, and give workshops on it, does not mean he or she is considered by peers as a great healer. (Note that a limitation of the Minnesota Master Therapist Studies is the lack of outcome measures to assess therapist effect; Spengler, White, Aegisdottir, & Maugherman, 2009b.)

Before we continue, we want to emphasize that the portrait that follows should be viewed as an ideal to strive for rather than a list of essential ingredients for any one individual. Every one of the ten master therapists studied did not possess every characteristic at the highest level. Rather, the master therapists had varying combinations of these characteristics. In the pages to come, we describe a prototypical portrait of mastery. Combining the efforts of the three dissertation projects during this time, the sample group was interviewed for over 100 hours. Each of the ten master therapists was interviewed an average of six times. Many, many more hours were devoted to research analysis of the interviews for the three dissertation projects and for a fourth project on ethics led by Jennings. In total, we estimate that 7,700 hours were devoted to this project. (A more detailed presentation of this portrait can be found in Skovholt, Jennings, and Mullenbach, 2004.)

Defining the Master Therapist

How should we define the term *master therapist*? We asked our expert group this question. One depicted master therapists this way:

> They are people who are not afraid to take risks. They are people who have a deeper understanding, a more universal understanding. They are people who have a lot of integrity. They are people who are comfortable with their power, and comfortable using it. . . . I think they're people who stretch themselves and stretch other people to go beyond what they think is possible . . . give a sense of hope. . . . It's a combination of challenge and giving that other piece that helps the other person feel not alone and to feel it is possible to do or achieve.
>
> —*Jennings, 1996, p. 111*

Another looked at the question from the perspective of choosing a therapist for herself and said:

> I'd want somebody that's accepting, somebody that's smart, somebody that's interesting, curious, stays informed, somebody who takes care of themselves, so that they have some energy to give; somebody who has that blend of being compassionate and empathetic, but also challenging. Somebody who's available. . . . Somebody that's wise. . . kindness, humility is a good word. . . . Willing to listen and grow, I'm thinking, an ability to see uniqueness.
>
> —*Jennings, 1996, pp. 111–112*

How can we describe master therapists' personal lives?

Significant but Not Overwhelming Stress Present in the Early Years

There may have been distress in the family or community: a person with a disability, part of a stigmatized group, in a distressed marriage, with an addiction, mourning a death, or social isolation from peers. In some form, human suffering seems to have been a companion for many of these individuals early in life.

> I think about all that I suffered as a child, the ways in which I felt I didn't get much that I wanted [yet] there was a solid sense that I always knew that my parents were grownup, I didn't have to be the grownup. I knew that I lived in a system that was basically just and fair.
>
> —*Mullenbach, 2000, p. 71*

Another example of some pain, but not too much, as ideal for early personal development comes from this master therapist:

> I think that [if] the therapist's life is one of deprivation and isolation and pain, I don't think it would work [to become an expert therapist]. However, I think this profession wouldn't be of interest if someone didn't know about emotional pain on a very personal level.
>
> —*Jennings, 1996, p. 101*

Reaction to Early Stress Was to Process Rather Than Cut Off

Many of these master therapists reported complex and stressful lives during the developmental years. Yet the level of stress was not so great that they chose to distance themselves from intense human relationships. Looking back, one person said about the positive aspects of the environment: "[I]t does not allow you to shut down, it does not allow you to build a fortress where you don't feel" (Mullenbach, 2000, p. 71). Faced with severe stress, another route is to stop the processing by use of emotional cutoffs. The master therapists studied did not take this route.

Taking on the Role of Helper

Members of our sample group may have been given or taken the family role of helper for others. Doing so meant they needed to attune themselves to others. For example, one master therapist said: "[P]art of what I tried to do in my youth was save my family, every way that I thought I could help be better in the family" (Mullenbach, 2000, p. 71).

Being assigned the role of helper meant early training in seeing the world through the eyes of the other and attempting to make things better. The practicum in helping started early. In our research, the earliest account of trying to help is this:

> [T]here are stories about me before he [the participant's father] died, I was four or five, going in one day when he was in bed sick, and without saying anything pulling down the shade because the sun was shining in his eyes. So I had it [emotional sensitivity], and I don't know where that came from precisely.
>
> *—Jennings, 1996, p. 100*

The master therapists may have had many years of experience by the time they started formal training. Imagine how far ahead such people are in graduate school, compared to peers who are just starting the helping role in their first practicum. One master therapist expressed this sentiment: "I know I'll be able to do this work because I'd already come out of that kind of environment [of helping others]. I already knew I could relate to a whole lot of the world" (Mullenbach, 2000, p. 70).

Human Suffering as a Positive Part of a Deep and Meaningful Life

Personal experiences with suffering during the developmental years may have made it easier for these master therapists to relate to the suffering world of clients. These masters may have been less frightened than people with other developmental histories. As one master therapist said: "I learned to see suffering as valuable" (Mullenbach, 2000, p. 81). Another said about suffering:

> It deepens me. I feel I understand pain awfully well. I think I know the issue isn't pain or suffering, the issue is not having to do it by yourself. It's really about . . . knowing that you're not alone in that core place.
>
> *—Mullenbach, 2000, p. 81*

About client suffering, a third said:

I think all in all, it leaves me with a certain kind of enthusiasm because I see people go through extraordinary pain and come out the other side.

—*Mullenbach, 2000, p. 81*

Overall, the early developmental years seemed to provide a laboratory for intensive learning about human life and early therapist development. A form of significant but not overwhelming stress was present. The people took on the role of helper, or at least acute observer of human behavior, and their approach involved immersion in human feelings rather than distancing and cutoff.

Early Professional Life

What characterized these master therapists' early professional development years? One key seems to be the buffering effect of strong mentoring against the elevated stressors of the novice practitioner. Here is a glimpse of the early vulnerability.

It was harder to do [apologize for mistakes] when I was less secure, probably less proficient and less adept as well.

—*Sullivan, 2000, p. 93*

Mentoring from Teachers, Supervisors, and Seniors

I remember those as good years. I'm sure they were stressful because a lot was new, but I felt very supported.

—*Mullenbach, 2000, p. 82*

Another said:

[A]t my first job, I was fortunate enough to have a really fine supervisor who I credit with the major amount of training and experience that I have. And that was totally geared to emotional self-awareness and use of self in ways in which I grew. . . . [I]t opened all the doors for me, and it also made what I was doing very vital and real, and I feel real grateful for that.

—*Mullenbach, 2000, p. 83*

A third said about mentoring in the early years:

I think that I had the good fortune or the good judgment to join a group of senior clinicians, all people 20 years older than I, very experienced. . . . [T]hey gave me the depth and breadth of clinical experience and an understanding of how practice works, and it was very important to me.

—*Mullenbach, 2000, p. 83*

A fourth said:

> [T]here were people along the way who believed in me and engaged with me because they believed in me. And I really thrived on that, more than I knew in the moment. I got so much from that. If I hadn't gotten that, my life . . . would have taken a different path.
>
> —*Mullenbach, 2000, p. 83*

PORTRAIT OF THE MASTER THERAPIST

The next portrait is a summary of characteristics of the ten master therapists (see Figure 11.1). First, we will start with what from the research process we described as Paradoxical Characteristics:

Some Important Paradoxical Characteristics
- Possess a drive to mastery yet never have a sense of having fully arrived—like traveling on an endless path.
- Have the ability to deeply enter the inner world of another, while often preferring solitude.
- Provide an emotionally safe environment for a client and yet can firmly challenge when necessary.
- Are highly skilled at harnessing the power of therapy to help others, while remaining quite humble.

Figure 11.1   Master Therapist Paradoxical Characteristics

Drive to mastery	**AND**	Never a sense of having fully arrived
Able to deeply enter another's world	**AND**	Often prefers solitude
Can create a very safe client environment	**AND**	Can create a very challenging client environment
Highly skilled at harnessing the power of therapy	**AND**	Quite humble about self
Integration of the professional/personal self	**AND**	Clear boundaries between the professional/personal self
Voracious broad learner	**AND**	Focused, narrow student
Excellent at giving of self	**AND**	Great at nurturing self
Very open to feedback about self	**AND**	Not destabilized by feedback about self

Source: Skovholt, Jennings, & Mullenbach, 2004, p. 132.

- Can thoroughly integrate the personal and professional selves yet with set clear boundaries between these worlds.
- Are voracious learners who often direct this energy to broad learning, as well as specific work-related topics.
- Excel at giving of self to others while nurturing a private self.
- Are very open to feedback about self, yet not personally destabilized by it.

SOME IMPORTANT CENTRAL CHARACTERISTICS

We describe the central characteristics using the three domains of Cognitive (C), Emotional (E), and Relational (R) (see Figure 11.2). An earlier description of this three-part CER model can be found in Jennings and Skovholt (2004).

Cognitive Central Characteristics

We will now describe the characteristics in Figure 11.2.

Figure 11.2 Master Therapist Central Characteristics

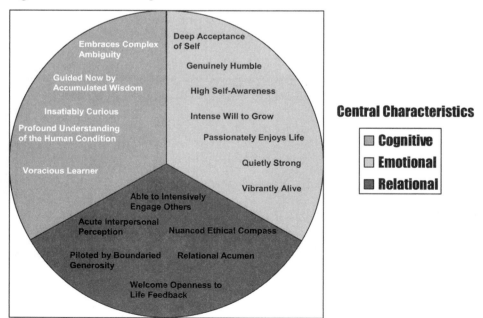

Embraces Complex Ambiguity

In Figure 11.2, both the known and unknown worlds have expanded. Just as answers have expanded, so have questions. There is a comfort with not knowing everything and an ability to not have answers for everything.

Guided Now by Accumulated Wisdom

The idea of wisdom fits well here with the definition by Bales and Staudinger (2000) of "wisdom as expertise in the fundamental pragmatics of life" (p. 124). Reflected data, book learning, and synthesized life experience have produced wisdom about human life, a deeper understanding.

Insatiably Curious

A simmering hunger for seeking, knowing, and for what is around the next corner seems present; at times it bursts out as intense curiosity. *Eager to learn, lifelong learner, active learner* are other terms that are appropriate for these therapists, who are eager to take on learning opportunities.

Profound Understanding of the Human Condition

Wisdom is in the center of this characteristic. Averaging 59 years in age at the time of the sampling, the therapists are experienced people, experienced in life. They have an acceptance, understanding, and appreciation of the wide latitude of ways that children, adolescents, and adults cope, manage, and interpret human life. Often a profound religious or spiritual dimension anchors their deeper and nuanced understanding of the human condition.

Voracious Learner

Learning is enthusiastically embraced as a magnificent renewal force. The world—everywhere and anywhere—is a potential classroom for the intensely inquisitive master therapist. Much of the learning is in the professional sphere; other learning is applied to the professional sphere.

Emotional Central Characteristics

Deep Acceptance of Self

What master therapists offer to others—acceptance—they provide for themselves. They have done the work to get there. Accepting the warts of the self takes pressure off the individual. Master therapists would talk of their failure experiences with clients with a sense that it was unfortunate but also real. For example, through experience, one master therapist learned she could not work with addicts. Rather than keep trying, she referred them elsewhere. Acknowledging and accepting weaknesses seemed to be a part of the picture.

Genuinely Humble

Self-consciousness about being described by others as master therapists indicates a self-perception of humility and their own humanness. Arrogance and its first cousin, narcissism, are seen as dangerous stances for therapists and are therefore actively resisted.

High Self-Awareness

Here we are describing a person who is highly observant of self. It is not a self-absorbed, narcissistic quality or the stance of an "intrusive shrink." These master therapists view knowing the self as an ethical duty. They are very introspective. This awareness of self is multidimensional, as seen in their demeanor and physical and verbal expression.

Intense Will to Grow

A central catalyst for mastery is an intense motivation to live a competent life. These therapists have dedicated decades to a concentrated will to grow. A parallel level of motivation is discussed in the gifted and talented literature with the term "rage to master" (Winner, 2000). Over the years of practice, preferred methods of growth have included participation in consultation, supervision, and personal therapy. High-level functioning is the outcome of the intense will to grow, which has been in operation for many years.

Passionately Enjoys Life

"Fun" is a big word here. "Zesty," "pleasure," "humor" are other descriptors. Master therapists seek novel experiences and seem to be healthy, happy people.

Quietly Strong

These individuals fight effectively against the raging power of clients' ineffective coping patterns—the hardened categories of coping possessed by many people who seek therapy help. Master therapists possess a toughness to continue excavating the pain when necessary. In the dissertation by Sullivan (2002), this strength is described within the Challenging Relationship Domain.

Vibrantly Alive

Master therapists can be described as energetic, and energetic for life. They have a deep appreciation for the entire human experience and really enjoy being alive. They are well-rounded, alert, and animated.

Relationship Central Characteristics

Able to Intensively Engage Others

An appetite for engaging others is present in these master therapists. Often it functions as an open willingness to be very present in the lives of others. A fondness for the interactive dimension of human life marks the lives of the master therapists.

Professionally, they are skilled and insightful as the therapeutic relationship is being formed, maintained, and ending. They are able to make clients feel very comfortable and very important.

Acute Interpersonal Perception

Hallmarks of the profession are interpersonal perception as well as the capacity to engage others, described earlier. Master therapists are able to quickly discern the emotional atmosphere and the interpersonal dynamics. These very human qualities, which master therapists hone to a level high above the norm, enable them to work with mastery.

Nuanced Ethical Compass

In master therapists, the moral compass is internal and deeply embedded in higher moral principles or virtue ethics. There is not an immediate turn to ordinary rules or worry about pleasing others. If this means risk taking, then they very seriously consider the risk. Their ethical beliefs permeated the interviews.

Piloted by Boundaried Generosity

Master therapists are kind-hearted, compassionate people. Within the professional therapy relationship, there is a commitment, generosity, and energy for clients. Yet there is also clarity about whose work is whose work—there is work for the therapist and work for the client.

Relational Acumen

The ability to "dance" with clients, using a wide variety of styles to fit with the other, marks master practitioners. In therapy language, this is often described as an accurate use of dose and timing. They are masterful at the relationship stances with clients.

Welcome Openness to Life Feedback

Master therapists are motivated to grow even if it is difficult. The ability to assimilate new information and constantly rebuild the framework is present in master therapists; they are not rigid. Professionally, they can learn from others, both clients and peers. They are able to integrate feedback—positive and negative—into an expanded understanding of self.

IMPLICATIONS OF THE MASTER THERAPIST PORTRAIT

Being a master therapist is just as much about optimal human development as it is about specific skill development within the narrow realm of the therapist's role. That was a big surprise for the researchers (Skovholt et al., 2004). We did not think its optimal human qualities would be so prominent in these portraits. We thought theoretical approach or an expertise with a specific population would rank more highly. What are examples of broader human development?

The development of wisdom is an example. Bales and Staudinger (2000) write: "We define wisdom as an expertise in the conduct and meaning of life. In this vein, wisdom is a key factor in the construction of a 'good life'" (p. 124). They go on to discuss how wisdom is about the fundamental pragmatics of life. This fits with our portrait of master therapists. Our results also dovetail with earlier descriptions from humanistic psychology of ideal human characteristics. For example, Jourard and Landsman (1980) list 15 characteristics of Maslow's self-actualized person. They are:

1. A low-defensiveness in perceiving reality
2. High acceptance of self, others and the realities of human nature
3. Spontaneity and naturalness
4. A focus on problems outside the self
5. Need for privacy
6. High degree of autonomy
7. Continual freshness of appreciation
8. Frequent "peak" experiences
9. A feeling of belonging—connecting to all humanity
10. A few close-loving relationships
11. Democratic character structure
12. Strong ethical sense
13. Nonhostile sense of humor
14. Creative/inventive
15. A resistance to enculturation

Overall, our findings of optimal human development parallel the new research in positive psychology. We would be remiss not to mention Rogers's (1961) model of the fully functioning person as described in his book *On Becoming a Person*. In this classic guide to personal growth and creativity, Rogers suggest that the fully functioning person approaches life as a process, not as an end point. He elaborates three parts: an increasing openness to experience, living fully in the moment (which he calls existential living), and an increased trust in oneself. Together, for Rogers, these three qualities produce the fully functioning person. These qualities, too, seem to fit with our master therapist portrait.

OTHER STUDIES OF MASTER THERAPISTS

Passionately Committed Therapists

Dlugos and Friedlander (2001) studied 12 therapists who received at least three peer nominations as "passionately committed." These therapists were not described as master therapists but rather as passionately committed. The results were described within four themes and categories of:

1. *Balance.* Maintaining physical and psychological boundaries between work and personal life. Recognition of the complementary of personal and personal development.
2. *Adaptiveness/Openness.* Obstacles as challenges and hunger for feedback. On an openness scale, the participants were 3 standard deviations above the mean for the normative population.
3. *Transcendence/Humility.* Here the spiritual nature of the work was most prominent.
4. *Intentional learning.* Personal and professional development described as complementary. A strong orientation to continual growth.

Singapore Master Therapist Study

Jennings et al. (2008) explored characteristics of Singaporean master therapists. Like other studies, the researchers used a combination of peer nomination and snowball sampling to identify master therapists. The criteria for nomination in Singapore were:

- Considered to be a master counselor
- Frequently thought of when referring a close friend or family member to a counselor because the person is considered the "best of the best"
- Would consider seeing the therapist for one's own personal therapy

Therapists who were nominated were asked in turn to nominate three master therapists. Among the total of 47 peer-nominated master therapists, 9 received 3 or more nominations. Thus, this distinct group of 9, each with 3 or more nominations, was chosen for the study.

Participants included five men and four women ranging in age from 40 to 59 years. Formal training among the master therapists varied greatly: There were two PhD clinical psychologists, one counseling psychologist, one master's-level social worker, two master's-level therapists, two bachelor's-level therapists, and one therapist with 34 years of applied training; experience ranged from 10 to 34 years. Each therapist was asked to respond to 18 open-ended questions, which were similar to those asked by Jennings and Skovholt (1999) regarding personal characteristics and therapy practices.

Using consensual qualitative research (Hill, Thompson, & Williams, 1997), the research team worked to identify themes through a consensus decision-making process for each master therapist. Researchers examined quotations and the number of therapists who represented each theme. Each theme was represented by at least four of the nine master therapists for a total of 16 themes within four categories.

The interview data indicated that Singaporean master therapists had several characteristics in these four categories: personal characteristics, developmental influences, approach to practice, and ongoing professional growth.

Personal Characteristics

The personal characteristics of Singaporean master therapists were: empathic, nonjudgmental, and respectful. They were mindful of expressing empathy and genuineness for clients, had a nonjudgmental attitude, and reflected on the importance of working with clients in a respectful way.

Developmental Influences

Singaporean master therapists emphasized four developmental influences: experience, self-awareness, humility, and self-doubt. They discussed the influence of learning from life experiences and self-awareness. Humility about one's limits and one's mistakes served as a source of growth. Having the experience of self-doubt encourages master therapists to keep growing their counseling skills.

Approach to Practice

Themes regarding the approach to practice included:

- Having a balance between support and challenge in working with clients
- Incorporating a flexible therapeutic stance in the work
- Utilizing an empowerment/strength-based approach
- Believing in the primacy of the therapeutic alliance
- Feeling comfortable addressing spirituality with clients
- Embracing a multicultural work context
- Having cultural awareness

Ongoing Professional Growth

Singaporean master therapists were mindful of professional growth, specifically professional development practices and the benefits of teaching/training others.

COMPARISON BETWEEN THE MINNESOTA AND SINGAPORE MASTER THERAPISTS

A qualitative meta-analysis was conducted to compare Jennings and Skovholt's (1999) Minnesota data on master therapists with the expertise findings in Singapore. Domains, categories, and themes from both studies were grouped together. This qualitative meta-analysis indicated several overlapping themes and categories to suggest a cross-cultural relationship between the studies.

The qualitative meta-analysis of the 25 themes between the studies revealed 12 themes that were strongly related between studies and 8 that were moderately related. The strongly and moderately related meta-analytic categories were relationship, therapeutic alliance, experience, professional development, humility, and self-awareness. These findings suggest that there may be underlying universal characteristics of expert psychotherapists despite cultural or nationality differences.

One difference related to working in a multicultural context. This was a theme in the Singapore study but not specified in the Minnesota sample. Singaporean master therapists embraced working within their multicultural context. This finding is not completely surprising, considering that Singapore is a country whose 4 million citizens, representing many ethnicities (Chinese, Malay, Indian, etc.) and religions (Buddhist, Taoist, Muslim, Hinduism, and Christianity), peacefully coexist on a very small island.

INGREDIENTS FOR MASTERY IN COUNSELING AND THERAPY

Next we present ideas for novices to consider about mastery. In this section we present a view of the novice-to-master therapist path and the markers along the way.

There are three preconditions for novice practitioners before setting out on the path toward mastery: (1) They must be relationship oriented; (2) they must be drawn to uncertainty; and (3) they must be affectively attuned to others.

Relationship Oriented

The work is so deeply interpersonal that a strong ability to relate well to others is a prerequisite. The Minnesota master therapists endorsed this perspective with comments such as: "The relationship is the whole thing," "I think that [the relationship] is . . . the most central part of psychotherapy" (Sullivan, 2000, p. 96), and "I have always maintained . . . that the primary tool that I use is the relationship. I have a lot of knowledge, I have a lot of skills, but they're wasted if the relationship isn't there" (Sullivan, 2000, p. 97).

Often the relationship focus starts early. Perhaps the therapist was inspired by a parent who was very skilled interpersonally. Perhaps the therapist benefited from the closeness of the family. Maybe a teacher served as a relationship model.

Drawn to Uncertainty

Sometimes trying to answer the simple question "How can I help people?" leads to a confusing, distressing, and lonely search through the fog. It is the fog of more questions than answers, the fog of the circle of not knowing expanding as fast as the circle of knowing, the fog of the reality of human complexity.

The helping professions are filled with uncertainty because of the complexity of human nature. Perhaps those of us in the helping fields should have worked with frogs or moles or loons—they are complicated enough. Humans! That is at a different level. It can be extremely stressful for high-achieving, doing-it-right, straight-A students suddenly to get hit with the human part of practicum. There is another person—the client—involved, and there is the interaction between the two individuals. That means there is uncertainty.

A basic condition for those in the helping fields is to have some comfort with ambiguity, because there is so much of it. Mark Vaughan, one of the coauthors of this chapter, calls this "the intrigue of ambiguity." The fog of not knowing can grow during a graduate school practicum. And it can start before graduate school with a human service job. And it can emerge later during one's career. It operates like a circle, there and then gone, then appearing later again.

Affectively Attuned to Others

The quality of being affectively attuned to others speaks for itself. The helping professions are about *helping others*. That is the core of the work. Being naturally empathic is central for expertise in therapy and counseling and other caring professions as well.

As discussed earlier in the chapter, often the capacity for empathy starts very early, as with childhood when the therapist felt caring and concern for the welfare of another family member. Perhaps a parent had frequent experiences of anxiety when addressing life dilemmas and the child tried to alleviate the parent's anxiety. Perhaps when young the therapist witnessed injustice being served to a parent and is asked to be empathetic toward the parent. Perhaps the therapist him- or herself suffered in one way or another and developed a depth of feeling as a result.

A great paradox of the work is that individuals are often drawn to the work because a personally meaningful part of their life has produced significant suffering. Perhaps they felt excluded by peers over and over again. Perhaps they failed in school and learned to know suffering this way. Perhaps they suddenly lost something of great value, like a home to foreclosure. These all can be valuable personal introductions to suffering. Yet at some point in a person's movement toward expertise as a helping professional, the focus must turn toward helping others.

These are preconditions, necessary qualities for people as they go forward on the path to mastery. Here are important markers on the road to mastery.

Marker 1: Rage to Master

Certain people put themselves through years or decades of punishing, intensive daily work that eventually makes them world-class great.

—Colvin, 2010, p. 204

A "rage to master" or "intense will to develop" is essential for mastery. Mastery takes concerted effort over a long period of time. It involves continual effort and increasingly difficult work tasks within the domain. This means there will be many periods of discouragement and failure for practitioners as well as times of great success, exhilaration, and praise by others. What keeps new practitioners pressing ahead? One ingredient is the rage to master, a term that comes from Winner (2000). Winner (2000) says: "Gifted children have a deep intrinsic motivation to master the domain in which they have high ability and are almost manic in their energy level. . . . This 'rage to master' characterizes children we have traditionally labeled gifted" (p. 163). In our Minnesota Master Therapists Sample, we found a similar intensity of motivation. Their "intense will to develop," over a long period of time, served as a major catalyst for their own mastery. We are reminded of the famous Thomas Edison quote about genius being 1% inspiration and 99% perspiration.

There is a snowball effect while on the path to mastery. As the person passes one marker, the possibility of getting to mastery increases.

Marker 2: Deliberate Practice Over Many Years

Two sayings are: "Practice makes perfect, no perfect practice makes perfect" and "All that you do, do with your might; things done in halves, are never done right." Both of these communicate the idea with Marker 2.

The job of the practitioner is to understand one of hundreds of versions of human behavior as expressed in the life of one person at one time. There can be so many options! After understanding, the task is to offer assistance to that person. Getting good at this takes a lot of time. Seasoned practitioners describe this long path in a highly engaging series of 15 first-person accounts edited by Goldfried (2001). The authors describe a wide variety of personal and professional events that served as channels for their development over many years.

Expertise in a particular domain is the result of years of study and exposure within that domain, which subsequently yields a high degree of specialized knowledge. We used Bob Dylan as an example earlier. In his biography of Bob Dylan, Spitz (1989) details the intense music playing of the young Dylan. Instead of going to class as a college student, Dylan played music and played music and played music. Through repeated practice, experts create complex cognitive representations within a domain, which subsequently allow them immediate access to integrated information relevant to a given situation or task (Feltovich et al., 2006).

Getting to an expert level requires lots and lots of practice at increasingly difficult levels—the scaffolding of skill, as Ericsson, Charness, Hoffman, & Feltovich (2006) state in their book, *The Cambridge Handbook of Expertise and Expert Performance*. The attainment of levels of performance that can be identified as expert requires a fervor to engage in rigorous, time-consuming practice sustained through periods of success as well as those of uncertainty and even failure (Ericsson & Lehmann, 1996, as cited in Feltovich et al., 2006).

This need to have extensive experience in the domain helps us understand why direct work with clients is so prized by practitioners. This is an inconvenient truth in the academic culture. In contrast to what academic researchers often say, experience with clients, not academic research, is the therapists' clear number-one-rated source of influence for growth. In a study of therapists in seven countries, the authors concluded: "The most salient positive influence on career development reported by therapists was direct clinical 'experience in therapy with patients'" (Orlinsky, Botermans, & Rønnestad, 2001, p. 4).

The accomplishments of expert performers arise as a result of the interaction between inheritance and environment, a feedback loop in which innate tendencies to motivation and ability lead people to engage in activities that improve performance. These improvements in turn lead to feelings of self-efficacy and increased self-esteem, which then feed back to further motivate people to broaden their engagement in deliberate intensive training. While they do not dispute the existence of specific heritable propensities that act as contributory factors to the attainment of high performance levels in specific domains, Ericsson, Prietula, and Cokely (2007) argue that in order for individuals to take advantage of these genetic predispositions, they must make use of certain indispensable environmental components, such as feedback, study with accomplished masters, and deliberate practice in order to progress through the stages of development toward the superior performance standards of the expert. Expert performance does not arise from nowhere due to specific heritable traits; rather, it arises incrementally as a result of long-accumulated observable experiences within the environment (Ericsson et al., 2007).

These specific deliberate practices are not a simple repetition of skills that individuals have already acquired but rather a progressive series of attempts to acquire new skills that currently are not part of the people's repertoire (Ericsson et al., 2007). However, these practice activities are not always enjoyable aspects of the journey.

Failure is a part of the journey on the path to expertise. Novices may not realize that failure is part of the process; but it is, in fact, an acceptable experience for all aspiring professionals. Opportunities for learning exist within the failures. For those aspiring to expertise, there will also be times of frustration when challenges to skill and theoretical understanding require that individuals adapt, using their current knowledge and skill to move through each challenge in order to reach another plateau in their quest. Holyoak (1991) asserts that this adaptation process, which has been referred to as adaptive expertise, moves individuals through unpredictable and ill-structured problems to the development of a "deeper conceptual understanding of the target domain" (p. 310). This deeper understanding results especially when a task is atypical and unpredictable, when the individuals are not under performance pressure to determine an effective solution in limited time, and when they are more sensitive to internally generated feedback (Holyoak, 1991). Adaptive expertise can be conceptualized as a process of "understanding" rather than "solving," as it requires motivation to learn for learning's sake, to reach a deeper, integrated, and holistic understanding both of the problem itself and of the processes that allow for effective and efficient problem resolution.

Feltovich et al. (2004) suggest that expertise is not simply a matter of skill acquisition but should be understood as a "complex construct of adaptations of mind and body" (p. 57). This integration of knowledge strengthens the existing scaffold, and through continuing to work on challenging tasks, individuals become more effective at decision making and problem solving.

As we said, in addition to the walking-the-path-to-mastery metaphor, we can also think of a snowball effect. As people pass one marker, and then another, the possibility of getting to mastery increases.

Marker 3: Open to Feedback but Not Derailed by It

One of the characteristics of the Minnesota master therapists is that they are open to feedback but not derailed by it. Wanting feedback on performance and then using it wisely is part of the portrait of master therapists. It is a bit paradoxical, being open to feedback but not derailed by it. "Derailing" means two things. One is being so discouraged by the feedback that individuals want to give up. The long path to mastery involves many successes and many failures mixed together. To continue through the failures, persistence is important, as indicated by Marker 1: Rage to Master. Another kind of derailing relates to the fact that some feedback is not accurate or helpful. Inaccurate feedback that people take in can cause serious derailing. For example, say another practitioner is giving you feedback. He has his own history as a person and practitioner, his own role in the situation, his own needs. All these shape his own perceptual reality and the feedback that he gives to you about your performance.

Feedback as a powerful catalyst for thrusting forward on the path toward mastery is described by Ericsson et al. (2007) in this way.

The journey to truly superior performance is neither for the faint of heart nor the impatient. The development of genuine expertise requires struggle, sacrifice, and honest, often painful self-assessment. There are no shortcuts. (p. 115)

Another kind of feedback involves people themselves monitoring how they are doing, all in the search to do better. Self-reflection and self-monitoring of the self as practitioner is important as part of expanding skill and knowledge through ever-increasing experiences. It is these emerging qualities that further serve as mediating factors in the progression to expertise.

Experience alone is not enough. The experience has to be used to grow. How is that done? One method endorsed for turning experience into expertise is the use of reflection (Neufeldt, Karno, & Nelson, 1996), a word that also means "deliberate practice." There must be a feedback loop so that people can learn from reflection. Professional baseball players have this with the intense feedback they get from video of their at-bats, from the hitting coach, and the numerous statistics that are used to gauge performance. Experience in activities like public school teaching, where increased pay is based on more academic credits earned and more teaching experience, does not necessarily produce more competence. The teacher can keep repeating the same mistake over and over again. A built-in system of feedback loops, such as clinical supervision, can make professional experience richer. Counselors and therapists can fall victim to not learning from their own practitioner experience when there is not a deliberate practice feedback system.

The path to mastery is long and twisted, with surprises around corners.

Marker 4: Humility

Humility is one of the markers on the road to mastery. We came to this idea because humility was a common description of the Minnesota Master Therapists. An example of humility was the comment from one participant that you should take a long enough vacation so that, after returning, it is clear that the world functioned just fine without you. The exact quote is: "[T]he trick is to be gone long enough . . . so you recognize your entire replaceability. That you are absolutely replaceable" (Mullenbach, 2000, p. 100). Humility is also a characteristic of the Singapore sample (Jennings et al., 2008).

In researching the topic of expert college teachers, Bain (2004) used the word "humility" to describe those he interviewed. He said one of them, David Bestanko at Northwestern University, attributed his success as a teacher to "how slow I am" (p. 142). Bain said that these expert teachers "even found power in their own ignorance" (p. 143). He goes on to say: "[T]hat humility, that fear, that veneration of the unknown spawned a kind of quiet conviction on the part of the best teachers that they and their students could do great things together" (p. 144). Another example is from the Dlugos and Friedlander (2001) sample of "passionately committed" therapists. They studied 12 therapists who received at least three peer nominations as "passionately committed." One of their major categories describing their sample was transcendence/humility.

Carl Sagan, the scientist who gained fame by explaining difficult science topics to the public, also expressed this attitude of humility. He was a skeptic even of his own answers, constantly reminding himself that he was "very new at this. You might be mistaken. You've been wrong before" (Sagan, 1996, p. 34).

Why is humility important? Perhaps for two reasons. First, it connects with the deeper existential reality of human life that we are all expendable. This truth can be so distressing that we can have a very hard time facing it. Yet one of the hallmarks of counseling and therapy is the search for truth. So, the practitioners' ability to face part of their own truth can help increase congruence.

A second reason that humility is important is because it can open people up to feedback. We think that humility is a signpost on the path to mastery and expertise because it works as a catalyst for the impact of experience. One of the surprising findings when studying expertise is that experience alone does not seem to produce expertise. As we said before, people have to *learn* from the experience. Openness to learning from experience is important. People cannot live in the shelter of their own safety that things are going well.

Feedback is oxygen to improving performance, yet it can be very difficult to accept. Practitioners must encounter a series of humiliations—and, it is hoped, learn from them—while moving forward in counselor and therapist development. But how easy it is for us as fragile human beings to turn away from the humiliations and bury ourselves in not knowing, in not learning. Palmer (1998) illuminates the humiliation and fog he feels from the allied field of teaching.

> [Sometimes] the classroom is so lifeless or painful or confused—and I am so powerless to do anything about it—that my claim to be a teacher seems a transparent sham. Then the enemy is everywhere: in those students from some alien planet, in that subject I thought I knew, and in the personal pathology that keeps me earning my living this way. What a fool I was to imagine that I had mastered this occult art—harder to divine than tea leaves and impossible for mortals to do even passably well! (p. 1)

Humility may also be a factor in experts continuing to push forward. As Colvin (2010) says:

> Great performers never allow themselves to reach the automatic, arrested-development stage in their chosen field. This is the result of continual deliberate practice—avoiding automaticity. (p. 83)

Narcissism, a polar opposite to humility, usually involves a rigidity of reality and a *closing off* of the oxygen of feedback. When discussing the topic of mistakes made by therapists, Freeman (2003) describes the danger of narcissism. He says the top three indicators of therapist narcissism are: "We think we are smarter than we are. We think we are more skilled than we really are. We think that charisma is an adequate substitute for skill" (p. 129). From Freeman's list, we can sense how more professional experience does not necessarily lead to learning.

We want to add that a person should not accept all feedback as accurate. We all know this from our personal lives. In the Minnesota Master Therapist sample, an applicable characteristic is called "Open to Life Feedback but Not Derailed by It."

Marker 5: Deep Coaching Attachments

> By watching the master and emulating his efforts in the presence of his example, the apprentice unconsciously picks up the rules of the art.
>
> *—Polanyi, 2002, p. 51*

We are using the term "coach" here to cover professional caring-instructional relationships. The exact work title may be mother, father, older sibling, teacher, professor, mentor, clinical supervisor, therapist, counselor, coach, manager, or something similar. We also believe that most deep coaching attachments are made with those who show both professional skill and caring for us as persons.

Coaches who know the knowledge area are essential. The best kind of coach for people usually changes as people move along the developmental path. A valuable first coach is like the classic kindergarten teacher: very encouraging, supportive, and instructional. This description also fits with the request of beginning students in counseling and related practicum who want a supportive clinical supervisor. In time, the best coach for moving people along the path changes, so that highly sought coaches for experts are often much more demanding and exacting in their coaching.

Being able to develop deep attachments with our coaches is important. Patricia Arredondo (2005), a leader in the counseling profession, tells of the importance of coaches in her life.

> My ninth grade and high school counselors took me under their wing and involved me as their aide. They encouraged and praised my performance and became important role models in my career development. (p. 35)

Coaches help in many ways. They motivate us and they teach us. Here is one story of the power of coaching: a mentoring relationship in counselor development. This is a long excerpt from James Benshoff (2010) and his article *The Power of Informal Mentoring in Counselor Development.*

> My first mentor appeared to me at the very beginning of my graduate counseling program. Gloria was an extraordinary teacher and group facilitator par excellence, but not at all the "warm, fuzzy" counselor or teacher type. She seemed

tough and formidable, with very high expectations for her students. In fact, Gloria was not a counselor at all but was an educational psychologist by academic training and a group facilitator by professional experience. As an excellent and experienced teacher she had an "eye" for students with potential—and fortunately, I was one of those students in whom she saw possibilities.

Her influence on me started early, in just the second course I took in my master's program. As a returning adult student and someone who had been a pretty marginal undergraduate student, I was highly motivated to do well in my graduate courses. Her course was a basic human development course that included my first exposure to a group approach to learning. The course required a major paper, developed over the course of the semester. Although this was supposed to be a 25-page paper, mine became more than 50 pages—longer than anything I had ever written before.

One day, Gloria and I walked out of class together. I was astounded when she not only commented very favorably on my paper but also suggested I should consider doctoral work. Here I was, just hoping I could make it through a master's program successfully, and an admired professor already was suggesting that I could be doctoral material. I am not easily flattered, but this was one of the biggest compliments I had ever received. I began to think seriously about how I could get my doctorate and the implications of that degree for my career opportunities.

I learned from this encounter how powerful that kind of affirmation or suggestion can be for students (as well as for clients); how planting that seed really can make a difference in people's lives and aspirations. This ability to see potential in clients and students—and to help them see and cultivate that—is a key tool in being an effective counselor or counselor educator.

Gloria ended up giving me an even bigger gift, though. Through her group counseling course—in particular the instructor-led experiential group—I learned clearly and deeply the profound power of process, in both group and individual work. For Gloria, facilitating the process was an art form and was a very powerful way of seeing and working in the world. Observing her ability to work in the here and now, to help group members focus on difficult issues, and to use process interventions to guide group members to deeper levels provided me with an extraordinarily powerful learning process. After the initial group course, Gloria invited me to co-lead the group with her the following semester. There were many aspects to this invitation, but most important was the fact that she had confidence I could do this.

For me, this was a rich learning opportunity since I had the chance not only to co-lead the group but also to process and plan group sessions with her. It was the opportunity to apprentice with a master, to be able to get inside her head to see how she thought about and intervened intentionally in groups. Although I could not know it at the time, this experience would dramatically alter my counseling and teaching styles. As I have continued to develop and hone these group facilitation skills over the years, they have become the basis for everything I do, including teaching, counseling, and professional leadership. A deep appreciation of, and respect for, the process of experiences also has extended into my personal life and my relationships. It's not just what I do—it's become a core part of who I am.

As I reflect on my experiences with Gloria, *mentoring* is the best word I can find to capture the nature of the relationship and the impact it had on me. Most definitions or descriptions of mentoring emphasize the variety of roles that mentors can play in the lives of their mentees. One university guide to mentoring graduate students suggests roles such as *guide, counselor, advisor, consultant, tutor, guru,* and *teacher*. The role that Gloria took with me, though, was primarily one of *guru*, or wise, experienced master teacher. Interestingly, I had to look elsewhere for good models for success in academia, research, or professional service and leadership. Gloria's unique gifts to me were about being a master teacher and an extraordinarily skilled group facilitator.

This is what I learned from Gloria: how to offer intuitive, well-timed support and encouragement in ways that have the potential to impact on students' lives; how to appreciate, create, and manage the process aspects of learning; and how to be an effective group facilitator, regardless of the type of group or group setting.

Along the way, she helped me discover some core parts of myself and to explore possibilities for how I could use these to be a more effective counselor, teacher, leader, and eventually a mentor myself.

I doubt that Gloria would have ever labeled our relationship as mentoring. Her influence, although very powerful, was subtle in many ways and reached me mostly because of the tremendous respect and admiration I held for her. I do not know whether she knew how closely I was watching her—*how* she managed groups, *how* she responded to students who were struggling to master course content, *how* she was able to make use of the process dimension to create self-awareness and change. (pp. 59–61)*

---

*Benshoff, J. (2010). The power of informal mentoring in counselor development. In M. Trotter-Mathison, J.M. Koch, S. Sanger, & T.M. Skovholt (Eds.) *Voices in the field: Defining moments in counselor and therapist development* (59-61). New York: Routledge.

Benshoff (2010) describes the ingredients of deep coaching attachments and why they are an essential for traveling on the path toward mastery and expertise. The mentor motivates the person to keep practicing to improve in the complex skills of the craft; watching the mentor do the desired skills provides very efficient learning; and as important as anything else, the mentor can change the person's view of self so that a more professionally skilled person can start emerging.

Marker 6: Boundaried Generosity

The term "boundaried generosity" came from our analysis of the Minnesota Master Therapists sample group. This term, which indicates both constraint, as in "boundaried," and deep giving of oneself, as in "generosity," is one of the essential features of long-term vitality in the helping professions. It is hard to balance other-care and self-care. Yet learning how to do this and do it well is a marker on the way to mastery and expertise in the counseling and therapy professions. See Chapter 7 of this book for more on this marker.

THE STUDY OF MASTERY AND EXPERTISE IS COMPLICATED

Although this topic of expertise is important, it is also complicated because of conflicting ideas. Although we believe a lot of experience is necessary for expertise, perhaps it is not necessary. Here are two examples. Since 2006, a Dutch company has been host to a chess competition between a team of older and younger players (McClain, 2009). The older players, those with more experience, lost in 2006, 2007, and 2008. Finally, in 2009, the older team, stacked with relatively younger players, won. For the 2009 competition, the older player of age 77 was replaced by a player who was 33. The younger team with players of 21, 17, and 14 almost won. This chess example presents a question that is central to the study of mastery and expertise: Is a lot of experience necessary for mastery?

Here is another example. Spengler et al. (2009a) recently completed a meta-analysis of clinical judgment within professional psychology. It was a Herculean effort wherein they reviewed 75 clinical judgment studies involving over 4,000 clinicians. They were attempting to stem the debate between academic researchers who argue that practice does not improve practice and practitioners who believe that professional experience is central to improved practice. The results support both academic and practice positions. The authors conclude that "greater clinical or educational experience leads to almost 13% more accurate decisions regardless of most other factors" (p. 379) and "An important consideration, then, for future researchers is why the experience-accuracy effect is so small" (p. 381). The authors point to the limitations to some of the studies, such as how the range of experience is often very narrow, thereby reducing researchers' ability to assess the true impact of experience (Spengler et al., 2009b). Adding to the lack of certainty, Lichtenberg (2009) comments that clinical judgment may not even be the critical area to measure because a contextual model of therapy and counseling seems to be ascending as the medical model descends in popularity.

Both of these studies—of chess and of clinical judgment—make us cautious in offering up a very definite view of mastery and expertise and how to get there. However, in this chapter, we have offered some ideas while also realizing that mapping out the path to expertise in our field can be confusing and unclear.

SUMMARY

We end this chapter with words from an expert therapist. At age 68, she described the pleasure and effectiveness of the work at the expert level. We have used this quote in other chapters of this book. It is such a favorite that we are including it again. The quote is from Skovholt and Rønnestad (1995):

> With diminished anxiety, I became less and less afraid of my clients and with that came an ease for me in using my own wide repertoire of skills and procedures. They became more available to me when I needed them. And during those moments it became remarkable to me that someone would have the willingness to share their private world with me and that my work with them would bring very positive results for them. This brought a sense of immense pleasure to me. (p. 96)

We hope this chapter on mastery and expertise will lead more practitioners down the path to both doing really good work and having such a positive stance as indicated by this quote.

REFERENCES

American Psychological Association. (2005, August). Policy Statement on Evidence-Based Practice. Approved by Council of Representatives at the August, 2005 meeting. Washington, D.C.

Arredondo, P. (2005). Mis inspiraciones y legados. In R. K. Conyne & F. Bemak (Eds.), *Journeys to professional excellence: Lessons from leading counselor educators and practitioners* (pp. 33–44). Alexandria, VA: American Counseling Association.

Bain, K. (2004). *What the best college teachers do.* Cambridge, MA: Harvard University Press.

Bales, P. B., & Staudinger, U. M. (2000). Wisdom: A metaheuristic (pragmatic) to orchestrate mind and virtue toward excellence. *American Psychologist, 55,* 122–136.

Belenky, B. L., Clinchy, B., Goldberger, N., & Tarule, J. (1986). *Women's ways of knowing.* New York, NY: Basic Books.

Benshoff, J. (2010). The power of informal mentoring in counselor development. In M. Trotter-Mathison, J. M. Koch, S. Sanger, & T. M. Skovholt (Eds.), *Voices from the field: Defining moments in counselor and therapist development* (pp. 59–61). New York, NY: Routledge.

Campbell, D. P (2007). *If you don't know where you're going, you'll probably end up somewhere else.* Notre Dame, IN: Ave Maria Press.

Chi, M.T.H., Glaser, R., & Farr, M. J. (Eds.). (1988). *The nature of expertise.* Hillsdale, NJ: Lawrence Erlbaum.

Colvin, G. (2010). *Talent is overrated*. New York, NY: Portfolio Penguin.

Dennett, D. (1991). *Consciousness explained*. Boston, MA: Little Brown.

Dlugos, R. F., & Friedlander, M. L. (2001). Passionately committed therapists: A qualitative study of their experiences. *Professional Psychology: Research and Practice, 32*, 298–394.

Dreyfus, H. L., & Dreyfus S. E. (1986). *Mind over machine: The power of human intuition and expertise in the era of the computer*. New York, NY: Free Press.

Ericsson, K. A., Charness, N., Hoffman, R. R., & Feltovich, P. J. (2006). *The Cambridge handbook of expertise and expert performance*. New York, NY: Cambridge University Press.

Ericsson, K. A., Krampe, R. T., & Tesch-Romer, C. (1993). The role of deliberate practice in the acquisition of expert performance. *Psychological Review, 100*, 363–406.

Ericsson, K. A., Prietula, M. J., & Cokely, E. T. (2007). The making of an expert. *Harvard Business Review, 85*(7–8), 114–121.

Feltovich, P. J., Prietula, M. J., & Ericsson, K. A. (2006). Studies of expertise from psychological perspectives. In K. A. Ericsson, N. Charness, P. J. Feltovich, & R. R. Hoffman (Eds.), *The Cambridge handbook of expertise and expert performance* (pp. 41– 67). New York, NY: Cambridge University Press.

Freeman, A. (2003). We're not as smart as we think we are. In J. A. Kottler & J. Carlson (Eds.), *Bad therapy: Master therapists share their worst failures* (pp. 123–130). New York, NY: Brunner-Routledge.

Gladwell, M. (2008). *Outliers: The story of success*. New York, NY: Little, Brown.

Glaser, R., & Chi, M.T.H. (1988). Overview. In M.T.H. Chi, R. Glaser, & M. J. Farr (Eds.), *The nature of expertise* (pp. xv–xxi). Hillsdale, NJ: Lawrence Erlbaum.

Goldfried, M. (Ed.) (2001). *How therapists change: Personal and professional reflections*. Washington, DC: American Psychological Association.

Hill, C. E., Thompson, B. J., & Williams, E. N. (1997). A guide to conducting consensual qualitative research. *The counseling psychologist, 25*, 517–572.

Hill, C. L., & Ridley, C. R. (2001). Diagnostic decision-making: Do counselors delay final judgments? *Journal of Counseling & Development, 79*(1), 98–118.

Holyoak, K. J. (1991). Symbolic connectionism: Toward third-generation theories of expertise. In K. A. Ericsson & J. Smith (Eds.), *Toward a general theory of expertise: Prospects and limits* (pp. 301–335). New York, NY: Cambridge University Press.

Jennings, L. (1996). *The personal characteristics of master therapists*. Unpublished doctoral dissertation. University of Minnesota.

Jennings, L., D'Rozario, V., Goh, M., Sovereign, A., Brogger, M., & Skovholt, T. (2008). Psychotherapy expertise in Singapore: A qualitative investigation. *Psychotherapy Research, 18*(5), 508–522.

Jennings, L., & Skovholt, T. M. (1999). The cognitive, emotional, and relational characteristics of master therapists. *Journal of Counseling Psychology 46*(1), 3–11.

Jennings, L., & Skovholt, T. M. (2004). The cognitive, emotional, and relational characteristics of master therapists. In T. M. Skovholt & L. Jennings (Eds.), *Master therapists: Exploring expertise in therapy and counseling* (pp. 31–52). Boston, MA: Allyn & Bacon.

Jourard, S. M., & Landsman, T. (1980). *Healthy personality*. New York, NY: Macmillan.

Lichtenberg, J. W. (2009). Effects of experience on clinical judgment. *Counseling Psychologist, 37*, 410–415.

Lichtenberg, J. W., & Wampold, B. E. (2002). Closing comments on counseling psychology's principles of empirically supported interventions. *The Counseling Psychologist, 30*, 309–313.

McClain, D. L. (2009, Sept. 6). Age showdown where players are considered "older" at 33. *New York Times*, p. 24.

Morell, V. (2008, Mar.). Animal minds. *National Geographic, 213*(3), 36–61.

Mullenbach, M. A. (2000). Master therapists: A study of professional resiliency and emotional wellness. (Unpublished doctoral dissertation). University of Minnesota.

Neufeldt, S. A., Karno, M. P., & Nelson, M. L. (1996). A qualitative study of experts' conceptualization of supervisee reflectivity. *Journal of Counseling Psychology, 43*, 3–9.

Orlinsky, D. E., Botermans, J.-F., & Rønnestad, M. H. (2001). Towards an empirically grounded model of psychotherapy training:

Four thousand therapists rate influences on their development. *Australian Psychologist, 36,* 139–148.

Paige, J. M., & Simon, H. A. (1966). Cognitive processes in solving algebra word problems. In B. Kleinmuntz (Ed.), *Problem solving: Research, method, and theory* (pp. 119–151). New York, NY: Wiley.

Palmer, P. (1998). *The courage to teach: Exploring the inner landscape of a teacher's life.* San Francisco, CA: Jossey-Bass.

Perry, W. G. (1970). *Forms of intellectual and ethical development in the college years: A scheme.* New York, NY: Holt.

Polanyi, M. (2002). *Personal knowledge: Toward a post-critical philosophy.* London, UK: Routledge.

Rogers, C. (1961). *On becoming a person.* Boston, MA: Houghton Mifflin.

Sagan, C. E. (1996). *The demon haunted world: Science as a candle in the dark.* New York, NY: Ballantine Books.

Scardamalia, M., & Bereiter, C. (1991). Literary expertise. In K. A. Ericsson & J. Smith (Eds.), *Toward a general theory of expertise* (pp. 172–194). New York, NY: Cambridge University Press.

Skovholt, T. M., & D'Rozario, V. (2000). Portraits of outstanding and inadequate teachers in Singapore: The impact of emotional intelligence. *Teaching and Learning, 40*(1), 9–17.

Skovholt, T. M., Hanson, M., Jennings, L., & Grier, T. (2004). A brief history of expertise. In T. M. Skovholt & L. Jennings (Eds.), *Master therapists: Exploring expertise in therapy and counseling* (pp. 1–16). Boston, MA: Allyn & Bacon.

Skovholt, T. M., & Jennings L. (Eds.). (2004). *Master therapists: Exploring expertise in therapy and counseling.* Boston, MA: Allyn & Bacon.

Skovholt, T. M., & Jennings, L. (2009). In paradoxical praise of common factors. *PsycCRITIQUES, 54,* 87–89.

Skovholt, T. M., Jennings, L., & Mullenbach, M. (2004). Portrait of the master therapist: The highly-functioning self. In T. M. Skovholt & L. Jennings (Eds.), *Master therapists: Exploring expertise in therapy and counseling* (pp. 125–146) Boston, MA: Allyn & Bacon.

Skovholt, T. M., & Rønnestad, M. H. (1995). *The evolving professional self: Stages and themes in therapist and counselor development.* New York, NY: Wiley.

Sounes, H. (2002). *Down the highway: The life of Bob Dylan.* New York, NY: Grove Press.

Spearman, C. E. (1927). *The abilities of man, their nature and measurement.* New York, NY: Macmillan.

Spengler, P. M., et al. (2009a). The meta-analysis of clinical judgment project. *Counseling Psychologist, 37,* 350–398.

Spengler, P. M., White, M. J., Aegisdottir, S., & Maugherman, A. S. (2009b). Time keeps on ticking. The experience of clinical judgment. *Counseling Psychologist, 37,* 416–423.

Spitz, B. (1989). *Dylan: A biography.* New York, NY: McGraw-Hill.

Stewart, M. (2002). *Jackie Stiles: Gym dandy.* Minneapolis, MN: Lerner Group.

Sullivan, M. (2000). Master therapist's construction of the therapeutic relationship. (Unpublished doctoral dissertation.) University of Minnesota.

Voss, J. F., & Post, T. A. (1988). On the solving of ill-structured problems. In M.T.H. Chi, R. Glaser, & M. J. Farr (Eds.), *The nature of expertise* (pp. 261–285). Hillside, NJ: Lawrence Erlbaum.

Winner, E. (2000). The origins and ends of giftedness. *American Psychologist, 55,* 159–169.

12

Vertical and Horizontal Nurturance for the Novice

Clinical Supervisors, and Many Other Peers

Thomas M. Skovholt and Yoonhee Sung

Learning through intense, extreme, and painful experiences, and using what has been learned to add meaning and depth to one's life and work is a recurring theme in the work of great writers. John Keats, who trained to be a surgeon, wrote, "Do you not see how necessary a world of pain and troubles is to school an intelligence and make it a soul?"

—Jamison, 2010, p. 66

What a task it is to use our own stretching, difficult, and painful experiences—including those while a novice therapist or counselor under supervision—so we can grow and become a "soul." To achieve this task in the quest to be an exceptional practitioner in the caring professions, we need a lot of people to help us. We all can be thankful that we have people, such as friends, classmates, family, supervisors, mentors, and teachers, to guide us, catch us, hold us, and encourage us. The need for people around us is the focus of this chapter.

As the famous song goes, the luckiest people among us are those people who need people. Just as children learn how to walk, trust others, and discover the world on their own, counselors learn counseling by struggling on their own. Yet, just like children, novice therapists need people, especially during difficult times. The novice voyage, or trek, is a time when it is important to have a lot of contact with positive people. The good news for novice counselors is that they do not have to travel solo. Many peers are walking on the same path; supervisors and mentors who have been there can help along the way too. These people do not free novice counselors from all their struggles, just as parents cannot take away all of their children's struggles and pain. Yet the support and encouragement from others helps beginners keep going. The people around novices provide wisdom, motivation, and inspiration.

Another way to think of this is to use the greenhouse analogy from Chapter 7. It is important for us to create a greenhouse for ourselves; in a greenhouse, there is water, light, and good soil. For novices, this means positive human contact, support, and challenging and expert instruction. Everything grows in a greenhouse. We need such a world for ourselves when we are going through the emerging practitioner experience.

We start our discussion with the importance of clinical supervision and go from there to another key relationship that sustains us: with peers. But before continuing, we want to note three references for you to have and read later. The first to a classic reference, one that describes preferred supervisor behavior, by Allen, Szollos, and Williams (1986). The second has a title that captures the long history of supervision: "Psychotherapy Supervision Since 1909: Some Friendly Observations About Its First Century" by Watkins (2011). A third, *The Ethics of Supervision and Consultation*, is the definitive book on supervision ethics by psychologist Janet Thomas (2010). Now, on to the sections of the chapter.

VALUE OF VERTICAL RELATIONSHIPS WITH CLINICAL SUPERVISORS

Clinical supervisors are very important for novice therapists. Who are they, and why are they so important?

Clinical supervisors come in a variety of sizes and shapes. Some are individual supervisors, others are classroom teachers, still others are academic advisors . . . and the list goes on. One consistent element is that they have more professional experience than novices do. Another is that they are responsible for the work of the novices. Some have a lot of training in clinical supervision, and some do not. Some really like doing supervision. Others end up in the role because no one else in the agency or school wants to or can do it. Some are really good at it; some are not so talented.

In Tom's M. A. and doctoral student counseling practicum classes, he has heard many, many students discuss their clinical supervisors, sometimes with great admiration and respect and sometimes with dread and dislike. And there are also many in-between reactions. Students have consistently loved some clinical supervisors. For Tom, years ago these people included Phyllis Epply, George Meyer, Joseph Johnston, Helen Roehlke, and Harry Grater. Thanks to them!

Why do we have such strong feelings toward our clinical supervisors? It has to do with our vulnerability. How do novices feel on the very first week of practicum? They may have many roller-coaster feelings—excitement and worry, joy and dread. They may wonder if clients will really see them as counseling professionals. They probably dressed in carefully chosen clothes, hoping they are neither too formal nor too casual. However, although beginners may appear comfortable and confident outside, they also may be terrified and clueless, feeling awkward walking in the hallway or running into staff members.

It can be wonderful to have someone to talk with, the person who is responsible for answering all of our questions and hearing all of our apprehensions. This is our supervisor. Compared to our relationships with peers, a supervisor provides more direct and practical help with clinical work, along with emotional support. The supervisor is the main person who helps novices get used to the counseling setting and answers novices' questions. In supervisory relationships, the supervisee is allowed to make a mistake, and it is okay not to know an answer.

Tom has asked some of his students' beloved supervisors to come to his clinical supervision class to help unveil the mystery of excellence in this field. These excellent clinical supervisors have the following attributes:

1. They are skilled at counseling/therapy practice. They have gone through the long professional process of becoming competent in the elusive art and science of counseling and therapy. This personal competence level gives them both the confidence to know what they are doing and to guide others on the practitioner path.
2. They are enthusiastic about clinical supervision and enjoy helping others develop professionally.
3. They do not get too fearful of supervisor responsibilities. Supervisors who are too fearful micromanage supervisees and truncate supervisees' developmental process.
4. They are able to balance the two—often in conflict—poles of supervision: supervisee development and supervisee evaluation.
5. They clearly describe to supervisees at the beginning of practicum/internship the criteria that will be used to evaluate them. Expressing the criteria used for supervisee evaluation is done clearly and fairly.
6. They are able to develop very positive working relationships with their supervisees.

Ideal supervisors for novices have all these characteristics. Yet, in reality, novices often have no choice in picking a supervisor—about as much choice as a person does in choosing his or her parents. Supervisors fall on a bell-shape curve: Some are great, some are poor, and some are average.

To help maximize the supervision relationship for novices, we are going to explore this topic more. Note that clinical supervision is one of the vibrant areas, one of the gems of the counseling and therapy professions. Excellent clinical supervision texts are available (e.g., Bernard & Goodyear, 2009; Ladany & Bradley, 2010; Ladany, Friedlander, & Nelson, 2005: Neufeldt, 2007). Having a chance to sit and talk with an interested expert about one's clinical work—the triumphs and the confusion—is a wonderful part of the field.

When researching professional development of therapists from different countries, Rønnestad and Orlinsky (2005b), a reference often cited in this book, discovered that novices rated clinical supervision, as a way to grow professionally, as more important than anything else, such as classes, research, direct work with clients, and reading books. For this novice research group, "formal supervision or consultation" (p. 154) was the most important source of influence. This is evidence of the central importance of clinical supervision for novices. Many other people-oriented professions do not have the same degree of clinical supervision as the counseling and therapy fields do.

Why is clinical supervision so important? One reason is because of the great gap between academic learning and actual experience with counseling and therapy clients. Novices who excel in the classroom can suddenly be lost in the confusing world of interacting with clients. Think of the lone sailor way out in the ocean who is doing just fine until gale winds arrive and the mast breaks. The air patrol arrives to great relief. So too novice practitioners need the air patrol—the clinical supervisor.

Here is an example of a beginner needing the wisdom of the supervisor:

> Lia, a beginning therapist, has her first session with a client. Coming from the interview she is exhilarated but exhausted—the task facing her seems daunting. After the client presented a series of problems, there was a silence, and Lia felt pressed to provide *the answer*, or at least guidance toward the answer.
> —*Ladany et al., 2005, p. 3*

What knowledge does the supervisor share with the supervisee? It is the knowledge from practice, as described in this example, in the world of medicine:

> The thousand stories of an experienced physician make a library, a vast accretion of personal and collective knowledge. The science is important, of course, but the stories too are important, and without them we know only halfway.
> —*Bardes, 2010, p. 111*

Clinical supervision is important because practitioner experience alone does not produce better performance—we have to learn from experience. The saying "A person can have 20 years of experience or one year of experience 20 times" captures this idea. The sorting-out process—the talking-through process of clinical supervision—helps all of us in our work. The performance arts is an example of a domain where performance is closely monitored and a form of clinical supervision (i.e. the dancing instructor in ballet) is used to increase skill level.

Catch-22 Dilemma for Novices as Supervisees

> Supervisors are not only admired teachers but feared judges who have real power.
> —*Doehrman, 1976, p. 11*

Although clinical supervision is a means for growth, it is also a place where novices are evaluated. To enter the professional field, novices must pass through the hands of a supervisor. Here, "through the hands" means they must be subject to great scrutiny. This scrutiny is captured by this poem, with permission from Lynn Moreland (1993, p. 13).

You supervisors dance
on the rim of
this machine
certain of your
power, your values
clear and calm in your purpose
I
trainee
am tumbled and
tossed
caught in the spin
jerked about by the hierarchy's
agitation
my vision
clouded by products
that whiten and soften the dark edge
of reality

And you and I know
that
the spinning always stops when
you open the lid to
check.

The strong evaluation atmosphere of clinical supervision points out the conflict for novices between the two poles of trying to look good and trying to learn and grow. One message is: "Look great and do great and be great and graduate and we all [the student and the professional gatekeepers] can be happy." At the same time, the message is: "Work on your personal development, show your flaws in supervision, and don't be phony because as Carl Rogers, one of our professional grandfathers, told us, being authentic is the way to real expertise." Consider psychologist Alexandra Stillman's (personal communication, May 15, 2007) explanation of these two orientations that pull on novices: "The performance to please/get the grade orientation versus performing for development orientation." Doing both *impression management* and *showing flaws* are like a catch-22 dilemma for novices.

In a parallel relationship, one lover tells the other of some hidden and unknown flaw. What will the lover do with the information? Leave, use it during a heated argument between them, or hold it, give suggestions, and offer support to the other? We just do not know what others will do with our vulnerabilities, and that is why it can be so difficult to reveal them to our supervisors.

Our suggestion is that novices try to balance these two orientations. That is what most supervisees do—they show flaws to the supervisor and ask for help but try to look good too. Clinical supervisors are there to guide novices and offer the invaluable support that novices need. Clinical supervisors are like sponges, ready to soak up excessive novice anxiety. It works best if supervisors feel that novices are open to feedback and appreciative of what the supervisors are doing for them. Supervisors often tell novice supervisees to be open to supervision and to share the struggles and dilemmas they face. Supervisors do this because they believe that more supervisee openness can lead to better work together and more growth for novices. This is true—except that supervisors have total control of how they use the information in evaluating supervisees, as Moreland expressed in the previous poem.

We recommend that novices ask to watch their supervisors actually doing their own clinical work with clients, but try to see the situation from the supervisor's perspective—understanding that the supervisor may have his or her own worries about doing everything just right when the supervisee is watching.

Having a less experienced supervisor—at practice and supervision—can be an advantage; so can having a more experienced practitioner/supervisor. The less experienced person is closer to the novice in terms of remembering the struggles of the novice years, yet his or her anxiety of inexperience may parallel that of the novice. The more experienced person is more removed from being a vulnerable beginner; yet novices may be fearful, as in the next quote from the world of medicine, that the supervisor is "so far removed from being an intern that he no longer remembers what it was like to be scared and alone" (Mintz, 2010, p. 173).

The more senior practitioner has more to give but sometimes has trouble translating expertise into easy-to-use steps for novices. This is because, in time, expertise tends to get internalized and automatic and can be harder for experts to articulate. An example is trying to tell someone how to get to a street that you drive to automatically. Sometimes it is hard to clearly explain the route to a visitor.

The most difficult situation for the new practitioner is *double traumatization*, a term that was discussed in earlier chapters (Rønnestad & Orlinsky (2005a)). The "double" refers to a combination of (1) clients who do not seem to improve and (2) a critical supervisor. Alone, each is stressful for novices. Novices look to client improvement as a way to gauge their own success. Over time, practitioners do not link their success so closely to quick client change. Also, with more supervision experiences, the reaction of one supervisor is less powerful.

The power of this double traumatization experience was evident to Tom when he has talked with practitioners many years after their novice years. Even after a span of many years, some have shown high distress when describing their earlier practicum/internship. While we are describing the negatives, we will also mention Magnusson, Wilcoxon, and Norem's (2000) six themes of lousy supervisors: unbalanced, developmentally inappropriate, intolerant of differences, poor modeling of professional/personal attributes, untrained, and professionally inappropriate. Quite a list! Ladany's (2010) article title also refers to this unhappy part of supervision: "Learning What Not to Do: Lessons from Lousy Educators and Supervisors."

Integrated Developmental Model

Stoltenberg and McNeil (2010) developed and expanded a popular developmental model of supervision, the Integrated Developmental Model (IDM); their book is now in its third edition. They offer a package of topics and a map through them for the Level 1, Level 2, and Level 3 supervisee. Supervisee awareness, motivation, and autonomy are markers of development through the levels. Piaget's classic developmental change process of assimilation, followed by accommodation, guides cognitive awareness. Many valuable topics are considered, such as the supervisee's intervention skills competence and client conceptualization within each level. They also consider common factors: the fundamental curative aspects across all approaches. IDM gives much-needed structure to the supervisee and supervisor working alliance.

CULTURAL CONSIDERATIONS AND CLINICAL SUPERVISION

When novices enter one of the therapy or counseling professions, they may experience a value clash between personal values and the professional values of the therapy and counseling field. For instance, a novice counselor with strong evangelical Christian beliefs may feel conflicted about supporting a client who wants to explore her sexuality by engaging in a same-sex relationship. This counselor may feel she is in a bifurcated reality with no easy way out: either give up her own personal values completely or maintain her religious beliefs and not become a counselor.

Handelsman, Gottlieb, and Knapp (2005) explain novice counselors' value conflict and resolution process by using Berry and Sam's acculturation model. This model conceptualizes the process of adjusting to a new culture with four possible states of value acculturation:

1. Marginalization (neither professionally nor personally engaged)
2. Separation (highly engaged personally while professionally unengaged)
3. Assimilation (low personal engagement and high professional engagement)
4. Integration (high value engagement in both personal life and professionally)

Novice counselors ideally can move to the integration state through various experiences, such as classes, readings, practicum, and supervision. In particular, the supervisor's role is critical in facilitating this process and preventing the novice therapist or counselor from being unable to cross a personal values–professional values chasm.

It is important for the supervisor to respect the supervisee's personal values and experiences and at the same time represent professional values.

How can a cultural conflict affect supervision? For instance, an Asian supervisee who grew up in a culture that values obedience to authority and humbleness may feel uncomfortable with a supervision style that encourages supervisees to choose supervision topics and set the supervision agenda in a collaborative way. If the supervisor does not understand this supervisee's culture, the supervisor may make a mistake in thinking the supervisee is dependent, passive, and not confident. Park (2010), a Korean who went to graduate school in the United States, described a defining moment in supervision when she experienced cultural conflict. Later, her supervisor showed cultural sensitivity. Park wrote:

> In the second semester of practicum, I was paired with a new supervisor, who informed me in our first supervision meeting that her supervision style was heavily influenced by the feminist approach. She enthusiastically emphasized that the main focus of her supervision work was the empowerment of her supervisees. She further explained that she tried to achieve that goal by letting her supervisees decide the content of supervision according to their self-identified needs. . . . Even though everything that my supervisor suggested sounded good in theory, it did not fit well with the schema of the evaluative relationship that I had in my mind. Having grown up in a hierarchical culture where paying respect to authority figures was considered an essential value, I had a hard time picturing myself as an equal partner in the egalitarian supervisory relationship that my supervisor was describing. . . . [At our next meeting] she apologized for imposing her ideas about supervision on me without first asking me about the nature of the supervision relationships that I had experienced in Korea and the type of supervisory relationship with which I would feel most comfortable. Suddenly, it felt as if a thick fog had lifted. I was very humbled by my supervisor's openness and honesty about her potential mistake. That was something that I never witnessed in my supervisors in Korea, where rules about saving face are deeply entrenched. . . . Our discussion paved the way for an in-depth exploration of what it would mean to me, as an Asian woman, to embrace a feminist approach. . . . [She] enabled me to process the internal conflicts I felt while negotiating between Korean and American cultures. . . . All of these positive experiences in supervision brought forth positive changes in my clinical work. I began to find my voice as a clinician. (pp. 88–89)

We hope the supervisor can help novices bridge any cultural conflicts they may experience. Culture is part of what defines us. Without integrating our personal values and beliefs, we cannot relate to a client as a real, genuine person, and we cannot use our "self" in counseling. Supervisors can provide modeling for managing cultural differences by helping supervisees to integrate different values.

SUMMARY OF THIS SECTION

We want to end this vertical relationship section by quoting one therapist on the transforming power of the clinical supervision he received years before.

> In that one magical transforming moment in supervision, David helped me move beyond my uncertainty. In receiving the gift of confidence, I was able to be confident in myself, for which I am forever grateful
>
> —*Osachuk, 2010, p. 66*

We hope you the reader will also have magical, transforming moments in clinical supervision that you will treasure for years after.

VALUE OF HORIZONTAL RELATIONSHIPS: PEERS, CLASSMATES, COLLEAGUES, AND FRIENDS

> Nothing compares to having a group of peers to whom you can reveal everything about your work and get thoughtful help in being more skilled with clients.
>
> —*Therapist Jane Brodie, personal communication,*
> *September 27, 2007*

The cohort model of graduate education was developed to take advantage of peers—and what we call the beauty of horizontal relationships. In this model, students take courses and go through the graduate program together. Being together a lot helps classmates bond with each other. Just as siblings in a family are invaluable and cannot be replaced by parents, so teachers, clinical supervisors, and professors cannot do for students what their peers can do.

Classmates do not have to worry about impression management with their classmates as they do with professors and supervisors. They can talk with each other about their fears, confusion, and uncertainty. Peers at a practicum site are usually at the same developmental level because they are going through similar challenges. Interpersonal support from those in the same profession is a critical component of counselors' cognitive and emotional changes. Since peers do not have authority or power as supervisors or mentors, the relationship with them is more mutual. Also, the relationship is voluntary and casual. As we found in our research, peers, especially admired peers, serve as strong models of how to do things professionally (Rønnestad & Skovholt, 2003).

The power differential is, of course, a big difference between a peer–peer relationship and a senior professional–student relationship. Because of their authority, influence, and power, seniors hold a different position in a person's life from peers. As we all know, this matters! We know this from being the child in the parent–child relationships in our own lives and, for some of us, the parent too. And we know it also from all the teacher–student relationships in our lives as students and, for some of us, as teachers too.

Take away the power differential, and we have the beauty and great nurturance of horizontal relationships—those connections we have with peers, classmates, colleagues, and friends. Kram and Isabella (1985) conducted research on 25 relationship pairs. They classified peer relationships into three types: the information peer, the collegial relationship, and the special peer. With an information peer, people benefit most from the exchange of information about their work with only occasional emotional support and confirmation. The collegial relationship is characterized by a moderate level of trust, self-disclosure, and direct feedback. Kram and Isabella called the most intimate peer relationship the special peer. This type of relationship is equivalent to best friends. There is a strong emotional bond and support for many aspects of the peer's life in both work and family. Self-disclosure and self-expression are present and expressed when talking about one's personal and professional dilemmas, vulnerabilities, and individuality.

The last of these peer relationships, the special peer relationship, offers the richest benefits for peers under stress (such as those in graduate school). However, to show how high distress produces peer closeness, nothing compares to combat. Junger (2010) lived with a combat unit and documented the intense fear that soldiers feel when in the ambiguous and uncertain danger of war. At any moment, they can be killed or in intense pain from a bomb or multiple bullets. How do humans cope with this horror? Junger says soldiers universally do the same thing: The welfare of the unit and other soldiers becomes more important than the self. If everyone has this level of esprit de corps, chances for survival increase. Junger says:

> Combat fog obscures your fate—obscures when and where you might die—and from that unknown is born a desperate bond between the men. That bond is the core experience of combat and the only thing you can absolutely count on. The Army might screw you and your girlfriend might dump you and the enemy might kill you, but the shared commitment to safeguard one another's lives is unnegotiable and only deepens with time. The willingness to die for another person is a form of love that even religions fail to inspire, and the experience of it changes a person profoundly. . . .
>
> A study conducted in the 1950's found that jumping out of a plane generated extreme anxiety in *loosely* bonded groups of paratroopers, but tightly bonded men mainly worried about living up to the standards of the group. . . .
>
> [O]ver and over again throughout history, men have chosen to die in battle with their friends rather than to flee on their own and survive. (pp. 239, 240, 242)

Wow! The novice years in the helping professions may be hard, but they are nothing like combat. Read Junger (2010) for yourself. However, the lesson here is how much peers help us when in adversity. Here are some specific benefits we all get from peers as we go through the roller coaster of the early novice years when our identity as a therapy-counseling practitioner is being shaped.

Three Benefits of Horizontal Relationships

Benefit 1: Normalization/Social Comparison

Peer relationships help us feel normal, and feeling normal is highly valued in the roller-coaster world of novice practitioners. The feeling of normality comes from what is called *social comparison information*. For instance, a client's request to switch to another counselor or a client's canceling of an appointment can be difficult experience for novice counselors because novices have not established a secured and confident professional self. Novices are easily threatened—this is not a statement about the individual; it is about the vulnerability and courage each of us must exhibit when going through the uncharted waters of the novice voyage. Novices can feel enormous relief when realizing that peers in practicum also had clients cancel an appointment. Seeing one's peers struggle like oneself can help novice counselors see the problem from a developmental perspective rather than from a sense of personal failure.

This is social comparison information in action. This normalizing of negative emotions can be explained by social comparison theory (Festinger, 1954), which states that people commonly compare themselves with others when evaluating their thoughts, opinions, abilities, and experience. Schachter (1959) proposed an *emotional* comparison theory, in which people currently experiencing a novel, high-stress situation are hypothesized to seek to affiliate with others who are facing the same threatening situation. In this way, we can assess our own emotional reactions and reduce uncertainty for the novel and stressful situation. Many years ago, Tom was part of a study (Skovholt & Brothen, 1981) where the authors found that people can increase self-esteem after comparing their experience with others by using the social comparison theory and the universality of experience.

Benefit 2: Emotional Support, Confirmation, and Belonging

Professionals in the helping professions such as counseling, nursing, and teaching are involved in the intensity of interpersonal interaction and thus are vulnerable to emotional exhaustion and burnout. Peer support mediates emotional exhaustion and burnout (Shoptaw et al., 2000). Having close relationships is strongly associated with subjective well-being and positive mood states. Genuine friendships give feelings of joy and well-being (Diener, Weiting, Harter, & Arora, 2010).

Benefit 3: Information Sharing and Honest Communication

Peers serve as an important channel for formal and informal information. Up-to-date, accurate information seems to reduce novice counselors' anxiety by decreasing their sense of uncertainty and giving them a sense of more control. Through informal peer relationships, novices have access to valuable information about so many things (e.g., degree requirements, teachers, unseen obstacles, and unseen possibilities) that they cannot learn about in any other way. Describing their experience in graduate school in counselor education, four classmates—Leake, Riding-Malon, Tzou, and Muhomba (2010)—catalog the joys and benefits of close friendship and how the friendships made things much better, easier, and richer for their own growth and meaning. The benefits they list include information sharing and honest communication.

The ease of peer relationships is related to the nature of friendships being equal and mutual. Compared to the supervisory or mentoring relationship, in peer relationships, people do not have the same concern about evaluation or approval. This allows novice counselors to express feelings and ideas more freely and serves as an emotional outlet for them. Expressing emotions about being a practitioner helps novices process the experience and learn at an intellectual level. Also, a forum for honest communication provides an opportunity for novice counselors to internally develop their own professional identity. With peers, people can express ideas and assert different viewpoints more freely. This helps individuals expand their own thinking and professional ideas.

Supervisors know us as people with a set of developing skills. Peers know us in a more complete way—across many different settings. Classmates meet each other for lunch, do projects together, and visit each other's home. This personal contact gives a more integrated perspective of who we are. Peers can give personal feedback. In the supervisory relationship, it is easy for supervisors to focus on supervisees' lack of skills. Yet in peer relationships, people know various aspects of each other, including values, personality, personal circumstances, strengths, and weaknesses.

We have just reviewed three big benefits of close, meaningful peer relationships: normalization/social comparison; emotional support, confirmation, and belonging; and information sharing and honest communication. Unfortunately, peer relationships also have an uglier underbelly.

PROBLEMS IN HORIZONTAL RELATIONSHIPS

Upward Comparison

Normalizing struggles and understanding them from a developmental perspective through social comparisons happens when all peers share their struggles equally. What happens when they do not? There can be more stress for the peer who thinks "It is only me who is struggling" because others are not sharing their vulnerabilities. It is kind of like the picture of the duck that looks calm on the surface but is madly paddling under the surface. Peers have to share the whole story.

Without knowing that their peers experience the same kinds of problems, novices will try to hide their insecure and incompetent feelings and present themselves as competent counselors. As a result, novice counselors may be left feeling they are the only ones who feel insecure and confused. In this case, social comparison works negatively. Novice counselors compare their most vulnerable inner selves with others' competent exteriors. Here is a "factory" for more frustration, insecurity and performance anxiety. The mountain to be climbed suddenly seems much higher.

This reaction can be explained by upward comparison. This happens to all of us at different times in our lives when we think the other is more X, Y, or Z than we are. Such comparisons are especially powerful when the X, Y, or Z is something highly desirable in our small, culturally encapsulated world. It could be a trait, a skill, a physical-intellectual-social attribute—whatever. Although the consequences of upward and downward comparisons vary depending on situations, typically downward comparisons lead to relief, joy, and more confidence while upward comparisons cause negative effects like anxiety and dejection and a feeling that one does not cope as well as others. Halbesleben and Buckley (2006) found this result in their study of burnout with 360 working adults. They used a social psychology term, "pluralistic ignorance," to explain findings about upward comparison and its long-term effects on burnout. Pluralistic ignorance refers to a mismatch between views of self and others (Katz & Allport, 1931).

In the case of novice counselors' struggles, pluralistic ignorance would mean that although a majority of novice counselors struggle, an individual incorrectly assumes that most others do not have the same problems, just he or she does. In Turkey, there is a saying that the farmer thinks that he only has chickens but the neighbor farmer over the hill has the more desirable geese. In fact, they both have chickens. Pluralistic ignorance in action!

Interpersonal Competition

Comparing the self with others is part of interpersonal competition. Negative emotions and negative self-evaluation are often by-products of these comparisons. Competition was the most frequent response of professional men and women concerning what they disliked about their friendships (Sapadin, 1988).

According to Tesser's self-evaluation maintenance (SEM) model (Campbell & Tesser, 1985; Tesser, 1988), people are motivated to maintain or increase their own self-esteem, which is influenced by three factors: psychological closeness of the other person, relevance of performance, and the performance outcome. That is, novice counselors' self-evaluations are more likely to be threatened when they compare themselves with school peers rather than with strangers, when the comparison is made on a key skill, and when peers do better on the important skill. One way to elevate self-evaluation is to use competition, meaning trying to perform better than others. Becoming very competitive is a natural response in this situation. But remember: Competing with peers reduces much of the benefits of going through the early struggles of therapy-counseling training with peers. People also deal with threats to self-evaluation by diversifying the traits for comparison—for example, "She does group work well, I'm better at assessment, and our other classmate really understands statistics." People may be the same in terms of their year in a graduate program, courses taken, and general field of work. Yet each person can be different in terms of career interests, life stage, personality, strengths, and weaknesses. If novice counselors compare themselves on only a few attributes that seem critically relevant for the work (e.g., who does individual therapy best), it is easy to feel competitive.

To try to reduce natural competitive feelings between graduate students, Tom has them consider the work "pond" as very big with room for all. For example, he told one graduate seminar of seven students that there were 7 billion people in the world; therefore, each of them had a pool of 1 billion people. He suggested that there was a meaningful place for each of them as a psychologist within a 1 billion person pool of human need. They seemed to appreciate the idea, although perhaps they did not say much because they thought it was ridiculous and it did nothing to dispel their anxieties about their own professional futures.

Limited Resources and Competition

The idea of limited resources and competition is closely related to the last topic of interpersonal competition. When there are limited resources, such as funding or job openings, peer *competition* rather than cooperation is likely to occur. This is explained by traditional views of competition as a zero-sum game, a rivalry between parties in which the success of one requires the failure of the other (Johnson & Johnson, 1989).

If you and your classmates both want to attain the same thing, it is hard to share important information with each other. In a competitive mode, people not only miss the opportunity to feel the joy and care of sharing but also feel an inner conflict and tension between their values of altruism and self-protection. This can be particularly distressing to counselors because they mostly value helping and caring for others.

In summary, relationships with peers can be of great use to novice counselors. We hope you have many more of the positives than the negatives that we describe regarding peer relationships.

A LAST COMMENT

Many, many other people sustain us on the novice voyage. We have described only some of these people, such as clinical supervisors and classmates. We have not given full credit to others: spouses/partners, parents, children, friends, mentors, advisors, professors, relatives—the list is long and the benefits are enormous. So many people keep us going. We end this chapter with a Parker Palmer quote about the mentor relationship.

> Mentors and apprentices are partners in an ancient human dance. . . . It is the dance of the spiraling generations, in which the old empower the young with their experience and the young empower the old with new life, reweaving the fabric of the human community as they touch and turn.
>
> —*Palmer, 1998, p. 25*

REFERENCES

Allen, G. J., Szollos, S. J., & Williams, B. E. (1986). Doctoral students' comparative evaluation of best and worst psychotherapy supervision. *Professional Psychology: Research and Practice, 17,* 98–99.

Bardes, C. (2010). The doctor in middle age. In L. Gutkind (Ed.), *Becoming a doctor: From student to specialist, doctor-writers share their experiences* (pp. 111–124). New York, NY: Norton.

Bernard, J. M., & Goodyear, R. K. (2009). *Fundamentals of clinical supervision.* Upper Saddle River, NJ: Pearson.

Campbell, J. D., & Tesser, A. (1985). Self-evaluation maintenance processes in relationships. In S. Duck & D. Perlman (Eds.), *Personal relationships, Vol. 1* (pp. 107–135). London, UK: Sage.

Diener, E., Weiting, N., Harter, J., & Arora, R. (2010). Wealth and happiness across the world: Material prosperity predicts life evaluation, whereas psychosocial prosperity predicts positive feelings. *Journal of Personality & Social Psychology, 99,* 52–61.

Doehrman, M. J. (1976). Parallel processes in supervision and psychotherapy. *Bulletin of the Menninger Clinic, 40,* 1–104.

Festinger, L. A. (1954). A theory of social comparison processes. *Human Relations, 7,* 117–140.

Halbesleben, J. B., & Buckley, M. R. (2006). Comparison and burnout: The role of relative burnout and received social support. *Anxiety, Stress & Coping: 19*(3), 259–278.

Handelsman, M. M., Gottlieb, M. C., & Knapp, S. (2005). Training ethical psychologists: An acculturation model. *Professional Psychology: Research and Practice, 36,* 59–65.

Jamison, K. R. (2010). On not becoming a doctor. In L. Gutkind (Ed.), *Becoming a doctor: From student to specialist, doctor-writers share their experiences* (pp. 59–67). New York, NY: Norton.

Johnson, D. W., & Johnson, R. T. (1989). *Cooperation and competition: Theory and research.* Edina, MN: Interaction Books.

Junger, S. (2010). *War.* New York, NY: Twelve.

Katz, D., & Allport, F. H. (1931). *Student attitudes.* Syracuse, NY: Craftsman.

Kram, K. E., & Isabella, L. A. (1985). Mentoring alternatives: The role of peer relationships in career development. *Academy of Management Journal, 28,* 110–132.

Ladany, N. (2010). Learning what not to do: Lessons from lousy educators and supervisors. In M. Trotter-Mathison, J. Koch, S. Sanger, & T. Skovholt (2010), *Voices from the field: Defining moments in counselor and therapist development* (pp. 98–100). New York, NY: Routledge.

Ladany, N., & Bradley, L. J. (2010). *Counselor supervision.* New York, NY: Routledge.

Ladany, N., Friedlander, M. L., & Nelson, M. L. (2005). *Critical events in psychotherapy supervision.* Washington, DC: American Psychological Association.

Leake, V. S., Riding-Malon, R., Tzou, Y. J., & Muhomba, M. (2010). United cultures of counseling. In M. Trotter-Mathison, J. M. Koch, S. Sanger, & T. Skovholt (Eds.), *Voices from the field. Defining moments in counselor and therapist development* (pp. 164–168). New York, NY: Routledge.

Magnusson, S., Wilcoxon, S.A., & Norem, K. (2000). A profile of lousy supervision: Experienced counselors' perspectives. *Counselor Education and Supervision, 39,* 189–209.

Mintz, L. E. (2010). Thirty minutes closer. In L. Gutkind (Ed.), *Becoming a doctor: From student to specialist, doctor-writers share their experiences* (pp. 171–179). New York, NY: Norton.

Moreland, L. (1993, May-June). Learning cycle. *Family Therapy Networker,* p. 13.

Nathan, M. J., & Petrosino, A. (2003). Expert blind spot among preservice teachers. *American Educational Research Journal, 40,* 905–928.

Neufeldt, S. A. (2007). *Supervision strategies for the first practicum.* Alexandria, VA: American Counseling Association.

Osachuk, T. (2010). The transforming moment with David. In M. Trotter-Mathison, J. M. Koch, S. Sanger, & T. Skovholt (Eds.), *Voices from the field: Defining moments in counselor and therapist development* (pp. 64–66). New York, NY: Routledge.

Palmer, P. J. (1998). *The courage to teach: Exploring the inner landscape of a teacher's life.* San Francisco, CA: Jossey-Bass.

Park, J. (2010). Paradoxical empowerment: Finding a voice in bicultural navigation. In M. Trotter-Mathison, J. M. Koch, S. Sanger, & T. Skovholt (Eds.), *Voices from the field: Defining moments in counselor and therapist development* (pp. 87–89). New York, NY: Routledge.

Rønnestad, M. H., & Orlinsky, D. E. (2005a). Clinical implications: Training, supervision, and practice. In D. E. Orlinsky & M. H. Rønnestad (Eds.), *How psychotherapists develop* (pp. 181–201). Washington, DC: American Psychological Association.

Rønnestad, M. H., & Orlinsky, D. E. (2005b). Comparative cohort development: Novice to senior therapist. Training, supervision, and practice. In D. E. Orlinsky & M. H. Rønnestad (Eds.), *How psychotherapists develop* (pp. 143–157). Washington, DC: American Psychological Association.

Rønnestad, M. H., & Skovholt, T. M. (2003). The journey of the counselor and therapist: Research findings and perspectives on development. *Journal of Career Development, 30*, 1, 5–44.

Sapadin, L. A. (1988). Friendship and gender: Perspectives of professional men and women. *Journal of Social and Personal Relationships, 5*, 387–403.

Schachter, S. (1959). *The psychology of affiliation.* Stanford, CA: Stanford University Press.

Shoptaw, S., Stein, J. A., & Rawson, R. A. (2000). Burnout in substance abuse counselors: Impact of environment, attitudes, and clients with HIV. *Journal of Substance Abuse Treatment, 19*, 117–126.

Skovholt, T. M., & Brothen, T. (1981). Social comparison theory and the universality of experience. *Psychological Reports, 48*, 114.

Stoltenberg, C. D., & McNeil, B. W. (2010). *IDM supervision: An integrative developmental model for supervising counselors and therapists* (3rd ed.). New York, NY: Routledge.

Tesser, A. (1988). Toward a self-evaluation maintenance model of social behavior. *Advances in Experimental Social Psychology, 21*, 181–227.

Thomas, J. T. (2010). *The ethics of supervision and consultation.* Washington, DC: American Psychological Association.

Watkins, C. E. (2011). Psychotherapy supervision since 1909: Some friendly observations about its first century. *Journal of Contemporary Psychotherapy, 4*(2), 57–67.

13

Worlds Apart

The Academic Research Culture and the Therapy Practice Culture and the Search for Common Space

Somehow we have entered the 21st century with research and practice often operating in separate spheres. . . .

The styles of publications and presentations that focus on science and that focus on practice are so vastly different, and there is a relative paucity of efforts to translate between these domains.

—*Lebow, 2006, pp. 3, 4*

The physician knows biology, chemistry, and physiology, knows how they work in the human body, knows the results of clinical studies that argue for or against a given therapy. Less recognized, but equally important, is a second way of knowing: the physician accumulates stories, layer upon layer. A few stories make only for isolated anecdotes. But the thousand stories of an experienced physician make a library, a vast accretion of personal and collective knowledge. The science is important, of course, but the stories too are important, and without them we know only halfway.

—*Bardes, 2010, p. 111*

Some of the least impactful theories of counseling in our field were proposed by people who have no sense of practice; they were too far removed from the phenomenon. You need to bring the art and craft of practice to your empirical research. It is hard to do both research and practice because they require different mind-sets—the researcher is skeptical and questions everything and needs to reduce ambiguity. In contrast, the practitioner can't question everything, but must

have confidence and must live with and enjoy ambiguity and have hope. . . .
[F]or good science and good practice, there must be a synergy between the two.
—*C. Gelso quoted by Hill, 2010, p. 585*

One of my greatest frustrations as president of APA [American Psychological
Association] is that I am not able to wave a magic wand and heal the science/
practice divide.

—*Brehm, 2007, p. 5*

PURPOSE OF THIS CHAPTER

In this chapter my aim is to express and explain a confusing part of the helping professions. It can be difficult for novices to understand how the academic research world and
the therapy/counseling practice world connect. For novices, practice is often jarringly
different from the academic research side of the profession, a difference that is felt in the
body and in the brain. Novices may or may not be aware at some level that the epistemology is also different. The existence of these two different worlds can be confusing for
emerging practitioners, because the cultural clash is usually not spelled out by professors
and academic advisors. We explore this issue here in this chapter.

In Chapter 9, we also explored ways of knowing in our field of therapy and counseling and examined the learning triangle of research, practice, and personal life. Here
the focus is on research versus practice and possible ways to heal this divide.

Some academic training models link academic research to practice; these include
the scientist–practitioner model (Lane & Corrie, 2007; Mellott, 2007) and the practitioner–scholar model (Peterson, Peterson, Abrams, & Stricker, 1997). These models
are presented as seamless ways that science impacts practice and practice impacts science. Unfortunately, in reality, the connection between these two worlds is often not as
seamless as the models suggest, despite admirable attempts to bridge these worlds (e.g.,
Stricker & Trierweiler, 1995).

It is hard to connect the two cultures when there are big differences in their phenomenological worlds. Practitioners focus on the human condition as captured in emotion. Most clients ask for help when they are experiencing one of the trilogy of the distress emotions: anger, anxiety, or depression. The world of practice is captured in movies
and novels and other affect-filled realities. Does the scientific, objective method fit here?
Researchers focus on the human condition as captured by the empirical method with its
emphasis on reducing error variance and having experimental control. Researchers like
to measure external things. Does the complexity and confusion of practice fit here? Here
is an epistemological clash for novices in practice: the objective world of the lab versus
the subjective world of the client.

MORE ON THE CULTURAL DIVIDE

> Over the last thirty years I've watched a lot of pain flow under the bridge. By
> now, I have a Ph.D. in human suffering.
>
> —*Pipher, 2003, p. xvi*

In this quote, used earlier in Chapter 7, Pipher describes the life of the practitioner.
Words spoken by the client in the therapy office often detail shattered lives, shattered
like glass breaking when hitting concrete. It is a scene of chaos, confusion, and great
sadness, and the practitioner's task—repairing the glass—is seemingly impossible. Practitioners do not work at joy clinics. There is suffering and disappointment all around.
This is what Pipher means about getting a PhD in human suffering. Although the work
can be meaningful and satisfying, it is not light and fluffy.

Compared to the practice world, the academic research world is more sanitized
with a view that the uncontrollable can be controlled. This culture puts high value on
small empirical studies. They are very difficult to complete because they must meet high
scientific standards. Only a few are accepted into high-prestige journals. Unfortunately,
from all this scientific effort, often there is little direction or meaning for practitioners
who are looking at the shattered glass, with pieces everywhere, and wanting desperately
to put it all back together.

Although much research and theory can be useful for practitioners, my experience
when interacting with many, many therapy and counseling practitioners is that research,
especially small, tightly controlled experimental studies offered without context, is not
sufficient and does not provide much fuel for them. It is like the difference between
reading about a foreign country and actually being there, interacting in the intense
cultural context. The reading is important but not sufficient.

What are the foundational differences between the culture of academic research and
the culture of practice? The ontology (basic assumptions about the nature of the world)
and epistemology (the fountain of knowledge) are profoundly different, as are the in-
centives for academic researchers compared to practitioners. These are the two cultural
worlds that pass each other, just like the famous two ships in the night.

The field of marriage and family therapy is a good example of the ongoing research–
practice cultural clash, or what Sexton, Alexander, and Mease (2004) describe as "the
persistence of the research-practice schism" (p. 638). In the field of marriage and family
therapy, researchers adopted the gold standard of high-quality research using statistical
methods. At the same time, Sexton et al. (2004) say practitioners rejected these methods because they are based on a logical, positivistic epistemology. The practitioners and
theory builders wanted to:

> capture phenomena thought to be reclusive, dynamic, [with] multidirectional
> processes of openness and growth, interdeterminate dynamic system trajectories,

and interpersonal transactions that absolutely could not be "dismantled" in a manner that represented the tradition of "good science." (p. 590)

As in other areas in the helping fields, these research and practice camps in marriage and family therapy have trouble finding common ground.

MY OWN BICULTURAL PROFESSIONAL LIFE

I have spent many years living professionally within these two separate cultures and at the place where they intersect. In one culture, I am a professor within a research university that is far removed from the world of practice; in the other, I am a part-time practitioner in a community clinic, far removed from the academic research culture. Living this bicultural professional life has had a very big impact on how I view the cultural gap in the therapy/counseling professions.

I have great respect for these two cultures. It has been a great privilege to be immersed in both of these work worlds. I have been enriched by the hardworking and talented people in both cultures who, in their own way, strive to make our human world a better place.

For many years, I have experienced the ebb and flow of two different cultures. It started when I took graduate courses in psychology, theology, and human development in the morning and then worked the afternoon shift at the University of Chicago inpatient hospital psychiatry unit when living in Hyde Park in Chicago in the late 1960s. Such different worlds in the classroom and the hospital! In the years since then, I have inhabited both these worlds of academic research culture and practice culture. My experience in both, and living this bicultural professional life, has led me to see the differences more than the similarities. It has been a version of what Tim Olson (1988) calls "bifocality and the space between" when he describes himself as both Japanese and American. The two cultures—research and practice—have different languages, different values; demand different skills; judge success differently; and respect different work skills. The cultures share few assumptions about what constitutes the good and noble professional life. There is very little overlap between the academic research and the practice world employment incentive systems. Practitioners get paid to work hard to help clients get better. Research professors get paid mainly for teaching, advising, publications, and obtaining grants. The academic terms "impact factor" and "citation index" sound as if they relate directly to practice. Mostly, though, academics use these terms to judge the value of a professor's intellectual ideas in the small circle world of research.

Yet, in my own therapy and counseling practice, I have been helped so much by theory and research. I have read and sorted through a mountain of theory and research over the years. Currently, as I sit and write, I am thinking about attachment research, working alliance research, readiness for counseling research, common factors research, marriage research, racial identity research, mindfulness research, and writing on ethics. The work in all of these areas has informed my practice.

An example of a specific research contribution comes from Wampold (2001, 2010). In a major analysis of many therapy outcome studies, he found that the practitioner's specific theoretical approach is of minimal importance in positive client outcome. That is important work, which I greatly appreciate and have cited in other chapters of this book. I have enjoyed reading *Research for the Psychotherapist* by Jay Lebow (2006). He does a wonderful job of laying out, in clear language, the research evidence and practitioner stance on numerous issues, giving equal attention to both camps.

Although research and theory have been so much help to me in the practice world, I cannot imagine knowing much about practice without practice. One major premise of the expertise literature is that experience in the domain is crucial for expertise (e.g., *The Nature of Expertise,* edited by Chi, Glaser, & Farr, 1988). I do not claim to be an expert, but I have learned a lot about practice by practicing. My 16,000 hours of counseling and therapy, accumulated in part-time practice over decades, have been very instructive. There are countless examples of having to experience something in order to understand it. Without doing it, can a person know a lot about canoeing in white water, giving birth, culture shock, being intensely in love, failing a class in college, winning a race, having a bad case of poison ivy, helping a loved one die, being a smoke jumper, parenting? The list goes on.

I think a central error of researchers is to discount the importance of practice experience to practitioner competence. It is ironic that academic researchers rely so much on their own experience as college teachers to guide their own teaching, and often do not attend to the scholarship on teaching (personal communication, psychology teaching award winner Thomas Brothen, September 22, 2007). Perhaps this reality is a statement about the epistemology of practice and how important professional experience is for making meaning. This use of one's professional experience is true, in my view, whenever intense human contact is at the heart of the professional work (e.g., social worker, teacher, therapist, counselor, physician, clergy).

ACADEMIC RESEARCH WORLD AS THE FIRST CULTURE FOR THE NEW THERAPY OR COUNSELING STUDENT

Early in graduate school, students in the helping professions, especially in research universities, are inducted into the culture of academic research. Usually student novices attend a series of academic classes and then later begin practicum/internship/field placement. During these classes, novices are introduced to research and theory through textbooks, class discussion, and presentations by professors.

When students are in a graduate class with a tenured, research-oriented professor, they are in one culture; when, later the same day, they go to a community clinic with a practitioner as supervisor, they are in another culture. Certainly the students know that the cultures are different; in one place, it is academic; in the other, it is practice. Yet the overt differences "hide the more profound fissures at the foundational, fundamental level" (L. Langenhahn, personal communication, June 20, 2007). Students go back and forth between these cultures without any clear discussion of how moving between the culture of research and the culture of practice is not seamless; since the cultures often clash, there can be an unarticulated confusion.

Since cultures tend to encapsulate and restrict one's worldview, it is only natural for academic researchers to omit telling students, at the start of the novice journey, about the culture of practice. Since the academic culture, especially in the large research universities, does not reward practice, it is hard for these professors to describe the nuances of a culture no longer visited. For these professors, practicum and internship are often far away in the rearview mirror.

There are highly credentialed and skilled practitioners within the research culture. Often they work in university counseling and mental health centers. Yet they often suffer by being practitioners in a research world. This means that they do not have an academic title, such as professor, they are not able to advise graduate students, and they have a lower pay scale.

Consequently, the culture of big research universities lacks professors who are highly experienced practitioners and know the pressing and difficult questions of the practice culture. Knowing the vexing problems of practice is important to keep the channels open between researchers and practitioners. Too often, each of these worlds operates in a small circle. Academics publish in high-status journals that are read and referenced by other academics; practitioners go to applied workshops and use peer consultation to understand the highly complex lives of clients.

Academic culture assumes that knowledge flows one way, from the high-status lab to the lesser knowledge-based world of practice. Practitioners do not believe researchers use practice-based data for answers. For example, in the book *The Great Ideas of Clinical Science: 17 Principles that Every Mental Health Professional Should Understand*, edited by Lilienfeld and O'Donohue (2007), the editors' biographic descriptions indicate stunning levels of productivity; one wrote 150 articles and the other edited 20 books. However, although the book is intended to enrich clinical practice, there is no mention of the editors' clinical experience. Neither writes about the illumination that came to him from hundreds and hundreds of intense, difficult, satisfying, and instructive experiences with clients. As I have noted in the expertise literature review of Chapter 11, a premise of the research on expertise (e.g., *The Nature of Expertise* by Chi et al., 1988) is that *experience* in a domain is central for expertise. For example, can a professor of European culture know much about Europe without occasionally being immersed in that culture? The editors of *The Great Ideas of Clinical Science* could at least note this major limitation regarding practice in their introduction. And the 20 chapter authors make almost no mention of active, enriching practitioner work. The chapters present many valuable ideas for practitioners. However, these academic research culture authors, cut off from practice, produce their ideas as culture outsiders and, therefore, their ideas are not as useful as they may think. For example, many ideas in the book suggest that practitioners use certain methods, such as clinical consultation, to learn from practice. But these methods are already used.

This debate about science versus practice is important. If the research products of the scientific method within the university context do little to affect practice, then the reason for existence for research-based university professors is in question. The status given to the "impact factor" and "citation index" would then eventually be perceived as part of a limited world of academics that is much less important than researchers assume. A major problem, as I have said, is that the well-designed, and difficult-to-complete, small empirical studies are often like seeds thrown onto the ground that never grow. The practitioner ground is not fertile for many of these seeds. Why? In order to control moderating and mediating variables, these studies must artificially reduce the real complexity of practice.

In the debate, academics have the publicity advantage. They know how to write articles that journals will publish. More important, they get credit and, indirectly, money for writing about research versus practice problems. Practitioners do not know the culture of journals and how to get published. Of more importance, although professors get paid indirectly for publishing because it is part of their job, practitioners do not get any fees for publishing journal articles because academic journals do not pay for publication. Publishing articles takes a lot of time and energy. Practitioners seldom write about the cultural war. They just keep doing practice work and do not read many of the scientist-practitioner articles. This is another example of ships passing each other in the night.

UNDERSTANDING CULTURE DIFFERENCES USING HOLLAND'S VOCATIONAL TYPOLOGY

We can look at these two cultures of research and practice by using research from career psychology, specifically the work of John Holland (Gysbers, Heppner & Johnston, 2009). Holland has developed a theory of career choice and satisfaction based on a model of person–environment fit. There is extensive research behind the Holland theory (Gottfredson, 1999). It can be used to understand differences between academic researchers and practitioners and their preferred work environments.

In Holland's theory, there are six personality types and six corresponding occupational environments. Two of the types of most interest to us in this discussion are investigative and social. Investigative-type individuals are drawn to college majors in math and science areas. They are drawn to analytical thinking and problem-solving patterns that are common in scientific, technical, and mathematical fields. Being methodical and precise are valued traits. Investigative-type individuals like the abstract data of the natural world and spend time and energy with theorizing and investigating in this world. They are drawn to jobs such as scientist, researcher, computer programmer, and technician. They usually do not find helping others in a personal way to be energizing. The language of numbers is more important than the language of words. A career daydream exercise (Skovholt, Morgan, & Cunningham, 1989) could, for an investigative-type person, involve discovery of an important but unknown scientific fact. Such work could be very fulfilling for such a person.

Social-type individuals, in the Holland theory, are drawn toward helping people with educational, social, emotional, spiritual, and physical needs. They are drawn to thinking patterns that are part of helping and understanding others. Often these patterns rely on emotion, nonsequential thinking, and understanding words and nonverbal communication as a whole. These individuals like jobs in teaching, counseling, and social work. They may find solving a scientific problem boring and uninteresting. The language of words is important, and numbers usually are not. A possible career daydream could involve helping a child resolve feelings about the traumatic loss of a parent.

In this brief comparison of Holland's investigative and social types, we can see how it is easy to have two cultures where there is not much connection or interest in the other. The logical, linear, sequential thinking of the scientist clashes with the creative, nonsequential, affect-centered thinking of the practitioner in the helping fields.

Table 13.1 shows some cultural differences in summary form.

Table 13.1	Culture of Practice vs Culture of Research	
	Culture of Practice	**Culture of Research**
Hero	Practitioner as hero	Researcher as hero
Epistemology	Words, N=1 stories of human life, especially of loss and recovery	Numbers, high-N studies using scientific methods
Reward System	Many referrals and thankful clients	Many empirical articles, grants, and tenure
Focus	Profoundly helping another	High research and grant productivity
Status	High respect of other practitioners and clients	High respect of other professors through citation index, impact factor, size of grants, and teaching ability
Get Paid	For clinical work	For research, teaching, and committee work
Accountability to Other Culture?	No; practitioners are concerned with reducing client suffering and pleasing referral sources. They sometimes feel used by researchers but not accountable to them.	No; academic researchers usually have little awareness of their impact, or lack of it, on practice influencing other researchers matters.
Does It Ultimately Matter if the Work Affects the Other Culture?	Yes; science and the medical model increase the status of the work, including money for practitioners.	Yes; the goal of improving human functioning is a major focus for academic work and the reason for grants and research support.

(continued)

Table 13.1   *(Continued)*

Holland Type	Social	Investigative
Popular Journals	*Psychotherapy Networker, Professional Psychology, In Session: Psychotherapy in Practice, New Therapist*	*Psychotherapy Research, Journal of Consulting and Clinical Psychology, Counseling Psychologist, Journal of Marriage and Family Therapy*
Popular Books	*The Gift of Therapy, Dialectical Behavior Therapy Skills Workbook, The Anxiety and Phobia Workbook*	Bergin and Garfield's *Handbook of Psychotherapy and Behavior Change, Bringing Psychotherapy Research to Life*

Next, we turn to the contributions and limitations of both cultures.

CONTRIBUTIONS, EPISTEMOLOGY, AND REWARD STRUCTURE OF THE RESEARCH CULTURE

Bergin and Garfield's Handbook of Psychotherapy and Behavior Change (Lambert, 2004), through its many editions, is considered the most respected book on research in therapy and counseling. In the chapter on efficacy and effectiveness of the work, Lambert and Ogles (2004) cite and discuss 313 research studies. It is hard to estimate the total number of hours that scholars have devoted to understanding the efficacy and effectiveness of our work when completing these 313 articles and books. I estimate that it is well in excess of 200,000 hours (a full-time job, defined as 40 hours/week for one year, equals 2,000 hours). These 200,000 hours equal four full-time researchers each working 25 years. So, the 200,000 hours may be an underestimate for the total research hours for the citations in just this *one chapter*. See the book and its 18 chapters for a full dose of this very impressive and valuable set of studies and reviews. There is so much in this one book that is valuable and insightful for practitioners.

There are, of course, many valuable research journals in the therapy and counseling professions. Just a few are mentioned in Table 13.1.

At a foundational level, theory and research are important. In the scientific-practitioner model, the information from classes serves as part of the inner framework for the student as practicum begins. Here are three examples of the great value of theory and research that serve as parts of the inner framework students develop for understanding human behavior:

1. Human behavior has both genetic and environmental roots.
2. There are systematic psychological ways of understanding human behavior.
3. Carefully researched psychological approaches enhance coping and significantly reduce human suffering.

As Murdock (2006) says, midlevel theory, between the most abstract and the most practical, offers the practitioner a lot from the research side. Murdock describes the usefulness of attachment, racial identity, and career development theory for practitioners. These theories have been very helpful to my work as a practitioner. And research on loss, coping, hope, resiliency, healthy traits, career and marriage transitions (as a few examples from many) give practitioners hypotheses to use in their work.

LIMITATIONS OF THE RESEARCH CULTURE FOR PRACTICE KNOWLEDGE

The limitations of contemporary research related to how therapy is studied greatly restrict the extent to which the results from therapy research are likely to be generalizable to clinical practice.

—*Kazdin, 2004, p. 560*

Even some of my colleagues who are both clinicians and researchers admit to using research sparsely in their clinical practice. . . .

The clinical phenomena is so complex that it never will be fully driven by research, only informed by it. . . . The process of treatment will never be amenable to a simple formula.

—*Lebow, 2006, p. 10*

The practice world is not one of logical, linear thought where independent variables and error variance are to be controlled. It is a world of affect, great ambiguity, confusion, creative and fluid thought patterns, a language of words, not numbers, and an intense focus on the needs of the other. If given a choice of knowledge that has rigor and knowledge that has meaning, meaning wins out. The complexity of love cannot be profoundly understood by counting hugs, as one does if counting is necessary for the research method.

In an attempt to improve practice, the scientific method has been used through the introduction of manualized treatments and empirically supported treatments (ESTs). Both are well-meaning attempts to move the research lab to the world of practice. Manualized treatments were developed to standardize treatments so that research could find the powerful ingredients of therapy (Hollon & Beck, 2004) and reduce incompetence in the field. Some academic leaders find them of great value. Yet Hollon and Beck (2004) review some of the problems with the manual approach:

[E]xtant manuals may be too rigid to be usefully applied in most clinical settings, and therapists may find that they stifle creativity. . . . [T]he most effective psychotherapists in controlled studies departed from manualized directives. . . . [T]herapist interpersonal skills were negatively correlated with the ability to learn a manual. . . .[H]igh level of adherence to specific models or procedures of psychotherapy may actually interfere with the development of a good working alliance.

—*Hollon & Beck, 2004, p. 245*

As stated earlier in this book, Reed (2006, p. 20) lists many variables as active in the counseling/therapy session. I count 33 on his list. That is a lot, but it does not explain the complexity, challenge, and confusion of the work. Reed describes these variables as interacting. When 33 variables are interacting with each other, there are 1,089 possibilities in each therapy/counseling session. This is a conservative number because many variables, such as establishing a therapeutic alliance or defining a client's desired role in treatment and the client's strengths, are not yes-or-no variables. The number 1,089 is evidence of the limited usefulness of a tightly controlled small study, and how it is not accessible to the practitioner in a useful way.

Professors get paid for valid research, which in the culture mostly means research that is empirically valid. For research to be empirically valid, investigators have to control many variables so that they can see how the independent variable directly affects the dependent variable. Using this method, the hard sciences have made tremendous strides in making discoveries and developing new ideas. The model of controlling variables often makes the lab a great contrast to the chaotic world of practice. And this is why research that works in a lab often does not translate to practice.

Slife (2004) presents the philosophical assumptions of the empirical research side of the therapy and counseling professions. He says that these fields, from the perspective of academic researchers, have adopted naturalism and empiricism, the central paradigm of the natural sciences, as the way to understand human life. He writes:

There is no empirical justification for empiricism, no scientific justification for science. Empiricism and the philosophies underlying science are just that—philosophies. Like all philosophies, they have philosophical axes to grind and pre-investigatory values to assert.

— *p. 50*

Slife's critique of the empirical method of naturalism—objectivism, materialism, and universalism—seems especially pertinent here because often the practice world does not operate on these theoretical assumptions. Here are Slife's views of the limitations of objectivism, materialism, and universalism for therapy and counseling practice.

Objectivism

> In its most basic form, objectivism is the study of "objects" that are external to the observer's mind.
>
> —*Slife, 2004, p. 49*

Education has heavily influenced us to be objective and to use the scientific method as the valid way of understanding. When psychology, as a discipline, moved away from philosophy, it adopted the scientific paradigm as a central method to acquire knowledge. A symbolic beginning of psychology as a science was the founding of Wilhelm Wundt's laboratory in Leipzig in 1879 (Hilgard, 1987, p. 3). Slife (2004) writes:

> Many psychologists . . . have long used the experimental and correlational methods of the natural sciences as though their scientific observations were the relatively accurate, unbiased renderings. (p. 49)

Being objective seems so right as a goal and as a sign of scientific progress. It seems to fit as a method for those who strive to understand the inanimate, such as illumination of streetlights, the metal basketball hoop, laser treatment for skin conditions, and resiliency of asphalt. Therapy methods have been deemed valid within the objectivism tradition. Most of the ESTs fit this mold, and the list of ESTs is heavily weighted toward cognitive and behavioral approaches. Approaches that are not as observable, such as existential, psychodynamic, person centered, and family, do not make the list because they do not produce data that are objective (Messer, 2001). The validity of some therapy methods seems to slip away because they cannot be objectively understood. Does this mean that subjective realities such as the world of emotions do not exist? Does it mean that psychologists cannot study profound human topics, like love and death, because they are not topics for objective study?

Materialism

The material assumptions of natural science highly value matter that can be captured by the senses or, as Slife (2004, p. 52) says, matter that is "tangible, visible and substantial." If there is no matter, it is not a candidate for scientific psychology. What happens to the client's unexpressed emotions toward self, the practitioner, the counseling process? These are central concerns of practitioners but are not tangible, so they do not exist in the materialistic assumptions of what counts. The newer biological focus in mental health work with psychotropic medications fits better with materialism than does a focus on existential therapy. One view ascends while the other recedes within the materialist values of the scientific method. Again, novices enter this swirling epistemological confusion when going from the classroom to the community practice site.

Universalism

Discovering laws of nature that apply universally is exciting for researchers. It is a holy grail hope in the animated pursuit of the scientific researcher, and many researchers in the counseling and therapy fields have adopted this paradigm. Yet when Slife (2004) examines universalism, he sees its limitations when applied to the counseling/therapy interview.

Practitioners are not searching for an abstract principle that applies universally; practitioners are interested in understanding the uniqueness of one person and using that understanding to help the one person. Nonuniversal principles that are unique, distinctive, and rare are prized if they help the therapy process.

Slife's (2004) critique of objectivism, materialism, and univeralism help us understand the limits of the direct application of empirical research to practice.

CONTRIBUTIONS, EPISTEMOLOGY, AND REWARD STRUCTURE OF THE PRACTICE CULTURE

How have we reached the point that intelligent people who are accepted into some of the most competitive doctoral programs in higher education, who complete a research-based doctoral degree, who undergo a minimum of two years of supervised clinical training, and who are able to pass national and state licensing exams are routinely discussed as though none of their knowledge is legitimate?

—*Reed, 2006, p. 14*

Therapy should not be theory-driven but relationship-driven.

—*Yalom, 2002, p. xviii*

Many of the most revered ideas, methods, and techniques used by therapists and counselors have come from family therapists Minuchin, Satir, and Bowen. Yalom and M. Erickson, as well as Jung, have also been very influential—very influential—in the work of therapists and counselors. All of these six giants in the field got their ideas from their active clinical practice. None developed their work from an epistemology based on empirical research ("The Top Ten," 2007). Practitioners might say, "Yes, the broader ways of knowing are what really provide insight." Researchers might say, "This is terrible; we need empirical research as the base for all of our work." More ships passing each other in the night.

A Big Issue: Do Practitioners Learn and Become More Skilled Through Practice?

The practitioner claim is that expertise develops through practice. Does it? A lot hinges on the answer to this question. If practice leads to expertise, then more practice is the right train to the right destination. If practice does not lead to more expertise, the best solution is to ask the academic researchers for answers. Then it is the practitioner's job to implement those answers. Unfortunately, all the different perspectives may be partially right. Let us review the topic and the evidence for "practice makes perfect."

We have all had experiences where doing more of something improves our performance. Examples include cooking, learning how to greet others in a different culture, driving a car, using a hatchet, shaving, pronouncing words. And if we really know something well, we can also improvise and, with moment-to-moment creativity, perform well. George Winston, the pianist, starts his performances by sitting on the stool and then lets his hands take him where they may. This, in my view, is how expert performers in the helping fields do their work. They have a deep schema of experience to draw on.

Donald Schön, who wrote the seminal book *The Reflective Practitioner* (1983), and followed it up with *Educating the Reflective Practitioner* (1987), worked in organizational development and the improvement of human performance. He also played jazz. From music, he learned that through practice and feedback about practice, we can learn a lot and continually get better. He called this process of practice-reflection-practice becoming a reflective practitioner. I do not imagine that he thought that a person can get better at jazz just by reading the research and applying it. For Schön, practice and learning from practice was crucial. So, here is a theoretical base for a certain kind of thoughtful professional practice in the helping fields: The formula is lots of practice, lots of feedback, better practice, and the cycle continues. In Chapter 11, we discussed this topic of expertise development in more detail. We continue with it here as part of the question of whether practitioners learn from practice.

The master therapists we studied (Skovholt & Jennings, 2004) seemed to learn a lot from practice. For example, three of the Paradox Characteristics (p. 132) in the study were:

1. Drive to mastery and never a sense of having fully arrived
2. Voracious broad learner and focused narrow student
3. Very open to feedback about self and not destabilized by feedback about self

Hitting a baseball in the major leagues is a difficult athletic skill. How do major league hitters do it? Everyday batting practice is one part of constant feedback. Watching videos is another; tracking statistics is a third; and, of course, constantly facing good pitchers is another. In their work on expertise, Ericsson, Charness, Hoffman, and Feltovich (2006) call this "deliberate practice." In the practitioner's world, counselors and therapists work on deliberate practice: by first seeing clients, then engaging in active reflection, case consultation, clinical supervision, and peer group supervision.

Feedback and processing are critical. When sitting with a client, practitioners are very focused and sensitive to the client's reaction. Hoshmand and Polkinghorne (1992) describe this kind of reflective judgment as a kind of expertise development. They affirm that skillful reflection enhances practitioners' skill in detecting the personal biases that are so destructive for really understanding and helping clients.

Teachers are like therapists in their use of the professional interaction (client and therapist, student and teacher) for learning. I remember listening to University of Minnesota professors who gave acceptance speeches after they had won teaching awards. When receiving awards, all discussed how much they learned from their students. Great teachers learning from their students? How does that work? Aren't professors supposed to profess: fill up empty, inert vessels with knowledge? No, these great teachers offered lavish appreciation for their students as teachers. Teaching them what? It seems that by really paying attention to their students, these professors learned how to teach them. These teachers were describing an intense interaction process where they tried out teaching methods on their students and modified things as they went along. This is an example of the classroom as a lab for learning about teaching.

All practitioners in the helping, teaching, and healing fields use interactions with the other in order to learn. As I wrote earlier, according to one psychology professor, a teaching award winner himself, most psychology professors use their own teaching, rather than the research on teaching, to guide their teaching style and method. This is a testament to the power of professional experience as a guide to competence. Listening intensively for feedback is a key to improvement. This spontaneous, interactive process is not part of the equation in small rigorous laboratory studies and helps explain why some studies never get applied in the real world of the clinical interview.

How do we learn from practice? McKenna, Boyd, and Yost (2007) examined this question by asking how senior professional clergy learn from experience. Professional ministry is a profession that parallels the helping professions, as "pastoral jobs involve interacting with a particularly wide variety of people in intensive, emotionally demanding situations" (p. 192). The researchers conducted 90-minute interviews with 100 senior clergy members. They coded the results under the two domains of situational factors and personal strategies.

The two highest-rated factors were (1) contact with role models or peers, times when others played a key role (McKenna et al., 2007, p. 196), and (2), learning focus, their lifelong desire to learn, to be teachable, curious, and have a sense of wonder (p. 197). The authors said these pastors cultivated a learning mentality by intentionally trying to learn from experience, which included watching how others react and reflect on events. From this study of senior clergy by McKenna et al. (2007), we have ideas of how experience can be the great teacher. And this helps us to think more about our earlier question: Do practitioners learn and become more skilled through practice?

In practice, the method of valuable knowledge acquisition is complicated. Goldfried's (2001) edited book of the professional development of 15 well-known practitioners captures the rich, multilayer, multisource, long-term development of experienced practitioners. The data for practice come from an integration of larger guiding principles from theory and research, the rich experience database of practice, and lessons from the personal life of practitioners. It is like a learning triangle. One side is the enormous knowledge base that comes from the insights gained from reflective practice. A second side comes from useful theory and research that is applied to helping clients live richer, more meaningful lives. The third side is the practitioner's own life, which offers wisdom about the human story. All three sides are necessary to form the triangle of the epistemology of knowledge for the practitioner. See Chapter 9 for more on details on the learning triangle.

In the large international study mentioned previously, there were many influences that affect how therapists do their work: Clients, supervision, personal therapy, and experiences in personal life were rated highest (Orlinsky & Rønnestad, 2005).

The world of loss and recovery is of great value to practitioners, because this is the expertise area their clients need. Many counseling and therapy clients make the pilgrimage to the practitioner's office because of loss. It could be the sudden end of a primary relationship, such as divorce, losing a job, or disillusionment with religious and spiritual beliefs. Perhaps the person is coping with a chronic illness. Or the loss may be from being cut from a sports team or artistic troupe. Scientific research and theory on many topics can be of use, but to really understand, practitioners must know and feel loss and suffering on an emotional level. That is why a book like *The Year of Magical Thinking* (Didion, 2006) is so valuable to practitioners as a data source. In this book, acclaimed writer Joan Didion describes a year of shocking grief in her life after her husband's sudden death and her only child's serious illness. Practitioners need to know the schema of grief: what it is, how it is expressed, how to enter it, and how to be helpful in the healing process. This personal, emotionally felt knowing is different than an intellectual version of knowing. Theory and research from the laboratory do not give practitioners this affective experience.

LIMITATIONS OF THE PRACTICE CULTURE FOR PRACTICE KNOWLEDGE

If we examine various theories and procedures in psychotherapy, we find a bewildering set of ideas and behaviors. There have been systems of therapy that had no therapist . . . systems in which the therapist says and does nothing . . . systems in which patients are asked to scream or strike out . . . methods in which the therapist makes fun of the patient, treating him or her with apparent disrespect . . . and methods in which the patient is treated with utmost respect . . . methods in which patients are treated as children . . . methods that stress religion . . .methods that are conglomerates of a wide variety of procedures.

—*Corsini, 2007, p. 2*

Without a scientific mind-set toward the work, it is easy for practitioners to run with theory and techniques they get exclusively from their own personal views and their own views of their own practitioner data. Their motivation may be to really help the clients. Conversely, the motivation for these ideas may be fame, money, self-healing strategies, or the inventor's own projections of what is important in human life. Sometimes it is all of these motivations together. All kinds of ideas emerge in the world of practice with good face validity but without a thread of external validity. When personal bias defines the work, client welfare is in danger.

Practitioners do go off in directions that emphasize their own projections of what is important in human development; for example, Harry Stack Sullivan thought it was anxiety, Albert Ellis thought it was being rational, Victor Frankel thought it was meaning and purpose (Corsini & Wedding, 2007). Although each of these views of the essential human concerns has made a significant contribution, each also has the limitation of not having an empirical base.

Inventors of methods find it powerfully seductive to present an approach, theory, or technique that works fast as an all-purpose balm. Just like any new diet plan that supposedly works wonders, the simple, quick, all-purpose therapy method gets attention. New methods in therapy and counseling often involve words such as "solution focused" and "brief" and some new mix of the words "cognitive-affective behavior" into an easily remembered acronym. Such methods can become popular if they offer hope for practitioners who may, as novices, be experiencing self-doubt about their effectiveness and are searching for a learnable yet comprehensive approach.

I remember one assessment method where people were asked to line up colors on cards, then get a code and read about their personality. The method was fun and engaging. Unfortunately, it had no construct validity. Here is another example: Encounter groups seemed like a good idea at the time, until research found that some participants got worse after participating. For more information, see *Encounter Groups: First Facts* (Lieberman, Yalom, & Miles, 1973).

Eye Program Desensitization and Reprocessing (EMDR; Shapiro, 1995) has been popular. Shapiro came upon this method by chance by using it on herself. It involves a series of eye movements that quickly reduce psychological trauma. There is research support for EMDR (i.e., Marcus, Marquis, & Sakai, 2004). Everyone wants such a method, one that quickly reduces horrific psychological wounds. Is it too good to be true? Perhaps. Proponents of the method are responsible for some of the positive outcome research with it. This investigator stance of theoretical allegiance has been cited as a factor in better outcomes for one method over another (Elliott, Greenberg, & Lietaer, 2004). Two studies have found EMDR and other approaches equally effective (Bradley, Greene, Russ, Dutra, & Westen, 2005; Seidler & Wagner, 2006). The theoretical rationale for how EMDR works—internal cognitive changes from eye movements—has not been proven. It may be that EMDR works because of the common/therapeutic curative factors that make many approaches effective—and, generally, equally effective. These include a positive healing ritual, a special place for the ritual, a one-way caring professional relationship, an explanation of the distress, and a path away from the distress to positive development. EMDR provides all of this, but so do other methods (Duncan, Miller, Wampold, & Hubble, 2010; Frank & Frank, 1991; Wampold, 2001, 2010; Wampold & Weinberger, 2010).

Practitioner-developed methods that suddenly become popular can have the ingredients of "too good to be true" for the slow train of the helping professions. The train usually gets there, but it takes a lot of effort, more like what was called the milk train. The bullet train is not for long-term, difficult problems. Remember in Chapter 1 where I discussed how people often come to us when they have an unsolvable problem that has to be solved. If it were so easy to find solutions, people would not need professional helpers.

Practitioners face intense pressure from overt and covert sources that act in concert. They hear: "Please do something magical, masterfully." Clients want it; insurance companies want it; referral agents, such as employee assistance programs, want it too. In a larger sense, we all want to believe that life is not so dangerous or difficult. We do not want to believe that psychic wounds can overwhelm us and not be easily or quickly fixed.

Yes, counseling and therapy can be effective and valuable to those who seek it out. However, a statistically average client result from the outcome research shows modest improvement after a number of sessions (Lambert, 2004). Yet quick-acting shamans or sorcerers with magical methods are in demand by both clients and new practitioners. Without scientific scrutiny, the culture of practice can be a slippery slope toward methods that, unburdened by a need for effectiveness and evidence, promise too much.

Under "Contributions, Epistemology, and Reward Structure of the Practice Culture," I discussed the importance of work in the domain as essential for practice improvement. The problem is that sometimes practice does *not* make perfect. Although a lot of practice and direct feedback can greatly improve practice (Ericsson et al., 2006), a problem with strong fidelity to a theoretical approach is that the feedback loop can be tuned to the wrong data. For example, in our study of senior psychologists (average age of 75), one practitioner told of being trained in a precise model of therapy (Rønnestad & Skovholt, 2001). If the clients did not return, he assumed that the model was not the problem, client readiness was. Then events in this therapist's personal life led him to confront the limits of the model for understanding human behavior and facilitating change. He then realized that client premature termination, during the many years of his therapy work, was feedback about lack of client readiness *and also* limitations in his therapy competence. For years, allegiance to a model and his seduction by the research support for it had blinded him from a complete understanding of client feedback. Sometimes, practice experience is more like going round and round on the merry-go-round, rather than making straight-ahead progress.

In a chapter titled "The Clinician as Subject: Practitioners Are Prone to the Same Judgment Errors as Everyone Else," Ruscio (2007) deflates the practitioners' balloon. Ruscio reviews research from cognitive science on the multiple errors humans make—including practitioners—when coming to conclusions from their own experience. Ruscio's work provides more evidence regarding the limitations of the practice culture for practice.

CONVERGENCE BETWEEN THE CULTURES OF SCIENCE AND PRACTICE

Does it make any sense to engage in practice without reference to relevant research or to engage in research that fails to be informed by the work of clinicians and bears no relation to practice?

—Lebow, 2006, p. 5

[Psychologist Enricho Jones] mastered the dialect of not succumbing to illusions generated by reductionism and simplification, while avoiding the trap of creating mystique and religion where the innocent questions can no longer be asked, and the truth is buried under multiple layers of false sophistication.

—Katzenstein, Fonagy & Ablon, 2010, p. 267

Carl Rogers is an example of a scientific practitioner. In two large surveys, in 1982 and 25 years later, in 2006, Rogers was rated by practitioners as the most influential psychotherapist ("The Top Ten," 2007). Rogers was not only a caring practitioner and talented writer; he was also a rigorous scientist who did extensive research on his methods using audiotape recordings to increase practice competence. See his chapter "Client-Centered Therapy in Its Context of Research" in Rogers (1961) for more specific information. He lived in both the practice and the research cultures. Today it is rare for individuals to live in both cultures because, as mentioned, the reward system divides the two worlds. However, if all academic jobs in the helping professions consistently had three active components—clinical practice, scholarship, and teaching—the cultural gap between the research world and the practice world would shrink.

A second way toward convergence could be the use of a "practitioner impact factor." We already have the academic indicators for good work of "impact factor" and "citation index." Both track how much a person's publications and scholarship affect the work of other scholars by, for example, how much other scholars cite a work. A limitation is that these criteria are only indirectly connected to competent practice. To ascertain a practitioner impact factor, an expert board of active skilled practitioners could judge the worth of publications. They could use this question to judge merit: Is this research methodically sound *and* directly applicable to a major practice topic?

Another way toward convergence is the use of research to monitor and provide practitioners feedback about their work. For knowledge from practice to act as a catalyst for expertise, Lambert and colleagues (Asay, Lambert, Gregerson, & Goates, 2002) have developed a feedback instrument for practitioners. Feedback is essential for the practice–feedback–practice loop that Schön (1983, 1987, 1992) describes as a way to promote expertise. Duncan, Miller, and Hubble (2007) and Lambert (2011) also describe how systematic feedback from clients can really improve practice. Here, through use of a research-based instrument, and with feedback data from sessions, we have a convergence of research and practice acting together to improve the lives of the clients we serve.

Note that limitations in using client feedback are the same limitations as using student evaluations as the sole criterion for teaching success. Sometimes teachers get high ratings without corresponding high student learning. Here is an example of the danger of exclusively using student/client reactions: The practitioner with the highest number of peer nominations in our master therapist study (Skovholt & Jennings, 2004) told me that, on occasion, a very positive outcome can be when the client leaves angry at the therapist. The therapist may be using a kind of paradoxical directive that leads to the client being angry and feeling, on leaving, of "I'll show you!" And the client may then make dramatic positive changes. The use of client rating scales would not capture the complexity of this kind of therapist expertise. Immediate feedback reaction may not capture a later, opposite reaction. For example, many high school students, years later, have changed their assessment of the skill level of a teacher, as when they say on reflection: "Mr. Rogers taught me more and cared for me more than I realized at the time."

A third convergence path is the use of qualitative research in the helping professions. The use of qualitative methods has increased greatly in recent years as witnessed, for example, by the explosion of books on the topic offered by the publisher Sage. Qualitative methods of narrative take advantage of the practitioner's "language of words" and reduces the need for the "language of numbers" that is alien to most practitioners. The results are more understandable, and the research designs do not demand the strict controls of the scientific method. In addition, some critical topics for therapists and counselors are best explored with qualitative or mixed methods. This was certainly true for Bill Cuff (1993) and his dissertation on courage.

Sexton et al. (2004) offer another way to think of convergence. They say that there is a dialectic—a tension between the two forces of research and practice—and that can be a good thing. They say we should savor the dialectic because the tension can bring a third force that is more complete than either the research or practice paradigm alone.

Fourth, one of the most prominent routes toward common ground is the focus on evidence-based practice (EBP). The term can mean many things to many people. According to one popular definition: "EBP integrates all scientific evidence and clinical information that is used to guide and improve psychotherapy processes, interventions, therapeutic relationships, and outcomes" (Goodheart & Kazdin, 2006, p. 3). This quote is from a book titled *Evidence-Based Practice: Where Practice and Research Meet* (Goodheart, Kazdin, & Sternberg, 2006). A hopeful part of this EBP movement is that learning from practice is an equal epistemology to research from the lab. As I have said over and over, practitioners learn from practice. My view is that we can only make progress when practitioner knowledge is given equal weight to that generated in the university science lab. Then we have the desired convergence between the practice culture and the research culture.

Last, a remarkable contribution to narrowing the gap between practitioners and researchers is a book published in 2010, with the hopeful title *Bringing Psychotherapy Research to Life,* edited by Castonguay and five other researchers. These editors publicly acknowledge the "elephant in the room" when they write:

> The marriage between research and practice has been long recognized as a troubled one. There are clinicians who reject research, and there are researchers who reject practice…this attempt of ours [with this book] is to make empirical findings clinically relevant, and thus reduce the gap between research and practice. (Castonguay et al., 2010, p. xix)

Such a stance by researchers is a breath of fresh air, to use that term, compared with the bitterness sometimes felt by those in applied work, as stated here by psychologist practitioner Jean Carter:

> I keep waiting to meet the practitioners described by our scientific-academic colleagues…The practitioners are thoughtless, reckless, cavalier, and do not learn from experience. Since they follow charismatic-leader driven treatment approaches without thought, they really need to be provided with manuals to tell them exactly what to do when… They do not read, they do not think; and above all, they have lost all capacity and interest in learning. (Cited by Reed, 2006, p. 14)

In *Bringing Psychotherapy Research to Life* there are biographical accounts of 28 prominent psychotherapy researchers. Many of these biographical essays detail how these researchers very actively attempted to make research relevant to clinical practice. Earlier in this chapter, I highlighted the career of Carl Rogers and described how he integrated clinical practice and scholarship. In *Bringing Psychotherapy Research to Life*, Rogers is honored by being the first of the 28 researchers described (Elliot & Farber, 2010).

Here is another example: Lester Luborsky worked in the psychoanalytic tradition and demonstrated that murky analytic concepts could be investigated through valid measures (Chits-Christopher et al., 2010). Hans Strupp made great contributions to practice with his work on the danger of therapist's negative reactions and the importance of healing ruptures (Moras et al., 2010). Aaron Beck is described as presenting a very carefully researched approach that is now used by practitioners everywhere (Hollon, 2010). The list goes on with this parade of great contributers, such as Jerome Frank, Marvin Goldfried, Gene Gendlin and his simple focusing technique, Laura Rice, and more.

No chapter is more inspiring than the one devoted to the work of Lorna Smith Benjamin (Critchfield, 2010). In this chapter, her research is used to illuminate the deep cancerous attachment patterns of individuals who have been mistreated in close relationships. Benjamin's work is based on her many years of working clinically with suffering individuals and the attachment pattern research of Harlow, Bowlby, and others. With Benjamin's research work, we have a way to understand and treat psychological cancer and "attachment gone awry." The researcher-practitioner gap narrows with this chapter—and the overall publication of *Bringing Psychotherapy Research to Life.*

SUMMARY

It is important for beginners in this profession to have an introduction to research and practice cultural differences. Graduate students in the counseling and therapy professions must live in, negotiate in, and succeed in these two separate knowledge cultures, which often conflict in basic values. Students are seldom told explicitly, and in detail, about these major cultural differences. I hope that by providing this information, I forearm readers by forewarning them. When we have knowledge cascading from many places—the lab, practice, and personal life—and when it is well integrated, our work with clients can be enhanced. And that is the whole point of the work.

Now we move to the last chapter in the book.

REFERENCES

Asay, T. P., Lambert, M. J., Gregerson, A. T., & Goates, M. K. (2002). Using patient-focused research in evaluating treatment outcome in private practice. *Journal of Clinical Psychology, 58,* 1213–1225.

Bardes, C. (2010). The doctor in middle age. In L. Gutkind (Ed.), *Becoming a doctor: From student to specialist, doctor-writers share their experiences* (pp. 111–124). New York, NY: Norton.

Bradley, R., Greene, J., Russ, E., Dutra, L., & Westen, D. (2005). A multidimensional meta-analysis of psychotherapy for PTSD. *American Journal of Psychiatry, 162,* 214–227.

Brehm, S. S. (2007). Neuroscience and prescriptive authority. *American Psychologist, 38*(6), 5.

Castonguay, L. G., Muran, J. C., Hayes, J., Ladany, N., & Anderson, T. (2010). *Bringing psychotherapy research to life.* Washington, DC: American Psychological Association.

Chi, M.T.H., Glaser, R. and Farr, M. J. (Eds.) (1988). *The nature of expertise.* Hillsdale, NJ: Lawrence Erlbaum.

Corsini, R. (2007). Introduction. In R. Corsini & D. Wedding (Eds.), *Current psychotherapies* (pp. 1–13). Belmont, CA: Thompson.

Corsini, R., & Wedding, D. (Eds.). (2007). *Current psychotherapies.* Belmont, CA: Thompson.

Critchfield, K. L. (2010). Lorna Smith Benjamin: Love, loyalty, and learning in close attachment relationships. In L. G. Castonguay, J. C. Muran, J. Hayes, N. Ladany, & T. Anderson (Eds.), *Bringing psychotherapy research to life* (pp. 221–231). Washington, DC: American Psychological Association.

Crits-Christopher, P., Barber, J. P., Grenyer, B. F., & Diguer, L. (2010). Lester Luborsky: A trailblazer in empirical research on psychoanalytic therapy. In L. G. Castonguay, J. C. Muran, J. Hayes, N. Ladany, & T. Anderson (Eds.), *Bringing psychotherapy research to life* (pp. 39–61). Washington, DC: American Psychological Association.

Cuff, W. (1993). The experience of courage and the characteristics of courageous people (unpublished doctoral dissertation). University of Minnesota.

Didion, J. (2006). *The year of magical thinking*. New York, NY: Vintage.

Duncan, B. L., Miller, S. D., Wampold, B. E., & Hubble, M. A. (2010). *The heart and soul of change* (2nd ed.). Washington, DC: American Psychological Association.

Duncan, B., Miller, S., & Hubble, M. (2007). How being bad can make you better: Developing a culture of feedback in your practice. *Psychotherapy Networker, 31*(6), 36–39, 42–45, 57.

Elliott, R., & Farber, B. A. (2010). Carl Rogers: Idealistic pragmatist and psychotherapy research pioneer. In L. G. Castonguay, J. C. Muran, J. Hayes, N. Ladany, & T. Anderson (Eds.), *Bringing psychotherapy research to life* (pp. 17–27). Washington, DC: American Psychological Association.

Elliott, R., Greenberg, S. S., & Lietaer, G. (2004). Research on experiential psychotherapies. In M. Lambert (Ed.), *Bergin and Garfield's handbook of psychotherapy and behavior change* (pp. 493–539). Hoboken, NJ: Wiley.

Ericsson, K. A., Charness, N., Hoffman, R. R., & Feltovich, P. J. (Eds.) (2006). *The Cambridge handbook of expertise and expert performance*. New York, NY: Cambridge University Press.

Frank, J. D., & Frank, J. B. (1991). *Persuasion and healing*. Baltimore, MD: Johns Hopkins Press.

Goldfried, M. R. (Ed.). (2001) *How therapists change: Personal and professional reflections*. Washington, DC: American Psychological Association.

Goodheart, C. D., & Kazdin, A. E. (2006). Introduction. In C. D. Goodheart, A. E. Kazdin, & R. J. Sternberg (Eds.), *Evidence-based practice: Where practice and research meet* (pp. 3–10). Washington, DC: American Psychological Association.

Goodheart, C. D., Kazdin, A. E., & Sternberg, R. J. (Eds.) (2006). *Evidence-based practice: Where practice and research meet*. Washington, DC: American Psychological Association.

Gottfredson, G. D. (1999). Holland's contributions to vocational psychology: A review and evaluation. *Journal of Vocational Psychology, 55*, 15–40.

Gysbers, N. C., Heppner, M. J., & Johnston, J. J. (2009). *Career counseling: Context, processes and techniques*. Alexandria, VA: American Counseling Association.

Hilgard, E. R. (1987). *Psychology in America: A historic survey*. Fort Worth, TX: Harcourt Brace Jovanovich.

Hill, C. E. (2010). Charles Gelso: The "real" person. *Counseling Psychologist, 38*, 567–599.

Hollon, S. D. (2010). Aaron Beck: The cognitive revolution in theory and therapy. In L. G. Castonguay, J. C. Muran, J. Hayes, N. Ladany, & T. Anderson (Eds.), *Bringing psychotherapy research to life* (pp. 63–74). Washington, DC: American Psychological Association.

Hollon, S. D., & Beck, A. (2004). Cognitive and cognitive-behavioral therapies. In M. Lambert (Ed.), *Bergin and Garfield's handbook of psychotherapy and behavior change* (pp. 447–492). Hoboken, NJ: Wiley.

Hoshmand, L. T., & Polkinghorne, D. E. (1992). Redefining the science-practice relationship and professional training. *American Psychologist, 47*, 55–66.

Jennings, L. (1996). Personal characteristics of master therapists (unpublished doctoral dissertation). University of Minnesota.

Katzenstein, T., Fonagy, P., & Ablon, S. (2010). Enrico Jones: Appreciating complexity. In L. G. Castonguay, J. C. Muran, J. Hayes, N. Ladany, & T. Anderson (Eds.), *Bringing psychotherapy research to life* (pp. 259–269). Washington, DC: American Psychological Association.

Kazdin, A. E. (2004). Psychotherapy for children and adolescents. In M. Lambert (Ed.), *Bergin and Garfield's handbook of psychotherapy and behavior change* (pp. 543–589). Hoboken, NJ: Wiley.

Lambert, M. J. (Ed.). (2004) *Bergin and Garfield's handbook of psychotherapy and behavior change*. Hoboken, NJ: Wiley.

Lambert, M. J. (2011, November). Becoming an Empirically Validated Psychotherapist: The Effective Use of Outcome Measure. Minnesota Psychological Association Conference. St. Paul, MN.

Lambert, M. J., & Ogles, B. J. (2004). The efficacy and effectiveness of psychotherapy. In M. Lambert (Ed.), *Bergin and Garfield's handbook of psychotherapy and behavior change* (pp.139–193). Hoboken, NJ: Wiley.

Lane, D. A., & Corrie, S. (2007). *The modern-scientist-practitioner: A guide to practice in psychology.* New York: Routledge.

Lebow, J. (2006). *Research for the psychotherapist.* New York: Routledge.

Lieberman, M. A., Yalom, I. D., & Miles, M. B. (1973). *Encounter groups: First facts.* New York, NY: Basic Books.

Lilienfeld, S. O., & O'Donohue, W. T. (2007). *The great ideas of clinical science: 17 principles that every mental health professional should understand.* New York, NY: Routledge.

Marcus, S., Marquis, P., & Sakai, C. (2004). Three- and 6-month follow-up of EMDR treatment of PTSD in an HMO setting. *International Journal of Stress Management, 11,* 195–208.

McKenna, R. B., Boyd, T. N., & Yost, P. R. (2007). Learning agility in clergy: Understanding the personal strategies and situational factors that enable pastors to learn from experience. *Journal of Psychology and Theology, 35,* 190–201.

Mellott, R. N. (2007). The scientist-practitioner model in professional psychology. *American Behavioral Scientist, 50,* 755–757.

Messer, S. B. (2001). Empirically supported treatments: What's a neobehaviorist to do? In B. Slife, R. Williams, & S. Barlow (Eds.), *Critical issues in psychotherapy: Translating new ideas to practice* (pp. 3–20). Thousand Oaks, CA: Sage.

Moras, K., Anderson, T., & Piper, W. E. (2010). Hans Strupp: A founder's contribution to a scientific basis for psychological practice. In L. G. Castonguay, J. C. Muran, J. Hayes, N. Ladany, & T. Anderson (Eds.), *Bringing psychotherapy research to life* (pp. 51–61). Washington, DC: American Psychological Association.

Murdock, N. L. (2006). On science-practice integration in everyday life. *Counseling Psychologist, 4,* 1–22.

Olson, T. (1988). Bi-focality and the space between. *Journal of Counseling and Development, 67,* 92.

Orlinsky, D. E., & Ronnestad, M. H. (2005). *How psychotherapists develop: A study of therapeutic work and professional growth.* Washington, DC: American Psychological Association.

Peterson, R. L., Peterson, D. R, Abrams, J. C., & Stricker, G. (1997). The National Council of Schools and programs of professional psychology educational model. *Professional Psychology: Research and Practice, 28,* 373–386.

Pipher, M. (2003). *Letters to a young therapist.* New York, NY: Basic Books.

Reed, G. M. (2006). What qualifies as evidence of effective practice? In J. C. Norcross, L. E. Beutler, & R. F. Levant (Eds.), *Evidence-based mental health* (pp. 13–23). Washington, DC: American Psychological Association.

Rogers, C. (1961). *On becoming a person.* Boston, MA: Houghton Mifflin.

Rønnestad, M. H., & Skovholt, T. M. (2001). Learning arenas for professional development: Retrospective accounts of senior psychotherapists. *Professional Psychology, 32,* 91–98.

Ruscio, J. (2007). The clinician as subject: Practitioners are prone to the same judgment errors as everyone else. In S. O. Lilienfield & W. T. O'Donohue (Eds.), *The great ideas of clinical science* (pp. 29–47). New York, NY: Routledge.

Schön, D. (1983). *The reflective practitioner: How professionals think in action.* New York, NY: Basic Books.

Schön, D. (1987). *Educating the reflective practitioner: Toward a new design for teaching and learning.* San Francisco, CA: Jossey-Bass.

Schön, D. (1992). The crisis of professional knowledge and the pursuit of an epistemology of practice. *Journal of Interprofessional Care, 6*(1), 49–63.

Seidler, G. H., &, Wagner, F. E. (2006). Comparing the efficacy of EMDR and trauma-focused cognitive-behavioral therapy in the treatment of PTSD: A meta-analytic study. *Psychological Medicine, 36,* 1515–1522.

Sexton, T. L., Alexander, J. F., & Mease, A. L. (2004). Levels of evidence for the models and mechanisms of therapeutic change in family and couples therapy. In M. Lambert (Ed.), *Bergin and Garfield's handbook of psychotherapy and behavior change* (pp. 590–644). Hoboken, NJ: Wiley.

Shapiro, F. (1995). *Eye movement desensitization and reprocessing: Basic principles, protocols and procedures.* New York, NY: Guilford Press.

Skovholt, T. M., & Jennings, L. (Eds.) (2004). *Master therapists: Exploring expertise in therapy and counseling.* Boston, MA: Allyn and Bacon.

Skovholt, T. M., Morgan, J., & Cunningham, H. N. (1989). Mental imagery in career counseling and life planning: A review of research and intervention methods. *Journal of Counseling and Development, 67,* 287–291.

Skovholt, T. M., & Rønnestad, M. H. (2001). The long, textured path from novice to senior practitioner. In T. M. Skovholt (Ed.), *The resilient practitioner: Burnout prevention and self-care strategies for counselors, therapists, teachers and health professionals* (pp. 25–54). Boston, MA: Allyn and Bacon.

Slife, B. D. (2004). Theoretical challenges to therapy practice and research: The constraint of naturalism. In M. Lambert (Ed.), *Bergin and Garfield's handbook of psychotherapy and behavior change* (pp. 44–83). Hoboken, NJ: Wiley.

Stricker, G., & Trierweiler, S. J. (1995). The local clinical scientist: A bridge between science and practice. *American Psychologist, 50,* 995–1002.

The top ten: The most influential therapists of the past quarter-century. (2007). *Psychotherapy Networker, 31*(2), 24–36, 68.

Wampold, B. E. (2001). *The great psychotherapy debate: Model, method, and findings.* Mahwah, NJ: Lawrence Erlbaum.

Wampold, B. E. (2010). *The basics of psychotherapy.* Washington, DC: American Psychological Association.

Wampold, B. E., & Weinberger, J. (2010). In L. G. Castonguay, J. C. Muran, J. Hayes, N. Ladany, & T. Anderson (Eds.), *Bringing psychotherapy research to life* (pp. 17–27). Washington, DC: American Psychological Association.

Yalom, I. D. (2002). *The gift of therapy: An open letter to a new generation of therapists and their patients.* New York, NY: Harper Perennial.

14

Epilogue

Promise and Meaning of the Work

To hope means to be ready at every moment for that which is not yet born.
—*Fromm, 1968, p. 9*

Voice shaking, knees shaking, hands shaking, mind cloudy when starting with my first ever counseling client. Later in the semester with new clients, the anxiety was like a small wave, not a HUGE wave.

Beginning counseling practicum student
May 3, 2012

In this last chapter I repeat some of the central points that I have made earlier and offer some new quotes and ideas. It is exciting to enter this career field, and I hope my writing about the struggles of beginners will not blind you to the joys and pleasures of the work. Actually, by discussing the struggles, I hope you will be able to negate negative factors and have even more positive experiences. So, now we turn back to some of the struggles.

"I had no idea what I was doing." This is the lament of the beginner in our field who is caught up in the swampy reality of early practice. You the reader have probably sung this lament. I did when I started out. It is a stressful position to be in. I salute all those who pass through this portal on the way to someplace else in the quest to be helpful to others. As Erich Fromm (1968), one of the great existential writers in our field, states, it takes courage to keep going without knowing the outcome.

"Petrified" was the word one of my students used to describe herself when embarking, for the first time, on the practicum journey. As I stated in an earlier chapter, when starting out in this work, our emotional reactions can be like a roller coaster of feelings (see Figure 14.1).

The roller coaster for the new therapist, as discussed in Chapter 3, with the new client naturally starts with *uncertainty*. Then there can be a quick plunge to the *worry* about what to do now. Then, suddenly, the roller coaster can move upward in a pleasant way as worry seems unnecessary. Things are going well . . . or at least the client has not suddenly left or expressed disgust. Such intense relief can bring on a bursting forth of *joy*. Suddenly there can be an unexpected moment of "What does the client mean by

Figure 14.1   Roller Coaster for the New Therapist

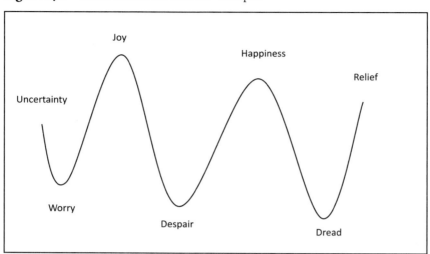

that?" and a crash down to the *despair* of being lost, as in "I have no idea, right now, at this point with this client, what to do." After a while, *happiness* may come when the cloud lifts for this reason or that. The roller coaster of the session with the client goes on as roller coasters do, up and down. There can be a sudden downward plunge into *dread*. But then the ride, unexpectedly, can turn toward, as the session ends, to *relief*. Novice practitioners experience all these emotions, and in only one session too.

The novice equation often can be stated as:

Client overt improvement = Successful therapist

Novice therapists really appreciate overt client improvement; lack of overt client improvement brings on lots of novice counselor stress. For the veteran practitioner, the client outcome equation is much more complex, as in:

Client improvement = Factors X + U + Z – W × P

Understanding this more complex formula, the veteran practitioner knows not to accept so much responsibility for lack of client success or so much credit for client success. This more complex formula means the veteran practitioner roller coaster does not have the sudden ups and downs of the novice roller coaster. So much goes into the equation for the veteran practitioner, such as client readiness, demographic connections (e.g., age, gender, socioeconomic status, ethnicity) between the two of them, quality of the early working alliance, cost of the professional help for the client, and the number and strength of other important issues for the client (e.g., How far away is the counselor's office? Do I have a final exam in college the next day? Do I have to address issues that I have skirted thus far?).

Novices in graduate school in the helping professions often undergo a loss of innocence. New graduate students often have been able to have control over school success by working hard, disciplining themselves, and following the rules of school. Now there is a rite of passage into the ambiguity of practice where practitioners cannot dictate what clients will do, feel, or think. All of a sudden one person (the client) with all of his or her complexity is interacting with the other person (the therapist). Suddenly, it is like the words of the poet Emily Dickinson: "To live is so startling it leaves little time for anything else." This startling explains the novice practitioner's sense of intensity when in practicum.

As I have said throughout this book, the major catalyst for the stress which novices face is the inherent (but often unknown to them) ambiguity of professional work. A counseling student can be told that the interaction with the client is full of ambiguity; experiencing it is often very different. The microscopic examination, understanding, and improvement of the emotional life of humans—the most complex of all species—is much more difficult than novices can imagine. Novices feel this loss of professional innocence most intensely when interacting with clients.

Before continuing, I want to put into perspective this wrestling with uncertainty. Perhaps all professional work—at the far edges of any field—involves lack of clarity. Read what scientist Martin Schwartz (2008), writing in the *Journal of Cell Science,* says about this.

> For almost all of us, one of the reasons that we liked science in high school and college is that we were good at it. . . . But high school and college science means taking courses, and doing well in courses means getting the right answers on tests. If you know those answers, you do well and get to feel smart. . . . I remember the day when Henry Taube (who won a Nobel Prize two years later) told me he didn't know how to solve the problem I was having in his area. I was a third-year graduate student and I figured that Taube knew about 1000 times more than I did (conservative estimate). If he didn't have the answer, nobody did. . . . That's when it hit me: nobody did. . . . . The scope of things I didn't know wasn't merely vast; it was for all practical purposes, infinite. . . . Science involves confronting our "absolute stupidity." That kind of stupidity is an existential fact, inherent in our efforts to push our way into the unknown . . . focusing on important questions puts us in the awkward position of being ignorant. . . . The more comfortable we become with being stupid, the deeper we will wade into the unknown and the more likely we are to make big discoveries. (p. 1771)

Here, Schwartz (2008) is presenting the bigger perspective on knowing and not knowing. Comfort with not knowing and simplicity is present in these words from therapist Mary Pipher who I have quoted often in this book.

> As a young therapist, I was seduced by wizardry, but I gradually realized that elaborate strategies, duplicitous techniques, and complicated paradoxes are not my strong suit…Straightforward methods are less likely to bewilder me or my clients. Plus, they feel more respectful.
>
> *Pipher, 2003 (p. 42)*

NOVICE CHALLENGES AND SOLUTIONS

Here I summarize eight novice challenges and solutions.

Challenge 1. Acute performance anxiety and fear

Solution. As a novice, prepare for the anxiety roller coaster.

Challenge 2. Heightened scrutiny by professional gatekeepers

Solution. Try to be open to developing while asking for clear clinical supervisor expectations.

Challenge 3. Porous or rigid emotional boundaries

Solution. Learn boundary generosity and deliberate self-care strategies.

Challenge 4. The fragile and incomplete practitioner self

Solution. Be patient with yourself when creating your practitioner identity.

Challenge 5. Inadequate conceptual maps

Solution. Learn the limits of global theories and the need for deliberate practice experience with specific client concerns.

Challenge 6. Glamorized expectations

Solution. Gradually learn to distinguish between realistic and idealized expectations without giving in to disillusionment and despair.

Challenge 7. Acute need for positive mentors

Solution. Find and attach to senior guides.

Challenge 8. To balance negative novice self-feelings with positive ones such as self-compassion

Solution. Big life beginnings always involve uncertainty and feelings of inadequacy. Remember, beginners also have great enthusiasm, hope, and energy.

Challenge 9. Initial interest for many novices is self-healing

Solution. Turn that interest to a broader focus that concentrates on healing the other.

BIGGER PICTURE OF HOPE, MEANING, AND EXCITEMENT

Although the struggles of the novice practitioner make the early years difficult, professional work as a practitioner can be very positive. And after the practitioner survives a difficult novice voyage, a productive and meaningful career can emerge.

As I wrote in an earlier chapter, lots of people do valuable and useful work:

- Starting a factory and then eventually employing 50 people, all of whom support families
- Running a snow plow all night, so that in the morning people can drive and get on with daily living
- Assessing toxicology levels in metals of consumer products
- Serving lunch to children at an elementary school
- Working for a union and defending cooks and maids against unevenly enforced rules
- Visiting preschools as an accreditation specialist to certify standards of care

- Developing instruments for airplanes to increase airline safety
- And, as a final example, developing a social network site so that people can connect on an important topic

Yes, many people do valuable work. Our field is included in this grouping of the valuable. Those outside the profession often consider it noble work. So, I salute you for choosing this career field and embarking on the journey to become a highly skilled counselor or therapist.

In our international human world, suffering is expressed in many forms. One prominent form is emotional distress and mental anguish. We have so much pain in the human family. The high level of joblessness and its effects, posttraumatic stress disorder, the shock of abandonment experienced in childhood, difficulties of immigration such as culture shock, the unrelenting pull of addictions, sexual trauma, severe depression and the danger of suicidal thinking, the pain of severe anxiety, unmitigated grief, the toxic effects of human cruelty—the parade of human emotional and mental pain is long.

All this pain produces so much that fights against the basic human hope for understanding and connection. When emotional distress is high, so much of the positive bounce of collaboration and compassion is lost. The rigidity produced when there is human pain has immense costs at the personal, family, state, country, regional, and world levels.

A primary way that we treat and lessen this human pain is by human compassion expressed by people caring for other people. Some of these people are professionals in the caring professions, such as the broad rainbow of psychological counselors, social workers, psychotherapists, physicians, nurses, teachers, clergy and religious workers, aid workers, allied healthcare workers, and human service providers. The human relationship of compassion, deep listening, and caring serves to vacuum in much distress, and offer hope—hope that the experienced difficulty will, in time, lessen in impact.

Exceptionally talented mental health practitioners can wade into this human distress and powerfully reduce the effects of the calamity being experienced. What makes for a master practitioner of the helping and healing arts? What are key components of expertise? What are significant training issues? These are key questions in the race to create enough high-level professional talent to battle human despair and assist others to lead lives of meaning, love, and joy. Emerging right now, at this time, is an inventory by Liam (2012) to measure mastery.

CYCLE OF CARING AS THE PRACTICE ESSENTIAL

Over and over again—with client, student, or patient—the practitioner must engage in a mini-cycle of closeness and later an ending of an often intense, professional connection. Being able to make professional connections with individuals in distress or need, of one kind or another, is at the heart of the helping professions, as described in detail in Chapter 8. After the connection is made—what in the professional literature is called the *working alliance*—the work of human growth begins. The practitioner and the client join together to make progress.

And then eventually the practitioner must say good-bye and have the connection end. And perhaps within only minutes, or perhaps with a longer break for renewal, the process repeats itself. Again and again the Cycle of Caring repeats, the essence of the helping professions in action. This process can activate the client's self-healing properties (Bohart & Tallman, 2009). Together, the client's work and the practitioner's efforts can produce positive gains.

WORDS THAT AFFIRM OUR WORK

Hubble, Duncan, Miller, and Wampold (2009) write:

> Psychotherapy continues to prove its effectiveness. The weight of quantitative studies consistently produces as effect size of about 0.8 standard deviations, which means the average treated person is better off than 80% of those who do not have the benefit of treatment. . . . When such findings are contrasted with results widely heralded as advances in the medical arena, psychotherapy yields significant benefits hand over fist. Rosenthal . . . pointed out, for instance, that the large trial for aspirin as a prophylaxis for heart attacks produced as effect size of .03 (compared with .80 for psychotherapy as a treatment for mental health problems). It is interesting that the magnitude of the effect was thought to be so astonishing that the trial was stopped prematurely because it was decided that delivering the placebo was unethical. (pp. 27–28)

In the next quotes, three veteran practitioners reflect on the honor of their calling after years of work.

> As a practitioner, I am so honored to be invited into people's lives. I almost do not have words to describe this honor.
> —*Expert therapist Jane Brodie, personal communication,*
> *September 27, 2007*

> As a therapist, my experience is that unhappy clients become happier, that feuding couples start to enjoy each other, and that families settle down and work together.
> —*Pipher, 2003, p. xvii*

> [I]t has always struck me as an extraordinary privilege to belong to a venerable and honorable guild of healers. We therapists are part of a tradition reaching back not only to our immediate psychotherapy ancestors—Nietzsche, Schopenhauer, Kierkegaard—but also to Jesus, the Buddha, Plato, Socrates,

Galen, Hippocrates, and other great religious leaders, philosophers, and physicians who have, since the beginning of time, ministered to human despair.

—*Yalom, 2003, pp. 258–259*

And last, I end this chapter and the book with two ideas. First, have fun in one's life while entering this serious work life. When doing serious work, it is important to also be playful in one's life. (Refer to Chapter 7 for more on being playful and having fun.) Second and last, although we search for answers, being open to questions is sustaining during the long practitioner career. Here are the very same words that came at the beginning of this book, words from Alice Walker.

I must love the questions
themselves
As Rilke said
like locked rooms
full of treasure
to which my blind
and groping key
does not yet fit.

and await answers
as unsealed letters
mailed with dubious
intent
and written in a very foreign
tongue.

and in the hourly making
of myself
no thought of Time
to force, to squeeze
the space
I grow into.

(Alice Walker, cited by White, 2004, p. 227-8)

REFERENCES

Bohart, A. C., & Tallman, K. (2009). Clients: The neglected common factor in psychotherapy. In B. L. Duncan, S. D. Miller, B. E. Wampold, & M. A. Hubble (Eds.), *The heart and soul of change: De-* *livering what works in therapy* (pp. 83–111). Washington, DC: American Psychological Association.

Fromm, E. (1968). *The revolution of hope*. New York, NY: Harper & Row.

Hubble, M. A., Duncan, B. L., Miller, S. D., & Wampold, B. E. (2009). Introduction. In B. L. Duncan, S. D. Miller, B. E. Wampold, & M.A. Hubble (Eds.), *The heart and soul of change: Delivering what works in therapy* (pp. 23–46). Washington, DC: American Psychological Association.

Liam, F. (2012). Master Psychotherapist Characteristics Inventory. Unpublished doctoral dissertation, University of Minnesota.

Pipher, M. (2003). *Letters to a young therapist.* New York, NY: Basic Books.

Schwartz, M. A. (2008). The importance of stupidity in scientific research. *Journal of Cell Research, 121,* 1771.

Yalom, I. D. (2003). *The gift of therapy: An open letter to a new generation of therapists and their patients.* New York, NY: Harper Perennial.

Index